Heidegger's Political Thinking

James F. Ward

Heidegger's Political Thinking

Amherst   *University of Massachusetts Press*

Copyright © 1995 by
The University of Massachusetts Press
All rights reserved
Printed in the United States of America
LC 94–38710
ISBN 0–87023–969–4 (cloth); 970–8 (pbk.)
Set in Bodoni Book by Keystone Typesetting, Inc.
Printed and bound by Braun-Brumfield, Inc.

Library of Congress Cataloging-in-Publication Data

Ward, James F., 1947–
    Heidegger's political thinking / James F. Ward.
      p.   cm.
    Includes bibliographical references (p.   ) and index.
    ISBN 0-87023-969-4 (cloth : acid-free paper). — ISBN
  0-87023-970-8 (pbk. : acid-free paper)
     1. Heidegger, Martin, 1889–1976—Political and social views.
    2. Political science—Philosophy. I. Title.
    B3279.H49W36   1995
    193—dc20   94–38710
                                                 CIP

British Library Cataloguing in Publication data are available.

To my wife, Barbara, with love

But what is essential in the revolutionary is not that he overturns as such; it is rather that in overturning he brings to light what is decisive and essential. In philosophy that happens always when those few momentous questions are raised.

Martin Heidegger,
Nietzsche: The Will to Power as Art (N1 20)

The discovery of the best rules of society suited to nations would require a superior intelligence, who saw all of men's passions yet experienced none of them; who had no relationship at all to our nature yet knew it thoroughly; whose happiness was independent of us, yet who was nevertheless willing to attend to ours; finally one who, preparing for himself a future glory with the passage of time, could work in one century and enjoy the reward in another. Gods would be needed to give laws to men.

Jean-Jacques Rousseau,
On the Social Contract (2.7)

Contents

Abbreviations

Heidegger's *Gesamtausgabe*

The following volumes of Heidegger's *Gesamtausgabe* have been used. They are identified by volume number, title, year(s) of composition or semester delivered in the case of lectures or seminars (WS = winter semester, SS = summer semester), editor, and year of publication. All are published in Frankfurt by Vittorio Klostermann.

G1   *Frühe Schriften* (1912–16), Friedrich-Wilhelm von Herrmann, 1978.

G2   *Sein und Zeit* (1927), Friedrich-Wilhelm von Herrmann, 1977.

G3   *Kant und das Problem der Metaphysik* (1929), Friedrich-Wilhelm von Herrmann, 1990.

G4   *Erläuterung zu Hölderlins Dichtung* (1936–68), Friedrich-Wilhelm von Herrmann, 1982.

G5   *Holzwege* (1935–46), Friedrich-Wilhelm von Herrmann, 1978.

G9   *Wegmarken* (1919–58), Friedrich-Wilhelm von Herrmann, 1976.

G12 *Unterwegs zur Sprache* (1950–59), Friedrich-Wilhelm von Herrmann, 1985.

G13 *Aus der Erfahrung des Denkens* (1910–76), Hermann Heidegger, 1983.

G15 *Seminare* (1951–73), Curd Ochwadt, 1986.

G19 *Platon: Sophistes* (1924–25), Ingrid Schüssler, 1992.

G20 *Prolegomena zur Geschichte des Zeitbegriffes* (SS 1925), Petra Jaeger, 1979, 1988.

G21 *Logik: Die Frage nach der Wahrheit* (WS 1925/26), Walter Biemel, 1976.

G24 *Grundprobleme der Phänomenologie* (SS 1927), Friedrich-Wilhelm von Herrmann, 1975, 1989.

G25　*Phänomenologische Interpretationen von Kants Kritik der reinen Vernunft* (WS 1927/28), Ingtraud Görland, 1977, 1988.

G26　*Metaphysische Anfangsgründe der Logik im Ausgang von Leibniz* (SS 1928), Klaus Held, 1978.

G29/30　*Die Grundbegriffe der Metaphysik: Welt—Endlichkeit—Einsamkeit* (WS 1929/30), Friedrich-Wilhelm von Herrmann, 1983.

G31　*Vom Wesen der menschlichen Freiheit: Einleitung in die Philosophie* (SS 1930), Hartmut Tietjen, 1982.

G32　*Hegels Phänomenologie des Geistes* (WS 1930/31), Ingtraud Görland, 1980, 1988.

G33　*Aristoteles: Metaphysik Theta 1–3, Von Wesen und Wirklichkeit der Kraft* (SS 1931), Heinrich Hüni, 1981.

G34　*Vom Wesen der Wahrheit. Zu Platons Höhengleichnis und Theatët* (WS 1931/32), Hermann Mörchen, 1988.

G39　*Hölderlins Hymnen "Germanien" und "Der Rhein"* (WS 1934/35), Susanne Ziegler, 1980.

G40　*Einführung in die Metaphysik* (SS 1935), Petra Jaeger, 1983.

G41　*Die Frage nach dem Ding. Zu Kants Lehre von den tranzendentalen Grundsätzen* (WS 1935/36), Petra Jaeger, 1984.

G42　*Schelling: über das Wesen der menschlichen Freiheit* (SS 1936), Ingrid Schüssler, 1988.

G45　*Grundfragen der Philosophie Ausgewählte "Probleme" der "Logik"* (WS 1937/38), Friedrich-Wilhelm von Herrmann, 1984.

G50　Pt. 1: *Nietzsches Metaphysik* (1941–42); pt. 2: *Einleitung in die Philosophie Denken und Dichten* (1944–45), Petra Jaeger, 1990.

G51　*Grundbegriffe* (SS 1941), Petra Jaeger, 1981.

G52　*Hölderlins Hymne "Andenken"* (WS 1941/42), Curd Ochwadt, 1982.

G53　*Hölderlins Hymne "Der Ister"* (SS 1942), Walter Biemel, 1984.

G54　*Parmenides* (WS 1942/43), Manfred S. Frings, 1982.

G55　*Heraklit. Pt. 1: Der Anfang des abendländischen Denkens* (SS 1943); pt. 2: *Logik: Heraklits Lehre vom Logos* (SS 1944), Manfred S. Frings, 1979, 1987.

G56/57　*Zur Bestimmung der Philosophie. Pt. 1: Die Idee der Philosophie und das Weltanschauungsproblem (Kriegsnotsemester* 1919); pt. 2: *Phänomenologie und transzendentale Wertphilosophie* (SS 1919), Bernd Heimbüchel, 1987.

G61   *Phänomenologische Interpretationen zu Aristoteles. Einführung in die phänomenologische Forschung* (WS 1921/22), Walter Brocker and Kate Brocker-Oltmanns, 1985.

G63   *Ontologie (Hermeneutik der Faktizität)* (SS 1923), Kate Brocker-Oltmanns, 1988.

G65   *Beiträge zur Philosophie (Vom Ereignis)*, (1936–38). Friedrich-Wilhelm von Herrmann, 1988.

Titles of Heidegger's Works in German

AE   "Phänomenologische Interpretationen zu Aristoteles (Anzeige der hermeneutischen Situation)." Edited by Hans-Ulrich Lessing. *Dilthey-Jahrbuch für Philosophie und Geschichte der Geisteswissenschaften* 6 (1989): 237–69.

DR   *Das Rektorat, 1933/34. Tatsachen und Gedanken.* Edited by Hermann Heidegger. Frankfurt am Main: Vittorio Klostermann, 1983.

Heb   *Hebel der Hausfreund.* Pfullingen: G. Neske, 1957.

NI   *Nietzsche.* Vol. 1. Pfullingen: G. Neske, 1961.

NII   *Nietzsche.* Vol. 2. Pfullingen: G. Neske, 1961.

NH   *Nachlese zu Heidegger.* Edited by Guido Schneeberger. Bern, 1962.

PLW   "Platons Lehre von der Wahrheit." In G9, pp. 203–38.

SDU   *Die Selbstbehauptung der deutschen Universität.* Edited by Hermann Heidegger. Frankfurt am Main: Vittorio Klostermann, 1983.

SG   *Der Satz vom Grund.* Pfullingen: Neske, 1978.

UA   "Zur Überwindung der Aesthetik. Zu 'Ursprung des Kuntswerks.'" *Heidegger Studies* 6 (1990): 5–10.

UK   "Vom Ursprung des Kuntswerks: Erste Ausarbeitung." *Heidegger Studies* 5 (1989): 5–22.

US   *Unterwegs zur Sprache.* 3rd ed. Pfullingen: G. Neske, 1965.

VS   *Vier Seminare.* Frankfurt am Main: Vittorio Klostermann, 1977.

ZS   *Zollikoner Seminare: Protokolle-Gespräche-Briefe.* Edited by Medard Boss. Frankfurt am Main: Vittorio Klostermann, 1987.

Translations of Heidegger's Works

AWP   "The Age of the World Picture." In QCT, pp. 115–54.

BC   *Basic Concepts.* Translated by Gary E. Aylesworth. Bloomington: Indiana University Press, 1993.

BPP   *Basic Problems of Phenomenology.* Translated by Albert Hofstadter. Bloomington: Indiana University Press, 1982.

BT   *Being and Time.* Translated by John Macquarrie and Edward Robinson. New York: Harper & Row, 1962.

BWr   *Basic Writings.* Edited by David F. Krell. New York: Harper & Row, 1977.

CH   "A Cassirer-Heidegger Seminar." Translated by Carl Hamburg. *Philosophy and Phenomenological Research* 25 (1964–65): 208–22.

CT   *The Concept of Time.* Translated by William McNeill. Oxford: Blackwell Publishers, 1992.

DT   *Discourse on Thinking.* Translated by J. M. Anderson and E. H. Freund. New York: Harper & Row, 1966.

EB   *Existence and Being.* Edited by Werner Brock. Chicago: Regnery-Gateway, 1949.

EGT   *Early Greek Thinking.* Translated by David Farrell Krell and Frank Capuzzi. New York: Harper & Row, 1975.

EPh   *The End of Philosophy.* Translated by Joan Stambaugh. New York: Harper & Row, 1973.

ER   *The Essence of Reasons.* Translated by Terrence Malick. Evanston, Ill.: Northwestern University Press, 1969.

ET   "On the Essence of Truth." In BWr, pp. 113–42.

HCE   *Hegel's Concept of Experience.* Edited by J. Glenn Gray. New York: Harper & Row, 1970.

HCT   *History of the Concept of Time: Prolegomena.* Translated by Theodore Kisiel. Bloomington: Indiana University Press, 1985.

HH   "Heidegger's Letter to the Boss' Daughter." Translated by Russell A. Berman and Paul Piccone. *Telos* 77 (1988): 125–27.

HS   *Heraclitus Seminar.* (1966/67) (with Eugen Fink). Translated by C. H. Seibert. University: University of Alabama Press, 1979.

ID   *Identity and Difference.* Translated by Joan Stambaugh. New York: Harper & Row, 1969.

IM   *An Introduction to Metaphysics.* Translated by Ralph Manheim. New Haven: Yale University Press, 1959.

KPM   *Kant and the Problem of Metaphysics.* Translated by James S. Churchill. Bloomington: Indiana University Press, 1962.

KTB   "Kant's Thesis about Being." Translated by Ted E. Klein, Jr., and William E. Pohl. In *Thinking about Being: Aspects of Heidegger's Thought,* ed. Robert W. Shahan and J. N. Mohanty, pp. 7–33. Norman: University of Oklahoma Press, 1984.

LH   "Letter on Humanism." In BWr, pp. 193–242.

MFL   *Metaphysical Foundations of Logic.* Translated by Michael Heim. Bloomington: Indiana University Press, 1984.

MHPT   "Martin Heidegger: Political Texts, 1933–1934." Translated by William H. Lewis. *New German Critique* 45 (Fall 1988): 96–116.

N1   *Nietzsche.* Vol. 1: *The Will to Power as Art.* Edited and translated by David Farrell Krell. New York: Harper & Row, 1979.

N2   *Nietzsche.* Vol. 2: *The Eternal Recurrence of the Same.* Edited and translated by David Farrell Krell. New York: Harper & Row, 1984.

N3   *Nietzsche.* Vol. 3: *The Will to Power as Knowledge and as Metaphysics.* Edited by David Farrell Krell. Translated by Joan Stambaugh, David Farrell Krell, and Frank A. Capuzzi. New York: Harper & Row, 1987.

N4   *Nietzsche.* Vol. 4: *Nihilism.* Edited by David Farrell Krell. Translated by Frank A. Capuzzi. New York: Harper & Row, 1982.

OTB   *On Time and Being.* Translated by Joan Stambaugh. New York: Harper & Row, 1972.

OWA   "The Origin of the Work of Art." In PLT, pp. 15–88.

OWL   *On the Way to Language.* Translated by Peter D. Hertz and Joan Stambaugh. New York: Harper & Row, 1971.

PA   *Parmenides.* Translated by André Schuwer and Richard Rojcewicz. Bloomington: Indiana University Press, 1992.

PG   "The Principle of Ground." Translated by Keith Hoeller. *Man and World* 7 (1974): 207–22.

Phy   "On the Being and Conception of *Physis* in Aristotle's *Physics* B.1." Translated by Thomas J. Sheehan. *Man and World* 9 (1976): 219–70.

PLT   *Poetry, Language, Thought.* Translated by Albert Hofstadter. New York: Harper & Row, 1971.

PR   *The Principle of Reason.* Translated by Reginald Lilly. Bloomington: Indiana University Press, 1991.

Pr   "Preface." Translated by William J. Richardson. In William J.

Richardson, *Heidegger: Through Phenomenology to Thought,* pp. viii–xxiii. The Hague: Martinus Nijhoff, 1963.

PT   *The Piety of Thinking: Essays by Martin Heidegger.* Translated by James G. Hart and John C. Maraldo. Bloomington: Indiana University Press, 1976.

QB   *The Question of Being.* Translated by William Kluback and Jean T. Wilde. New York: Twayne, 1958.

QCT   *The Question concerning Technology and Other Essays.* Translated by William Lovitt. New York: Harper & Row, 1977.

R   "The Rectorate, 1933–34: Facts and Thoughts." Translated by Karsten Harries. *Review of Metaphysics* 38 (1985): 481–502.

RA   "The Self-Assertion of the German University." Translated by Karsten Harries. *Review of Metaphysics* 38 (1985): 470–80.

RAW   "The Self-Assertion of the German University." Translated by William S. Lewis. In *The Heidegger Controversy,* ed. Richard Wolin, pp. 29–39. Cambridge: MIT Press, 1993.

Sp   "Only a God Can Save Us: *Der Spiegel*'s Interview with Martin Heidegger." Translated by Maria P. Alter and John D. Caputo. *Philosophy Today* 20 (Winter 1976): 267–84.

SR   "Science Reflection." In QCT, pp. 155–82.

ST   *Schelling's Treatise on the Essence of Human Freedom (1809).* Translated by Joan Stambaugh. Athens: Ohio University Press, 1985.

WCT   *What Is Called Thinking?* Translated by Fred D. Wieck and J. Glenn Gray. New York: Harper & Row, 1968.

WGM   "The Way Back into the Ground of Metaphysics." Translated by Walter Kaufmann. In *Existentialism from Dostoevsky to Sartre,* ed. Walter Kaufmann, pp. 265–79. New York: New American Library, 1975.

WHN   "The Want of Holy Names" (1974). Translated by Bernhard Radloff. *Man and World* 18 (1985): 261–67.

WM   "What is Metaphysics?" In BWr, pp. 91–112.

WNZ   "Who Is Nietzsche's Zarathustra?" Translated by Bernd Magnus. *Review of Metaphysics* 20 (1967): 411–31.

WP   *What Is Philosophy?* Translated by William Kluback and Jean T. Wilde. New York: Twayne, 1958.

WT   *What Is a Thing?* Translated by W. B. Barton and Vera Deutsch. Chicago: Regnery, 1967.

Other Abbreviations

BGE   Friedrich Nietzsche, *Beyond Good and Evil.* Translated by Walter Kaufmann. New York: Vintage Press, 1966.

MHUD   *Martin Heidegger—Unterwegs im Denken. Symposion im 10. Todesjahr.* Edited by Richard Wissen, Freiburg: Verlag Karl Alber, 1987.

Preface

Every question specifies as a question the breadth and nature
of the answer it is looking for. At the same time, it
circumscribes the range of possibilities for answering.

(N4 206)

IN THIS BOOK I examine Martin Heidegger's political thinking. There
can be little question of Heidegger's importance in philosophy as well
as in the wider intellectual life of the West in the late twentieth century.
To trace his manifold influences on phenomenology, existentialism,
theology, literary theory, psychoanalysis, feminism, aesthetics, and
ecology would require a project of encyclopedic proportions. Postmod-
ernism in virtually all of its expressions is unimaginable without him,
for the central postmodern teachings that there can be no genuine
foundational thinking or discourse and that Western philosophy has
reached the end of its history, or its end simply, are understood as
Heidegger's teachings. The only political regime to which Heidegger
committed himself in speeches and deeds was that of National Socialism, and the significance of that fact for his philosophy has been debated from the 1930s to the present day. It is by "neither accident nor
error," in Lacoue-Labarthe's felicitous phrase, that Heidegger's "philosophy" and his "politics" are interwoven.[1]

Interpretations of Heidegger's political involvement with National
Socialism have ranged from dismissals of it as an aberration, or a mere
fact of biography, to attempts to determine whether or in what ways
Heidegger's thinking exhibits either a defect that makes it vulnerable
to Nazism or a quality that ensures its connection with Nazism. Most
discussions of this issue have depended until recently on what is now
often called the "official" account—prepared and sustained by Heidegger and some of his students, ratified wittingly or not by many of his

interpreters—that his political activity was brief, limited to the period of his rectorate, and that he came to regard it as a mistake he soon corrected. In the early 1980s the German historian Hugo Ott began to publish the results of archival research which showed that the extent and duration of Heidegger's political activity was far greater than had been generally known.[2] The publication of Victor Farias's *Heidegger et le nazisme* in France in 1987 elevated the question of Heidegger's politics to a prominent place in contemporary French intellectual life, contributing to a many-sided, ongoing debate that now transcends its origins, for the widening circle of issues raised in connection with Heidegger's Nazism reaches the question of the nature and legitimacy of modernity.[3] It is now not unusual to find that students of philosophy issue warnings concerning Heidegger's thinking. Debates among leading schools of philosophy, Stanley Rosen believes, have been "seriously distorted" by his influence, while Jacques Derrida writes of the "necessity of showing—without limit, if possible—the profound attachment of Heidegger's texts (writings and deeds) to the possibility and reality of all nazisms."[4] The claim that Heidegger's thinking is apolitical cannot be taken seriously. It tells us more about the limitations of those who make it than about Heidegger's views. Certainly such themes as the crisis of the West, the significance of science, the impossibility of grounding practice in any first philosophy, the end of philosophy, nihilism, the significance of Greek antiquity in and for the present crisis, and the possibility of a new beginning are recognizably "political" on all but the narrowest understandings of politics. Heidegger is a political thinker if by "political" one means, in the manner of classical antiquity, the order of human things. Indeed, one assessment of his influence names Heidegger as the "weightiest critical authority since the death of Marxism."[5]

The findings of the new Heidegger scholarship show that all interpretations of Heidegger's political activity that depend upon its supposed brevity and superficiality are no longer tenable. The facts appear now to be incontrovertible. Heidegger attempted to implement National Socialist aims during his rectorate, including efforts to reform the teaching of science to meet the needs of the revolution, complied with racial "cleansing" laws that excluded Jews and others from financial assistance, and promoted National Socialism to students and workers in public addresses. After his rectorate, he refused to accept Jewish doctoral students, engaged in political denunciations of colleagues and former students, and remained active in attempts to organize German academics to support the Nazi regime. His defenses or explanations of his political activity are characterized by evasions and lies. Most damning of all, he remained silent, or very nearly so, about the Holocaust.

In this study I shall keep the "Heidegger case" on the periphery of my readings of Heidegger's texts because I am convinced that his political thinking transcends his political engagement. Through close reading of a number of Heidegger's texts, I show how politics is inscribed in his manifold lines of thinking concerning his chosen philosophical theme, the question of Being. The direction of his thinking was toward what he understood as ever-more fundamental conditions for this question. For Heidegger, thinking and acting are intimately linked, and the conditions that affect how or even whether the question of Being can be asked are constitutive of what he will come to call various "epochs" in the "history of Being." Moreover, against the tradition of Western metaphysics, Heidegger will argue that genuine "thinking," which surpasses "philosophy," is not universalistic but is and must be rooted in the particular; a determinate historical location, a "people," is the necessary soil from which thinking may grow. As a political thinker, Heidegger is concerned with the *German* people. While this people is, or has the possibility of being, exemplary for the West, I emphasize that for Heidegger this destiny can *only* be that of a people, specifically, one whose language is said to equal or surpass that of the Greeks as more powerful and more spiritual (IM 47; OWL 178–80).

If we must locate Heidegger ideologically, he is clearly a thinker of the European Right. The principles of 1789, liberal democracy, the emergence of mass society, and industrialization are all to be explained and opposed by a relentless and ever-deepening reflection on modernity. Heidegger is, however, neither a "reactionary modernist" seeking to harmonize romantic irrationality and modern technology nor a conservative seeking a restoration of the German state.[6] He belongs, rather, to the tradition of German *völkische* nationalism; a number of texts evoke the *völkische* vision of a homogeneous, rural, and pastoral people, deeply rooted in the soil of a place, suspicious of, if not simply hostile to, industrialization, capitalism, urbanization, and even national unification. "Rootedness" (*Bodenständigkeit*), necessary for all great things, is threatened by the "spirit of the age into which all of us were born" (DT 48–49).[7]

Heidegger's political thinking, however, is no more reducible to the simplicities of *völkische* nationalism than it is to official National Socialism, for ranges far beyond even the most generous intellectual boundaries one might establish for these positions. What had been recognized by Heidegger's best students from almost the beginnings of his philosophical activity has become impossible to ignore with the ongoing publication of his early writings and lectures: Heidegger is a revolutionary thinker, surely one of the most radical thinkers in the history of philosophy. His radicalism is comprehensive. In the words of one of his translators, David Farrell Krell, he "yearned for a 'fundamental change,' *Aufbruch* or *risorgimento,* that would totally recast the social, political, and academic order in Germany" (N4 267). It is as grievous a misreading of Heidegger to attempt to sever this aim from his philosophical enterprise as it is to interpret that enterprise solely or even primarily in terms of its apparent distance from or nearness to National Socialism. Like so many other Germans, he was convinced that the National Socialist revolution would bring about a renewal and reinspiriting of Germany, but unlike most of those who expected much from National Socialism, Heidegger wanted the radical questioning of genuine philosophy to energize the revolution and the German people.[8] The question of Being has as its political correlate the most radical of revolutions. *The* political question, the crucial question for Heidegger's political thinking, is:

> What if it were possible that the human, that peoples [*Völker*] in their greatest practices [*Umtrieben*] and legacies [*Gemachten*], are linked to beings [*Seienden*] and yet had long fallen out of Being [*Sein*] without knowing it, and that this was the innermost and most powerful source [*Grund*] of their decline [*Verfalls*]? (IM 30)

My inquiry is an extended commentary on this question.

Even during his rectorate, Heidegger's political teaching became known as a "private" or even "Freiburg" National Socialism.[9] Certainly there is evident in many of his writings, as we shall see, a stance critical of the racism, manipulative propaganda, and mass mobilization of the German people integral to official Nazism. What outrages us, once it is thought, is the notion that there is, or could be, an "ideal" Nazism, an original, of which the reality of the Third Reich was the monstrous image.[10] I do not think, however, that it is necessary to identify Heidegger's political thinking as an "ideal" Nazism. Rather, his political thinking, to generalize a point made by J.–F. Lyotard in connection with BT, permits, but does not necessitate, his engagement with Nazism.[11] Put concisely, thinking in its radical and therefore decisive sense is for Heidegger correspondence with, standing exposed to, and enduring, Being. National Socialism, as he understood it initially, was the only political possibility radical enough to serve as the political correlate of thinking because its basic movement appeared to him as an authentic retrieval of German rootedness.

Although I am not concerned thematically with postmodernity in this book, I cannot avoid noting the irony inherent in the thought that the philosopher, after Nietzsche, most crucial to postmodernity, whom many consider the greatest thinker of the twentieth century, is a thinker profoundly hostile to much that belongs to the twentieth century. In another and possibly more profound sense, Heidegger's *völkisch* nationalism makes him an extraordinarily timely thinker, for it is impossible today to ignore nationalism, what John Lukacs has called the "most powerful political force in the world," at the end of modernity.[12] Precisely because it is *not* superficial, not an ideological rind easily separated from the core of his thinking, Heidegger's teaching raises a crucial problem for much of the postmodern political thought indebted to him. A recitation of some familiar postmodern themes, often overlapping or interpenetrating, must suffice here to make my point: the impossibility of or incredulity toward metanarratives; the rejection of any foundational or grounding principles (and thus of any political or ethical teaching grounded in first philosophy); the endings of metaphysics, the subject, modernity, Enlightenment, and the West; the stances of antihumanism, transgressive delegitimizing of power; oppositions to "Western rationality," to technology, to any and all compounds of these (Europophallologocentrism); the irreducibility of plurality and difference. If this inventory is folded into the last theme named, then the motto of postmodernity is René Char's line in the strategic location given it by Reiner Schürmann: "demain le multiple."[13]

And yet, it may be questioned whether the "multiple" is truly thought by postmodernists if nationalism is ignored. The differences celebrated by postmodernists seldom appear to include the "nation," however understood; politics—democratic-anarchic, agonistic, delegitimizing, "pagan," and so on—is seldom nationalist politics. Postmodern understandings of politics have not yet challenged sufficiently the dismissive universalism, inherited from liberalism and the Left, for which nationalism is, in Stanley Hoffmann's words, "an atavistic anachronism that was bound to disappear sooner or later in a rationally organized universe."[14] Is it conceivable that Heidegger's thinking lies, not merely behind or at the roots of postmodernity, but also, as he claims truly essential thinking must do, *ahead*, returning back to postmodern political thought, deconstructing not only the obvious targets—what Derrida identifies as "those discourses which possess some authority today in our Western culture"—but eventually also the discourses that celebrate the "manifold," which can look suspiciously like yet another universal?[15]

If we remain, or attempt to remain, closer to Heidegger's understanding of himself as found in his writings, however, we cannot simply identify him as a critic or opponent of modernity, for he insists that what he attempts to do is to follow the path and pursue the matter of thinking, that the decisive questions do not arise from an opinion or preference but rather belong to the movement of thinking (IM 30–31). I want to remain, that is, with Heidegger's self-interpretation, according to which the movement of thinking traced in his work is itself inscribed in what he tries to think about, because my aim is to bring to light the political dimension of that thinking. What *appears* as criticism and opposition is reached, according to Heidegger, in and by the unfolding of the question of Being, itself of necessity historically situated (36). It is this philosophical dimension that distinguishes Heidegger's political thinking from that of crude *völkisch* nationalists, which is to say that his ideological location does not suffice to explain, or explain away, his thinking.

In this study I am concerned primarily with texts, and I wish to make clear at the outset what that means for my examination of Heidegger. First, I am not concerned here in any detail with the enormous literature that has developed concerning the "Heidegger affair." I doubt that our understanding of Heidegger's thinking is best served if it is refracted through quarrels rooted in the collapse of Marxism or the emergence of the postmodern. Several decades ago, one wrote about Heidegger in connection with existentialism, with Sartre, or with theology; today it is Derrida, and tomorrow it will be someone else. Second, I am not interested, in this study at least, with the question of how to do political philosophy in the Heideggerian or post-Heideggerian age; this task, if it is to be undertaken seriously, must depend upon a sound understanding of Heidegger, to which I attempt to contribute.

It remains to offer some thoughts on how I have tried to read Heidegger. I cannot claim to have deployed anything so formal as a theory of the text; there is indeed something ironic in the fact that a philosopher deeply critical of all that can conceivably be associated with Cartesianism and methodology generally elicits a methodological frenzy in many of his interpreters. It has even been suggested that we "don't know how" to think about the connections between Heidegger's thought and his politics.[16] As the volumes of Heidegger's *Gesamtausgabe* continue to appear, I have become convinced that interpretive questions of precedence and subsequence, of precisely when Heidegger first announced a theme or employed a term, should be given less emphasis than has often been the case. Moreover, the order in which various writings have been composed is a necessary but limited indication of the order in which Heidegger's thinking took place. Everything in a lecture, Heidegger says, depends upon "decisive [*entscheidenden*] steps" (IM 71). Philosophy, unlike the sciences, has no object with which it can begin, for it is a "happening [*Geschehnis*] which must at all times achieve Being (in its appropriate manifestness) anew. Only in this happening can philosophical truth disclose itself." For the student or listener, then, the steps in this happening must be taken "after and with" (*Nach und Mitvollzug*) those of the lecturer. The lecturer has taken these decisive steps in advance, or has prepared the way for them. The thinking required for such preparation precedes both the preparation itself and its eventual articulation in the lecture. Thus, the thinking brought to writing and speech in the first Hölderlin lectures of 1934/35, the first Nietzsche lectures of 1936/37, and so on, precedes them. The texts of lectures and unpublished manuscripts, then, allow us to ascertain early, perhaps even the earliest, appearances of a thought in writing but cannot tell us when a thought was first thought. I agree with David Farrell Krell's point that no matter how interpreters subdivide Heidegger's thinking, "the problem remains that the moment we begin to think about any element of any part that element itself turns back and forth to all the remaining elements in Heidegger's thought. Heidegger began to think about these matters earlier than we ever imagine he could have, and his pondering of them lasted longer than we can ever anticipate."[17] Lines of thinking are projected, reworked, occasionally abandoned, expanded in one text, condensed almost to the vanishing point in another. A sentence or two in one text may present a distillation of a massive undertaking elsewhere. Heidegger's thinking is dispersed across the most diverse texts and surface periodizations. His interweaving and untangling of the lines of thinking in his texts exhibits his self-transforming inquiry. The task of the interpreter is to attempt to understand what governs the multiple transformations of this inquiry.

While Heidegger's motto for the *Gesamtausgabe* is "ways—not works," the ways of his thinking are and must be exhibited in works, and these works have an integrity or wholeness as works, a coherence that is not opposed to their openness or provisionality (G1 437). A reading of Heidegger's texts must attempt to do justice both to what is ordered, thematized, unfolded in its particularity in a given text—itself an ensemble of these undertakings—and to their dense interplay of disseminations and inscriptions across texts.

The diversity of Heidegger's works is remarkable: lecture courses on a single text or part of a text, on a single thinker, or on a poem; studies of individual philosophers and poets; public lectures; treatises on fundamental concepts of philosophy; meditations; poetry. And yet the interpreter must also recognize the rigor evident in virtually any Heideggerian text. It is necessary to learn, Heidegger claims, to read *Thus Spoke Zarathustra* in "the same rigorous manner as one of Aristotle's treatises; the same manner, be it noted, not the identical manner" (WCT 70). A text that must be read in this way has also been composed in this way. A rigorous manner of reading, however, is not a "universal schema which could be applied mechanically to the interpretation of the writings of thinkers, or even to a single work of a single thinker" (71). Heidegger writes that "all true thought," such as a dialogue of Plato, is open "by reason of its nature" to a "multiplicity of possible interpretations," for "multiplicity of meanings is the element in which all thought must move in order to be strict thought." The inexhaustibility of a Platonic dialogue belongs to the dialogue and does not represent a failure to reach some "formal-logical univocity" or, I would add, any other sort of univocity. At the very least, one must be open to the possibility that what Heidegger says concerning the works of the greatest thinkers may be true of his own works as well.

One must also bear in mind Heidegger's insistence that a lecture must speak propositionally and thus will be an obstacle to thinking and saying what cannot properly be thought and said propositionally (OTB 24). Heidegger is seldom, if ever, interested in breaking a lance in defense of the irrational; rather, his challenge is to think, when necessary, in ways more fundamental or essential than those enshrined in the tradition.

That "what must be thought about"—Being—withdraws from us; the happening of withdrawal "could be what is most present in all our present, and so infinitely exceed the actuality of everything actual" (WCT 8–9). Knowingly or not, we are drawn toward what "draws, attracts us by its withdrawal" (9). Accordingly, we are "pointers"; "we are who we are by pointing in that direction." It is in the movements of being drawn into what withdraws and pointing into the withdrawal that "man first *is* man. His essential nature lies in being such a pointer." When one is drawn into what withdraws, one is thinking, "even though he may still be far away from what withdraws, even though the withdrawal may remain as veiled as ever" (17). Socrates, because he "did nothing else than place himself into this draft, this current, and maintain himself in it," is the "purest thinker of the West," which is "why he wrote nothing." One who writes out of "thoughtfulness" must "inevitably be like those people who run to seek refuge from any draft too strong for them." The hermeneutic lesson I draw from this is the opposite of that evidently drawn by deconstructionists. We follow a text carefully not because the text is all we have but precisely because it is the best, or even the only, guide to what we do not have, to what is not a text. A hint as to what we do not have is given in Heidegger's next sentence: "An as yet hidden history still keeps the secret why all great Western thinkers after Socrates, with all their greatness, had to be such fugitives." When inquiry into the meaning of Being is understood in terms of what has "dominated our historical Dasein since antiquity," such inquiry "becomes explicitly what is, namely a reflection on the source of our hidden history" (IM 77).

A chronicle of Heidegger's way would record his engagements, both exhibited and concealed in his works, with, among others, Parmenides, Heraclitus, Aristotle, Plato, Descartes, Kant, Hegel, Schelling, Hölderlin, Kierkegaard, Nietzsche, Trakl, Dilthey, Rilke, Husserl, and Ernst Jünger. I have not attempted that most tempting of the scholar's tasks—"corrections" of his interpretations of the philosophers and poets. It is easy to show that Heidegger's interpretations often, although not always, disagree with more conventional readings, just as one may show that Aristotle misreads Plato, Hegel misreads Kant, and so on. I am concerned, however, with interpreting *Heidegger*'s thinking, which is conducted—again, often, if not always—in and through a setting-apart, an *Auseinandersetzung,* with other thinkers and poets. I accept, for the purpose of interpreting Heidegger, his own distinction between philology and philosophy, which emphasizes the latter's concern with the matter for thinking (KPM xxv).

An example may suffice to make my point. For an eminent contemporary interpreter of Heidegger, the name "Heidegger" takes the place of "a certain discursive regularity," a text or collection of texts.[18] For Heidegger, in the foreword to his Nietzsche volumes, the name "Nietzsche" "stands as the title for *the matter* of his thinking" (N1 xv). A lecture on Schelling suggests how Heidegger understands interpretation: "As with every actual interpretation of a work of thought," he writes, "it is true here that it is not the opinion which a thinker ends up with that is decisive, nor the version in which he gives this opinion" (ST 106). What is decisive is "rather the movement of questioning that alone lets what is true come into the open."

I am also not concerned here with the closely related issue of Heidegger's translations, especially of classical Greek. Again, Heidegger's principal concern is rarely, if ever, entirely philological. The "basic words" with which Heidegger is concerned are not recovered to arrive at an understanding of what the Greeks meant but rather to attempt to gain access to that to which these words somehow correspond, to that which they articulate. Here I shall simply state with dogmatic brevity that philology cannot be neutral; as a science, it is conditioned by presuppositions, not the least of which include a tacit understanding of Being, as has been the case since at least the Greeks (BT 209). Differing or opposing schools of philology exhibit, and cannot at once question and yet employ, differing or opposing tacit understandings of Being. At a more fundamental level, philology as such is intelligible as a distinctively modern science or as decisively constituted by modern science, and for Heidegger, as for Nietzsche, what the scholars dig up they first buried themselves: "What help are impressive-sounding epithets like 'basic word,' if the bases and abysses of Greek thinking so little concern us that we cover them up with labels picked at random from representational quarters that have become common for us?" (EGT 111). What philology takes for granted (indeed, what it must take for granted) is precisely what philosophy or thinking must question—

that we have, or can have, a science of language. The horizon of inquiry into the Being of language is "veiled" (BT 209). Because we are within language, we "can never step out of it and look at it from somewhere else" (OWL 134). What we seem to see of the nature of language is always conditioned, for we "remain committed to and within the being of language" "in order to be who we are." This condition gives us our appropriate dwelling, that "realm where we, who are needed and used to speak language, dwell as *mortals*."

Finally, I want to draw attention to the limits of psychological and ideological interpretations of Heidegger to which Heidegger directs us himself. First, on the notion that a philosophical problem is solved by uncovering psychological impulses alleged to lie beneath it, Heidegger writes: "One can pacify himself with the satisfaction of such world-view psychological curiosity, but it must remain clear that hunting for instinctual motivations in the history of the mind would have neither a possible object to study, nor any justification whatever, nor the possibility of accomplishing anything, if the problems were identical with the psychological motivations that play a part in mastering problems" (MFL 115).

Second, ideological interpretations of Heidegger are inherently limited, at best, in their power to illuminate his thought. The reduction of Heidegger's thinking to ideological discourse is perhaps the best way to persuade us not to read him. A former teacher of mine remarks: "A Locke bent on justifying child labor, a Montesquieu glorifying the nobility of the robe, a Machiavelli advising a Medici to scheme and fight, are figures too reduced to be even worth criticizing."[19] Can we add to such a list a Heidegger praising the Nazi revolution? Only through a close reading of texts in which Heidegger's political thinking is present can contribute to a decisive answer to this question.

I turn to Heidegger for some hints on how to read him when we reach, or suspect we have reached, the limits of explanations of his thought and action which depend upon the times. He writes: "When a thinker's work, or pieces and traces of his work, are available, the 'life' of a philosopher is unimportant for the public. We never get to know what is essential in a philosophical life through biographical descriptions anyhow" (ST 5). In one of his lectures on Nietzsche, Heidegger asks how thought can exert a shaping force and notes the teaching of the "classical English and French sociologists concerning the milieu—meaning both the general atmosphere and the social order" (N2 22). To this doctrine Nietzsche would reply, Heidegger tells us, that thoughts determine a person more than do other things: "They alone determine him with respect to these very foodstuffs, to this locality, to this atmosphere and social order." Heidegger then ascends to the level of fundamental principles: "In 'thought' the decision is made as to whether men and women will adopt and maintain precisely these circumstances or whether they will elect others; whether they will interpret the chosen circumstances in this way or that way; whether under this or that set of conditions they can cope with such circumstances. That such decisions often collapse into thoughtlessness does not testify *against* the domination of thought but *for* it. Taken by itself, the *milieu* explains nothing; there is no *milieu* in itself" (22–23). Obviously, one may disagree with Heidegger on this point. I refer to it to signal my intention to show, in and through his texts, how Heidegger understood his milieu, for his political thinking is not simply a distillation of his influences.

Chapter 1 combines a general introduction to Heidegger's political thinking with an examination of the crisis of science and its place in the university as the crucial site in which the wider crisis of the present age becomes visible. The second chapter is concerned primarily with Heidegger's inscription of the crisis in his account of "world" in a lecture course given in 1929/30, "The Fundamental Concepts of Metaphysics." It is here that one finds a massive statement of the basis in Heidegger's thinking for his opposition to any naturalistic understanding of human beings such as the "biological" racism of official National Socialist ideology. Here as well can be seen his deepening appropriation of Nietzsche as the decisive thinker for the present age. In chapter 3 I turn to *An Introduction to Metaphysics,* originally a lecture course from 1935/36, to show how Heidegger unfolds his understanding of the crisis of the West and of Germany from his inquiry into the question of Being. Here I emphasize the internal relation between his philosophical itinerary and his politics.

Chapters 4 and 5 are concerned with what I call Heidegger's "political science," by which I mean his attempt to rethink modern science and to mobilize it as the crucial element in his political thinking. This project brought him close to, and yet ultimately helped distance him from, National Socialism. It is in connection with this theme that I examine some of his most direct—and infamous—political utterances. In chapter 4 I show that the question of science is linked in Heidegger's thinking to the question of work, or, as I call it, borrowing from Aristotle, "properly human" work. Here I examine his understanding of work, his critique of Marx, and the relation of his view of work to the ideological doctrine of work found in National Socialism. In chapter 5 I turn directly to Heidegger's teaching on science, with an emphasis on what I believe to be his most significant discussion of science, found in the recently rediscovered and published *Beiträge zur Philosophie* (Contributions to Philosophy), written during 1936–38, which explains why science could not, in the final analysis, furnish a suitable basis for a response to the crisis.

In chapter 6 I am concerned with Heidegger's understanding of the Greeks. The issues here are two: what is the political sense of Heidegger's interpretation of Plato, and how does Heidegger understand the *polis?* Chapter 7 considers Heidegger's understanding and use of the German poet Friedrich Hölderlin. Just as "Nietzsche" marks the present age as the culmination of the Western tradition of philosophy in and as nihilism, "Hölderlin" marks the present age as determined by the absence of the gods. Heidegger's engagement with Hölderlin, and also with Georg Trakl, gathers the threads of his political thinking into an interweaving of his reflections on the present and his concern with the destiny of the Germans, with their historical task. Put briefly, Heidegger uses Hölderlin to show the depth and severity of our present condition, and he shows that the authentic appropriation of the poet by the Germans is precisely what has not yet happened. Central to these reflections is Heidegger's teaching concerning the gods. Finally, I offer in the Epilogue a brief reflection on some of the most important implications of Heidegger's political thinking.

Each chapter begins with a passage or passages from Heidegger's rectoral address, which I employ to provide access to the principal themes of the chapter. Estimates of the philosophical significance of the address differ greatly. The author of one of the standard commentaries of Heidegger, William J. Richardson, tells us that its "theme is ordinary enough" and that it is of "clear but decidedly minor importance," while Harry Neumann identifies it as a reflection of "the only serious attempt in our century to recover awareness of philosophy's necessarily political rootedness."[20] I incline more toward Neumann's assessment than that of Richardson. As we shall see, Heidegger inscribes the address in his thinking. There is no Heideggerian principle which allows us to distinguish degrees of importance among his addresses and writings. If, as Heidegger insists, his only concern is the question of Being, and if the volumes of the *Gesamtausgabe* exhibit a "being-underway in the field of a self-transforming inquiry into the manifold meanings of the question of Being" (G1 437), then the rectoral address, as well as the political speeches he gave during his rectorate, belong in the inventory of his path of thinking.

Heidegger's Political Thinking

Introduction

The most durable and unfailing touchstone of genuineness
and forcefulness of thought in a philosopher is the question as
to whether or not he or she experiences in a direct and
fundamental manner the nearness of the Nothing in the Being
of beings. Whoever fails to experience it remains forever
outside the realm of philosophy, without hope of entry.

(N2 195)

TO READ HEIDEGGER politically is to reflect on how the political
is thought in his work. For Heidegger, "Thinking the most difficult
thought of philosophy means thinking Being as time" (N1 20). My aims
in this introductory chapter are to unfold further some of the fundamental themes or lines of thinking in Heidegger that I believe join this most
difficult thought with the political. "What I name with the word Being, a
word which is of long standing, traditional, multifaceted and worn out,"
Heidegger writes, "needs man for its revelation, preservation and formation" (Sp 278). This teaching inscribes all human things, including
political things, in the question of Being. For Heidegger "every philosophical—that is, thoughtful—doctrine of man's essential nature is *in
itself alone* a doctrine of the Being of beings. Every doctrine of Being is
in itself alone a doctrine of man's essential nature" (WCT 79). In the
strict sense, however, there are neither "members of the relation, nor
the relation as such," and thus dialectic fails. What cannot be done is
to *begin* with human nature or with Being, for "every way of thinking
takes its way" within the "total relation" of Being and human nature
(80). In this text Heidegger both employs and deconstructs "relation";
if we try to put the thought contained here into an older philosophical
idiom, it is that the relation between man's nature and the Being of
beings is "internal," albeit in such a sense or to such a degree that

"internality" fails to convey the belonging Heidegger seeks to articulate. The political is to be found in this belonging.

The question of Being is the question of the meaning of Being. From its beginnings, Heidegger's thinking distinguishes beings from Being—the ontological difference. The latter is not a different sort of being or substance but rather the process or movement—"movedness" (*Bewegtheit*) as distinguished from the motion of beings (BT 427)—in and by which beings disclose themselves, becoming intelligible as present. As early as 1923 Heidegger characterizes the basic problem in thinking facticity—later, Dasein—as thinking Aristotelian *kinēsis* decisively (G61 117). This presence, however, is incomplete, for the movement of presencing has as its correlate the movement of absencing, that is, the absence of complete presence, and this absence is, moreover, somehow present.[1] Where it seems appropriate, I will represent this movement as presencing ↔ absencing and the structure of a being thus understood as presence ↔ absence. The movement of disclosure, which necessarily includes withdrawal, is one of unconcealing and concealing—which will be represented as unconcealing ↔ concealing—and comes into intelligibility, what is named "world" in Heidegger's thinking. I suggest eliminating the definite article "the" to emphasize that intelligibility happens, takes place, *as* "world." Such expressions as the "worlding of world" in Heidegger's "later" works are less enigmatic, if no less worthy of reflection, than they may seem initially. The structure of this process of disclosure—the temporality of Being (more precisely, temporality *as* Being)—has as its correlate the temporal structure of what Heidegger calls Dasein.

It is quite misleading, as Heidegger himself often notes, to understand Dasein as "man," "human nature," "consciousness," or any equivalent notion. Dasein is not derived from a "concept" of human nature (BT 226–27; cf. CT 6E–9E). This is because traditional understandings of "man" regard him as a being "available" (*vorhanden*) like other beings; they fail to comprehend that what is most important about man is the Dasein within man (KPM 337). While Dasein may be understood as human "life" (i.e., the distinctive way human beings are), "life," in turn, must be distinguished from animality, for the being of animals is also that of a thing in the world (HCT 160–61, 236–37). Ultimately, however, the existential analytic, the analysis of Dasein, is and must be distinguished from any treatment of "man" in traditional

2

philosophy and theology, as well as in such disciplines as anthropology, psychology, and biology (BT 71–72).

Dasein is a way of Being of the being in and for which the question of Being becomes possible, a way characterized by temporality (BT 32–40; HCT 147–50; G21 146; BPP 267–74). The difficult thought here is that "Dasein" is the name not of a being but rather of a *site*, a location in or at which beings are at once disclosed and concealed, in or at which Being is thereby exhibited, and which also must be understood as happening, as temporal movement (BT 32, 171, 224; G21 146; BPP 267–74; N2 26–27; EPh 70–71). The later essay on Trakl contains a succinct discussion of "site" and "siting." What Heidegger's "discussion" (*Erörterung*) does is "first, to point out the proper place or site of something, to situate it, and second, to heed that place or site," leading to the question that "asks for the location of the site" (OWL 159). A site must not be understood as a neutral location. Rather, it "suggests a place in which everything comes together, is concentrated. The site gathers unto itself, supremely, and in the extreme." The gathering power, Heidegger goes on, "penetrates and pervades everything. The site, the gathering power, gathers in and preserves all it has gathered, not like an encapsulating shell but rather by penetrating with its light all it has gathered, and only thus releasing it into its own nature" (159–60).

Being as movement and site must be thought together. Since a site is a location where something is *as* something, it is necessarily a location where what is withheld from presencing is also "there." This means that the site exhibits the other of what is disclosed, its darkness, scarcely recognized by the philosophical tradition, and corresponded to with greater fidelity by poetry and "thinking."[2] Any seemingly substantive claim or positive teaching of Heidegger must, I am convinced, be understood as incorporating in some way its own conditionality, which is to say, its own darkness, thus understood. Accordingly, a Heideggerian account never claims to bring its matter to anything like complete discursive clarity. "Everything spoken stems in a variety of ways from what is unspoken" (OWL 120). "What is unspoken is not merely something that lacks voice," he writes; "it is what remains unsaid, what is not yet shown, what has as not yet reached appearance. That which must remain wholly unspoken is held back in the unsaid, abides in concealment as unshowable, as mystery" (OWL 122). Poetry and thinking are "each held in its own darkness" (90). There is, Heidegger writes, a darkness "older than truth," (OTB 71). As he puts it in "The Origin of the Work of Art," "Every being we encounter and which encounters us keeps to this curious opposition of presence and absence in that it always withholds itself at the same time in a concealedness. The clearing in which beings stand is at the same time a concealment" (PLT 53). Accordingly, he goes on, "the open place in the midst of beings, the clearing, is never a rigid stage with a permanently raised curtain on which the play of beings runs its course" (54).

As a siting or happening of a site, Dasein can be collective and historical; thus, Heidegger can write of the Dasein of a people ("our German Dasein") or of our "historical Dasein." Thus, in his answer to the question of how Dasein's Being is realized in and as the "most radical individuation" (BT 62), Heidegger says: "The becoming of Being is meant always for the historical human being. That is, for the Hellenic, the Christian, and so on."[3] The teaching on historicity, according to which the resolute taking over of tradition is an "originary happening" (*ursprünglicher Geschehen*) of individual Dasein and the "community of the people" as "fortune" and "common fortune" (*Schicksal, Geschick*) (BT 435–36), after all, answers the question of whether Dasein is intelligible in a "more originary way than in the projection of its authentic existence" (422). Because Dasein is never simply individual, it is not evidence of an incoherence in Heidegger's thinking that Dasein has or can have collective and historical senses. These possible senses of Dasein mark its political dimension, and since Dasein is Da-sein, the being-open to Being, needed by Being, Being also has a political dimension.

I

Heidegger's thinking is always concerned with conditions; the question of Being as the question of the meaning of Being is everywhere and always thought in and through thinking conditions of and for this questioning. Questioning subordinate to or in service of the question of Being traces movements of thinking concerned with conditions in more specific domains of inquiry. Such inquiry is carried on in the most diverse of Heidegger's works, with or without anything that resembles a "technical" philosophical idiom, but always with great rigor. The reflections on Parmenides and Heraclitus, Hölderlin, and Trakl and the meditations on the basic words of Western thinking exhibit this rigor as much as do the works on fundamental ontology in the 1920s. Regardless of its periodization, Heidegger's thinking, then, is "transcendental."

Heidegger's transcendental discourse encompasses history in its reflection on conditions. Thus, when we ask the question What is a thing? we "seek what makes the thing a thing . . . what conditions [*bedingt*] the thing," which cannot itself be a thing (WT 8–9). This question is historical, for any definition of "thing" is invariably historical (39–54). Thus, what is called "natural" is always historical, which means, against Husserl for example, that there is no simply natural understanding of the world (40). It is possible that "in our natural world-view we have been dominated by a centuries-old interpretation of the thingness of the thing, while things actually encounter us quite differently." Thus, when we reflect upon the condition of a science, for example, "we take the step into the line of vision and onto the plane of transcendental reflection" (179). When we "ask about the thingness of the thing and endeavor to place ourselves into the realm of this question, it is nothing else than the exercise of this transcendental view point and mode of questioning." Taking possession of this realm, "being able to walk and to stand in its dimensions, is the fundamental presupposition of every scientific Dasein which wants to comprehend its historical position and task." Transcendental questioning—here concerning science—is necessary for Dasein's understanding of the conditions for its action. Such questioning is necessarily political questioning. The recognition that our "natural" world-view is historical, that when we understand a thing as a bearer of properties "it is not we who are seeing and speaking but rather an old historical tradition," brings us to a decision (40–42). We can avoid thought and adjust ourselves to what we think of as "natural," thereby taking this "thoughtlessness as a standard for the things," or we can think through and come to recognize the limits of modern science. The decisions take place "in the sphere of historical freedom, that is, where a historical Dasein decides its ground, as well as how it decides, what level of freedom of knowledge it will choose and what it will posit as freedom" (42). Heidegger goes on: "These decisions are different at differing periods and among different peoples. They cannot be forced. With the freely chosen level of the actual freedom of knowledge, that is, with the inexorableness of *questioning*, a people always posits for itself the degree of its Dasein" (42).

The "formulas" of philosophy concerning the essence of the thing are "only the residuum and sediment of basic positions taken by historical Dasein, toward, and in the midst of, things taken as a whole, and which it took itself." These "basic positions" are, contrary to their appearance, still movements, for a movement can remain "in the state of repose [*Ruhe*]" (44).

In the history of philosophy, Heidegger writes, "faulty interpretations" are not "mere defects of thoughts." Rather, they "have their reason and their necessity in Dasein's own historical existence" (BPP 321–22). There is even a "faulty interpretation conceded within the temporal interpretation of Being as such and again no arbitrary one" (322). This suggests an important point about Heidegger's project of fundamental ontology as a whole: it is not only inscribed in the historical site within and from which the question of Being must be raised, but of necessity it is inscribed as "error." The presencing of a being exhibits temporality, which thereby constitutes such presencing as having a history. The intelligibility of a being—that it is in world—is articulated in discourse as "meaning" prior to the elaboration of any technical sense of intelligibility, such as interpretation or assertion (BT 203–4); this apriority also has, or is, a history.

With thematic reflection on history comes the necessity to speak of the "turning," the *Kehre,* in connection with Heidegger. The "turning" is misunderstood as an acknowledgment of the failure of Heidegger's project of fundamental ontology, or as a matter of changes in his philosophical style or language. Rather, it is inherent in the matter for thinking (Pr xviii). In my view, there is no rupture or radical break within Heidegger's thinking but rather a deepening of the questioning of Being through deepening reflection on the condition of this questioning, whose site is now thought in terms of a movement, which Heidegger calls the "history of Being," understanding of which is necessary to think the "truth of Being." Being, "stamped as presence [*Anwesen*] by its time-character [*Zeit-Charakter*], makes the approach to Da-sein." The "turning" is Being's approach, its movement; its "time-character" requires that it is "stamped as presence" in some determinate manner. There are, in other words, many ways in which beings presence; the principles according to which they presence are those of *epochs*—the "various fundamental positions among beings" taken up by Western man as corresponding to the ways in which the presencing of beings is stamped (EPh 19).

As it illuminates beings, Being exhibits the human essence, which "unfolds historically as something fateful, preservd in Being and dispensed by Being, without ever being separated from Being" (EGT 25). In and as this movement of unconcealing ↔ concealing, Being "withdraws" and thereby "sets beings adrift in errancy"; they "come to pass in that errancy by which they circumvent Being and establish the realm of error. . . . Error is the space in which history unfolds" (26). Indeed, "without errancy there would be no connection from destiny to destiny: there would be no history."

Epochē names Being's "luminous keeping to itself in the truth of its essence," its concealment from which "comes the epochal essence of its destining, in which world history properly consists" (EGT 26–27). The way in which Being gives itself, the "way in which it clears itself," is a "historical, always epochal character" (ID 67). What will be understood and experienced as beings "has in every case already been decided by the epochal clearing and lighting of Being" (PR 84). The belonging together of man and Being, their, "toward-each-other," is a "realm of mutual appropriation," entry into which makes "thinking" in its Heideggerian sense possible (ID 33). The "leap" into such thinking gives us the "insight that we do not reside sufficiently as yet where in reality we already are." When we ask for our location, we ask, then: "In what determinate joining of Being and man?" This means, In what epoch? Epochs mark "transformations of presencing," which "shows itself as the *hen*, the unifying unique One, as the *logos*, the gathering that preserves the All, as *idea, ousia, energeia, substantia, actualitias, perceptio, monad*, as objectivity, as the being posited of self-positing in the sense of the will of reason, of love, of the spirit, of power, as the will to will in the eternal recurrence of the same" (7). As epochal, that is, as metaphysical, principles, these principles "are such as stands in the first place, in the most advanced rank . . . [they] refer to rank and order," and "we follow them without reflection" (PR 19–20). When any epochal principle, such as the principle of sufficient reason, is heard as a principle of Being, "its nature is such that it lays claim to us in our essence. . . . This is to say that the claim of Being first ushers humans into their essence" (68). An epoch, however, is not a "span of time in occurrence, but rather the fundamental trait of sending [*Geschick*]—its holding-back, for each while, so that what it gives may be received" (OTB 9). Heidegger's historical periodizations name ensembles of presencing and absencing organized around ways in which Being takes place, for Being "takes its essential stamping each time from one being that gives the measure" (EPh 20).

Geschick names the way in which Being "bestows itself, proffers itself to us in beings." "We usually understand *Geschick*," Heidegger writes, "as being that which has been determined and imposed through fate: a sorrowful, an evil, a fortunate *Geschick*. This meaning is a derivative one. For *schicken* originally denotes: 'preparing,' 'ordering,' 'bringing each thing to that place where it belongs' " (PR 61). *Geschick* is a "verdict" (*Spruch*) "on the basis of which all human speaking speaks" (94). While *Spruch* translates the Latin *fatum,* Heidegger explains, "fate" is not fatalistic: "Because Being, in proffering itself, brings about the free openness of the temporal play-space and, in so doing, first frees humans unto the openness of whatever fitting essential possibilities they happen to have." The nature of this play is not to be thought with and from an understanding of Being as ground/reason; rather, Being as ground/reason is to be thought in terms of the play "which engages us mortals who are who we are only insofar as we live in proximity to death, which as radical possibility of existence is capable of bringing what is most elevated to the clearing and lighting of Being and its truth" (PR 111–12). "Death is the as yet unthought standard of measure of the unfathomable," Heidegger writes, "which means, of the most elevated play in which humans are engaged in on earth, a play in which they are at stake" (112).

Heidegger emphasizes that *Geschick* does not make the history of Being a "happening characterized by a passing away and a process"; rather, it is to be thought as "proffering and withdrawing," and these are the same (62). It is difficult to think the "*Geschick*-character of Being," for "rigorously thought, this means: Being." Moreover, " 'Being' means something different from 'Being' as it occurs in the various epochs of its *Geschick*," for "there reigns in the whole of the *Geschick* of Being something that is the same which, however, does not allow itself to be represented by means of a general concept or to be extracted as a lineament from the manifold course of history." What Heidegger calls the history of Being is "determined by the way in which Being takes place, and by this alone" (OTB 8). This means that the "history" of Being is not simply a succession of principles. It is "neither the history of man and of humanity, nor the history of the human relation to beings and to Being. The history of Being is Being

8

itself, and only Being" (EPh 82). "In every phase of metaphysics a portion of a way becomes visible each time that the sending of Being clears for itself in sudden epochs of truth upon whatever is" (QCT 54). The significance of this movement for human beings is evident, for the history of thinking is not fundamentally a sequence of the changing opinions of philosophers but rather "the bestowing of the essence of humans by the *Geschick* of Being" (PR 86). "Only in the *Geschick* of Being and from out of it are we *Geschick*-like," Heidegger writes, "and as beings that are *Geschick*-like, we are compelled to find what is fitting—and that means at the same time to be enmeshed in missing what is fitting" (68). Thus, the *Geschick* "is not only not a self-contained ongoing process, but it also is not something lying over against us. Rather, it is more likely that the *Geschick* is *as* the conjunction of Being and human nature" (94). There is, however, neither a linear succession of epochal principles graded according to progress nor a regressive movement of thought back to "there is" that is a "gradation in the sense of an ever greater originariness" (PR 91; OTB 45). Thus, the history of metaphysics "remains just as essentially remote from the origin in its start as in its finish" (EPh 81).

The same in the history of Being that cannot be represented conceptually is a "legacy [*Überlieferung*] from epoch to epoch, but it does not run between epochs like a band linking them; rather, the legacy always comes from what is concealed in the *Geschick,* just as if from one source various streamlets arise that feed a stream that is everywhere and nowhere" (PR 90–91). That source is the originary or origination, *Ursprung, ursprünglich.*[4] The originary is "the rise that presences at the same time as it withdraws into itself," "a going *back* into itself, that is, towards *itself* as always going forth," (G55 365; IM 14; Phy 363; PLT 77); it is what the Greeks named *phusis,* "the originary mode of appearing," and does not "let itself be immediately experienced" (WT 83; G39 131): "Being is the self-concealing revealing, *phusis* in the originary sense" (Phy 269). Beginning with Plato, *phusis* becomes understood "in view of its relation to humans who either grasp or do not grasp it" (G55 140). *Phusis,* as Heidegger will always teach, is not to be understood from later concepts of "nature"; it is presencing ↔ absencing as such, *said* in Greek thinking, but never *thought* in that thinking, which is why, despite the inestimable significance of the Greeks in and for the West, Heidegger's "step back" from metaphysics can never be simply or essentially a return to the Greeks (ID 50–52; EGT 76–77; G55 68). To think or attempt to think this sheer movement is not to think an ultimate referent.

Anfang (inception) and *anfänglich* (inceptive) name the initiating of an epoch that belongs to that epoch, while *Beginn* (beginning) usually designates the birth or start of thinking as situated in an epoch and governed by an epochal principle (G55 78–80). Thus, the division of Being into whatness and thatness, decisive for metaphysics, at once exhibits and conceals "oblivion of Being" and thus "points to an event in the history of Being" (EPh 3–4). The originary withdraws in favor of the inceptive—a determinate understanding of Being *as* thus divided— and Western thinking (metaphysics) begins. Heidegger's remark concerning the movement of thinking in Aristotle from experience to the notion of divine substance deconstructs understandings of the subsequent course of metaphysics as progressive: "The illusion that the transformation proceeding from the essential beginning of metaphysics preserves its genuine assets while at the same time progressively developing them" (10) Inception is the happening of an age, and the inceptive comprises an epochal order of "its gods, its art, its polity, its knowledge" (WT 50). Far from bringing about the epochs, human thought and action follow the strife, the *polemos,* of unconcealing ↔ concealing (IM 92). What seems, especially in the Hölderlin lectures, to be an emphasis on founding, what may suggest to some readers a projection by Heidegger of the poet as a Machiavellian armed prophet, is ultimately conditioned by this struggle. It is certainly correct to find in Heidegger an abiding affinity for the tragic, which "is a position of the will and therewith of knowledge in regard to Being in its totality whose fundamental law lies in struggle as such" (N2 61). Thinking and epochal order occur together; their relation is not one of production or causality (EGT 94; QCT 130). The relation between the "gathering"— as Heidegger understands the Greek *legein*—of human thinking and the Heraclitean *logos* of presencing is a "pure relation, originating nowhere" (G55 328). It is essential to understand that for Heidegger inception and the inceptive are not mere appearance. Thus, today's *Geschick* "of Being into its truth is *Being itself* as initiating" (G55 345). Thus, the truth of Being is given in and as the manifold inceptions found in and as the history of Being but the originary, presencing ↔ absencing, remains unthought. At least as early as IM, and thematized

10

most prominently in *Beiträge,* is the notion of "an other inception" (*andere Anfang*). I resort to this awkwardness of "an other"—and not "another," let alone, "*the* other"—inception to signal the fact that for Heidegger the present epoch intimates the possibility of a different inception, as if the entire Western metaphysical tradition is ultimately no more than one possibility. Such an inception is most emphatically *not* a repetition of Western philosophy from the early Greeks onward, with various corrections and emendations, but rather something radically other. When we read the texts in which Heidegger speaks and writes of a preparation, it is an other inception for which we are to prepare. The difficult *political* thought in this teaching is that the *German* people, suitably prepared, are somehow a correlate of this happening.

II

The task of Heidegger's political thinking is to understand the present age in the most comprehensive possible way, to gain, to use the title of one of his lectures, "insight into that which is." To utter this insight is, ultimately, not merely to "describe the situation of our time," for "it is the constellation of Being that is uttering itself to us" (QCT 48). What determines "today" is "reckoned neither by the calendar nor in terms of world-historical occurrences, for it is determined by the period in the history of metaphysics that is most our own; it is the metaphysical determination of historical humanity in the age of Nietzsche's metaphysics" (N4 195). That determination, "the fundamental movement of the history of the West," is nihilism (QCT 62). In our age "nihilism" names Being, for "the essence of nihilism is the history in which there is nothing to Being itself" (N4 200–201). Nietzsche cannot overcome nihilism because he understands overcoming metaphysically as a revaluation of values grounded in the will to power, which is still an epochal and thus a metaphysical principle (203). Metaphysics is itself nihilism: "The essence of nihilism *is* historically as metaphysics, and the metaphysics of Plato is no less nihilistic than that of Nietzsche. In the former, the essence of nihilism is merely concealed; in the latter, it comes completely to appearance. Nonetheless, it never shows its true face, either on the basis of or within metaphysics." Metaphysics "determines the history of the Western era. Western humankind, in all its relations with beings, and even to itself, is in every respect sustained and guided by metaphysics. In the equation of metaphysics and nihilism one does not know which is greater—the arbitrariness, or the degree of condemnation of our entire history heretofore" (205).

Heidegger's various lists of problems of the present age—technology, loss of rootedness, mass society, even nihilism—were common intellectual currency for the European Right between the world wars or, mutatis mutandis, for much of the Left at the present time. What differentiates Heidegger's inventories is his teaching that what unifies them and makes them intelligible is their inscription as the end correlates of the decisive inception with and as which Western philosophy, and therewith the West, began. This is why he can write that nihilism is the " 'inner logic' of Western history" and that the technology that now dominates the earth exhibits the completion of metaphysics (N4 204–5; QCT 67; EPh 80). Thus, the question of whether the tradition's understanding of human beings as rational animals, grounded on the teaching that Being is ground/reason, exhausts the "essence of humanity," is the "world-question of thinking. Answering this question decides what will become of the earth and of human existence on this earth" (PR 129).

Metaphysics is the "realm for the essence and coming-to-pass of nihilism," within which the "disessentializing" (*Verwesung*) of the suprasensory—what Nietzsche speaks with his word "God is dead"—takes place (QCT 65). That this movement has decisive implications for the political is made evident by an inventory of principles thus deconstructed in "history's open space" that is metaphysics: "It becomes a destining that the suprasensory world, the Ideas, God, the moral law, the authority of reason, progress, the happiness of the greatest number, culture, civilization, suffer the loss of their constructive force and become void." Metaphysics can only think being "with a view to Being. Being is first and last what answers the question in which the being is always what is interrogated. What is interrogated is not Being as such. Hence, Being itself remains unthought in metaphysics, not just incidentally, but in accord with metaphysics' own inquiry" (N4 207). While it thinks Being as such in terms of being, metaphysics never thinks the "as such itself," which names unconcealment, "which is unthought in its essence" (212). Now this means that "Being itself would unfold essentially as such unconcealment—as revealing." Since this unconcealment is itself concealed, Being "stays away" (*ausbleiben*); that Being is "as such staying away," that its unfolding is withdrawing, is unthought in metaphysics (214–15; PR 54; EGT 25–26). With the movement of withdrawal, the staying away of Being, "there comes to be a relation to something like a place, away from which staying away remains what it is: the staying away of unconcealment as such" (N4 216–17). The place is our own location; the staying away of Being is exhibited in the present age as nihilism, and in the danger that is the correlate of this *Geschick*, that indeed *is* the "epoch of Being coming to presence as Enframing [*Gestell*]," the nontechnological essence of the technology that dominates man and the earth, and exhibits the "flashing of Being," that is, the happening of Being in and as which epochality as such becomes intelligible (QCT 42–43, 47).

Human comportment in its essential or most profound sense is receptive to and prepares for the turnings of epochal principles. It is impossible, Heidegger says in many texts, to return literally to an earlier epoch such as classical Greece. We cannot return to Greece "by means of a leap" anymore than we can make Christianity vanish; "the only possibility is to transform history, that is, truly to bring about the hidden necessity of history into which neither knowledge nor deed reach, and transformation truly brought about is the essence of the creative" (ST 145–46). The beginning of the West, he reminds us, was not from nothing; rather, it had to overcome "its greatest opposite, the mythical in general and the Asiatic in particular, that is, it had to bring it to the jointure of a truth of Being, and was able to do this." In his attempt to think how Being and time are related, Heidegger reaches the difficult thought that what can be said of Being and time is "there is"/"it gives" (*es gibt*) Being and time; indeed, "to think Being explicitly requires us to relinquish Being as the ground of beings in favor of the giving which prevails concealed in unconcealment, that is in favor of the it gives," which is to say, the originary (OTB 5–6). The "way in which Being takes place" is the "way in which it gives Being," which is to say, the movement of presencing that approaches and reaches man (8, 12–13). The "giving" thought here is not meant to suggest anything like a deeper ground somehow behind Being (17–22). Rather, "it gives Being" shows itself as "a sending and a destiny of presence in its epochal transmutations" (17). The presencing of presence—its movement—is the "extending reach," the "approaching, being not yet present, [that] at the same time gives and brings about what is no longer present, the past, and conversely what has been offers future to itself" (13). The structure of the relation of future, past, and present—the "time-space"—is the "mutual reaching out and opening up," the three "interplaying ways of giving, each in virtue of its own way of presencing," of the three dimensions of "true time" (14–15). The interplay of these ways of giving is the unity of the three dimensions of time—time's fourth dimension—and is the "true extending," which at once holds future, past, and present apart in their own nearness (15–16). That is, the "giving" in "it gives time" "grants the openness of time-space"—grants sitedness—"and preserves what remains in what has-been, what is withheld in approach"—conditions unconcealing ↔ concealing (16).

Ereignis—often translated as "appropriation" or "eventuation," but which I shall leave untranslated—names the determinant of the belonging together of time and Being, "that which makes any occurrence possible," but which, again, is not a ground or metaphysical first (19). Thus, *Ereignis* is neither Being nor time nor any sort of ground but rather "the neutral '*and*' in the title *On Time and Being*" (43). The "inflashing" (*Einblitz*) of Being is the "disclosing *Ereignis*," a "glancing" that at once gives light and "keeps safe the concealed darkness of its origin as the unlighted" (QCT 45). The "withdrawal," the withholding, that plays within giving, together with the sending and extending conditioned by it, belongs in *Ereignis,* which "grants the time from which history takes the granting of an epoch" (OTB 22; EPh 83). In the *Beiträge* Heidegger explains that *Ereignis* is not an "earliest" (*Früheres*) or an a priori but is rather the "time-spacelike contemporaneity [*zeitraumliche Gleichzeitigkeit*] for Being and beings" (G65 13). Acknowledging the difficulty of this thought, he writes: "*Ereignis* remains the most strange [*Befremdlichste*]" (27). It is in *Ereignis* that there arises the possibility of an overcoming of the "mere dominance of Enframing," indeed, a "transformation of Enframing into *Ereignis,* by virtue of *Ereignis*" that "would bring the appropriate recovery—appropriate, hence never to be produced by man alone—of the world of technology from its dominance back to servitude in the realm by which man reaches more truly into *Ereignis*" (ID 37). If Enframing addresses itself to us "as *Ereignis* which first surrenders man and Being to their own being, then a path would be open for man to experience beings in a more originary way—the totality of the modern technological world, nature and history, and above all their Being" (40). When thinking reaches *Ereignis*, then, it reaches the end of the history of Being, for it is now concerned with concealment as such and not with the concealment of concealment (OTB 41). Moreover, *Ereignis* is "without destiny"; it conditions *Geschick*. This cannot mean that it is without movement; "rather, it means that the manner of movement most proper to *Ereignis* turning toward us in withdrawal—first shows itself as what is to be thought." Put for the moment into a transcendental idiom, what is to be thought is conditionality as such, which for Heidegger is event-like. With this task, thinking takes leave of epochal principles and finds no replacement for them; it is the correlate of presencing ↔ absencing as such.

What has not yet been thought is the "silent word" to which thinking is the response (G55 27; OWL 121). What has not yet been done justice is that inceptive thinking "sees Being itself, imageless in its initially simple essence as a constellation" (G55 146). When the constellation of man and Being is thought as constellation, when thinking enters into *Ereignis,* then each of these terms is "set free into the freedom of its own essential richness and thereby left to the site to which, of itself, it belongs" (WCT 52). There is, or can be, a way of human comportment, a way of man's being, and thus a way for the political to be, that is the correlate of *Ereignis.* A more decisive thinking of action understands that "human bringing-forth," *poiēsis,* "depends on *phusis* as arising prior to everything else and coming toward man. *Poiein* takes *phusis* as its measure. It is *kata phusin*" (G55 367; QCT 10). Such "originary compliance" with *phusis* would be action undertaken without reference to a first principle (G55 247). Such action would not resemble the direction of practice by theory; world as intelligibility exhibited in action would retain, just as it has within epochality, "something unmastered, hidden, confusing"—its own darkness (PLT 55). Purely compliant action is attuned to and by the play of Being, which "as the abyss" "plays the play" that is "without 'why,'" and answers the question "whether and how we, hearing the movements of this play, play along with and accommodate ourselves to the play" (PR 113).

Since it is a *"withdrawal of Being* in which we stand," the "most characteristic feature for the forgetfulness of Being (and here forgetfulness should *always* be considered from the Greek *lēthē;* that is, from the self-concealing, from the self-with-drawing of Being), the characteristic feature of *our* destiny is the fact that the *question of Being,* which I pose, has not been *understood* yet" (PR 83). Heidegger's question, then, is inscribed in and is constitutive for the present situation; the movement of thinking thus exhibited is internally related to the age

which is its correlate. In "having given up the preeminence of consciousness for the sake of a new domain, the domain of Dasein, man has
but one possibility left, to attune himself to this new domain, namely,
to enter into it" (G15 390). Such attunement—called "releasement"
(*Gelassenheit*)—lies "outside the distinction between activity and passivity," a distinction that belongs to metaphysics; it is a "higher doing"
that is not an activity (DT 61). Attunement to Being as movement is, in
regard to its necessary relation to political things, the aspect of Heidegger's thinking I characterize as his political *paideia*. In the 1920s
Heidegger writes of Aristotle that "the most important thing is the
correct *paideia*, originary [*ursprünglich*] assurance in a matter, emerging from a familiarity with the matter itself, the assurance of the appropriate manner of dealing with the matter" (CT 21E–22E). The immediate context of this remark is a reflection on what is involved in
understanding time, history, and retrieval. It is unwise, I think, to
suppose that Heidegger had only "technical" issues of philosophy in
mind. His political thinking intends to be a correct *paideia* governed by
the question of Being.

1 | Retrievals and Settings-Apart

The masters always have an indelible and therefore deeper
knowledge of their roots than their disciples can ever achieve.
(WCT 184)

AT THE END of the rectoral address, Heidegger says that "no one will
even ask us whether we do or do not will" the essence of the German
university "when the spiritual strength of the West fails and the joints of
the world no longer hold, when this moribund semblance of a culture
caves in and drags all that remains strong into confusion and lets it
suffocate in madness" (RA 480). In this chapter my chief concern is to
shed light on the evolving basis in Heidegger's thinking during the
1920s for his understanding of the crisis of the West—what he will call
in *Beiträge* "the hour of the fall of the West" (G65 396). The political in
Heidegger's thinking is inseparable from his reflections on this crisis,
which are to be found in his understanding of relations between science
and the course of modern, and especially, German philosophy.

A few remarks on Heidegger's early writings and lectures are in
order. In the light shed by these works, BT must now appear as *one*
gathering of themes in his early thinking, one way in which his manifold attempts to comprehend "life" in order to comprehend Being are
worked out.[1] As such, it is a station in his path of thinking and is not
the only text from this period that must be considered carefully. In
the 1920s Heidegger seeks a conceptual apparatus freed from defective—that is, insufficiently self-reflective, theoretical—determinations,
rooted in human life and therefore capable of comprehending human
life philosophically. Phenomenology, itself rethought fundamentally in
and through Heidegger's mutual inscription of Husserl and Aristotle, is
opened up to Dilthey, and therewith to the *Geisteswissenschaften*, because Heidegger conceives the history and the "systematics" of philos-

ophy together. Human facticity, exhibited in and as self-interpreting historical conduct, action, is the site for the convergence of these two conventionally sundered traits of philosophy. Heidegger's inquiry is systematic and formal, issuing in categorial frameworks that deploy structures that attempt to exhibit ways of human facticity. The various ensembles of "factical life," culminating in the existential analytic of BT, resemble to some extent the categorial distinctions that appear in the efforts of such theorists of the *Geisteswissenschaften* as Max Weber and Georg Simmel to theorize invariant features of human experience from transcendental presuppositions such as "meaning."[2] For Heidegger, such categories are understood as ways of Dasein's Being, that is, as forms of temporality. Temporality, in turn, is understood in and through the experiential structure of early Christianity.[3] Thought more essentially, temporality leads to the question of "time," and therewith to the question of Being. In turn, such issues require attention to and a rethinking of the philosophical tradition. All of Heidegger's engagements—with Aristotle, Scholasticism, Husserl, Dilthey, the neo-Kantians, Kierkegaard, Luther, Augustine, and others—are critical appropriations, *Auseinandersetzungen,* in which he deconstructs conventional interpretations of received wisdom and attempts to retrieve the experiential structures and their deeper grounds hitherto obscured. Questioning the tradition must begin in and with the present, with present-day conditions, or with the present *as* the condition for inquiry. This moment in Heidegger's thinking makes possible his reflections on politics, for the political is a part of the present as condition.

I shall begin with a brief look at Heidegger's earliest published philosophical writings in order to show that for him the technical issues of philosophy are inscribed in human life and history, in what he calls "living spirit," from the beginnings of his thought.[4] Close study of these writings, in my view, renders implausible the notion that Heidegger somehow turned to history *after* the supposed "failure" of BT. I understand the lines of thinking in these early writings as preparation for Heidegger's thematizing of the history of Being.

The problem of "meaning" with which Heidegger is concerned, and which, I must add, already portends his engagement with theorists of the "sciences of spirit," for whom this issue is also central, requires a site (*Ort*), a "world" with its own logical structure, a domain that can belong only to philosophy (G1 212, 277, 280, 292, 302). The categorial theory required for a theory of meaning requires an account of the conditions of meaning which must, in turn, have its own spiritual and historical conditions (24–26, 227, 270). What Heidegger seeks is a categorial theory that is closely related to "life," indeed one that is somehow rooted in and thus an exhibition of "life," which was Dilthey's aim as well.[5] Hence, his expression "living problems" (174). The thinking of Duns Scotus, for example, is closely linked to the "multiplicity and tension-potential" (*Mannigfältigkeit und Spannungs-möglichkeit*) of life, which gives it the power to move from the fullness of life to the abstractions of mathematics (203). Nor are these features of Scotus's thought accidental, for they exhibit for Heidegger, who borrows Hegel's line from the preface to the *Philosophy of Right,* the forms of life of an age grown old, on which can be found the "gray on gray" of philosophy. The breadth of Scotus's theory of categories, which comprehends the thinkable by understanding "Being" as what is common to all domains of reality, is itself an exhibition of the conditions of its historical appearance, a claim that, mutatis mutandis, Heidegger will come to make for his own thinking as well (201–11). Attributing the thought to Duns Scotus, Heidegger says that our *existing* provides the ground of meaning, and the *freedom* inherent in our existing is related to the multiplicity of realms of meaning (301–2). It is crucial to recognize that for Heidegger this freedom has nothing to do with arbitrariness; rather, recognition of the conditionality of meaning brings with it awareness of the objective character of the domain of meaning (341–98).

In his explanation of the reasons why the history and systematics of philosophy must be treated together, Heidegger writes that the differences in the essential thinking of the philosophers, as exemplified in the differences between Aristotle and Kant concerning knowledge, are intrinsically related to differences in the "spiritual-historical milieu" (*geistes-geschichtliche Milieu*) (49–50). The domains of religion, politics, and the issue of the meaning of the present moment of culture are indispensable for understanding the "formation" (*Entstehung*) and historical "conditionality" (*Bedingtheit*) of philosophy (196). Even the constancy of human nature in terms of which philosophizing is often understood is itself intelligible only when philosophical problems are "retrieved" (*wiederholen*) in history. In an early statement of a pervasive theme in his thinking, Heidegger writes that philosophy, "like every other science, is regarded as having a cultural value," but "what is most proper to philosophy is its claim to be of worth and to function as a *value of life* [*Lebenswert*]" (195). Thus, "philosophical ideas are more than a scientific material with which one might concern oneself out of personal preference and the will to further and to participate in the formation of culture." There is "at the bottom of every philosophical conception a personal taking of position of the philosopher concerned." As testimony, Heidegger invokes Nietzsche, who comprehended this fact "in his implacably severe manner of thinking and in his capability of plasticity in representation with the well-known phrase, 'the drive that philosophizes' [*Trieb der philosophiert*]" (195–96).

While there is no extensive reflection on time in these early writings, Heidegger does tell us that "time, understood here as a historical category, becomes as it were the point of departure" for the understanding and practice of philosophy (195). Because philosophical issues have an inner relation to ways or forms of life, any serious study of Scholasticism, for example, must recognize the unity of medieval thinking and medieval life (198). For the medieval philosopher there is a "submersion" (*Versenkung*) in the "matter for thought handed down in and as tradition (*überlieferten Erkenntnisstoff*)" almost unthinkable in the present day. The matter for thinking dominates the thinker. Accordingly, the individuality of thinkers is subordinate to the matter for thinking, a situation which is exhibited in the dominance in medieval thinking of issues concerning universals and principles. Moreover, the medievals lack our consciousness of methodological issues because they lack the freedom from restraint characteristic of the modern epistemological subject (199). Indeed, the medieval man is not a self in the modern sense at all. He exists in a metaphysical tension (*Spannung*) toward transcendence. Reality as such is for the medieval a phenomenon bound to, to the extent that it is dependent upon, transcendent principles. Such confinement is not experienced as "unfreedom" but rather as the "right direction for the life of the spirit" (*Blickrichtung des Geisteslebens*). Heidegger asks whether modern methodological consciousness is superior or a sign of a lack of productivity (200). For the medievals, there is method in the sense of a determination of thought by the matter for thinking to the extent that Scholasticism is grounded in the thinking and spirit of Aristotle (201).

Heidegger claims to have shown both the necessity and possibility of leaving the "fundamental problem-sphere of subjectivity" (402). His thinking moves from epistemology to metaphysics, for it is only in terms of a higher objectivity, itself a rapprochement of realism and idealism, that the issues surrounding the validity of judgments can be approached (403–4). The ground for a multiplicity of domains of validity must lie in a multiplicity of regions of objectivity (404). The only suitable approach to such objectivity lies in our recognition of the concept of "living spirit" (*des lebendigen Geistes*) which encompasses such possibilities for understanding validity as "Being" and "Ought" and overcomes traditional oppositions between mental life and ideal meanings (405). "Living spirit" is the "translogical context" of transcendental inquiry. The horizon of conventional, or Kantian, transcendental logic is modern epistemology, which is inadequate. It is the living spirit in the fullness of its activities, which is to say in its history, that determines the meaning of categories (407). The ahistorical epistemological subject is an absurdity; it is an unsuitable basis for understanding living spirit (407–8). We can now see why philosophy cannot proceed without its "genuine optic," which is metaphysics, and moreover metaphysics already construed historically (406). Heidegger's program requires a "metaphysical-teleological interpretation of consciousness" in order to clarify the ways in which meanings condition the determination of objects without simply reducing them to logical objects.

The relation between living spirit and philosophy should not be thought under the heading of "world-views," a mistake which prevents recognition of the possibility of a genuine "breakthrough" (*Durchbruch*) into "true actuality" and "actual truth" (*wahre Wirklichkeit* and *wirkliche Wahrheit*) (406). In order to recover the genuine depth-dimension (*Tiefendimension*) of categorial problems, we must understand that living spirit "is as such essentially historical spirit in the broadest sense of the word." An adequate concept of spirit can only be reached in terms of its history (408). I go, I believe, only slightly beyond the letter of Heidegger's text in adding that history in turn is intelligible only in terms of spirit. Heidegger does say clearly that history and "culture-philosophic-teleological explanation" (*kulturphilosophisch-teleologische Deutung*) must become the meaning-determining elements for the problem of categories (408). As an illustration of his proposal, Heidegger argues that the manner in which the medievals lived their relation with God cannot be detached from their understanding of such technical philosophical issues as judgment and logic. Thus, the scholastic doctrine of analogical predication exhibits "the conceptual expression of the world of experience of medieval man, qualitatively fulfilled, charged with value, and drawn into relationship with the transcendent; it is the conceptual expression of the determinate form of inner [*inneren*] Dasein anchored in the transcendent and originary relationship of the soul to God" (408–9). The multiplicity of relations between God and the soul, between *Jenseits* and *Diesseits,* is the context for scholastic metaphysics. Transcendence does not cancel out man's immersion in the world but provides a necessary orienting reference to the divine. The world-view of the Middle Ages is teleological and hierarchical; the world is understood in terms of differentiations of value. Today, the life of the soul is caught in a meaningless flux without transcendence. As a consequence, contemporary man experiences "insecurity" (*Unsicherheit*) and "disorientation" (*Desorienterung*) where medieval man did not (409). We are led by Heidegger to the possibility about which he remains silent here, that *our* philosophical concepts are related to these present-day experiences. The concept of living spirit gives Heidegger an approach to the principal concerns of metaphysics that allows him to grasp the medieval conjunction of mysticism and Scholasticism, which is not reducible, he insists, to the modern opposition of rational and irrational (410). There can be an excessive rationalization of and in philosophy, for philosophy detached from life is powerless (*machtlos*), while mysticism as irrational experience is purposeless (*ziellos*). Heidegger concludes with the observation that a philosophy of living spirit finds itself of necessity committed to an *Auseinandersetzung* with Hegel (411).[6]

For Heidegger, relations between science and the university are crucial aspects of the present situation. His reflections on them, in turn, are inscribed in the larger theme of the crisis of our present condition. The 1919 lecture course on philosophy and the problems of world-views begins programmatically. Philosophy can and must become scientific; the idea of science and its realization calls for a "formative operation" (*umgestaltenden Eingriff*) that brings with itself a transport into a new "standpoint of consciousness" (*Bewusstseinsstellung*) and thereby "a unique form of the stirring of the life of the spirit" (*eine eigene Form des Lebens des Geistes*) (G56/57 3). In the Aristotle/phenomenology lecture course of 1921/22, he argues that philosophy cannot simply be "defined," nor can formal logic substitute for philosophical reflection (G61 16–26). Nor will it suffice to understand philosophy from some other supposedly firm foundation such as science or a world-view, or even from "experience," which is itself a philosophical concept (36–39). Philosophy is "original science" (*Ur-wissenschaft*), "pre-theoretical" and thus more fundamental than any other science (G56/57 3–4, 95–117; HCT 1–2). Thought radically, this conception of philosophy is the "end of philosophy" as traditionally understood (G61 35). It is also a way of "personal Dasein."

Each Dasein's personal life has a moment in which its determination, its understanding of the world, its "life-horizon" (*Lebenshorizontes*), is exhibited (G56/57 4). The life-horizon, which has as well the senses of "with-others" (*Mitmenschen*) and "society" (*Gesellschaft*), is exhibited in a variety of genuine "forms of performance and forms of life" (*Leistungs-und-Lebensform*) such as "the scientific, the religious, the cultural, the political." Heidegger's primary focus here is on the scientific form of life. The life of the man of science, like those of the religious man and the artist, is exhibited in his characteristic activity. This activity is neither theory nor practice as conventionally understood but rather "exemplary" (*vorbildlichen*) life-activity, a "mode of action" (*Wirkung*) that exhibits originary "personal-impersonal Being" (*personlich-unpersonlichen Sein*). Only as such does the scientific type of life and life-world construct itself. Science as a way of life is a "ruling habitual element in an unscientific life-world" (*mitherrschendes habituelles element in nicht-wissenschaftlichen Lebenswelten*) and possesses a significance that cannot be lost. Heidegger concludes the opening of the lecture with an injunction from Angelus Silesius—"Man, become essential!"—and a verse from the New Testament: "Who can receive this, let him receive it" (Matt. 19:12). Celibacy is the divine gift to which these words of Jesus refer; it is not immediately evident how the life of science is its contemporary counterpart, although in a book review for *Der Akademiker* in 1910 Heidegger had written that to "every *genuine* presuppositionless scientific work, belongs a certain depth of ethical power, the power of self-control and self-renunciation."[7] We begin to understand why fundamental crises in and for science have significance beyond science.

The scientist does not stand alone but is bound to a "community" (*Gemeinschaft*) of research, a "school," and the like. The "living continuity" (*Lebenszusammenhang*) of scientific consciousness takes objective form and organization in scientific academies and universities. Reform and renewal of the university is crucial, since the "real revolutionizing of the spirit" (*echten Revolutionierung des Geistes*) taking place today is totally misunderstood, and this in the university, which should be its home (4–5). "Today we are not ripe for genuine reform in the sphere of the university," Heidegger writes, for "becoming ripe for it is the matter of a whole generation [*einer ganzen Generation*]." Heidegger's use of "generation" here shows his indebtedness to Dilthey, for whom the term designates a shared historical formation and politico-cultural task.[8] Renewing the university signifies a "rebirth of genuine scientific consciousness and life-relations," which are "renewed only in regress into the genuine origins of spirit [*echten Ursprunge des Geistes*]."

I

A deeper account of the crisis of science is required. In HCT (1925) Heidegger raises the possibilities, against conventional understandings of history and nature and of the sciences concerned with them, of, first, a more fundamental inquiry capable of asking whether history as understood by spiritual or historical science truly *is* "the authentic reality of history," history in its historicity; second, whether the separation between history and nature might suggest that an "original and undivided context of subject matter remains hidden and that it cannot be restored by a subsequent effort to bring the two, nature and spirit, together within the whole of human Dasein" (HCT 1–2). I note here that Heidegger already rewrites the distinction between nature and history as a distinction between nature and spirit. In BT it is made clear that historical science is inadequate to the task of thinking historicity (BT secs. 76–77).

There is today a "crisis of the sciences" in at least two senses. Heidegger identifies the sense in which "contemporary man, especially among the young, feels that he has lost an original relationship to the sciences" (HCT 2). In 1923, Heidegger says that the present stage of science and the university have become questionworthy but thus far to no avail. In what can only be taken as a reference to Max Weber's "Science as a Vocation," he remarks that men write brochures on the crisis of the sciences, on the vocation of the sciences, but do not yet reach the fundamental issues involved (G63 32). In the 1925 lecture Weber is mentioned by name as the author of a lecture "which was so despairing over the sciences and their meaning." In Heidegger's view, Weber's position amounts to "despair and helplessness," and the solution he proposes to restore meaning to the sciences is to cultivate a world-view of science and construct from it a "mythic conception of the sciences." The absence of further comments on Weber's views suffices, in my view, to indicate Heidegger's opinion both of Weber's grasp of the problem and his solution. The second, and deeper sense, the real crisis, is internal to the sciences. Their relationship to their own subject matter has become questionable. Genuine progress occurs only when there is reflection to secure the fundamental concepts of a science in a "more originary understanding of its subject matter" (HCT 3). As Heidegger puts it in BT: "The real 'movement' of the sciences takes place when their basic concepts undergo a more or less radical revision which is transparent to itself. The level which a science has reached is determined by how far it is *capable* of a crisis in its basic concepts" (BT 29). It is important to recognize that for Heidegger the crisis is not simply that the sciences now have a questionable relationship to their subject matter, for it is the attempt to "reclaim their particular domain or objects originally" that constitutes the deeper sense of crisis. If we recognize the necessity for a "mode of experience and interpretation in principle different" from those within the sciences so that research assumes a philosophical character, the crisis, which cannot be dissolved, can be "directed" in fruitful ways *for* the sciences (HCT 3). Heidegger's teaching calls for bearing up in the face of the crisis and turning it to our advantage. A larger point may be made as well. Our decision with regard to science, if it is to be authentic, can correspond only to what essentially *is* with regard to science, to its present-day condition. It must be, in the idiom of BT, an authentic appropriation of the sciences.

The "sciences of spirit" are distinguished from the natural sciences in a crucial way. In his account of the "determination of the basic structure of worldhood as meaningfulness," Heidegger argues that references, and not things, have a primary function in the structure of the encounter of belonging to world (HCT 200–201). Heidegger mentions the Marburg school's distinction between substances and functions but finds this inadequate because the primary sense of "function" is derived from mathematical physics. "Reference" must be understood as a technical term with many senses, one of which, under discussion here, is the sense of reference as integral to the structure of the encounter of belonging to world which is "to mean" (201). In Heidegger's analysis "meaningfulness" is not a matter of rank or value as it is in everyday language. The ordinary use of "meaningful" or "meaningfulness" is "laden with predicates of value," and Heidegger questions whether "value" is an original phenomenon or rather a construction based on some presupposed ontology of nature. "Meaning" is also used in the sense of the "meaning" of a word (202). Heidegger recognizes that *this* conventional sense is related to his own but takes this opportunity to remark that "meaningfulness" is itself an inadequate name for the phenomenon under consideration. The phenomenon of "meaningfulness" does have an intrinsic connection with discourse, which Heidegger recognizes he has not yet explored. Finally, if Dasein is possible only because there is world, a problem arises. "Dasein exhibits itself as an entity *which is in its world*," Heidegger writes, "*but at the same time is by virtue of the world in which it is*" (202). There is, then, a "peculiar *union of the being of the world with the being of Dasein*," a relation intelligible only to the extent that the structures of Dasein are clarified.

If the structure of worldhood, the worldhood of the world, lies in meaningfulness, the structures of the world are correlations of meanings (203). While contemporary philosophers such as Husserl, Spengler, and Cassirer have drawn attention to signs, symbols, and the like, Heidegger finds that the universality claimed for such notions conceals both a distinctive feature of the spiritual sciences and a danger to which they are vulnerable. The spiritual, which is the object of the human sciences, is more vulnerable than nature to the necessary violence of science. It is more easily misinterpreted because a misinterpretation of the spiritual is itself spiritual. As such, it becomes a semblance of its subject matter in a way impossible for the natural sciences. The spiritual "offers less resistance than in the field of natural science, where nature immediately takes its revenge on a wrong-headed approach" (203). The "world of objects" of these sciences "seems to be easily understood and defined by anyone and by arbitrary means," which is to say that there is a "peculiar lack of need for a suitable conceptuality, without which the natural sciences, for example, simply could not advance." Heidegger's targets are interpretations guided by "universal phenomena from which all and sundry can be made—for ultimately each and every thing can be interpreted as a sign; these "pose a great danger for the development of the spiritual sciences" (204). "Nonrelationship" names our relationship to the spiritual as a relationship to its absence, or at least to its seeming indeterminate character. I will not go so far as to claim an equivalence of the spiritual and Being for Heidegger in this text, but the understanding of the spiritual which he criticizes here could be characterized as a "vapor and a fallacy," to use Nietzsche's phrase to which Heidegger will attach enormous importance (IM 29–30). The indeterminateness of the spiritual is the basis for the apparent ease with which it can be understood. There is seemingly no need for any "suitable conceptuality" for it. We are directed, of course, to the need for such conceptuality and the failure of the contemporary notion that everything is a sign or symbol to do anything more than cover over whatever may be the actual determination of the spiritual.

The crisis has another dimension not included in the 1925 lecture. "Phenomenology and Transcendental Value-Philosophy," presents Heidegger's *Auseinandersetzung* with Windelband, Rickert, and Lask, and, beyond them, with value-philosophy as such. The historical motivation of the problems of value-philosophy must be understood in terms of its conditionality in and through the nineteenth century (G56/57 124). What is decisive in the present era, and what value-philosophy has never understood, is not the originality of world-views as responses to contemporary problems but the originality of the problem posed by, and, I am tempted to interpolate, *as* science. In the face of *the* issue of the age—the significance and consequences of science—conventional philosophy is distinguished by its lack of originality and its derivative character.

What philosophy requires is an "authentic path" back to the Greeks, for its present is inauthentically related to them (AE 238–39). Accordingly, "the critique of history is always only critique of the present (*Gegenwart*]" (239). This insight helps to explain why Heidegger attempts to retrieve the Greeks and present his own teaching simultaneously. "The philosophy of today's situation moves itself," Heidegger writes, "inauthentically" (*uneigentlich*) in "Greek conceptuality" (*der griechischen Begrifflichkeit*) (249). To the extent that it has a genuine relationship to this conceptuality, it possesses a "piece of the genuine tradition in its originary meaning [*echter Tradition ihres ursprünglichen Sinnes*]." Philosophy in the present situation proceeds according to a "taking up" (*Ansetzung*) of the "idea of men, the ideal life, the representation of Being from human life in the growing of fundamental experiences," although thus far present-day approaches to these issues stand in the way of an understanding of Greek conceptuality. The "phenomenological hermeneutic of facticity" will proceed from the present situation in its interpretation of the history of philosophy, going beneath the

"the traditional and dominant interpretation for covered-over motives and unexpressed tendencies" to accomplish a "deconstructive return" (*abbauenden Rückgang*) to break through to the "originary motive-source." Hermeneutics works "only from the way of destruction" (*auf dem Wege Destruktion*). Philosophical research, then, understood in terms of thematization of factical life, is "in the radical sense 'historical' knowing." It is a "destructive setting-apart" (*destruktive Auseinandersetzung*) with its own history. We cannot have in "genuine preservation" (*eigentlicher Verwahrung*) what is not "originarily exposed [*auslegen*] and expressed [*ausdrucken*]." In his phenomenology of religion, Heidegger speaks decisively: "Philosophy is the return [*Rückgang*] to the originary-historic [*Ursprünglich-historische*]," a teaching that emphasizes that his retrieval of the originary is from its beginning in his thinking precisely not a return to earlier philosophy.[9] The "positive power" of any answer to the question of Being "must lie in its being *ancient* enough for us to learn to conceive the possibilities which the 'Ancients' have made ready for us" (BT 40). The recovery of the Greeks, then, has nothing to do with any recovery or restoration of antiquity, or of the thoughts of antiquity, but rather must be an uncovering of the possibilities of antiquity, which are not merely ancient possibilities. Philosophy is philosophizing; it is a way of life or of being, and its concepts are drawn from factical life, as both Plato (G61 48–50) and Aristotle (AE 248–67) have shown. Thus, Heidegger characterizes philosophy as "a how of self-comportment" (*ein Wie des Sichverhaltens*) (G61 50). For Plato, he goes on, philosophy cannot be "determined as *technē*" (*als technē bestimmen*). Inscribed in the present-day question of the university, this teaching means that genuine philosophy cannot be anything like a university discipline.

As his "phenomenological existential topic," Heidegger proposes to examine the "site" (*Ort*) of "factical life" as the "origin" (*Ursprung*) of meaning (G61 31). Against any traditional notion of intuition, Heidegger advances his own notion of "indication" (*Anzeige*), a formal, preconceptual definition which "is at the same time characterized as not fully and properly giving the object to be determined, but merely pointing to it and pre-giving it in a basic way" (32). This method takes Husserl's concept of an unthematic or ordinary intentionality exhibited in what is experienced but not yet known and transforms it into the theme of a distinctive kind of motion of factical life—a falling toward beings. Husserlian phenomenological reduction does not reach any sort of transcendental consciousness but rather indicates what Heidegger here will allow to be called "hermeneutical intuition" as an a priori condition *in* facticity (39). Heidegger had already arrived at an even more decisive formulation in 1919 concerning Husserl: "The pure ego would derive from the 'historical ego' via the repression of all historicity."[10]

The inscription of the movement of phenomenological reduction in facticity will also of necessity be its inscription in historicity. This is to say that factical life and philosophical research are not radically separated, for the former is exhibited in and as the Being of life, with which the latter is thematically concerned (AE 239). Philosophy, however, encounters a difficulty in understanding life (*zōē, vita*) which is centered on the "ambiguity" or "multiple senses" (*Zweideutigkeit, pollachōs legomenon*) of "human Dasein" in and for the Greeks, the Old Testament, the "New Testament–Christian" and the "Greek-Christian" (240). Indexical for this multivocity is "care" as a name for the determinate intelligibility and engagement of factical life, which must itself be analyzed in terms of its structure of "to which" (*Worauf*) and "with which" (*Womit*), encompassing death and fallenness as exhibitions of the temporality of the factical.

The contemporary understanding of Being comes from the "Greek-Christian interpretation of life," which determines the philosophical anthropology of Kant and therewith the thinking of German idealism (250). Theology lies behind the speculation of Fichte, Schelling, and Hegel and comes from Luther's "new religious fundamental position [*Grundstellung*]," which in its turn comes from his interpretations of Paul and Augustine, and his *Auseinandersetzung* with medieval Scholasticism. Finally, Scholasticism is grounded in its understanding of Aristotelian physics, psychology, ethics, and ontology. It is from this "anthropology" of the medievals, Heidegger claims, that we must understand medieval hymnology, music, architecture and the like (251). They are only "spiritually-historically" accessible from "an originary phenomenological interpretation of the philosophical-theological anthropology of the Middle Ages." "Phenomenological destruction" can reach the origin of medieval anthropology in Aristotle's physics, from which his ontology and logic "awaken." Thus, "the central phenomenon, which is the explication thema of physics," Heidegger writes, "becomes beings in the How of their being-moved" (*das Seiende im Wie seines Bewegtseins*). Even Aristotle, however, is not the beginning, for in an authentic recovery of Aristotle can be found the doctrine of Being of Parmenides and "thus the decisive step [*entscheidende Schritt*] is taken in which the meaning and fate [*Schicksal*] of western ontology and logic is decided" (252). With this step is decided, in consequence, the meaning and fate of the West.

II

In the 1919 lecture Heidegger chooses to identify the field on which the issues are contested as "culture." What is needed for genuine philosophy is a "phenomenological-historical *Auseinandersetzung*" with the philosophy of the present period (G56/57 125). Heidegger traces the origin of value-philosophy, as the culture philosophy of the present, to its roots in modern philosophy in general (129–39): "At the end of the nineteenth century, specific achievements were held to be technology [*Technik*] and the theoretical basis making it first possible: natural science. One speaks of the age of natural science, of the century of technology" (130). Heidegger's theme is the "spiritual-historical genesis" of "culture" (131). The concept of "culture" around which philosophy has revolved in the last years of the nineteenth century and the first years of the twentieth century is understood in terms of "acquisition" (*Errungenschaft*), which Heidegger employs here as a master category of modernity. The paradigm of modern acquisition is science, to which culture—also understood in terms of acquisition, as something that can be had or lost—is a response. Among the casualties of Heidegger's criticism is the very idea of "absolute values" as thought by value-related contemporary philosophy (G61 111, 165–66). The "cultural values" of the present, which he had previously invoked to constitute the intelligibility of the historical (G1 431–32), are given up when he parts with notion that the "validity" of values can furnish "genuine objectivity" (G1 273, 167–72, 216–17, 221; cf. G56/57 140–76; BT 198). Thus, Heidegger writes in BT that ontology is not "philosophy of culture" (BT 221).

The deeper roots of "culture" lie in the Enlightenment and the historical consciousness it produces (G56/57 132–35). While "Enlightenment" was not originally a historical category, it becomes such with the idea of universal history, which is grounded in the "absolute rule of mathematical natural science and rational thinking" (132). The triumph of pure thinking is the idea of "spirit" as such, as the experi-

30

ence of mankind. The universality exhibited in various theories of historical stages such as those of Turgot and Comte is predicated of mankind as a whole, and the individual becomes an instance of the human species, a "historical atom" (132–33). A crucial deficiency of Enlightenment is that "the poet was not evaluated (by Enlightenment rationalists) as a shaper within a genuine experiential world, but instead as an improver of language, which in its refinement and polish brought public and social life to an elevated stage" (133). The sun of the first friendly morning after battle—Heidegger cites Hölderlin's translation of a passage from Sophocles' *Antigone*—is not that of the astronomer or astrophysicist, which cannot touch Thebes with glory and does not acknowledge our battles (74–76). With Herder, however, the movement of history reaches beyond cosmopolitanism to the nation, now understood to have determinate qualities or a distinctive form of life, and historical reality appears other than what can be comprehended in a "schematic-rulebound, rationalistic-linear direction of progress" (133–34). Against "an abstract, rational happiness and goodness" as the goal of progress, what emerges is the importance of "individual, qualitatively original centers of reality and contexts of reality; the categories of 'ownness' [*Eigenheit*] become meaningful and related to all shapes of life, that is, *this* first becomes visible as such." In Heidegger's words, "The singing of the people teaches one to see himself as a unique value-stuff of historical Dasein [*geschichtlichen Dasein*]." The Schlegels, Niebuhr, Savigny, and Schliermacher all contribute to this line of thinking, but it is only with Hegel that the Germans reach the "decisive idea of German movement as the highest point" of the history of spirit.

The modern understanding of philosophy as its own history, which is the accomplishment of German idealism, is the spiritual context for the modern notion of culture as acquisition and performance (135). Heidegger's tracing of this history exhibits several political tendencies. First, he shares the conservative criticism of Enlightenment rationalism and progressivism. Second, he takes over the nationalism exemplified by Herder and inscribes it in the development of German idealism. Third, he articulates a radical criticism of "culture," a theme which will appear in many of his works throughout the 1930s. It is essential to understand that Heidegger is not simply endorsing the cultural politics of the German Right; rather, his criticism is directed at "culture" as such, which will always carry for him a sense of the superficial and merely contemporary. "Liberalism" will be its political embodiment. Modern natural science seems to be able to answer the traditional questions of philosophy, however, which means that the domain of culture, cultivated now by philosophy, is derivative and inessential (136). The "modern life-direction" is toward "the formation of technology in its widest sense." The resources of German thinking exhibited in the history of spirit have thus far proven unable to meet the challenge posed by science. Phenomenology alone is radical enough for this undertaking. It will take up the historical mission of German idealism and thereby show itself to be a new and originary force in the history of spirit.

The situation of German philosophy in the second half of the nineteenth century was determined by the transformation of scientific consciousness which occurred after the collapse of idealism. The attempt to make philosophy scientific was carried on in the context of the growing independence of the sciences, which led to the notion that philosophy should have the character of a theory or logic of science. Taking its bearings from the sciences, philosophy was philosophy of science and subordinate to science (G63 67–74). Thus conceived, philosophy understood itself as a return to or renewal of Kant. In Heidegger's view, this understanding, because it did not return to the actual subject matter under investigation, was essentially traditionalist and fundamentally mistaken in its reduction of Kant to a philosopher of science (HCT 13, 16). Within the sciences "empirical facts" were predominant, bringing their weight to bear on history and nature, which were already separating as subject matters. Dominated by the search for a "science of consciousness," scientific psychology penetrated and became the basic science of philosophy (G63 69). Heidegger compares this situation unfavorably with that of the Middle Ages and the Greeks, for whom "the whole man was still seen; inner psychic life, what we now so readily call consciousness, was apprehended in a natural experience which was not regarded as an inner perception and so set off from an outer one" (HCT 15). The reigning world-view was a crude scientific materialism; the historical sciences, in imitation of the natural sciences, were avowedly nonphilosophical and dominated by "facts." What passed for fundamental reflection within them was methodological inquiry. First principles were left to the "particular mental-set of the historian," which meant that whatever "impulses operative" in the historian prevailed. Since the 1870s, these impulses were "essentially nourished by politics" (13–14). Heidegger is silent here about the nature or consequences of this nourishment.

I turn again to Heidegger's discussion of the university. As the site of philosophy, the university is vulnerable to a number of objections (*Einwanden*) Heidegger raises. If "philosophy" today is "university philosophy," then its rejection of Nietzsche marks its confusion and irrelevance (G61 65–67). Leadership is called for. The situation of philosophy and the university is "without prophets and Führer-illusions [*Führeralluren*]" (69–70); "One writes today of the leadership problem [*Führerproblem*]!" (70). Indeed, the question is whether the university can do anything except exhibit "degenerate dispositions" (*degenerierte Stimmungen*). At issue are the decisions of whether our work and research simply continue on or whether we are to be seized by a "radical idea" and bring it to dwell in our Dasein, and whether, in our "going under," we allow ourselves to be brought to the most profound distress or remain with the comfort of myth and mysticism of religiosity. In the absence of passion, we are deprived of the "resolution [*Entschlossenheit*] of understanding" and fall into either a "surrogate of spiritual advertisement" or a specious objectivity (71). We can only begin to think philosophy in a way "appropriate to the situation" (*situationsbebuhrend*), and the situation of the university is "not originary" (*nicht ursprünglich*). The university must come to stand in an "objective connection to its history" to come into its own. As a historical thing, its decision must be made historically, which is to say, from its "today" (*Heute*) (73). The decision is for or against genuine philosophy in the context of the crisis of the present, a crisis inseparable from science (62–78).

The decisive question, then, is how the present is to be understood. His own generation, Heidegger claims, is unlike others because it stands at the end of one tradition and the beginning of another (73–74). It is a generation with historical consciousness; "in it we see ourselves, and out of it we see our future" (74). Spengler exemplifies this point of view, but his thinking is deficient, for his is a "philosophy of history without the historical, *lucus a non lucendo*." Moreover, his *Prussian Socialism* betrays his own teaching in *The Decline of the West:* "All was not meant so darkly, the restless activity [of decline] can go on undisturbed." I suggest that Heidegger found Spengler's celebration of Prussian virtues and *Lebensphilosophie* in *Prussian Socialism* insufficiently radical. "The talk of decay, technologization (Bergson, Spengler) is so far confused," Heidegger writes, "that the phenomena in which and for which and by virtue of which the decay is carried out are not positively made the problem" (26). Heidegger asks: How do we stand in the claim of tradition? (75) The problem of the university is the problem of the "meaning and right" (*Sinn und Recht*) of tradition (76), that is to say, the problem of authority, and therewith *the* political problem. This problem is inscribed in the problematic of history, which is to say, in our own facticity.

The university "*is* in factical life," and "the facticity of life, Dasein, is in itself historical." The university belongs, then, to the problems and crises of the present. The renewal of the university calls for a recovery of history and therewith "life," for it is "only life" and not any sort of "culture program" that "makes an 'epoch'" (*macht "Epoche"*) (G56/57 125). It is only "active Spirit" (*tätige Geist*) that does this, a truth recognized today only in the inadequate notion of philosophy as world-view. Genuine philosophy requires a "phenomenological-historical *Auseinandersetzung*" with the philosophy of the present age.

Heidegger's proposal to understand the nature of philosophy from our comportment in the university, to understand this comportment as the concrete mode of access to the fundamental question, is a call to approach this question in terms of the historical movement of the university, its "what-how" (*Was-Wie*), which makes his account a "genuine expression" (*echte Ausdruck*) of the fallen situation of the university (G61 77). "Our problematic" is to understand the determinants of our own sense of Being; this can result in bringing our "Dasein-sense" (*Daseinssinn*) to a "withdrawal" (*Abhebung*) in the direction of what is originary, which makes this sense "timely and historical" (78). The movement of withdrawal will of necessity be a mode of our Being, a comportment, an action. Our withdrawal toward the originary is also of necessity a political movement.

This withdrawal is a movement toward a reawakening of the question of Being, which for Heidegger underlies, because it discloses, the conditions for the sciences (BT 31). A history of the question of Being is "more accurately *the history of the decline and the history of the distortion of the basic question* of scientific research into the Being of entities," a "history of the incapacity to pose the question of Being in a radically new way and to work out its first fundaments anew—an incapacity which is grounded in the being of Dasein" (HCT 6). The crisis of the sciences, in its technical and political dimensions, is inscribed in the question of Being and in the history of the decline and distortion of this question. To the extent that Dasein is intelligible as the site of Being, there is already the possibility that Dasein's incapacity to pose the question of Being radically is itself related to Being.

The task of philosophy is not merely contemplative. As presented in the 1921/22 lecture, the ensemble of categories that exhibits factical life is governed by limits and is thus deployed against teachings which fail to recognize the finite. Formalized as the infinite (*Unendlichkeit*), all versions of endlessness (*Endlosigkeit*) are opposed to the "meaningful-world-having" (*bedeutsamwelthaften*) that life lives (G61 107). The infinite is a mask worn by factical life that it "sets into" (*aufsetzt*) its world and plays a central role in modern philosophies of life (107–8).

Heidegger's hermeneutics of facticity is an attempt to "restore to life its original difficulty" in the face of Dasein's tendency for the "easy" (108–10). (Heidegger cites Aristotle's teaching [*Nicomachean Ethics* 1106b28ff.] that evil belongs to the unlimited, good to the limited.) His *paideia* will be concerned with a possibility of Dasein that must, in his view, be mobilized against an inherent tendency of Dasein. The categorial structure of this hermeneutics is built upon *kinēsis*, or the "movement characters" (*Bewegungscharaktere*) of life (112). Since Heidegger understands "the Being of life as its 'facticity,'" it is necessary to be able to follow the fundamental structure of living "as movement" (114). Hermeneutics must accomplish the movements of a backward look and a forward look (*Rückblick und Vorblick*) along Dasein's path (110–17). Dasein's movement toward the unending, a basic tendency, is "hyperbolic"; its path the easy way (109). Questions concerning our access to and explication of facticity are not at bottom, Heidegger insists, merely methodological or conceptual. Rather, a decision must be made whether it is "seizing or not seizing" (*Ergreifen oder Nichtergreifen*) our Dasein (116).

At stake is whether philosophy is "disposed" appropriately in "its contemporary spiritual state of righteousness [*Rechtschaffenheit*]" and in the ground of its completion and the "reach" (*Reichweite*) and "originariness" (*Ursprünglichkeit*) of its aim, as well as concerned with the "factical relevance" of its research. That is, can questioning "bring to experience and thus to its genuine seizing-possibility [*Erfassungsmöglichkeit*]" "life as factical life in its objectivity-and-Being-direction [*Gegenstands- und Seinsweise*]"? This question prepared for BT's status as both an elucidation of and yet made possible by the question of Being, insofar as that question remains to be asked. That the work is, in Heidegger's sense, concerned with comportment, with action, is evident when we understand the question of Being is "nothing other than the radicalization of an essential tendency-of-Being which belongs to Dasein itself," which is to say that the question is itself integral to Dasein's way of Being, which means, among many other things, its action in world (BT 35). The effect of thinking the question of Being is a modification of our way of Being. Accordingly, all aspects of the question of Being in BT stand in relation to possibilities for action, which makes BT as a whole necessarily "political."

The phenomenologies of Husserl and Scheler are insufficiently radical to address the decisive issues for two crucial reason. First, they fail to understand that "what a phenomenon is as a possibility is not directly given as a phenomenon," which means that phenomenology must be *"precisely the work of laying open and letting be seen,* understood as the methodologically directed dismantling of concealments" (HCT 86, 80–89; cf. G63 67–74). Phenomenology has a critical dimension which is ignored when it is misunderstood as anything like a passive reception of appearances. Instead, *"Being-covered-up* is the *counter-concept to phenomenon,* and such concealments are really the immediate theme of phenomenological reflection." Reflection on this relation requires consideration of the question of Being, which Husserl and Scheler did not grasp (HCT 95–135). This neglect of the question of Being, however, is neither accidental nor merely the result of a philosopher's negligence (129). The question of the meaning of "Being," raised by Plato in the *Sophist,* muted in Aristotle, and even more so since, is shown in "the *history of our very Dasein,"* where history is not "the totality of public events" but rather the *"mode of happening of this Dasein"* (129). Neglect of the question is possible and "reigns in this manner for thousands of years" because what is exhibited is a "particular mode of the being of Dasein, a specific tendency toward decadence [*Verfall*]." Accordingly, Dasein, "in this mode of being of *falling,* from which it does not escape, first really comes to its being when it rebels against this tendency" (129–30).

Second, Husserl and Scheler had unwittingly (i.e., traditionally) continued the philosophical tradition. Husserl had resumed the tradition of Descartes and thus had reached the problematic status of reason, beyond which his own thinking could not go. Scheler, in contrast, had turned to Augustinian-Neoplatonic and Pascalian thought motives. In both cases, the deeper tradition of Greek philosophy is latent, which can be seen in Husserl's orientation toward a secular understanding of man as rational animal and in Scheler's Christian perspective. In an earlier version of this argument, Heidegger makes clear that facticity or Dasein is to be distinguished decisively from "man," a term which he would reserve to both the classical understanding of a rational living being and the biblical understanding of a person with personality (G63 21–33). Indeed, the concept of person would seem to have an entirely religious, and especially biblical, provenance (25–29). Heidegger's summary criticisms lead to a remarkable observation with which the preliminary part of the lecture concludes (HCT 130–31). Scheler's understanding of man as an eternal "out-toward," as a God-seeker, is derived from Pascal and therewith from medieval theology (G63 24–29). A determination of the essence of man based on transcendence and being-directed-out toward something appears in such theologians as Tatian, Calvin, and Zwingli (HCT 131). The doctrine of Genesis that man was made in God's image dominated medieval thought and had a decisive effect on Kant, who took over the Christian understanding of man "detheologized only to some extent." Then Heidegger's final lines: "This very rough account is presented only in order to come to understand the neglects uncovered by our critique, not as 'mistakes' which can be easily corrected, but as the power of the historical Dasein which we ourselves are condemned or called to be. To this last alternative we can surely respond only out of personal conviction. No scientific judgment is possible here. Perhaps even the alternative is no longer a genuine one."

This passage divides Heidegger's introduction and criticisms of his predecessors from his own substantive teaching. The division is not merely textual. A line has been drawn; on the far side of the line, from the location from which it was drawn, the Christian understanding of man appears as a historical possibility nearing its possible eclipse. The experience from which *Being and Time* was to be thought—articulated by Nietzsche's word that "God is dead"—looms ahead unnamed. From its place as the last word of Heidegger's introduction, it stands as the gateway to, or perhaps as the last condition for, Heidegger's own teaching.

III

In BT the account of historicity, which understands Dasein in a way more "originary" (*ursprünglicher*) than the existential analytic, shows that our facticity is *never* exclusively individual; it is always inscribed in a context which, as a "heritage" (*Erbe*) resolutely appropriated, brings Dasein into its "originary happening" (*ursprüngliche Geschehen*) and the "happening [*Geschehen*] of the community, of the people [*der Gemeinschaft, des Volkes*]," into its *Schicksal* and *Geschick* (BT 435–36). While *Schicksal* is often translated as "fate" and *Geschick* as "destiny," in order to distinguish individual and community or people, this decision creates the problem of thinking similarities and differences between "fate" and "destiny." Thus, Macquarrie and Robinson suggest that "*Schicksal*' [our 'fate'] might be described as the 'destiny' of the resolute individual; '*Geschick*' [our 'destiny'] is rather the 'destiny' of a larger group, or of Dasein as a member of such a group" (436 n. 1). Heidegger himself, however, makes clear that *Geschick* is no more compounded from "individual *Schicksalen*" than "Being-with-one-another" (*Miteinandersein*) is compounded as a "happening together" (*Zusammenvorkommen*) of individual subjects. A more illuminating and less makeshift translation, though not free of difficulties, is Richardson's "fortune" and "common fortune" for *Schicksal* and *Geschick* respectively.[11] Dasein, whether regarded individually or collectively, chooses its heritage resolutely and freely, which for Heidegger always means within and in terms of historically specific possibilities. Thus, Dasein's originary happening "lies in authentic resoluteness" in which the possibility it takes over is both inherited and chosen (435).

Ultimately, the distinction between individual and collective historizing is tenuous; what is said concerning individual Dasein is everywhere and always already inscribed in collective Dasein. In his account of the structure of Dasein's understanding of Being in BPP, Heidegger argues that Dasein's projection is and must be a projecting on a determinant possibility and not merely an empty or, we may say, an imaginary possibility. That upon which Dasein projects itself is a possibility of itself (BPP 277). Moreover, projection as projection *of* . . . rests upon something. Understanding as projection is and must be Dasein's existential understanding. That is, the unveiling of things is not a transformation of things into objects of contemplation. Rather,

Dasein's insight about itself has the character of truth, of uncovering. As a self-projection, understanding exhibits its fundamental mode of happening, which makes projection the authentic meaning of action. In understanding, the happening of Dasein is characterized in its historicity. Understanding is not fundamentally a mode of cognition but a basic determination of existence. It is existential because "in it existence, as the Dasein's happening in its history, temporalizes itself" (278). Since Dasein is necessarily being-with, in a world, its projection is never subjective. Dasein is never a *first* among others (278–79).

It is because Dasein *is Schicksal* that it can be affected by the "blows of *Schicksal*" (*Schicksalsschlagen*) (BT 436). "Fortune" is an awkward translation here. What is needed is perhaps the coupling "fortune/fate" or "fate/fortune," with the priority remaining to be decided in each instance. "Fortune" unsettles and deconstructs "fate," while "fate" specifies that "fortune" is experienced by Dasein determinately. A similar approach could be taken with *Geschick*. Where it seems appropriate, I shall represent these relations with fortune ↔ fate. In any case, existing thus, Dasein is "disclosed as Being-in-the-world both for the 'fortunate' circumstances which 'come its way' and for the cruelty of accidents." Fortune—or fate—does not "arise first from the clashing together of events and circumstances," for one who is "irresolute gets driven about by these—more so than one who has chosen; and yet he can 'have' no fortune." On the basis of its anticipatory resoluteness, free for death, Dasein "understands itself in its own *superior power* [*Übermacht*], the power of its finite freedom," which *is* only in its choosing to make this choice. In its choice, Dasein takes over the "*powerlessness* [*Ohnmacht*] of abandonment" to its own having chosen to choose. This assumption of powerlessness lets Dasein have a "clear vision for the accidents in the Situation that has been disclosed."

"Fortune" and "common fortune" as translations direct us to Heidegger's emphasis on the conjunction of necessity and possibility: "In Being-with-one-another in the same world and in our resolution for determinate possibilities, our fortunes [*Schicksale*] have already been guided in advance." That Heidegger has in mind nothing like the passivity often associated with "fate" is made evident by the next sentence: "The power of common fortune [*Geschickes*] first becomes free in communicating [*Mitteilung*] and in struggle [*Kampf*]," two fundamental modes of political action in Heidegger. He employs Dilthey's concept of "generation" here as we have already seen him do in the early 1920s—to name the historical site of Dasein's action: the "full authentic happening" of Dasein is found "in and with its 'generation.'"

Fortune ↔ fate not only is given as a deliverance but is also "that powerless superior power" which, grounded in temporality as its condition (which encompasses death, guilt, conscience, freedom, and finitude), allows Dasein to exist historically (436–37). Only a being essentially futural—which is to say, free for death and able to let itself be thrown back upon its "there," only a being which as futural is in the process of "having-been"—can "by freeing up for itself the possibility it has inherited, take over its own thrownness, and be in the moment of vision for 'its time.'" "Only authentic temporality which is at the same time finite," he goes on, "makes possible something like fortune ↔ fate [*Schicksal*]—that is to say, authentic historicity." Since Dasein's historicity is crucial for its authenticity, we can see the necessity for it to reach an appropriate understanding of its own time or generation. What must be stated clearly is that there can be nothing like a neutral or independent verification of this understanding, just as no such verification is possible either for any aspect of the hermeneutic of Dasein or indeed for that hermeneutic as a whole. The circularity of both the analysis and the Being of Dasein makes a "leap" into these circles "originarily and wholly" (*ursprünglich und ganz*) necessary (363). We must, then, be able to recognize our time in Heidegger's account and therewith acknowledge its illuminating power.

Authentic retrieval (*Wiederholung*) is grounded in anticipatory resoluteness. This is the possibility that Dasein might "choose its hero," since "it is in resoluteness that one first chooses the choice which makes one free for the struggle of loyally following in the footsteps of that which can be retrieved." Again, Heidegger is emphatic that retrieval neither simply brings about somewhat that is "past," nor does it "bind the 'Present' back to that which has already been 'outstripped'"; rather, in projecting possibilities, retrieval makes a "reciprocative rejoinder" (*Erwiderung*) to the possibilities retrieved (437–38). This reply is a response made in resolution, and thus in a "moment of vision" (*Augenblick*), which means it is as well a "disavowal" or a "rebuff" (*Widerruf*) of "that which in the 'today' is working itself out as the 'past'" (438). It is not, then, anything like a passive acceptance of what is fated. What follows immediately shows, I think, that retrieval outstrips a pair of alternatives that may be called, if not humanistic, then

40

perhaps, human—all too human: "Retrieval does not abandon itself to that which is past, nor does it aim at progress. In the moment of vision authentic existence is indifferent [*gleichgültig*] to both these alternatives." From these accounts of retrieval and the historicity of Dasein, it is evident that the importance of history lies in the "authentic historizing of existence which arises from Dasein's *future*." History is a "way of Being" (*Seinsweise*) of Dasein that "has its roots so essentially in the future" that death, as Dasein's ownmost possibility, "throws anticipatory existence back upon its *factical* thrownness, and so for the first time imparts to *having-been* [*Gewesenheit*] its peculiarly privileged position in the historical." Here, then, is the answer to the question of why the past has a privileged position in the ordinary understanding of history (431). The next sentence is crucial, for it exhibits the relation between the existential analytic and Dasein's historicity: "Authentic Being-toward-death—that is to say, the finitude of temporality—is the hidden basis of Dasein's historicity" (438).

Schicksal, which continues to have the force of both "fortune" and "fate," names the freeing up of oneself to the "there" of the moment of vision and is the ground of *Geschick*, which Heidegger explains here is the "historizing [*Geschehen*] of Dasein in Being-with with others." I suggest that *Geschick* retains its duality. "Fortune" and "common fortune" can translate the German here, but in the very next sentence the relationship is more complex: "*Das schicksalhafte Geschick* can in repetition be disclosed explicitly in its joining with the heritage that has come down to us." Here it appears necessary to employ something like "fateful destiny" for the Germans, but if we do, it is also necessary to remove any sense of passivity, for Heidegger goes on to write that by "retrieval Dasein has first made its ownmost history manifest." Moreover, historizing is grounded in Dasein's ecstatic temporality, as is the "disclosedness which belongs to historizing," which is "the way in which we make this disclosedness our own" (438).

Dasein's understanding of itself in terms of that which it encounters and that with which it is circumspectively concerned is not primarily cognitive but is a projecting of oneself upon one's possibility of being-in-the-world, that is, existing *as* this possibility. This is true even of the "they." Given this involvement, Dasein's connectedness is intelligible in terms of what it is concerned with and what it experiences (440). Heidegger is now able to tell us what history is *not:* it is "neither the connectedness of motions in the alterations of Objects, nor a free-floating sequence of Experiences which 'subjects' have had." Indeed, Heidegger makes clear that he is not concerned here with anything like the traditional epistemological subject: "The thesis of Dasein's historicity," he explains, "does not say that the worldless subject is historical, but that what is historical is the entity that exists as Being-in-the-world. *The historizing of history is the historizing of Being-in-the-World.*" That is, the historicity of Dasein *is* the historicity of world, which itself is grounded on the temporalizing of temporality. Dasein as factically existing "already encounters that which has been discovered within-the-world." Dasein's Being-with-others—that is, its necessarily "social" character—is inscribed in the account of historicity. Indeed, the existential analytic as a whole is set into motion in the following sentence: "With the existence of historical Being-in-the-world, what is ready-to-hand and what is present-at-hand have already, in every case, been incorporated into the history of the world."

From the sequences of arguments in BT by which Heidegger severs Dasein's historicity from historical science, I turn to an operation which allows a correct account of historicity to compare the understandings reached by historical science with the object of historical science (secs. 76–77, esp. 445–48). Heidegger's inscription of Nietzsche's understanding of historical science in *Untimely Meditations* exhibits the "use" and "abuse" of history as conditioned by the historicity of one's life, which is to say that one has already decided for "authentic or inauthentic historicity" in understanding history according to Nietzsche's classifications of the monumental, the antiquarian, and the critical (448–49). Nietzsche's classification of three kinds of history—monumental, antiquarian, and critical—is "adumbrated [*vorgezeichnet*] in the historicity of Dasein." It is on the basis of *Heidegger*'s teaching on historicity that we can grasp that these orientations must be united in any "authentic history." *Nietzsche*, however, did not draw these distinctions accidentally: "The inception of his 'study' allows us to suppose that he understood more than he has made known to us."[12]

Dasein's historicity is inscribed in Nietzsche's conception of monumental history. "Coming back resolutely to itself," Dasein, Heidegger writes, is "by retrieval, open for the 'monumental' possibilities of human existence." Monumental history has its origin in and from monumental historicity. Now since in such retrieval there is the possibility of "reverently preserving the existence that had-been-there, in which the possibility seized upon has become manifest," authentic history is antiquarian to extent that it is monumental. Through its temporalizing, Dasein unites the future and having been in the Present, which discloses the "today" authentically and "as the moment of vision" (449). However, to the extent that "today" is understood as a possibility of existence which has been seized upon and is thus futural, "authentic history becomes a way in which the 'today' gets deprived of its character as present." As Heidegger puts it, such history "becomes a way of painfully detaching oneself from the falling publicness of the 'today.' As authentic, the history which is both monumental and antiquarian is necessarily a critique of the 'Present.' "

The political sense of Heidegger's critique is to be found in his discussion of the correspondence between Dilthey and Yorck (449–55). From Heidegger's account of temporality as the ground for authentic history, it is possible to rethink historical science so that it can assist Dasein in opening itself up to the possible (449). Heidegger finds in Yorck and Dilthey the possibility of a political pedagogy informed by authentic historical science. Dasein's historicity, exhibited in resolve and retrieval, inscribed as fortune ↔ fate in what is necessarily collective, in Being-with others, conditioned by its time, self-interpreting in terms of its generation, and disclosing to itself its possibilities, also provides itself with its own political pedagogy. We glimpse this pedagogy, in the passages from Yorck. Authentic historical science exhibits a reciprocal inscription of pedagogy and science; that is, it exhibits a conjunction that outstrips the specific content and limits of historiology. What historiology may fail to provide, in other words, may well be provided either by another science or, more likely, by a deeper reflection on science. Yorck's pedagogy may be summarized, I think, as concerned with the formation of genuine individuality, a matter of *Bildung,* which is for him a "state-pedagogical task" (*Staatspaedagogische Aufgabe*). What must be explained is Heidegger's "technical" summary which follows Yorck's talk of "dissolving elemental public opinion" and making "conscience" powerful. That summary leads to the limits of Yorck and Dilthey, which are the limits of the tradition, and ultimately, as Heidegger tells us, of the *ancient* way in which the question of Being is presented. Heidegger has shown as well the limits of conventional historiology and therewith the power of his own understanding of Dasein's historicity. That thematic is not self-sufficient; it is governed by both Heidegger's overall aims in BT and by the subordinate concerns I have tried to identify. What is called for is the historical destruction of the history of philosophy. That history is ultimately what defeats the political pedagogy of Yorck and Dilthey. When that history is destroyed, the pedagogy is freed from the incoherence of the defective conceptuality in which it has been formulated. My point is not that Heidegger simply shares the project of *Bildung* as understood by Yorck and Dilthey. Rather, it is that unlike Yorck and Dilthey, Heidegger understands the interpenetration of the political task and fundamental philosophizing. The right *paideia* cannot exhibit itself apart from attention to such philosophizing, and *that* is the way in which Heidegger takes up and contributes to the "spirit of Count Yorck in the service of Dilthey's work" (455).

I conclude this chapter with a look at an argument in BPP. Section 20 (BPP 274–302) discusses temporality as the condition for the possibility of an understanding of Being. Put briefly, all comportments toward beings rest on an understanding of Being. Such an understanding is related to Dasein's existence in that it is among the possibilities for which Dasein is freed. Heidegger grasps "understanding" as know-how, which is the condition for all other comportments. As know-how, understanding has the structure of projection, which is to say, as a possibility. This possibility is *not* "an empty possibility into which I could enter and, as it were, just gab about it" (277). Projection is analyzed into that upon which Dasein projects itself, which is its own possibility and that upon which the projection rests, or that which the projection is a projection *of.* The core of understanding as projection is Dasein's existential understanding. The unveiling involved here does not mean that what is unveiled is turned into an object of contemplation. Rather, as self-projection, understanding of Being is Dasein's fundamental mode of happening. This means that understanding of Being is the authentic meaning of action (277). In and through such understanding, Dasein's happening is characterized in its historicity. Thus, understanding of Being is only derivatively a mode of cognition. Its primary sense is as a basic determination of Dasein's existence.

Now since Dasein is Being-in-the-world, its projection is always a possibility of Being-in-the-world (278–79). Dasein is never somehow initially among others or among beings, whom or which must subsequently be encountered. Accordingly, Heidegger explains, the problem for which the I-Thou relation is a proposed solution does not arise. We cannot solve the problem of solipsism with "solipsism *en deux.*" The I-Thou relation is possible only because Dasein is already in the world.

What Dasein finds in the world is inauthentic understanding, that is, Dasein's understanding of itself other than by "that apprehended possibility of itself which is most peculiarly its own" (279). The understanding of Being found in the world, however, makes possible both the experience of nature and the self-apprehension of history.

Understanding of Being is grounded in Dasein's temporality (302–18). "Temporality exists—*ist da*—as unveiled," Heidegger writes, "because it makes possible the 'Da' and its unveiledness in general" (307). Temporality is exhibited, therefore, wherever a *Da* is "intrinsically unveiled." With the horizon of the ecstatic unity of temporality, the series of projections—"understanding of beings, projection upon Being, understanding of Being, projection upon time"—reaches its end, a terminus which in its turn calls for an account of the finiteness of time (308). Since temporality as the constitution of Dasein is the source of the possibility of understanding of Being, it "as origin is necessarily richer and more pregnant than anything that may arise from it." The rank of the origin, we may say, is what elevates the possible over the actual. Accordingly, "all origination and all genesis in the field of the ontological is not growth and unfolding, but degeneration," Heidegger writes, "since everything arising *a*rises, that is, in a certain way runs *away*, removes itself from the superior force of the origin." This insight governs Heidegger's understanding of the present and of the tradition which is exhibited in and as the present. It is his transcendental deduction of the necessarily fallen condition of his age and thus the ground of his understanding of the place and significance of his own thinking.

There is one final passage from the 1927 lecture to be considered. While philosophy may regard Being as a being, the ontological difference—the difference between Being and beings—is latent in Dasein (318–19). The existence of Dasein is "to be in performance of this distinction." "Only a soul that can make this distinction," Heidegger writes, "has the aptitude going beyond the animal's soul, to become the soul of a human being" (319). The ontological difference is always temporalizing itself. Indeed, it *is* only in and as the carrying out of the distinction. Thus, ontological difference is intelligible as temporal difference. The thematizing of temporal difference yields the history of Being. The demonstration of Dasein's thoroughly public character yields collective Dasein. The *Kehre* is the thematic interweaving of these products as the exhibition of their inscription in the crisis of the West.

2 | The Happening of Crisis

Before Being can occur in its inceptive truth . . . the world
must be forced into ruin and the earth must be driven to
desolation, and humans to mere labor. Only after that decline
does the event take place in which, in a long span of time, the
sudden abiding of the inception occurs. The decline has
already taken place. The consequences of that event are what
has happened in the world history of this century.

"Overcoming Metaphysics" (EPh 85)

HEIDEGGER'S ASSUMPTION OF the rectorate is a commitment to the
"spiritual leadership" (*geistigen Führung*) of this "'high' school"
(*hohen Schule*), the German university (RA 470). The following (*Ge-
folgschaft*) of this spiritual leadership is the corporate body (*Korper-
schaft*) composed of the bodies of teachers (*Lehrerschaft*) and students
(*Schulerschaft*). The relation of leading to following, which is the fundamental political relationship in the address, is a relation between spirit
and bodies. The body of teachers, moreover, leads the body of students
(475), from which will come the leaders of the German people (471,
476, 477, 479). Indeed, the faculty is truly a faculty only if it is capable
of "spiritual legislation" (*geistiger Gesetzgebung*) (478). The German
university is the school in which the leaders and guardians (*Hüter*) of
the German people are educated and disciplined (477). The German
people (*Volk*) is characterized as a community (*Volksgemeinschaft*), a
people that knows itself in its state (471), and a people (476) in the
midst of other peoples (*Völker*). Throughout the address, Dasein is
understood collectively and historically (471–78). The following of
teachers and students "awakens and grows strong only from a true and
joint rootedness in the essence of the German university" (470). In
turn, this essence gains "clarity, rank, and power" when its spiri-

tual leaders are themselves led by "that unyielding spiritual mission [*geistige Auftrags*] that forces the fate of the German people to bear the stamp [*Gepräge*] of its history."

The conjunction of "spirit" and "force" appears in the address under the heading of the "stamp."[1] Thus, Heidegger asks if the essence of the German university has the strength to stamp (*Prägekraft*) our Dasein (470) and teaches that science must become the force that stamps, or shapes (*prägende Kraft*), the body of the German university (477). What is at issue is nothing less the failing "spiritual force" (*geistige Kraft*) of the West (479).

Derrida notes that nowhere in his work does Heidegger furnish a thematic treatment of "spirit" (*Geist*) and suggests that spirit is inscribed in "contexts that are highly charged politically"; it "perhaps decides as to the very meaning of the political as such," or "would situate the place of such a decision, if it were possible."[2] The action of the rectoral address occurs entirely in the realm of spirit. Heidegger refrains from offering his definition of "spirit" until he has both identified its task and presented the teaching on science. While we are not yet told *what* the spiritual mission is, we are told *how* this mission leads: it "forces the fate of the German people to bear the stamp of its history." Moreover, this mission is "unyielding," which is to say that its force is exerted continuously as the fate and fortune of the German people.

A succession of events in time *becomes* history only when a people is carried toward and inserted into its site and thus into the locus of the tasks set for them to which they commit themselves, which is the sense of Heidegger's understanding of the manner in which a people bears the stamp of its history. In Heidegger's words in "The Origin of the Work of Art": "History means here not a sequence in time of events of whatever sort, however important. History is the transportation of a people into its appointed task as entrance into that people's endowment" (PLT 77).[3] In becoming what it truly is, a people takes over its stamping, giving itself its destiny, which we have seen is also its fortune.

The "stamp" designates the order of an epoch; the ruling principle of an epoch is called a "stamp" (*Prägung*), and the various ruling principles "stampings." In a later text: "There is Being only in this or that destinal stamp," which is to say that within any epoch Being is exhibited only in and as a determinate stamp (ID 66). This understanding appears as well in the 1930s. There is a "saying that projects," exemplified in and by, but not limited to, poetry in a very broad sense, in which "the concepts of a historical people's essential way of being, that is, of its belonging to world history, are stamped in advance" (*vorgeprägt*) (PLT 74). Heidegger's political pedagogy is and must be brought to bear in and on a specific here and now. In the rectoral address Heidegger joins with the *Volk* in subscribing to and bearing the stamp, which is to say, the conditionality, of its history. The deeper condition of modernity which makes possible the very idea of the *Volk* is and must be set aside, given the political intention of the address and its author.[4] In this chapter I want to bring to light Heidegger's understanding of the crisis of the present, of the here and now to which his political thinking responds and corresponds, through a reading of his lecture course of 1929/30, *The Fundamental Concepts of Metaphysics: World—Finitude—Solitude* (G29/30).[5] These lectures, which contain some of Heidegger's most politically energized thinking, are crucial for an understanding of "spirit," and thus of politics, in his thought, because they present the basis in his philosophy for his criticisms not only of Nazi racist biologism but of any naturalistic understandings of human beings, through an attempt to distinguish the essence of animality as "world-poor" (*weltarm*) from the essence of Dasein as "world-building" (*weltbildend*). This project in turn is inscribed in his account of "boredom" as the "fundamental determination" (*Grundbestimmung*) of our contemporary situation. "Spirit," although not treated thematically in these lectures, is nonetheless clarified indirectly, through Heidegger's exploration of "world" and his arguments that separate decisively "world" and therewith humanity from any naturalism.

The structure of the lectures is an inversion of that of BT. The first part provides an account of the temporal structure of boredom and the "moment of vision" (*Augenblick*), while the second part furnishes an account of "world," an arrangement that reverses the order of the earlier work, in which the analysis of Dasein and world precedes the treatment of time. More important is how this inversion registers the distinctively and strongly political character of the lectures. The first part provides not merely a treatment of the fundamental determination of Dasein and its temporal structure but presents our present situation, its salient features, and a defense of Heidegger's understanding set over against other interpretations, all offered in Heidegger's own name.

For Heidegger, *the* basic feature of the present situation, exhibited in and as "deep boredom" (*tiefe Langeweile*)—examined at length—is the "remaining away" of "essential distress"; it is the *absence* of the "mystery" and "inner terror" of existence, the distressing fact that we are not sufficiently distressed, that constitutes the distress of our present situation. Formally, this condition resembles our situation with regard to the question of the meaning of Being in BT. As absence, it is the correlate of the forgetting of this question. Heidegger's aim in investigating boredom is to contribute to its awakening and therewith to a recovery of or intensification of our distress. The movement of thinking leads to the question, What is the "whole" or "totality," from which affliction has remained away? The wideness or expanse, the "as a whole" or "in totality," is "world," which leads then to the thematic issue of the lectures: What is "world"? The teaching of the second part is carried over into IM in a single sentence: "Animals have no world, nor do they have a world-environment" (IM 45).

Derrida has drawn attention to what seem to him and others to be symptoms of a fundamental aporia, if not an incoherence, in Heidegger's account. In attempting to distinguish decisively between animal and human, is not Heidegger at bottom attaching himself to the tradition? Is he not adding another chapter to the history of categorial distinctions between animal and human when he presents the decisive differences as registered in human world-building, in which, as Derrida argues, he attaches "spirit" to "world"? To the extent that Heidegger appears to place human as world-builder above animals as world-poor, he succumbs against his own deepest aims, in Derrida's view, to a "humanist teleology" that has remained "the price to be paid in the ethico-political denunciation of biologism, racism, naturalism, etc."[6] For Krell, Heidegger takes over Hegel's move from philosophy of nature to philosophy of spirit, "*the* move of metaphysics," which makes the teaching of these lectures a "very traditional sort of story."[7] What remains unasked in this line of criticism is whether there is for Heidegger the kind of animus exhibited in these readers toward any distinction that is intelligible as traditional.

The beginning of the lectures introduces philosophy as situated problematically both in the university and as related to science, worldviews, art, and religion (G29/30 1–6). It is essential, I think, to follow this opening section with care, for it forges connections between themes specific to these lectures and Heidegger's continuing attempt to understand the nature of philosophy in conjunction with the present situation.

Although genuine philosophy exhibits an ambiguity (*Zweideutigkeit*) which makes it seem to lie somewhere between science and world-views, it is ultimately unlike world-views and ranks above the sciences (15–31; cf. MFL 12–14, 179–80). Philosophy must be understood "only from itself and determinable as itself—comparable with nothing," a position from which it is "something stubbornly fixed, the extremity" (3). Understood from its "essential determination" (*Wesensbestimmung*) as "philosophizing," philosophy appears "as our own, as human doing" (4–6). From this understanding it is necessary to ask in turn, What is human? Heidegger asks: "The crown of creation or a path of error, a great misunderstanding and an abyss?" Philosophizing is a "human doing in the darkness covering the essence" of the human, which makes philosophy "something in totality and extremity, wherein an extreme utterance and dialogue of humans happens" (6, 12). Philosophy is not simply something human beings can do, nor is it centered on them; rather it comes upon or over us: "Do we know by what we admit ourselves?"

Heidegger proposes to understand philosophizing from Novalis's remark: "Philosophy is actually homesickness [*Heimweh*], the drive [*Trieb*] to be at home everywhere" (7, 12). He draws attention to the novelty—indeed the seeming impropriety—of beginning with a poet, "only a poet" and a romantic poet at that, and not a "scientific philosopher." Indeed, he reminds us that Aristotle himself tells us that "many a lie is told by singers" (*Metaphysics* 983a3f.). "Homesickness" is a principal theme of Heidegger's Hölderlin interpretations, as we shall see in a later chapter. The very word "homesickness," moreover, is "unintelligible" for traditional philosophy, for it is drawn from everyday life and is hardly a part of the philosophical vocabulary. It is also worth noting that Heidegger is silent here, but not elsewhere, about Nietzsche's characterization of German philosophy as "homesickness" for the Greek world, as the way that must follow the "rainbow bridge of concepts," which is the only way now open to it, back to the Greeks in order to rejoin the bond with them, "the hitherto highest type of human."[8] Philosophy can only be a *drive* to be at home because in philosophizing we are *not* at home. Now to be at home, Heidegger explains, is to be not only here and there, or at one's site, but rather "at all times and especially being in the whole [*im Ganzen*]" (7–8).

The whole in which we always are is "world," in which we are "always already" involved or in or to which we are "underway" (*unterwegs*) (8). "We are this on the way itself," Heidegger writes, "this passage, this 'neither one nor the other' [*Weder das Eine noch das Andere*]." This "oscillation" between the "neither-nor" is neither one nor the other; it is "yet and not yet and yet" (*Doch und doch nicht und doch*). The "unrest" (*Unruhe*) of nothing is "finitude" (*Endlichkeit*), which is not a property but rather the "fundamental type" (*Grundart*) of our being, and as such something we must "preserve" (*behüten*): "This preserving is the . . . innermost way-of-being-finite [*Verendlichung*]" (8). Finitude *is* only in preserving this "way-of-being-finite."⁹ An "isolation" (*Vereinzelung*) of the human from Dasein happens in this finitude, which has nothing to do with one's "slim and small ego"; it is a "becoming isolated" (*Vereinsamung*) in which humans achieve a nearness to things and thus to world. Accordingly, in order to understand world, finitude, and solitude, we must inquire into what happens with us and must ask what is human that they happen in our ground (9). The questions of world, solitude, and finitude owe their possibility to a "necessity in the need of our Dasein"; it is only when these questions are and remain "engrained" (*verwurzelt*) that we are "authentic" (*echt*) (252–53). Heidegger asks if what we know of human beings, "the animal, the fool of civilization, the guardian of culture, even personality," is like a shadow in us of what is "completely other," that is, Dasein (9).

It is necessary for us to decide whether to ask the questions of world, finitude, and solitude, whether we have the strength to endure them "throughout our whole existence." As Heidegger explains later, the question of world arises from the question of the meaning of "in totality"; the question of solitude arises when we reflect on the moment of vision in which Dasein resolutely appropriates its ownmost situation, and together these questions bring us to the issue of understanding how and as what deep boredom exhibits itself in its "*originary unity and joining*" (252). This reflection leads further to thinking concerning how world and solitude are related. What seems to characterize the movement of Dasein into its authentic existence is "exhaustion" (*Gebrochenheit*). Heidegger asks: "What does this exhaustion of Dasein in itself mean?" We cannot ask these questions as if they, or we, are "undetermined and irresolutely indulged." The drive to be at home is already a seeking (*Suchen*) of the way and questioning the "opening of the right path." This is to say that philosophical concepts cannot be understood correctly if we ignore what is at stake in and with them. The concepts of philosophy seize us; we are in the grip of them. This means that they are not, and cannot be, accessible unconditionally. There must be a fundamental determination (*Grundstimmung*) which conditions our philosophical conceptualization and has the character of a totality, a determination of Dasein which makes the question What is metaphysics? transform itself into the question What is human? (10–13). No ready answer is forthcoming; one becomes a puzzle for oneself. After a repetition of the question, Heidegger lists some possibilities: "an overcoming, a direction, a storm that sweeps over our planet, a recurrence or a weariness of the gods?" While "we do not know," we see that it is in "this puzzling essence that philosophy happens" (13). Genuine philosophical questioning is concerned not with "inscribing on the consciousness of humans, but rather at evoking the Dasein" in us (257–58). The questions of philosophy are its "others" (*Anders*) that are at once "the Same" (*Selbe*) as philosophy; they are reached in and through a "transformation" (*Verwandlung*) which "gives to the *happening [Geschehen]* of the history of philosophizing its own *quite original historicity [Geschichtlichkeit]*" (259). Accordingly, philosophical concepts have a "completely other and originary" provenance in our coming to stand in philosophical questioning.[10]

The aim of reflection on these questions is the "freeing of the Dasein in men" in the face of the affliction and the removal of mystery (*Geheimnis*) from Dasein (255). We must call to our Dasein in order to attend to the "horror" (*Schrecken*) that now characterizes it. The entire problematic of the lecture course is inscribed in Heidegger's enterprise because "the fundamental determinant of boredom is engrained in the temporality of Dasein," which means the "the *essence of time* itself" grounds the questions of world, finitude, and solitude; the "ground-question of metaphysics" is thus "the question concerning Being— Being and Time" (256).

The philosopher is "taken up" in and by philosophizing and is moved "in an entirely different kind of relating, originally, fundamentally different from every scientific manner of relating" (G29/30 9). One of Heidegger's most electrifying statements on philosophy expresses his teaching: "Philosophy is the opposite of all comforting and assurance. It is the whirlwind, whirling the human being into it, in order that he or she thus alone without phantasy might grasp human existence. Precisely because this truth of such grasping is something final and ultimate, it has the uttermost uncertainty as its constant and dangerous neighbor. No knower stands at every moment necessarily so close to the edge of error as the one who philosophizes" (28–29).

A fundamental determination is a *how* of Dasein and must be distinguished decisively from psychological process, mental events, consciousness, and the conceptualism of the philosophical tradition (83–103).[11] Both fundamental determinations and our effort to understand have far-reaching consequences: "The awakening of a determination and the attempt to work our way closer to this remarkable thing coincide at the end with demanding a complete recasting of our conception of the human" (93). Our "spiritual life" today is constrained in a "cul-de-sac" (*Sackgasse*) of psychological and anthropological interpretations, and our self-understanding in terms of enlightenment, tolerance, and freedom "is in its ground a comfortable and undangerous tyranny" (271). In learning and awakening our fundamental determination, which determines us "in a way as if there is no determination" (102), we learn what determines "genuine action" (*wirkliches Handeln*) and learn that "*our* action here is a *determined question*" (272). Thus, if we intend to ask the question of Being, we must know "our present situation" (*unserer heutigen Lage*) as the condition for philosophizing (103–16).

Heidegger then argues against several interpretations of the present situation, positions he regards as both inadequate and derivative, in consequence unable to awaken the determination that is both required for and in fact conditions philosophy. Before his criticisms, Heidegger sets the stage by asking: Who are the "we" who figure in these teachings? Are we individual human beings who come together in this space (*Raum*)? Or are we those who are in the university and thus to a degree determined by the sciences or by our part in the process of the formation of spirit? (103–4). And, he asks, is the history of spirit "only as a German or as a Western and furthermore European happening [*Geschehen*]" (104)? The question of "in which situation" do we stand means from or out of what demarcation or boundary (*Abgrenzung*) of the situation do we stand?

I

Spengler, Ludwig Klages, Scheler, and Leopold Ziegler all share a common standpoint for their critical accounts of the present situation based on an antithesis between our organic "life" and "spirit" (103–7). Heidegger inscribes his criticisms of them in his ongoing opposition to naturalistic conceptions of the human. Because they are insufficiently radical and do not reach what is essential, their teachings offer only spurious comfort in the midst of crisis (111–12). They exemplify the "higher journalism" of our age that trades in second- and third-hand thinking and creates the "spiritual space" (*geistigen Raum*) in which we live (106). It is instructive to note that Spengler, Klages, and Ziegler are theorists of the political Right.

I reproduce briefly Heidegger's specific criticisms. In *The Decline of the West,* Spengler traces the world-transformations accomplished by spirit against the soul and life of human beings in and through technology and the modern economy that produce a "complete unbuilding" of Dasein, exhibited in the modern large state (*Grossstadt*) (105). Klages, in his *Spirit as the Antagonist of the Soul* (1929), calls for a liberation from spirit through a return to "life," where "life" means, in Heidegger's words, "the dark boiling of the instincts, which simultaneously get taken as the fertile soil of the mythical." It is evident here that Heidegger has no sympathy for the vitalism and irrationalism of Klages's position.[12] Heidegger rejects what he portrays as Scheler's solution, the maintenance of an *Ausgleichs,* a "balancing" between or "equalization" of life and spirit, a teaching presented in his *Man in the Age of Equalization* (1929) (106). Ziegler's *European Spirit* (1929), "unoriginal and philosophically flawed," attempts to explain the conflict of life and spirit historically and presents the resolution of the conflict through a recovery of the Middle Ages. I note that one of Ziegler's earlier works, *The Holy German Empire* (1925), presented the Reich as a permanent historical mission for Germany.

Each of these interpretations of the age—indeed, the opposition of life and spirit as such—is derived from and limited by the horizon of Nietzsche's distinction between the Apollonian and the Dionysian (107). Heidegger provides a brief account of Nietzsche's teaching which prepares for his own understanding of the true importance of Nietzsche, and thus of his own thinking as measured by this understanding (107–11). In interpreting Heidegger, it is wise, I think, not to pass over any discussion of Nietzsche too quickly. What interests Heidegger here is the correlation of the opposition of Dionysus and Apollo and Nietzsche's knowledge of its importance in and for his own philosophy (108). Heidegger is clear that "Dionysus and Apollo" does not name a cultural theme of the Greeks but a matter for Nietzsche's think-ing. Thus Heidegger sets aside the issue of whether or to what extent Nietzsche's understanding of the opposition is historically correct. Hei-degger turns to the treatment of Dionysus and Apollo in *The Will to Power*, which for him is already Nietzsche's "greatest and most decisive work." He cites four aphorisms, in whole or in part, from the second division of book 4, labeled "Dionysus"; 1005, 1049, 1050, and 1052 (pp. 520–21, 539–40, 542–43). The order of the aphorisms is one of the development or transformation of the opposition, which for Heideg-ger represents the internal development of Nietzsche's thinking and shows the necessity for change in anyone who would be related in thought to Nietzsche.[13]

The first aphorism resisters Nietzsche's emerging differences with Wagner and his recognition that his own instinct, unlike that of Scho-penhauer, went "toward a *justification of life*, even at its most terrible, ambiguous, and mendacious; for this I had the formula *'Dionysian.'* " Without comment, Heidegger moves to the second aphorism, which formulates "*Apollo*'s deception" as "the *eternity* of beautiful form; the aristocratic legislation, *'thus shall it be forever!'* " The Dionysian is marked by "sensuality and cruelty. Transitoriness could be inter-preted as enjoyment of productive and destructive force, as *continual creation.*"

For Heidegger, the "most beautiful and decisive form" of the opposi-tion appears in the next aphorism, which is cited in full, but interrupted by Heidegger. I quote the first three paragraphs:

The word "*Dionysian*" means: an urge to unity, a reaching out beyond personality, the everyday, society, reality, across the abyss of transitoriness: a passionate-painful overflowing into darker, fuller, more floating states; an ecstatic affirmation of the total character of life as that which remains the same, just as powerful, just as blissful, through all change; the great pan-theistic sharing of joy and sorrow that sanctifies and calls good even the most terrible and questionable qualities of life; the eternal will to procrea-tion, to fruitfulness, to recurrence; the feeling of the necessary unity of creation and destruction.

The word "*Apollonian*" means: the urge to perfect self-sufficiency, in the typical "individual," to all that simplifies, distinguishes, makes strong, clear, unambiguous, typical: freedom under the law.

The further development of art is as necessarily tied to the antagonism between these two natural artistic powers as the further development of man is to that between the sexes. Plenitude of power and moderation, the highest form of self-affirmation in a cool, noble, severe beauty: the Apollonianism of the Hellenic will.

The last paragraph of the aphorism contains, Heidegger tells us, Nietzsche's distinction of the origin (*Ursprungs*) of his interpretation and thus his "deepest interpretation" (*tiefste Ausdeutung*) of the Greeks (110).

Nietzsche's text resumes:

> This antithesis of the Dionysian and the Apollonian within the Greek soul is one of the great riddles to which I felt myself drawn when considering the nature of the Greeks. Fundamentally I was concerned with nothing except to guess why precisely Greek Apollonianism had to grow out of a Dionysian subsoil; why the Dionysian Greek needed to become Apollonian; that is, to break his will to the terrible, multifarious, uncertain, frightful, upon a will to measure, to simplicity, to submission to rule and concept. The immoderate, disorderly Asiatic lies at his roots: the bravery of the Greek consists in his struggle with his Asiaticism; beauty is not given to him, as little as is logic or the naturalness of customs—it is conquered, willed, won by struggle—it is his *victory*.

The final decisive transformation of the opposition exhibited in the last aphorism is Nietzsche's distinction of the types "Dionysus" and "the Crucified." Here Heidegger does not cite the passage in its entirety. He provides the following:

> *The two types: Dionysus and the Crucified.* . . . It is here I set the *Dionysus* of the Greeks; the religious affirmation of life, life whole and not denied or in part (typical—that the sexual act arouses profundity, mystery, reverence). Dionysus versus "the Crucified": . . . The god on the cross is a curse on life, a signpost to seek redemption from life; Dionysus cut to pieces is a *promise* of life: it will be eternally reborn and return again from destruction.

It takes only a few words, Heidegger claims, to see that it is in *Nietzsche*—Heidegger italicizes his name throughout three paragraphs—that the opposition is "living" (*lebendig*), something that cannot be said of the four writers Heidegger has discussed, whose understandings of Nietzsche and what is at issue in his thinking are grounded in a "truly vulgar and metaphysically most questionable 'psychology'" (111). If the sequence of transformations of the Apollonian/Dionysian opposition ends in Dionysus and the Crucified, then the question of Christianity cannot be ignored. Accounts of the present based on oppositions of life and spirit suffer not only from naturalistic understandings of life but from superficial understandings of spirit which fail to recognize that spirit in the present situation, the situation which forces itself upon us, is linked to Christianity. The "journalists" Heidegger criticizes have not been able to bring themselves to ask a question Heidegger had raised, as I have shown, by 1925, if not earlier: What if the Christian alternative, humans as god-seekers, is no longer possible? Nietzsche's thinking is "where the site [*Stelle*] of an authentic [*eigentlichen*] *Auseinandersetzung* lies."

In his Nietzsche course "The Will to Power as Knowledge" (1939), Heidegger furnishes an interpretation of Nietzsche that rejects the latter's "alleged biologism" and thereby explains more fully his claim in the 1929/30 lectures that Nietzsche's understanding of "life" is itself misunderstood (N3 39–47). This account is crucial to Heidegger's aim of saving Nietzsche from Nazi distortions. Put concisely, Heidegger removes Nietzsche's basic thought that "comprehends beings as a whole as 'life' " from biology as a science (39). Given Nietzsche's discussions of "Discipline and Breeding," not to mention the blond beast, Heidegger does not deny that he uses biological language, and yet even though it is "in a way, correct" to understand his thinking as biologism, this view "presents the *main obstacle* to our penetrating to his fundamental thinking" (41).

The realm of "living beings" that is the object of biology is grounded in "metaphysical propositions" "about beings—about what they are—propositions that posit and delimit the area," and such propositions do not and cannot belong to biology as a science (41–42). Thus, "Biology as such never decides *what* is living and *that* such beings are" (42). Indeed, even if a biologist makes such a decision, he does so as a "metaphysician, as a human being who, beyond the field in question, thinks beings as a whole." Metaphysics is not simply continuous with scientific thinking as something like a more general version of it (43). Rather, a leap is required to reach it, for such reflection on a science is "something essentially different" (*etwas wesentlichanderes*) from the sort of thinking that belongs to the sciences. Now such thinking cannot regulate science any more than science can ground metaphysics (43–44). Science and its customary form and level of self-reflection are both "historically grounded on the actual dominance of a particular interpretation of Being, and they always move in the dominant circle of a particular conception of the essence of truth. In every fundamental self-reflection of the sciences it is always a matter of passage through metaphysical decisions that were either made long ago or are being prepared now" (44). The belief in the very idea of a scientific world-view, that is, a world-view grounded in or justified by science, is a result of the "intellectual confusion in the public mind that emerged more and more strikingly in the last third of the previous century and attained remarkable success in those half-educated circles who indulged in popular science." The source of this confused relationship between science and metaphysics, in turn, lies in the essence of modernity. When Nietzsche is thought "decisively enough," this essence becomes intelligible. Biologism transfers doctrines dominant in biology to "the other realms of beings" such as history, which, as an "arbitrary misuse" of biological thinking, is a "groundless violence [*grundlose Gewaltsamkeit*] of thinking" and a "confusion of knowledge" (45). The error of biologism, however, is not simply an unwarranted extension of concepts that belong to a science to areas that do not, but rather lies in "total ignorance of the fact that biological thinking itself can only be grounded and decided in the metaphysical realm and can never justify itself scientifically."

Nietzsche's thinking produces an "illusion" (*Anschein*) of biologism, which leads Heidegger to ask first whether Nietzsche takes over concepts from biology without understanding that such concepts "already contain metaphysical decisions," and second, whether he intends to ground the "privileged position" he seems to give to life in a ground that "has nothing more to do with the phenomena of life in plants and animals," and finally, why "the grounds of this pre-eminence [*Vorrang*] of life and of living beings comes into its own precisely in the consummation of Western metaphysics" (45–46).

Thus, when Nietzsche thinks "beings as a whole and prior to that Being" as "life" and "when he defines man in particular as 'beast of prey,'" he is thinking metaphysically, rather than biologically (46). Heidegger's claim is that in thinking "life," Nietzsche "brings the essence of Western metaphysics to completion on the historical path that is allotted to it," that is, that he brings to words what was "preserved spoken in the inceptive [*anfänglichen*] essence of Being as *phusis.*" The illusion of biologism belongs to the "foreground" of Nietzsche's thinking, within which conventional interpreters of Nietzsche move (46–47). The "form" of Nietzsche's writings, the fact that his "words and sentences provoke, fascinate, penetrate, and stimulate," inclines one to think that "if only one pursues one's impressions, one has understood Nietzsche." Instead, Heidegger writes: "We must learn to 'read'" (47). Now it is evident that he has not removed biologism from Nietzsche altogether. An *illusion* of biologism remains an illusion of *biologism* and not of something else. That is, Heidegger must both affirm that Nietzsche employs a biologistic idiom and deny that he intends it biologistically.

I return to the 1929/30 lectures. After his criticisms of the "journalists," Heidegger then speaks in his own name, from his own understanding of what is, and does not go on to address directly the issue of thinking with and against Nietzsche. Doctrines that are at bottom only examples of culture philosophy cannot reach what is decisive: the "deep boredom" (*tiefe Langeweile*) that determines all cultural-philosophical understandings of the present situation (G29/30 111–16). In standing with our culture, Heidegger writes, "we ourselves are through these world-historical site-determinations [*Ortsbestimmung*]" (111–12). The "characteristic ephemerality" (*Kurzlebigkeit*) of the teachings of culture philosophy ensures that these "these world-historical diagnoses and prognoses of culture fail us," he claims, for "they *do not attack us*" (*treffen nicht uns*). Culture philosophy as such cannot comprehend the present situation but can see, as Heidegger puts it, "at the most only today," which "completely without us" is merely the "eternal yesterday" (*ewige Gestrige*). Its very idiom of "diagnoses" and "prognoses" is alien, for its essence is not in an "originary growth" but rather leads a purely "literary existence." Culture philosophy would seem to belong to the "they" and inauthenticity. Heidegger's criticism extends to "culture" itself. He rejects as superficial the notion of culture as the "expression" (*Ausdruck*) of soul or spirit that grounds the present-day culture philosophy of "expressions, symbols, symbolic forms" (113).

Although Heidegger does not refer to Ernst Cassirer by name here, the use of "symbolic forms" makes it evident that Heidegger includes Cassirer in his criticism. Before delivering the 1929/30 lectures, Heidegger had registered his profound disagreements with Cassirer in their well-known encounter at Davos in March and April of 1929. Cassirer was not only an eminent philosopher of the academic establishment but also a liberal; to an admirer he was the "representative of the best in the universalistic tradition of German culture."[14] To the extent that this liberalism is grounded in his understanding of Kant, a criticism of this understanding is ultimately a criticism of his liberalism. A brief look at the dispute between Heidegger and Cassirer is in order.

Because Heidegger understands Kant as an ontologist and not an epistemologist, as do neo-Kantians like Cassirer, he presents his own question of Being as continuous with Kant's project (CH 214; KPM; BPP 125–29). In Cassirer's view, Kantian synthesis—"the basic power of all pure thought"—leads to the "very core of the culture- and symbol-concepts." Through reflection on how finite humans can understand necessary and universal truths, Kant had reached "objectivity" and even "absoluteness," thereby showing, in such notions as the categorical imperative, how finite humans can "achieve a conception of entities which, by definition, are not finite themselves" (CH 214–15). In contrast, Heidegger argues that Kant's work exhibits the priority of the finite. The "very idea of an 'imperative,'" Heidegger writes, "betrays its inner relationship to a finite creature." The supposed transcendence of Kantian ethics "thus remains within the bounds of the finite." The decisive issue is "what is the inner structure of existence itself, is it finite or infinite?" Since "the infinite of the ontological is essentially tied to the experience of the ontic," that is, the finite, ontology itself is "an index of finitude" (216). Unfortunately, however, Kant's ontology of the person, as exhibited in his teaching concerning moral personality, required him to conceive the person in terms of "objective ends" that are things or thinglike (BPP 132–45). The mode of being of the moral person is free action, which Kant recognized but could not theorize coherently. Against Kant, Heidegger argues that it is possible to understand the ego "in the way in which it gives itself" (145). What is called for, then, is a "suitable ontological interpretation of the subject, one that is free from the entire tradition" (146). Kant's dual ontologies of nature and morals, impossible to unite, are carried over into the thinking of his present-day disciples.

Cassirer produces a philosophy of culture and cannot reach the question of Being, because he accepts uncritically the traditional demarcations of philosophy, including those ratified by Kant (CH 217–19). The foundation Cassirer believes he possesses is "the position of idealism from which I have never wavered" (218). This position is more than a philosophical doctrine, as Cassirer's use of Goethe in his responses to Heidegger's questions shows. Heidegger's antagonism is directed against the cultural ensemble in and for which this use of Goethe sufficed to address fundamental issues.

Toward the end of a restatement of some of the principal themes of BT in which he emphasizes the finitude of existence, Heidegger says that while the philosopher does not offer a world-view directly as a doctrine, "it may become possible" in philosophizing "to realize radically the transcendence of existence itself, that is, the inner possibility of this finite creature to confront Being as such" (217). Unlike Cassirer, or for that matter, Kant, Heidegger will not ask for anything like a transcendental condition for freedom, because freedom cannot be encountered like an object of theoretical knowledge but "can be confronted only in philosophizing. All this can only mean that there is not, and cannot be," Heidegger writes, "any liberty except in acts of liberation. The only and proper way for humans to grasp freedom is this liberation of freedom in humans." Such liberation is more fundamental than the free creation of cultural forms that is for Cassirer the "hallmark of [the human's] infinity" (218). Unlike Heidegger, Cassirer projects the "common human world" as an objective world, exemplified by language, which in its capacity to bridge differences among individuals shows the "objectivity of symbolic forms" (220). Cassirer's belief that we live in and possess a world of "objective spirit" is his reason for remaining within Kant's transcendentalism (220–21).

Heidegger emphasizes that Cassirer's "form-creative consciousness" is not Dasein. Nor is Cassirer's freedom what is to be liberated through acts of liberation. For Heidegger, "liberation" means "becoming free for the finitude of existence" and thus entering into thrownness. Because it is not determined by "life" or "spirit" as traditionally understood, Dasein cannot be translated into Cassirer's philosophy. It is rather "the original unity and structure of the immanent commitment of the human who, bound to his body, is thereby bound to 'what there is' [Seiendem], in the sense that existence (being thrown into what there is) breaks through to it."

Heidegger reinscribes the discussion in Kant's question, "What is man?" (220). His answer is unequivocal. The human is "open to Being and to himself." This transcendence places him into "the whole of Being as such." The task of "philosophical anthropology" must be "rooted in the basic problematic of philosophy itself," to turn the human "beyond himself and back to Being in its wholeness, thus revealing to him, despite his freedom, the nothingness of his existence," which is "no cause for pessimism or sadness." Rather, this disclosure shows that there is "productivity only where there is real resistance, and that it is up to philosophy to turn man around from the passive preoccupation with the products of the spirit to the hard severity of his destiny." Although Cassirer replies that Heidegger's "last point was indeed an important one," he offers, presumably as a reply, his acceptance of the supposed objectivity of symbolic forms and his adherence to Kant. Cassirer's idealism cannot speak either of destiny or its hardness and thus cannot address the crises of the present. Cassirer's liberalism, therefore, is powerless.

II

We must ask of any diagnosis of the present condition: "Is this study of the human essential?" (G29/30 113). The question remains whether such teachings "hit and seize" (*trifft und ergreift*) our Dasein. Strictly speaking, we do not even need to ask "where we stand" but "must ask rather: *how does it stand with us? [wie steht es mit uns?]*" "We know well enough" about our situation, Heidegger writes, to know that it produces interpretations that show "the rule of philosophy of culture" and that "determine Dasein." Heidegger's use of the formulation "it gives" (*es gibt*) transfers to the situation the determinant of the interpretations that determine Dasein. Dasein is attuned to the present situation to the extent that it, or its condition, is indeed intelligible in terms of culture philosophy. This cannot be all, however, for it is still possible to ask: "What happens when these diagnoses of culture are given a hearing, even if in quite diverse ways?" (115).

Culture philosophies detach "us from ourselves" and lead (*führen*) us to ourselves in a "world-historical situation and role" (112). Why is it necessary for us to have this role? A torrent of questions follows:

Are we ourselves becoming insignificant that we need to have such a role? Why do we find ourselves without significance, that is, without essential possibilities for our Being? Is it perhaps that an indifference yawns at us from all quarters, an indifference whose deep grounds are hidden from us? But who will speak thus, where the inverted world, technology, the economy of men tear themselves and stop in their movement? And nevertheless we seek for ourselves after a *role?* What occurs in us, that we ask this anew? Why do we have to make ourselves interesting again? Why do we have to do that? Perhaps because we are bored with ourselves? Should one become bored with himself? Why is that? *Is it in the end with us thus, that a deep boredom draws in and out in the abysses of Dasein like a silent fog?* (Cf. WM 101; ML 42)

To comment: Culture philosophy, in diagnosing the present situation as the result or expression of a conflict between life and spirit, gives us a historical *role*, a surrogate significance in the face of boredom and indifference. Such a role, cast in the terms of culture philosophy, is *merely* a role. What Heidegger objects to in the teachings of Spengler, Klages, Scheler, Ziegler, and Cassirer is the comfort we evidently derive from having our situation explained to us so that we may prepare for what is coming "in order to be still less burdened and taken into claim and attacked" (112). The naturalistic misreading of Nietzsche which Heidegger finds in culture philosophy results in diagnoses that provide no challenge to us, while what is truly at stake in the opposition of Apollo and Dionysus in Nietzsche is ignored. If we are compelled to make ourselves interesting *again*, then we must have been compelled to make ourselves interesting *before*. Our need and capacity to make ourselves interesting diverts us from what is, while it is also a response to it. What Heidegger seeks is a response more profound than making *ourselves* interesting, for this perennial project of humanism fails in the present age, concealing from us the inscription of the age in us, exhibited as boredom. A sentence from the "Letter on Humanism" is apposite: "What still today remains to be said could perhaps become an impetus for guiding the essence of man to the point where it thoughtfully attends to that dimension of the truth of Being which thoroughly governs it" (LH 209). We cannot find ourselves by any "detestable sniffing of the soul" of the sort so popular today, for we must "return back" (*zurückgegeben*) to ourselves so that we can "rise" (*aufgegeben*) to become what we are (G29/30 116). Neither an "extensive cultural discourse" nor a new psychology will help us to find ourselves. Rather, "we must find ourselves so that we bind ourselves into our Dasein and that Da-*sein* becomes for us the *sole binding* [*einzig Verbindliche*]." Deep boredom, as a possibility of Dasein, must be understood if we are to know how it is to be awakened (211–17).

The account of boredom combines a phenomenological treatment, carried out with close attention to nuances of experience, with an equally intricate temporal treatment, made possible and necessary by the fact that *Langweile* has a sense of lingering, and thus of temporality missing from the English "boredom" (117–23).[15] In and for boredom, lingering and "passing away" (*Zeitvertrieb*) are the pivotal aspects of time. I shall abridge Heidegger's analyses in order to concentrate on the political significance of boredom.

Throughout his account, Heidegger employs a basic definition of boredom: "that into which we are held out [*das Hinhaltende*] and yet that which leaves us empty [*Leerlassende*]" (130). We cannot understand, much less overcome, boredom if we treat it as a conscious experience, that is, something objectifiable, into which we can place ourselves through an act of will or imagination (132–39). In all of these errors, "we do not *establish an originary* [*ursprüngliche*] *relation* with boredom, which is to say that it does not come to us" (136). In order to grasp it, we require "only the composure [*Gelassenheit*] *which is peculiar to the free gaze of the daily life*," free of any theory of consciousness or of the stream of experience (137).

The "being-left-empty" (*Leergelassenheit*) of things, a characteristic quality of boredom, is connected with being held out into "lingering time" as the deepening of boredom detaches itself from specific situations, objects, and experiences (138–80). The empty (*Leere*) thus builds itself into Dasein (180). Throughout these analyses Heidegger attempts to exhibit the articulations of emptiness. The emptiness into which we are held is not undifferentiated. It differs as the various modes of being held out differ. Thus, philosophy and science have their own ways of holding themselves out into emptiness, and the emptinesses encountered in and by them differs from those encountered in and by poetry, for example (194–98). When "it is boring for one" (*Es ist einem langweilig*) is a correct characterization of our attunement to our situation in its totality, we recognize the unity of "being held out into" and "being-left-empty" (206–10). The emptiness of deep boredom, in which reference to an identifiable self disappears and one is no one in particular (*niemand*), comes when "we as Dasein find ourselves entirely forsaken by beings in totality" and experience an emptiness that "is not a hole located between what is filled but concerns the entirety of beings and is nevertheless *nothing*, is *no-thing*" (210).

The time character of deep boredom is the excessive lingering of the "while" (*die Weile*); the "while" lingering in and as Dasein is the "while" that measures Dasein's lingering (217–28). As the "while" lingers and widens, deep boredom deepens still more as the condition of Dasein (230–49). The question of how does the Dasein in us stand can be asked as: "Is the human himself at bottom [*am Ende*] bored?" (241). It is precisely the *question* that cannot be understood from the standpoints of the common understanding, the "so-called praxis of life," and "all programatism" (*Programatismus*), which seek only an answer in the form of a "fixed proposition, a dogma, a conviction." Rather, the question should lead us to inquire into the structure and structural moments of boredom, the relations "being held out into" and "being-left-empty," their originary unity, and its grounding in the temporality characteristic of boredom. Against the dogmas of intellectuals, Heidegger insists on keeping the issue as a whole open and inquiring phenomenologically into it. His repetition of "we see" (*sehen wir*), in contrast with dogmatic philosophical teachings, is hardly accidental. Since we know that in the present situation the crucial questions of philosophy arise from deep boredom, it is clear that the distress of the present furnishes an opportunity. Again, destiny divides Janus-like into fate and fortune.

The emptiness, the vacuum, is not "stark nothingness" (*vollige Nichts*) but is rather "emptiness in the sense of denial, avoidance, thus emptiness as deficiency, privation, *need*" (243). Again, it is evident that emptiness is differentiated. What responds to the emptiness of *this* time, *this* situation, is "convulsions, crises, catastrophes, afflictions: contemporary social misery, political confusion, the impotence of science, the hollowness of art, the groundlessness of philosophy, the weakness of religion." The responses of men to these problems, their efforts to reach solutions, to gain order and satisfaction, involve not only individuals but "groups, Bunds, circles, classes, parties," all "organized against the afflictions, and each organization has its program." Such reactions, however, are insufficiently radical, for "these nervous defensive measures against the afflictions," Heidegger writes, "*prevent one from noticing precisely the need [Not] of the whole.*" Indeed, the afflictions themselves do not provide sufficient evidence for the emptiness of the whole, which means that a deeper questioning is necessary (243–44). What we ask is something that does not have the same character as the various afflictions but is more fundamental (244). Heidegger repeats the list of problems that begins with "contemporary social misery" to indicate precisely what the sort of affliction he is searching for is *not*. The "deepest and hidden" distress is rather the "remaining away [*Ausbleiben*] of the essential distress [*Bedrangnis*] in our Dasein in the whole." The "remaining away" of Dasein's "essential distress" is the "emptiness in the whole," which means that neither the individual nor the "community" (*Gemeinschaft*) "stands in the deeply rooted unity of an essential way of acting [*eines wesentlichen Handelns*]." While "we are those assigned by a slogan, followers of a program," "no one is the manager [*Verwalter*] of the inner greatness of Dasein and its necessities. This being-left-empty in the end vibrates in our Dasein." Because mystery is lacking, "the inner horror which every mystery bears in itself and which gives to Dasein its greatness" remains away.

Heidegger says no more about the "manager" in these lectures; it is impossible to decide the political sense of his remark solely on the basis of the text. Rockmore suggests, plausibly, I think, that Heidegger means here that "no one is really master of himself or herself" in the present situation.[16] What cannot be ignored is that the essential distress of Dasein and its response are essentially political. The remaining away of distress is concealed but yet exhibited in the practice of everyday activities, and the "organizing and program-building and experimenting" of the age are merely attempts to seek "comfort in the absence of danger [*Gefahrlosigkeit*]" (244–45). Our contentment deceives us into believing that it "is no longer necessary to be strong in the ground of our essence" (245). Heidegger claims that we are concerned "only with acquired competences," while "the present is full of problems and questions of pedagogy." That is, the skills that are so easily acquired—and here I believe Heidegger is attacking established academic ways of thinking again—are insufficient to respond to the crisis of the present. As Heidegger puts it, "Force and power can never be replaced by the accumulation of competences." What must be learned is the specific way in which we are held out into and belong (*gehören*) to the nothing as it is exhibited in Being-left-empty (246).

Dasein must come to demand of itself the great demand (*Zumtung*) of rising into its Being. Heidegger asks: "But do we all not know this?" His answer is: "Yes and no." No, to the extent that we have forgotten that when one becomes "what he *is*, he must throw the Dasein itself on his shoulder." We try to evade the "danger zone" (*Gefahrenzone*) (247). In doing this, we show that do not presume "too much of Dasein" but instead "complain about the misery of life." "Human beings must first decide anew," Heidegger writes, "for this great demand." The necessity of these decisions (*Entschlusses*) is concealed and yet revealed in "the moment of vision of our Daseins." To make this decision Dasein needs "genuine knowledge" (*echte Wissen*) of what stands in "authentic enabling" (*eigentlich Ermöglichende*). Dasein must always stand in the moment of vision so that it can give to itself an "authentic binding" (*eigentliche Verbindliche*). Such binding is never a matter of following an "ideal and fixed original"; rather, Dasein must wrest and take possession of its own possibility. Moreover, what is demanded in our situation is that the remaining away of distress must be understood and seized as Dasein's "innermost necessity" (*innerste Notwendigkeit*). "Co-announced [*Mitangesagt*] is the necessity of understanding," Heidegger writes, "that first and foremost must bring itself into freedom anew, must conceive [*begreifen*] itself as Da-sein." When we are truly distressed by the remaining away of distress, there must return with this absence a "hunger after the utmost and first possibility of this moment of vision."

Heidegger asks a series of questions announced by the phrases "we can ask" (*Wir können fragen*) or "we can only ask" (*Wir können nur fragen*) "whether" something is or is not the case (247–48). The questions may be considered rhetorical, for Heidegger has already prepared us to agree with his assessment of our condition. These questions are preceded by two positive statements. First, "we cannot maintain and make firm objectively or in itself that the emptiness empties us and thereby forces us into the peak [*Spitze*] of this moment of vision." Second, "we cannot make firm the swinging between the wideness of the emptiness and the peak of this moment of vision." That is, we cannot stabilize the movement of emptiness; we cannot ensure that it moves us to the moment of vision. Neither can we stabilize the oscillation exhibited in and by this movement. If, as I think likely, *Gelassenheit* remains the way of our being correlate to the emptiness into which we are extended, then an authentic response to our condition must be marked by a "letting go" of theory-governed action and a "letting be" of what is exhibited in and as our condition (cf. BT 344; ID 32). We cannot simply register the deep boredom of our Dasein as a "state of affairs" to which we remain indifferent. Rather, "we can ask" whether our Dasein is at bottom determined by deep boredom, whether our "present everyday humankind" in the manifold of its "doings" acts against deep boredom; "we can only ask" whether present-day humanity is forced from needs by the "wideness of its concealed deepest need," for it now finds a self-defense in "satisfying and tranquilizing itself"; whether present-day humanity "has already broken and bent around the peak of the sharpest moment of vision" and made "obtuse and preserved obtuse through the haste of [its] reactions, through the suddenness of [its] program, with which haste and suddenness [it] repulses the resolve of the moment of vision" (G29/30 248). While we cannot make firm the deep boredom in the Dasein of present-day human beings, "we can only ask" whether we today do not "suppress deep boredom precisely in and through" our present-day "humanenesses" (*Menschlichkeiten*), and thus hide from our own Dasein.

The questions we ask or can only ask are followed by statements that specify what we can do. "We can understand deep boredom only in such questioning," Heidegger writes, "by giving it space." But, he notes, questioning about the fundamental determination does not mean the "further apologizing and carrying on of [our] present-day humanenesses," but rather the freeing of the humanity, that is, the "essence" (*Wesen*) of the human, which is to say that "the Dasein in him becomes essentially released" (cf. 252–55). The freeing of Dasein in us has nothing to do with arbitrariness. The former is taken on "as its ownmost self-imposed burden," for one is free only when one can truly give oneself a burden. To ask about the fundamental determination is to ask "what the determination as such gives to ask." Only in such questioning can it be decided whether we bring courage (or "spiritedness" [*Mut*]) to what we know is given to us by this fundamental determination (248–49). We must "truly" (*wirklich*) question, asking what afflicts or distresses us in the determination and what "at the same time recedes as a *decisive possibility*"; it is necessary to attend to the "horror" (*Schrecken*) that marks our situation (249, 255). What Dasein says about itself in speaking from the fundamental determination "puts us in the path of the word" (*zum Wort verhelfen*) not for us to accomplish idle speech (*Geschwätz*) but rather for the word that addresses (*anspricht*) us to "action" and to Being (*Handeln, Sein*). The "word we ought to understand," Heidegger writes in the last sentence of part 1, is the "truth of the fundamental determination set forth from its essential content," the truth, as we may otherwise put it, of the present epoch in the history of Being.

III

Heidegger's inquiry into the world-poverty of animals and human world-building belongs of necessity to philosophy because the question of world cannot arise in and for the natural sciences (274–83, 374–88).[17] "World" in the animal's world-poverty must be distinguished from "world" in human world-building so that the former is not merely a deficient form of the latter. To anticipate Heidegger's result: What the animal lacks in lacking "world" is the "accessibility [*Zugänglichkeit*] of beings as such" grounded on an "exhibition [*Offenbarkeit*] of beings as such" (411–12). "World has the character of 'wholeness' [*Ganzheit*]" (412–13). The world-poverty of the animal, however, remains "above all obscure [*dunkel*]" (288). Heidegger's thesis requires an "insight" (*Blick*) into the animal kingdom, as in the following example. A lizard sunning itself on a rock cannot grasp the rock as rock; it has neither openness nor an absence of openness to the rock as an entity, nor yet any access to the difference between openness and its absence (cf. 361). While the rock on which the lizard rests is given to it in "some way" (*irgendwie*)—which allows us to say that the animal has world—it cannot be given to the lizard *as* a rock, and thus the animal does not have world (291–92).[18] The antinomy arises only if we have failed to distinguish adequately between the logic of "metaphysics and essentiality," which allows for such claims because it can think the manifold senses of "time," "world," and "accessibility to beings," and that of the "sound understanding of human beings," which does not (293).

What has been reached is not a resolution of the question but rather the setting within which the question must be taken up. A "resolution," or perhaps one should say a "loosening" (*Auflosung*), is possible only when we look into the "knotting of the knots" (*Verknotung des Knotens*); the "interlacing [*Verschlingung*] of the propositions: the animal has world—the animal does not have world" (294). "The extremes of world-absence and world-building" interlace, and it can only be "here in the originary loosening of the problems [that] what is called world must show itself." What we already know is that "the world of the animal . . . is not a kind and a grade of the world of men." The animal is "not only something ready-to-hand" but is determined in its "kind of Being" (*Seinsart*) in terms of that to which it has access. What is required is an account of the essence of animality.

A lengthy chapter attempts to work out this essence (295–388). I prescind from details to some of the principal features of Heidegger's account of how animals are related to world (311–18). Animals have a "capability-to" (*Fähigkeit-zu*) which relates them to their own behavior and environments (319–44). The fundamental determination of the animal, however, is *Benommenheit,* which is for animals what "comportment" (*Verhalten*) is for human beings (341–42, 346). Krell translates *Benommenheit* as "benumbedness," for *Benommen,* as the past participle of *benehmen,* means "disturbed, dazed, dizzy, dazzled, confused, mildly anesthetized"—that is, benumbed; Heidegger's choice of words "seems to rest on the essentially *privative* and *passive* sense of *Benommensein.*"[19] For Krell, the distinction between *Benommenheit* and *Verhalten* "drives from an ancient prejudice, that Heidegger's *sachliche* interpretation is in fact guided by what Nietzsche would have called a *moral* prejudice, indeed *the* moral prejudice." As Haar notes, however, Heidegger remarks that *Benommenheit* is used in psychiatry to, in Haar's words, "designate a state of confusion between consciousness and unconsciousness" (348) and may be translated by "compulsion."[20] In my view, "compulsion" indicates the quality of the *motion* Heidegger claims is peculiar to animals; *Benehmen* may be translated as "behavior," which is conditioned by the animal's "self-absorption" (*Eingenommenheit*) (348). "Compulsion" is then, he explains, "this absorption of the animal in itself at the interior of which only directed movement is possible." Haar glosses this definition: "to behave" and to be "numb," *benommen,* must be heard together, for they name "a movement of being carried off to oneself which closes the animal drive in on itself, even more than leading it toward its goal."[21]

The animal has no way of being in the strict sense; it simply *is.* The animal "*as such does not stand in an openness of beings,* but rather is *as* a being" (347, 361). Thus, "compulsion and its indices are without radiance," which means that the self-relation, if indeed we want to call it such, is "without reflection." The animal is by-itself in a way radically unlike the selfhood the human being has as a person. Compulsion is the condition for the possibility of the animal to be self-benumbed in its "surroundings" (*Umgebung*), but it is "never in a world" (347–48). The animal does not *truly* see, conceive, and so on as human beings do (348–49). As a corollary, our characteristic ways of comportment cannot be understood as "organic occurrences." Even analogies between what animals do and what we do are inappropriate, since the animal's seizing of the completeness of Being, of beings in their totality, is as compulsion and thus essentially unlike the ways in which human beings are or can be. Compulsion is the "inner possibility of animality as such"; it is the "bearing" (*Bezogenheit*) of the animal (349–50).[22]

In place of genuine "openness," Heidegger argues that animals are surrounded by an environment intelligible to us, but not to animals, as a "ring" of processes (362–74). One sort of process Heidegger calls "eliminations" (*Beseitigens*), that is, transitionless changes from one condition to another. For the female wasp, the male is either a sex partner or prey, but never is *as* any other condition, such as being alive (363–64). While the animal has some sort of connection with beings, beings cannot be for the animal as they are for us—to be seized, related to, and so forth (369–74). The ring surrounding the animal is also a "ring of de-inhibitions" (*Enthemmungsring*), that is, the animal moves from one inhibition to its other, but this other cannot be open as a being (369). This, then, is *how* the animal is "open" (370). The essential distinction that concerns Heidegger is between how things are as available (*vorhanden*) for humans and how things are for the animal as ringed with de-inhibitions (370–71). This ringing belongs to "the innermost organization of the animal and its fundamental form." What happens in and with the being-open of the animal is not an exhibition of itself, for the animal can only have a "so-called inner," but is rather simply lying in the circle of de-inhibitions (372). This is because there can be nothing "remaining" after an instance of de-inhibition; the animal "cannot-let-itself-in" (*Sich-nicht-Einlassen-können*). The animal's "openness" is the openness of de-inhibitedness, which is a having that is not a having. It is, more precisely, a "not-having of world in having the openness of de-inhibitedness" (392). Thus characterized, compulsion is the condition for other conditions of animality such as irritability and other supposed properties of "living substance" (372).

Biology is unable to understand that compulsion is a "determinant movedness" (*bestimmte Bewegtheit*) and not a static condition. Now this characterization raises a profound question. The animal has, or seems to have, a course of life with such moments as birth, awakening, maturing, aging, death, as do human beings, for whom these are as temporal and historical (386). Can the organism have a history? These motions are the "Being-character" of the living. Can the animal kingdom as a whole be said to have a history, that is, to *be* a history as Dasein can? Now if it is the case that Dasein's ability to be a history can be understood as its ability to be political, we are faced with the question of whether politics is or can be in any sense a possibility for or within the animal kingdom. If we cannot speak of such a history, then what can be said? Again, these issues cannot arise in and for biology as a science (387).

The question of death belongs to the "innermost essence of life" (387). Again, can this problem be related intelligibly to the scientific disciplines with which Heidegger is concerned? Heidegger's criterion is stringent: "The touchstone for the suitability and originality of every inquiry into the essence of life and vice versa is whether the inquiry has sufficiently grasped the problem of death; and whether it is able to bring that problem in a correct way into the question concerning the essence of life." Death is surely something more or other than a mere occurrence. Indeed, the question of the essence of death is prior to the question of the essence of life. The question of death is like the question of whether an organism is or has a history in that a categorial issue is at stake. Is the death of an animal a "dying" (*Sterben*) or a "demise" (*Verenden*), where the latter, as in BT, differs essentially from authentic dying (388; cf. BT 290–93)? As Heidegger explains, the animal's death is a "demise," "insofar as we address the dying of men." Indeed, what is problematic is the issue of the essence of the "natural, physiological death" of the animal, which contemporary biology cannot address, for its observations are "already completely without an inner relation with the basic problem of the essence of animality" and life.

Whatever its limits are with respect to animality, the thesis of world-poverty illuminates human-being (388–96). It clarifies the *Erörterung*, the situating of the human, in clarifying world-building (394–95). The incompetence of biology here does not affect metaphysics, although Heidegger remarks that only a poet may be able to address these issues (396). His admission that he has not arrived at a suitable understanding of the problem of death, which is necessary to understand the essence of life, is not a "failure" (386–87, 395–96).[23] Rather, he reaches a limit in terms of which the issues have become more visible. This limitation exhibits the conditionality of the enormous exposition of the problem of world and the thesis that the human is world-builder (397–532). In much of this discussion Heidegger is at his most technical, his emphasis propaedeutic. The stakes are high: "Perhaps the essential determination of the human is identical with the unfolding of these problems of world-building" (419). His presentation of the "as" as the structural moment of openness stands over against the tradition's understanding of *logos* as ground and therewith the priority of logic in metaphysics, which exhibits only a "non-originary unfolding" (*nicht-ursprüngliche Entfaltung*) of the problems of world (418–21).

Although Heidegger registers his familiar criticisms of the tradition, he makes abundantly clear that his own account is provisional. Indeed, he seems to return—or is it a retreat?—to the orchestration of methodological issues as a kind of swerve away from the problems he has posed, which all revolve around the opacity, the unintelligibility, of animality. The intricate and laborious presentations of fundamental conceptual issues in metaphysics (421–25) stands before—indeed, is held out into—what he will later call "our appalling and scarcely conceivable bodily kinship with the beast," our nearness and distance from animals that makes them of all beings "perhaps the most difficult to think about" (LH 206).

The thematic presentation of world-building distances itself from and ascends over the constellation of issues having to do with the world-poverty of animals. It is only from some determinate mode of Dasein's being that the animal kingdom appears as a domain of beings at all; this is conditional for access to the animal kingdom and for the intelligibility of the compulsion and the determinate ringings of animals (397–404). In the ringing of animals there is open to us an "inner ruling character" in what is living (403). This is what is traditionally understood as "nature," but Heidegger argues that "nature" is not simply given; rather, it is already what stands over against our science. We see and speak of the "naturality" of nature conditionally, for we are always "in the midst of beings" in some determinate way, which conditions any notion of "nature." "Living nature," then, is not any sort of given but is rather a conditioned projection (404). The immediate access to, or unconditioned comprehension of, nature required by naturalistic or biologistic social theory is impossible; such theory is categorially confused. "World" is not the totality of beings but rather the exhibition (*Offenbarkeit*) of beings as intelligible (404–9). This intelligibility, however, is itself conditioned, for we can then raise the question of how it stands with this exhibition of beings (405). Thus, we are prepared for historically determinate *ways* in which beings are intelligible. What "happens" (*geschieht*) with beings? (406). If beings require world and world is conditional (i.e., historical), then the question of the human as world-builder is necessarily historical—and I must add, political—for we must look into our "whole history," into the "originary tradition" (*ursprünglichen Überlieferung*), to understand the Dasein that conditions the human as world-builder (407–8). We thereby ask about ourselves in the "right manner" (*rechten Weise*). Inquiry into what the human is "delivers up" our Dasein to us, a deliverance which "is an index of inner *finitude* [*Endlichkeit*]" (408).

When we understand that in asking the question of the human, we exhibit an awakening of a "fundamental determination of our Dasein" (*einer Grundstimmung unseres Daseins*), the connection between the two parts of the lecture course becomes visible. In the first part, Heidegger reminds us, he has said nothing about world-building (408–9). Now Heidegger turns to "the problem of the exhibition of beings and the way of its happening [*Art ihres Geschehens*]" (409). Heidegger's agenda requires a return to the direction opened up by his account of deep boredom in order to present the "moments of the world-concept" from deep boredom "as a fundamental determinant of human Dasein." This determinant, he explains programmatically, "is to be set in relief against the what we asserted the essence of animality to be," that is, "compelled behavior."

This positioning is crucial, for the essence of animality "appears to slip into closest proximity" to the "*binding* [*Gebanntheit*] of Dasein within beings as a whole" that is characteristic of deep boredom. "It will of course be shown," he goes on, "that this closest proximity of the two essential constitutions [*Wesensverfassungen*] is merely deceptive, that an abyss lies between them, an abyss that cannot be bridged by any kind of mediation in any way at all. But then the complete bifurcation of the two theses, and thereby the essence of world, will become luminous to us."

Because the way in which our Dasein places us before beings in their totality is governed by boredom, this placing is not a "condition of the soul" (*seelischen Zustanden*) but rather a "becoming-carried-out" (*Hinausgetragen-werden*) of our being (410, 409–16). This thought precedes a crucial turn in the direction of Heidegger's thinking. We learn that humans do not build world in any "subjective" sense; rather, "world-building happens, and from its ground can the human first exist" (414). This means that it is the Da-sein in us which is equated with "the human qua human," that is, as world-builder. "The Dasein in the human *forms* [*bildet*] world," Heidegger writes, and goes on to explain: it "sets up" (*stellt*) world "hither" (*her*); "it gives a form [*es gibt ein Bild*], a look [*Anblick*] of itself"; it sets up world "thither" (*dar*); "it makes it from, is framing, surrounding [*Einfassende, Umfangende*]." None of this, he reminds us, is somehow about consciousness or the experiences of the soul (415). Rather, this "fundamental determination opens an originary perspective to us concerning human Dasein." It is only, however, because we are already "there" that we can ask these questions (416).

Heidegger's treatment of the as-structure here presents it as the structural moment of manifestness, which relates this inquiry into "as such" to the issues raised in the account of world-building (416–21); this inquiry is not a search for a metaphysical first or a self-sufficient concept, for the former must be something "available" (*Vorhandenes*) and the latter is impossible, given Dasein's historicity (421–35).

The "originary dimension" of "as" is the condition for "propositions" or "assertions" (435–40). A proposition is "something decided"; put somewhat speculatively, the decision integral to proposition or assertion is the proper motion of the as-structure (436). Heidegger emphasizes that in proposition or assertion, "something becomes set up over something," a process further analyzed into ways in which such setting up is done and the "law" (*Gesetzte*) governing setting up (436–37). These operations, in turn, are grounded in the comportment of everyday Dasein toward beings as available (438). Here, as so often in Heidegger's thinking, lies an opening to antiquity, for what is sought is the ground of discourse and logic comprehended by the Greeks as *logos* (438–39). What is sought is the "completely other" (*ganz Andere*) in which "as" and "in totality" are grounded (440).

This section is a preface to an inscription of Heidegger's understanding of Aristotle in the problems of these lectures. In a dense and massive section amounting to a treatise on *logos apophantikos*, Heidegger employs Aristotle to deconstruct predication and thus to reach the prepredicative openness which is the condition for predication and thus for logical discourse as such (441–83). This long-standing interpretation of Aristotle leads to Heidegger's claim that Aristotle anticipates the as-structure, which we now learn is *world*, the manifestation of beings as such in totality (483–507). There must be prepredicative, prelogical conditions for the use of predication and logic (501). I pass by the details of Heidegger's closer look at *logos* in order to draw attention to his principal claim that there is a "prelogical being-open for beings," a "preceding forming (*Bilden*) already ruling 'in totality' " (505). World is this preceding forming. It is the "fundamental happening" (*Grundgeschen*) of world-building in Dasein (507). Three moments of this happening are distinguished: the holding out, or of, or into bindingness (*Verbindlichkeit*); the process of completion (*Erganzung*); and the unveiling (*Enthüllung*) of the Being of beings (506). World-building is, in effect, an instantiation of the as-structure, a possibility animals do not and cannot have.

Heidegger claims to be within sight of a "direct unmediated interpretation of the world phenomenon" and inscribes his analysis in his understanding of the history of philosophy (507). The problem of world runs through all philosophy; it is what underlies the problems of *logos* and all of its subsequent variants such as ratio, reason, and spirit (508). Our failure to recognize the importance of world only shows that we are "historyless" (*geschichtslos*). As traditionally understood, *logos* is insufficiently radical for the problem of world. No movement forward on this problem is possible as long as *logos* is understood such that metaphysics can be, as it is for Hegel, the "science of logic." Rather, it is necessary to allow the "old fundamental questioning" to arise anew. The ruling of world and Dasein's awakening to it are possible only for the human, and Heidegger's analysis itself, he argues, is reached only from the fundamental determination of our Dasein (509–10). The happening of awakening is a sending, a *Geschick* that befalls or does not befall us; it is neither a matter of our "good will" nor even our historicity. Rather, the strength required for waiting can come only from that "which respects a mystery."

In freeing ourselves from the tradition we release or free the tradition and have an "ever-new appropriation" (*Immerneuaneignung*) of its power (511). The condition for this is a "transformation" (*Verwandlung*) in Dasein. There are two paths (*Wege*) for this transformation: from a fundamental determination that is explored *to* problems and from problems that are explored *to* this determination (512). The paths converge. Thus, from inquiry into deep boredom as the fundamental determination of our present situation and from reflection on the problem of world which does not refer explicitly to deep boredom, a transformation in Dasein is possible. The transformation can neither be forced (*erzwingen*) nor effected, for it is found only in what "philosophy alone" can do—"to prepare" (*vorbereiten*).

Heidegger begins to complete the circuit of his thinking in these lectures when he joins his analysis of world to the theme of ontological difference (516–23). Put concisely, ontological difference is not so much a philosophical thesis as it is a characterization of Dasein's way of being. As such, it cannot belong to the way an animal is, and indeed does not belong to the vulgar understanding either (517). I shall forgo any further commentary on Heidegger's treatment of ontological difference here except to note his awareness of the necessity to find a "new basis" for discussion of it (518–20).

In the concluding section of the lecture Heidegger assimilates projection as the "originary structure" (*Urstruktur*) of world-building to the ruling of world as the Being of beings in their totality as world projection (524–32). In order to understand the happening of ontological difference, it is necessary to inquire into the originary structure of fundamental happening (524). The self-extending of binding (i.e., our own conduct) is already exhibiting this structure in and with our doings among beings (525). Heidegger explains, as he had always maintained, that we do not begin, indeed we do not have to begin, with anything like some ostensibly primary relation of subject and object or consciousness. Rather, any such foundation is a derivative sort of binding.

A new and important question is to inquire into the "coherent" (*einheitliche*) character of fundamental happening that allows for the various features Heidegger's account has uncovered (526). Here we learn that this structure is conceptualized as "projection" (*Entwurf*). The essence of the human, the Dasein in us, is determined in and through this "projection character." Projection, as the originary structure of happening, is the "fundamental structure of world-building" (527). "Projection is world-projection," Heidegger writes: "World rules [*Waltenlassen*] in and for a dispensation from the character of projection." He explains that projection is not arbitrary (527–28). It is a binding as a condition for possibility, which is to say that projection is the happening of binding, which Heidegger clarifies as a determinate spreading and gathering. All of this has the character of opening, which is the condition for the possible in its possibility (529). Projection is the opening of "enabling" (*Ermöglichung*), which is in turn the "originary relatedness" (*ursprüngliche Bezogenheit*) of possible and actual, of possibility and actuality. Moreover, projection as the "revealing of enabling" is an authentic happening of ontological difference: "Projection is the irruption [*Einbruch*] in the 'between' of differences. It first enables the differentiating in its differentiatedness. Projection *unveils the Being of beings.*" In the unity of the originary structure of projection the "dispensation of the Being of beings in their totality" happens "in its particular possible bindingness. In projection world rules" (530).

Heidegger assimilates his account to Aristotle's teaching that *logos* "grounds its possibility" in the "originary unity of *sunthesis* and *di-airēsis*." As the latter, projection happens as a "releasing/thrown-forward" (*enthebend-vorwerfendes*), a taking-apart, and as the former as binding and connecting. Thus, projection is the "originary happening that—formal-logically speaking [*formallogisch genommen*]—unites contradictories in itself: binding and loosing [*Verbinden und Trennen*]." Heidegger explains that projection—"as the formation of the differences of possibility and actuality in enabling, as irruption in the difference between Being and beings, strictly as the breaking open of this between—is also that which 'self-relates [*Sich-beziehen*],' in which the 'as' originates." Projection, we may say then, is the movement of the "as" in the as-structure. The "as," Heidegger writes, "is the marking [*Bezeichnung*] for the structural moment of that originary *breaking open* [*ein-brechenden*] 'between'" (531). We do not first have a determinate "something" or even the possibility of something *as* something; our location in projection, our "moving in the 'as,'" is the condition for givenness. "In the happening of projections the world builds itself," which is to say that a "something" breaks out of and from possibility and breaks into actuality in projection. Dasein is the being of a "quite original kind" (*ureigener Art*) of which alone can be said that it *exists*, that it is "in the essence of its Being a coming out of itself without leaving itself behind." This sentence bears the weight of the analysis of Dasein as it is inscribed in Heidegger's account of projection as the originary structure of world-building.

We are, then, "unable-to-remain" and lack the power to situate. In throwing the Dasein in the human into its possibilities, projecting holds it "exposed to" (*unterworfen*) actuality. "Thrown thus in projection," Heidegger writes, "the human is a *passage* [*Übergang*], passage as fundamental essence of happening [*Grundwesen des Geschehens*]." This means that "the human is history, or better, history is the human." In passage, the human is "carried off and from there essentially '*absent*' [*abwesend*]," where "absence" has the "fundamental sense" of the way in which the human "makes his way" (*wegwest*) in the past and future, never simply "available" but rather "*existing* in ab-sence [*Ab-wesen-heit*]." "Displaced" (*Versetzt*) into possibilities, [our] actuality in existing in and as the movement of absencing means that [our] being must be a permanent "Being-mistaken" (*versehensein*), for it is only as "mistaking and displaced" that we can be "deranged" (*entsetzen*) In turn, "only where the dangerousness [*Gefahrlichkeit*] of derangements is, is there the bliss of wonders," Heidegger writes. This is the "awakened rapture that is the breath of all philosophizing," what is named *enthousiasmos* by the greatest of philosophers and is announced in "The Nightwanderer's Song" (*Das Nachtwandler-Lied*) of Zarathustra, by the "last of the greatest," Nietzsche. Then Heidegger cites the song whose title is "Once More" and whose meaning is "into all eternity," the song Zarathustra teaches to the higher men, in which we as well experience the world:

> O man, take care!
> What does the deep midnight declare?
> "I was asleep—
> From a deep dream I woke and swear:
> The world is deep,
> Deeper than day had been aware.
> Deep is its woe;
> Joy-deeper yet than agony:
> Woe implores: Go!
> But all joy wants eternity—
> Wants deep, wants deep eternity."

It is essential to recall the action and the argument of the text from *Thus Spoke Zarathustra* for the song if we are to understand its role here for Heidegger.[24] The higher men have just celebrated the ass festival with and for Zarathustra. The Ugliest Man, the murderer of God, who had been unable to affirm life and who had created and spoken the litany of the ass festival, announces—in the "most astounding event" of that astounding day—that he has learned from Zarathustra to "love the earth." He also utters the name of Zarathustra's song in his affirmation of life: " 'Was *that* life?' I want to say to death. 'Well then! Once more!' " As midnight approaches, Zarathustra takes his companions into the night and whispers to them the teaching of the eternal return as the midnight bell whispers it to him. Each line of the song except for two lines not thus prefaced—"I was asleep— / From a deep dream I woke and swear"—concludes a short passage of Zarathustra's teaching before the song appears in its entirety, having been learned by the higher men.

In the following resume, the numbers in parentheses are those of the numbered sections in the text and follow the sections they identify. What midnight teaches cannot be heard clearly by day but now "steals into nocturnal, overawake souls" (3). The hour has come that asks the question of who shall be the lord of the earth. Zarathustra cautions the higher man to take care, for "this speech is for delicate ears, for your ears." The song asks what deep midnight declares (4). The higher men have not flown high enough, for they have not redeemed the dead, as the tombs of the dead now ask. Now Zarathustra can say that midnight declares that the world is deep (5). The sound of the sweet lyre registers the pain of fathers and forefathers and thus ripens, sweetening, and bringing the fragrance of eternity that sings of the depth of the world that day cannot reach (6). Against the impure day, Zarathustra invokes the brighter midnight, for the "purest," the "midnight souls who are brighter and deeper than any day," shall be "lords of the earth." The day cannot reach the world's deep woe (7). Zarathustra is a drunken sweet lyre, a drunken poetess. In the sobriety of overintoxication comes the truth that joy is deeper than woe (8). What is ripe wants to die; what is unripe, marked by woe, wants to live, but does not want itself. Deep joy exceeds deep woe, for joy wants itself and "everything eternally the same" (9). In the moment of midnight, Zarathustra tells the higher men, his world became perfect; "midnight too is noon; pain too is a joy; curses too are a blessing; night too is a sun," and, he adds, "a sage too is a fool." In saying yes to any joy, the higher men have said yes to "*all* woe," for "all things are entangled, ensnared, enamored," and if "ever you said, 'You please me, happiness! Abide, moment!' then you wanted *all* back." This is what loving the world means (10). In wanting eternity, joy wants the "eternity of all things" including itself, and thus the world, which means it also wants agony; hence, "*all* things" (11).

Heidegger teaches in these lectures that our position is as world-builder on the earth, existing in and as the site of the movement of presencing and absencing. Human being is as passage, and thus as happening, as history. At bottom the critique of naturalism and biologism, and the demonstration of the essential differences, the gulf, between human and animal, rejects a shallow rootedness in the name of a deeper rootedness. The teaching of science concerning animality is a teaching of daylight and cannot reach the depth illuminated by the midnight brightness of Heidegger's teaching. This is to say that the animal, finally, does not truly dwell upon the earth because it cannot build world. In the final pages of the lectures, Heidegger offers a technical account, so to speak, of dwelling exposed to, and enacting, all that is entangled; this is the deep eternity wanted by joy. Such dwelling, Heidegger explains, is of necessity being mistaken, being deranged. It is dwelling as the eternal movement of displacement. Only such dangerous dwelling, which wants "*all* back," brings the awakened rapture of philosophizing. No understanding of the human as animal explains the happening of world; teachings inattentive to the essential distinctions between a being in which Dasein can be and a being in which it cannot be are rendered unable to comprehend the present determination of the human and therewith cannot tell us what is to be done. Heidegger never solves and disposes of these issues. Decades later he still maintains that "the body phenomenon is the most difficult problem" for philosophy (HS 146): "The bodily [*Leibliche*] in the human is not something animalistic. The manner of understanding that accompanies it is something that metaphysics up till now has not touched on." The criticism that Heidegger reinstitutes a discredited traditional distinction between spirit and nature rests upon the conviction that the critics have available what Heidegger is modest enough to acknowledge he does not have: the complete understanding of the nature and significance of human embodiment. What must be asked of those thinkers and nonthinkers who assimilate the human to the animal is whether their understandings of animality may bear the weight of what Heidegger attempts to think under the heading of "world-building."

3 How It Stands with Being

> Prior to all comfortable calculations about validity and
> objectivity for humanity stands the reflection on what we
> actually have and can have before us, on the available ways of
> fulfilling this.
>
> (G61 165)

THE RECTORAL ADDRESS opens philosophy and the political to
each other by showing how philosophy—presented as "science"—is
grounded in the present condition. Heidegger's discussion of the metaphysical question and his characterization of philosophy in IM touch
the political essentially. I am concerned in this chapter with tracing the
mutual inscription of philosophy and politics in IM, a central text for
Heidegger's political thinking.[1]

The metaphysical question, with which IM is concerned at its outset,
is first in rank, for it is the widest, deepest, and "most originary"
(ursprünglichste) of questions (IM 2–3). It is impossible to ignore the
human in asking the question, even when our inquiry seems to call for
an "unrestricted range" in which "all beings are equal," for our being
"persists in coming to the fore." With the first reference in the lecture
to Nietzsche, to "Concerning Truth and Falsehood in an Extramoral
Sense," Heidegger invokes the immensities of space and time to show
the seeming insignificance of human beings (3–4). It is the case, however, that a "unique relation" (einzigartige Beziehung) arises between
what is as a totality, when it is questioned, and questioning, through
which it is "for the first time opened up as such" and "kept open" (4).
Thus, questioning cannot be merely a "contingency" (Vorkommnis)
within the whole but rather, in confronting the whole, seems to step out
of it, although not completely. Here, then, is why questioning is "distinguished" (Auszeichnung); "what is asked in the question reacts upon

the questioning itself," and the ground of the question becomes the occasion for further questioning into the "why."

Although beings are not affected by questioning, the genuine carrying out of questioning in which what is questioned reacts on questioning makes questioning not simply an "occurrence" (*Vorgang*) but rather a "distinguished contingency that we call a *happening*" (*Geschehnis*). With "happening" Heidegger indicates the true rank of this questioning, inscribing it in the idiom in which he writes of the political. Questioning does not affect the movement of beings but does affect, because it is a constituent of, the proper motion of Dasein.

In the "recoil" (*Rückstoss*) of the question "why" upon itself, then, there is a "significant happening" which we must bring about (5). The recoil does not happen "freely of itself" but rather requires sufficient "strength of spirit" (*Kraft des Geistes*) for the "experience" to come to us that the why-question "has its ground in a leap [*Sprung*]" through which we "leap out of [*Absprung*] all the previous security, genuine or supposed," of our Dasein. The question "is only in the leap and as the leap," which "opens up its own ground, brought about leaping," and is thus called "in the genuine meaning of the word an origin [*Ursprung*]: Self-grounding-leaping [*das Sich-den-erspringen*]." That is, with the fundamental question of metaphysics, as with the circular structure of Dasein's Being in BT, it is necessary to leap into the circle; no "gradual pedagogy," as Richardson calls it, is possible (BT 363).[2] It is because "all genuine questions" spring from this question, which is their origin, that the question must be understood as the "most originary question." It is impossible to determine "objectively" whether "we truly question, that is, leap" or not (IM 5–6). What can be said, however, is "the question immediately loses its rank in the circle of a human-historical [*menschlich-geschichtlichen*] Dasein in which the questioning as originary power [*ursprüngliche Macht*] remains alien" (6).

Without pause Heidegger turns to one such Dasein. For those for whom the Bible is "divine revelation and truth," the question is answered before it is asked.[3] The biblical doctrine of creation is no answer to the metaphysical question. One who "stands from the soil of such a faith" cannot truly ask the question and continue to have it, but can only ask "as if" (*als ob*) the question retains its force. Heidegger goes on to write, however, that "a faith that does not perpetually expose itself to the possibility of unfaith is no faith but a convenience" which is "neither faith nor questioning, but rather the indifference of those who can busy themselves with everything," including an interest in faith and questioning.

Now since the question is first in rank or fundamental or the question of all authentic questions, we may well ask about the rank of a condition of Dasein in which the question cannot be asked with genuine attention to its importance. For Heidegger there can be no "Christian philosophy." "Theology," as he explains in his lecture "Phenomenology and Theology," given at Marburg in 1927 and 1928, is the positive science which arises from, theorizes, and thus objectifies "Christianness" (*Christlichkeit*), what in IM is called the "Christian-experienced world" (*christlich erfahrene Welt*)—that is, faith (PT 6–8; IM 6). It is neither speculative knowledge of God understood as an object, nor a study of the relationships between man and God, which would be philosophy or history of religion, nor a psychology of religious experience, nor even an application of philosophy of religion to Christianity (PT 15). As the science of faith, theology requires philosophy, even though faith does not, because while theological concepts may seem to be "disclosed only through, for, and in faith," they are as *concepts* necessarily conditioned by Dasein's preconceptual understandings of Being, and thereby related to an ontological context in its "originary totality" (*ursprünglichen Ganzheit*) that not only is presupposed but is specifically a "pre-Christian" understanding of Being (17–19). Thus, while faith as rebirth neither produces itself nor can what is revealed throughout it be found by the use of autonomous reason, "the sense of the Christian happening as rebirth [*Geschehen als Wiedergeburt*] is that one's pre-faith-full [*vorglaubige*], that is, unbelieving, human existence is sublated [*aufgehoben*] therein" (18). *Aufgehoben* is understood here as "raised up, kept, and preserved in the new creation." In the overcoming of one's pre-Christian existence, that existence is "ontologically included within faith-full existence," for "to overcome does not mean to dispose of, but to have one's disposition in a new way." Thus it is "precisely because all basic theological concepts, considered in their full regional context, include meanings which are existentially (factually) powerless, that is, *ontically* sublated, they have *ontological* determinants which are pre-Christian and which can thus be grasped purely rationally." While the concept of sin is conditioned by faith, an account of this concept requires explication of "guilt," which is for Heidegger an ontological determination of Dasein. "The more radically and appropriately the basic constitution of human existence is brought to light in terms of genuine ontology," he writes, "for example, the more the concept of guilt is grasped in its origin, the more clearly can it function as a guide for the theological explication of sin" (19).

Philosophy does not direct theology, for the relation of sin to guilt has nothing to do with rational deduction, nor can one discern sin on the basis of the ontological concept of guilt, nor yet even show the "factual possibility" of sin. Rather, philosophy furnishes to theology a "correction" as "co-direction" (*Mitleitung*) required because the "existential concept [of sin] has pre-Christian meanings," although the "primary direction (derivation) as origin [*Ursprung*] of its Christian content is given only by faith." The correction offered by philosophy "formally points out [*formal anzeigend*] the ontological character of *the region of Being* [*Seinsregion*] to which the concept of sin as *concept of existence* [*Existenzbegriff*] must necessarily adhere." I remind the reader that "formal pointing out" names a relation of thought to its matter in which the former holds itself back from any constitutive role. Thus, philosophy allows the theological content of the concept of sin to rise "out of and within the specific existential dimension of faith which was pointed out," accomplishing a "freeing and indicating" (*Freigabe und Anweisung*) of the "belief-composed originary disclosure [*glaubensmassige Ursprungsenthullung*] of theological concepts" (20).

There is no necessity for philosophy to take on this task for theology; indeed, it is theology, and not philosophy, that makes this request. Thus, philosophy is only a "possible" corrective for theology, and "can be what it is without functioning factically [*faktisch*] as this corrective." Heidegger reminds us that "*faith*, as a specific possibility of existence, is in its innermost core the mortal enemy [*Todfeind*] of the *form of existence* which is an essential part of *philosophy* and which in fact is ever-changing." In a note he explains further that what is involved here is a "basic (existential) confrontation of two possibilities of existence."

My next point can be stated with greater brevity. The way in which the tradition, in which metaphysics and ways of thinking shaped by metaphysics, understands God is as creator/producer. If, as is the case with Kant, for example, the Being of a being is theorized as being produced, then God is understood as the highest being capable of producing, which is to say, as a *being* (BPP 147–54). This is "ontotheology," prefigured in WM (109–10), examined in Heidegger's writings from the 1930s onward, and receiving its classic formulations in the

1941 manuscripts "Metaphysics as History of Being" and "Sketches for a History of Being as Metaphysics" (EPh 1–74), the 1949 introduction to WM (G9 379–80), and the 1957 lecture concerning Hegel, "The Onto-theological Constitution of Metaphysics" (ID 42–74). In the last work he explains that metaphysics has been both ontology and theology; this is why WM understands it as the "question about beings as such *and* as a whole" (54). "The wholeness of this whole is the unity of all beings that unifies as the generative ground," a concise formulation which means that "metaphysics is onto-theo-logy." To understand how God enters philosophy it is necessary to accomplish the "step back" (*Schritt zurück*) to inquire into the origin of the ontotheological constitution of metaphysics (56). If Being exhibits itself as the "ground that gives itself ground and accounts for itself," then metaphysics, in thinking of Being as both the "ground-giving unity of what is most general" and the "unity of the all that accounts for the ground, that is, of the All-Highest," thinks as an account, a *logos*, a "logic" that thinks Being as the "ground of beings" (58–59). When this ground is thought as the "first ground," then Being is represented as *causa sui*, which is to say, as God (60).

Now when this essential character of metaphysics is understood epochally, when Being as presence—necessary if Being is to be thought as ground—is recognized as a way in which presencing takes place, a *Geschick* (OTB 7–10), the conditions identified as "pre-Christian" in PT are inscribed in the history of Being. This means that they are ontical concepts embedded in the movement of ontotheology. Since the disclosure of God, even if understood as inconceivable, must be thought, the conditions for thinking are grounded in the understanding of Being as presence taken epochally. Theology as such, but not faith, is subordinate to the larger order of epochality. Philosophy parts company from faith, as it must, but cannot do the job of theology, for to ask the fundamental question calls for pushing "our questioning to the very end" (IM 6–7). Faith and theology cannot accomplish this. Heidegger turns again to philosophy.

I

Philosophical questioning is "untimely" because philosophy is either projected in advance of its time or because it "binds today back to its antecedent and what *inceptively* was [*anfänglich Gewesenes*]" (7).

"Philosophy always remains a knowledge which not only cannot be adjusted to a time," Heidegger writes, "but on the contrary imposes its measure on its time." While philosophy cannot be applied or judged in terms of its usefulness "in the manner of economic or other professional knowledge," it can still be a force. The political premise of philosophy in IM follows: "What has no immediate echo in everyday life can stand in an intimate accord with authentic happening in the history of a people" and even as an "anticipation" (*Vorklang*). It is not possible to determine "once and for all what the task of philosophy is," for "every stage and every inception of its unfolding bears within it its own law [*Gesetz*]."

These remarks are a preface to a longer treatment of philosophy, in which Heidegger makes clear that the metaphysical question "has nothing in common with our habitual concerns," for there can be no "gradual transition" to it from what is familiar. It would appear that the common and unrecognized encounters we have with the question mentioned at the beginning of IM have no further role to play in Heidegger's inquiry. The phenomenology of such encounters gives way to Heidegger's increasingly explicit teaching.

Since "every essential shape of spirit [*wesentliche Gestalt des Geistes*] stands in ambiguity [*Zweideutigkeit*]," philosophy, as one such shape, is misinterpreted if its ambiguity is not recognized (8). Such misinterpretation is more likely the less "commensurate" (*unvergleichlicher*) a shape of spirit is with other shapes of spirit. Philosophy is "one of the few autonomous creative possibilities and at times necessities of human-spiritual [*menschlichgeistlichen*] Dasein." What I shall call the "foundational" misunderstanding thinks philosophy is able to furnish a "foundation" (*Grundlegung*) for the "meaning and goals of human-being" (*Menschenseins*) and thus for the "future historical Dasein and time of a people." What I shall call the "instrumental" misunderstanding thinks philosophy can furnish a "system" and "world-construction" (*Weltbild*) of the "totality of beings" from its reflection on the sciences that will facilitate the "promotion" (*Forderung*) and "acceleration" (*Beschleunigung*) of the "practical-technical business of culture" (9).

Against the foundational error, Heidegger argues that since it is a concern of the few, philosophy cannot "directly" (*unmittelbar*) bring about the "forces," "methods," and "opportunities" required for a "historical condition" (*geschichtlichen Zustand*) (8). The few are the "creative transformers, transposers" (*Verwandelden, Umsetzenden*). Philosophy follows paths that cannot be laid out in advance, working itself out into a "breadth" (*Breite*) until it "finally in one way or another becomes forgotten as originary [*ursprüngliche*] philosophy," sinking to become a "self-understanding of Dasein" (9).[4] Nowhere does Heidegger say that philosophy can avoid this fate. Philosophy in its essence, he writes, "can and must be: a thinking opening [*denkerische Eroffnung*] of the paths and perspectives of the measure and rank-setting knowledge in which and by which a people comprehends its Dasein in the historical-spiritual [*geschichtlich-geistigen*] world and brings it to fulfillment [*Vollzug*]." Such knowledge "kindles, threatens, and necessitates all questions and values."

Against the instrumental error, Heidegger argues, as he had done in 1921–22, that it is in the essence of philosophy to make things more difficult and not more easy (*leichter*) (cf. G61, 108, 182). The "authentic sense of accomplishment [*Leistungssinn*] of philosophy is to challenge historical Dasein and therewith the ground of Being simply." Philosophy "gives back to things, to beings, their weight (Being)" because its challenge is an "essential ground-condition [*Grundbedingungen*] for the birth of all greatness," which for Heidegger is here the "fortune ↔ destiny [*Schicksal*] of a historical people and its works." *Schicksal*, he explains, can be spoken of only "where a true knowledge of things rules Dasein."

Both sorts of errors share the mistaken belief that the correctness of the commonplace that nothing can be done with philosophy exhausts philosophy. What should be asked is whether philosophy "ultimately does not do something inceptive [*anfangt*] *with us*." This reversal, crucial to Heidegger's understanding of philosophy, is followed by two references to Nietzsche, whom Heidegger joins in characterizing philosophy as "an extra-ordinary [*ausser-ordentliches*] questioning into the extra-ordinary [*Ausser-ordentlichen*]."[5] The fundamental question takes us out of the ordinary and the everyday, and such questioning is itself extraordinary, for it is "completely voluntary, wholly and uniquely set up from the completely mysterious ground of freedom, what we have called the leap" (11).

The Greeks asked the question concerning being as such in totality in its "true inception" (*Anfang*) (11). We must recognize that it is to the "first and most decisive unfolding [*massgebenden Entfaltung*] of philosophy among the Greeks" that his inquiry turns, and not simply to the Greek philosophers. *Phusis* is the Greek name for what is. Here, as he will do at greater length elsewhere (cf. Phy 221–56), Heidegger distances *phusis* from its Latin translation, *natura,* and thereby from the subsequent vocabulary of medieval and modern philosophy. With *phusis,* as with all "Roman translations of the Greek philosophical language," what is lost is the "originary meaning" of the Greek word; "the authentically philosophic naming-force [*Nennkraft*] of the Greek word is destroyed." Subjected to this misunderstanding, Greek philosophy appears to be a philosophy of nature and thus a primitive anticipation of modern science (12–13).

The word *phusis* "says" (*sagt*): "the emerging [*Aufgehende*] from itself (such as the blooming of a rose), the self-opening unfolding, what exhibits, maintains, and endures in such unfolding, briefly, the emerging-lingering holding-sway" (11–12). *Phusis,* thus understood as the "emerging holding-sway," is visible in, but is not identical with, the phenomena we call "natural." Rather, "this emerging and inward-standing-beyond-itself [*In-sich-aus-sich-Hinausstehen*]" is not one "process" (*Vorgang*) among others but "Being itself, by virtue of which beings first become and remain visible." It was "through a poetizing-thinking [*dichtend-denkenden*] fundamental experience of Being" that the Greeks found what they called *phusis,* a discovery that was conditional for their "insight into nature in a narrower sense." The originary sense of *phusis* presented here is the sense it has throughout Heidegger's writings. This sense clearly includes the political, as the following sentence indicates: "Hence *phusis* originarily means heaven as well as earth, the stone as well as the plant, the animal as well as the human, and human history [*Menschengeschichte*] as the work of men and gods; finally and first of all, the gods themselves under *Geschick*."[6] As emerging and enduring, *phusis* encompasses "Becoming" and "Being" as traditionally understood, for it is both the "emerging holding-sway" and "what endures" under this holding-sway. Thus, Heidegger emphasizes the movement character of *phusis,* for it is the "a-rising [*Ent-stehen*] out of which the hidden [*Ver-borgenen*] first emerges and brings itself to stand."

While the originary sense of *phusis* did not vanish in and for the Greeks, it was narrowed in two ways: by contrast with *nomos* and *technē* (13–14). Encompassing what we, although not the Greeks, regard as the opposition between the living or psychic and the physical, *phusis* is contrasted with *thesis* and *nomos*, with "ordinance" and "law, rule in the sense of the ethical [*Sittlichen*]," where the latter means what is accepted as "binding out of freedom and allotted out of tradition; what concerns free conduct and attitudes, what shapes the historical Being of men, *ethos,* which under the influence of morality is degraded into the ethical" (13).

Technē accomplishes an additional restriction of *phusis.* In its Greek sense, *technē* is a "knowing ordering [*wissende Verfügen*] concerning the free planning, instituting, and ruling of institutions"; it is "creating, building, as knowing bringing-forth [*Hervor-bringen*]" (13–14). Parenthetically, Heidegger remarks that "it would require a special study to explain what is essentially the same in *phusis* and *technē.*" Put briefly, *technē* in its original Greek sense is understood in terms of the disclosure of what is and the "know-how" required to let this happen, to release what is, a teaching that assimilates *technē* to "art." *Poiēsis*—the disclosing and producing of art—is assimilated to *phusis,* for the latter is "bringing-forth," *poiēsis,* which means that *phusis* is "*poiēsis* in the highest sense" (QCT 10–11).[7]

Phusis is experienced primarily as "what in a way imposes itself most immediately on our attention" (IM 14). It is essential to note that this experience does not exhaust *phusis.* The question "what is being as such" is asked from what we experience as first for us, *ta phusika,* although the movement of questioning necessarily reaches beyond it, that is, *meta ta phusika,* to "metaphysics." In a note Heidegger explains that "physics" has determined "metaphysics" throughout the history of philosophy, for the determination of what lies beyond "physics" is conditioned by what is regarded as lying within "physics" (cf. Phy 224).

The whole of what has appeared thus far in IM is taken up into a larger domain of thinking when Heidegger writes that the "question concerning Being as such" has a "different essence and origin" from that of metaphysics as determined by physics (15). This question, of course, is Heidegger's own question. Now if this question is understood simply as a "mechanical repetition" of the question of metaphysics, the former is "just another transcendental question." BT's use of "transcendental horizon" contributes to this interpretation, but Heidegger distinguishes the conventional sense of "transcendental" in terms of subjectivity from his own sense of the "existential-ecstatic temporality of Da-sein." In any case, the two questions resemble one another, in large part because the "essential source" (*Wesensherkunft*) of the metaphysical question remains obscure. The question of Being, conventionally understood, Heidegger explains, *is* the question of metaphysics, which is *not* a thematic inquiry into Being, which "remains forgotten." Indeed, Being is hidden from metaphysics, and the "forgottenness [*Vergessenheit*] of Being that itself falls into forgottenness" is the "unknown, but enduring impetus to metaphysical questioning" (15–16). The question with which IM is truly concerned, then, is the question of Being as *Heidegger* understands it, and not the question of metaphysics. IM is "introductory" in that it introduces the asking of the fundamental question. By questioning in the manner of BT into the meaning of Being, which is to say into the "disclosure of Being," the hidden essence of metaphysics comes to light (16).

Fundamental questions *are* only "as they are actually asked" and not as ready-made. A "leading into [*Hineinführen*] the asking" of such questions must "first awaken and create the questioning," which is a "questioning preceding" (*fragendes Vorangehen*, a "pre-questioning" (*Vor-fragen*). The "way of thinking" (*Gesinnung*) of genuine questioning consists in a "*willing* to know" (*Wissen-wollen*), in which one who wills is resolved (17). "Resoluteness" (*Entschlossenheit*) "acts from the moment of vision and does not stop," for it is "no mere decision to act, but is rather the deciding inception (*Anfang*) that anticipates and reaches through all action." Willing is being resolved (17). In a note Heidegger adds that the "essence of willing is here carried back into resolve" and that the "essence of resolve lies in the revealedness [*Entborgenheit*] of human Dasein *for* the clearing of Being and not in a storing up of energy for 'action,'" and refers the reader to sections 44 and 66 of BT, as well as to ET. Willing as resolving is related to Being, is grounded, as "letting-be." In BT Dasein's resoluteness is "what first makes it possible to let the Others who are with it 'be' in their ownmost potentiality-for-Being, and to co-disclose this potentiality in the solicitude which leaps forth and liberates" (BT 344). Here "letting be" translates Heidegger's " 'sein' zu lassen." Resoluteness is salvaged from a decisionist reading, and its inscription in IM's account of willing to know gives the character of action to questioning.

Knowing is a kind of action, for to know means "to be able to stand in the truth." Since "truth is the exhibition of beings," knowing is "the ability to stand in the exhibition of beings, to endure [*bestehen*] it" (cf. WM 105). Heidegger's further development of the metaphysical question is intended as "training" (*Einübung*) in questioning to help us endure our standing. It is not possible to ignore the "nothing" in the metaphysical question "why are there beings rather than nothing" (IM 19). We are not, however, "as free as it may have seemed to us up to this point," for we stand in a tradition in which the questions of Being and nothing have been raised together (20). Both our fear of nihilism, which some suppose is the result of concern with nothing, and our traditional belief in the authority of logic, understood as prohibiting discourse about nothing, are based on a misunderstanding rooted in a failure to understand the metaphysical question that in turn arises from "an increasingly hardened [verhartenden] forgottenness of Being."

The problem of nihilism is not discussed thematically at this point, but only the objection from the standpoint of logic to discourse about nothing. What is at issue is the authority of logic. As Heidegger had made clear elsewhere, such as in MFL, logic as such is "grounded in a very definite answer to the question about what is" (20–21). This means that thinking regulated solely by logic cannot understand, let alone answer, the question. It is necessary to become "unscientific" to speak of nothing, but this is a misfortune only if we believe that scientific thinking is and must be the standard for philosophical thinking and that it is the only rigorous thinking (21). Such thinking is derived from philosophical thinking, which remains prior in rank to it. "Philosophy stands," Heidegger writes, "in a completely different domain and rank of spiritual Dasein." Only "philosophy and its thinking" and poetry are in this order, and only they can speak of nothing, although they are not for that reason the same. The great poet's power to speak of nothing comes from the "superiority of spirit" (Überlegenheit des Geistes) of poetry over science that lets him speak as if Being is "expressed and invoked for the first time" (21–22). "In the poetizing of poets and in the thinking of thinkers there is always so much world space [Weltraum]" that things "lose completely their indifference and commonplaceness" (22).

With this preparation, which establishes the authority of poets and thinkers and deconstructs the authority of logic, Heidegger returns to the question. When we ask "Why are there beings?" we begin with what is given and question it as to its ground, an inquiry that is an extension of a way of thinking practiced in everyday life (22–23). When we add "rather than nothing," this path is closed to us, for instead of moving from one given to the next, the being with which we begin is "held out into the possibility of Nonbeing [Nichtseins]" (23). The sense of "why" in the question changes: "Why is the being torn away from the possibility of Nonbeing? Why does it not simply keep falling back into it?" The effect of this reversal is to exhibit the motion internal to, but hitherto unrecognized in, the question. That is, the being is now not simply something available (*Vorhandene*). As drawn into the question, it now "oscillates" (*schwankt*) between being present and falling into Nonbeing. What is sought now is a ground that will explain the "rule [*Herrschaft*] of beings as an overcoming [*Überwindung*] of Nonbeing." The ground asked for is asked "as ground of the decision for the being against nothing, or more precisely, as ground for the oscillation of beings, which sustains and unbinds us, half being, half not-being, which is also why we can belong to no thing completely, not even to ourselves; yet Dasein is in every case mine." This turbulent sentence attaches a familiar teaching of BT to an account that situates us in the sheer motion of beings. Parenthetically, Heidegger explains that Dasein is "in every case mine" because it is "*itself* by virtue of its essential relation to Being *überhaupt*" and not in any sense of subjective positing or an individual ego (23–24). Thus, while questioning cannot change what is, what remains "what it is and as it is," it nonetheless moves us into the "open" and thus lets us "belong entirely to ourselves." When we recall that such belonging marks authentic Dasein, it becomes evident that philosophical questioning is inherently political.

II

The metaphysical question transforms itself into the question of Being when we understand the "twofold sense of the word 'Being' "—*that* something is and *what* "brings it about"—leaves unclear how to distinguish between Being and what is, registered in the Greek *to on* as both *ta onta* and *to einai*. This question, however, calls for us to ask: "How does it stand with Being?" (*Wie steht es um das Sein?*) (27). That Being has a standing means that the question of Being is thoroughly historical. This becomes evident when Heidegger writes that since we cannot simply grasp the Being of a being, we must "make it clear from the very outset how it stands at present with Being and with our understanding of Being." In Heidegger's working out of the question of metaphysics, we are led to the present situation.

A few examples suffice to show that while we know that things *are*— the high school building, a storm, a mountain range, a state, a painting—our acquaintance with beings does not seem to lead us to Being (27–29). Our attempts to apprehend Being amount to reaching into a void. Heidegger then turns to Nietzsche, who was "perfectly right" in the "last analysis" when he called such "highest concepts" "the last cloudy streak of evaporating reality" (29). Nietzsche's understanding of Being as a vapor and a fallacy—Heidegger cites *Twilight of the Idols*— is an essential part of his thinking, indeed the "fundamental support and determinant of his philosophy" (30). Heidegger makes clear that his reference to Nietzsche, whose philosophy "holds its ground against all the crude importunities of the scribblers who cluster round him more numerous with each passing day," has nothing to do either with such abuse of Nietzsche's work or with "blind hero worship." Rather, in order to understand Nietzsche, it is necessary to bring "his accomplishment to a full unfolding." If Nietzsche speaks the truth about Being, the fundamental question of metaphysics must be abandoned. Again, as we have seen him do in the 1929/30 lectures, Heidegger moves Nietzsche to a decisive position, presenting his thinking as a fundamental alternative. Is Nietzsche correct, "or was he himself only the last victim of a long process of error and neglect, but as such the unrecognized witness to a new necessity?" It is Heidegger who can unfold Nietzsche's thought and comprehend both his true rank, against the misunderstandings of his followers, as the unrecognized witness to a new necessity and the new necessity itself, which Nietzsche himself did not grasp.

The apparent emptiness of the concept of Being is the fault neither of Being nor of its concept, neither of us nor our ancestors. Rather, should we not say that the fault, the emptiness, "lies in something that runs through Western history from the very beginning, a happening which the eyes of all the historians in the world will never perceive, but which nevertheless happens, which happened in the past and will happen in the future?" Heidegger then asks the decisive question about the significance of Being for us, what I have called *the* political question in Heidegger's thinking:

> What if it were possible that the human, that peoples [*Völker*] in their greatest practices [*Umtrieben*] and legacies [*Gemachten*], are linked to beings [*Seienden*] and yet had long fallen out of Being [*Sein*] without knowing it, and that this was the innermost and most powerful source [*Grund*] of their decline [*Verfalls*]? (30)

The correlation of the question of Being with human things is exhibited in Heidegger's question. We already know from "The Essence of Truth" that our historical comportment is always attuned to some way in which what is becomes manifest and thus conceals itself (ET 131–32). We have also seen that the unfolding of any philosophical concept or the elucidation of any structural feature of Dasein eventually proves to rest in some fashion upon an understanding of Being. As Heidegger puts it in "What Is Metaphysics?" insofar as we exist, we are already "within" metaphysics. Dasein's character as "going beyond" what is shows that metaphysics as "going beyond," as *meta*physics, belongs to the "nature of the human" or is the "ground-phenomenon" of Dasein, or simply *is* Dasein (WM 111–12). In his formulation of the fundamental political question, Heidegger speaks explicitly of what must be called the rank of our attunements to Being. We learn that the "greatest practices and legacies" of peoples are linked to Being. This thesis furnishes us with criteria for discerning whether or to what extent peoples have fallen out of Being, for the absence of greatness is now disclosed as an index of such falling. We now understand the true nature of the greatness and the decline of peoples because these conditions are now placed in their proper setting. While we may dispute Heidegger's account of human things, it is absurd to charge him with indifference to them. Heidegger claims to disclose the true horizon for the understanding of human things. He claims to have truly grasped the essence of what is highest in greatness and of what is lowest in decline.

A parenthetical and thus later reference to BT follows (BT 219–24, esp. 223). Heidegger directs us to his account of "Falling and Thrownness" and in particular to his understanding of falling as a disclosure of a structural feature of Dasein, and not as a matter of human corruption. If the falling out of Being by a people is to be understood along the lines of the falling of Dasein, then the latter as constitutive of "all Dasein's days in their everydayness" has as its counterpart in the former, the everyday life of a people (224). We are left with the possibility that the greatness of a people inheres in the extraordinary achievements of extraordinary men. If the correlation with BT is complete, however, we must also consider the possibility that greatness is a modification of everydayness, just as authentic existence does not float above, but consists of a distinctive grasp of, the everyday.

Heidegger does not ask such questions from "any particular sentiment [*Gemüt*] and world-view." Rather, we are forced (*zwingt*) to these questions by the question "How does it stand with Being?" (IM 30–31). The political question is inscribed in the necessity of thought to which we are compelled by the movement of questioning. While this question is "sober" (*nuchterne*), it is also "quite useless" (*sehr nutzlose*). Nevertheless, it is "*the* question": "Is 'Being' a mere word and its meaning a vapor, or is it the spiritual destiny of the West [*geistige Schicksal des Abendlandes*]"? (31). Heidegger's use of *Schicksal* preserves the play of meanings around fortune and destiny which characterizes the historical situation.

The remainder of the first chapter (31–42) provides Heidegger's account of the present situation. I shall proceed slowly because the account exhibits an articulation, the recognition of which is crucial to an adequate understanding of Heidegger's teaching. There is first a general characterization of the crisis (31), which is followed by an anticipatory glance at what is required for its resolution (31–32). The middle part establishes the historical sense and significance of the question of Being, which means that it inscribes the political, as Heidegger understands it, in the history of Being (32–37). It is a technical philosophical discourse framed by the issues which call for it. Heidegger then offers a deeper account of the crisis of the West as grounded in the "deprivation" (*Entmachtung*) of spirit through inquiry into one of its elements, the "misinterpretation" of spirit (37–41). Finally, Heidegger proclaims the necessity for an inquiry into language: "Because the destiny of language [*Schicksal der Sprache*] is grounded in a people's *relation* to *Being*, the question of Being will involve us deeply in the question of language" (42). Thus, it is no accident that we must turn to language in order to "set forth, in all its implications, the fact of the evaporation [*Verdunstung*] of Being."

Within what I have identified as the first part of Heidegger's account, there is yet another articulation consisting of four responses to the governing question "How does it stand with Being?" The first response explains the present situation and crisis. Heidegger is emphatic; his opening sentences exhibit no hesitation or qualification:

> This Europe, in its ruinous blindness forever on the point of cutting its own throat, lies today in a great pincers, squeezed between Russia on one side and America on the other. From a metaphysical point of view, Russia and America are the same; the same dreary technological frenzy, the same unrestricted organization of the average human being. (31)

In this passage there is the first of two appearances in the lecture of the assertion that Russia and America are "metaphysically" the same. Rather than indulge an understandable impulse to indignation to be found in some who defend liberal democracy against Heidegger's assault, I propose to try to follow the lines of thought which encompass his assertion.[8] The list which follows is often passed over quickly by readers who see in it little or even nothing more than an expression of reaction, a familiar itemization of the superficiality of modern society in the age of technology. Let us take a closer look. The position of the list *after* Heidegger's assertion of the metaphysical sameness of Russia and America suggests that its contents clarify this sameness. There seem to be two unifying grounds for the items on the list, one of which is found within it, while the other comes directly after it. We have before us:

First: The conquest of the globe and its opening to exploitation. Here Heidegger refers to instantaneous communication, a theme present in his thinking since the early 1920s. His example is the simultaneous "experience"—placed in quotation marks—of the assassination of a king in France and a symphony concert in Tokyo. The condition, the unifying ground, for this sort of "experience" is stated in the next clause: "when time has ceased to be anything other than velocity, instantaneousness, and simultaneity, and time as history has vanished from the Dasein of all peoples." In *Beiträge* Heidegger argues that the modern emphasis on "velocity" is symptomatic of the modern forgetting of Being (G65 121). Ironically, there is a "slowing down" (*Verlangsamung*) of history marked by the appearing of the velocity and manageability (*Lenbarkeit*) of " 'historical' development and its anticipation" (441). Moreover, this condition is also the ground for the next pair of examples.

Second: "when a boxer is regarded as a nation's great man; when mass meetings attended by millions are looked on as a triumph." What is at issue is not merely the vulgar or the false—and it is obvious that Heidegger criticizes the mass public rallies of the Nazis. The way in which time is experienced, time as history, has disappeared, and in so doing its absence furnishes a decisive condition for the vulgar events of the present. A more urgent reformulation of Heidegger's questions follows: "Then, yes then, through all this turmoil a question still haunts us like a specter: What for?—Whither?—And what then? [*wozu?—wohin?—und was dann?*]."

The second response exhibits the second unifying ground of Heidegger's list. "The spiritual decadence of the earth [*Der geistge Verfall der Erde*]," Heidegger writes, "is so far advanced that the peoples [*die Völker*] are in danger of losing the last bit of spiritual energy [*die letze geistige Kraft*] that makes its possible to see the decadence." Heidegger distinguishes his "observation" (*Festellung*) from *Kulturpessimismus* and from such "childish categories as pessimism and optimism," which "have long since become absurd" in the face of the proportions assumed by the elements of the crisis, which follow in another list: the "darkening of the world" (*die Verdüsterung der Welt*), the "flight of the gods" (*die Flucht der Götter*)—elements drawn from Hölderlin—the "destruction of the earth" (*die Zerstörung der Erde*), the "transformation of men into a mass" (*die Vermassung der Menschen*), and the "hatred and suspicion of everything free and creative" (*der hassende Verdacht gegen alles Schöpferische und Freie*).

The next response identifies the location of the German people: situated in the "middle" (*Mitte*) of Europe, within the pincers—indeed, at the center of the European center and thus subject to the greatest pressure. The Germans have the most neighbors and are thus the most endangered people (*das gefahrdetste Volk*). They are also the most "metaphysical people" (*metaphysische Volk*). The conjunction of the greatest danger and the metaphysical status of the German people exhibits, when rightly understood, the possibility, the fortune, the opportunity, which may be seized by the German people. "We"—that is, Heidegger, speaking for the German people—are certain of this determination (*Bestimmung*). I translate *Bestimmung* as "determination" rather than "vocation," as Manheim does, because here we find an affirmative counterpart, an alterity, to the determination of "boredom" in G29/30. The people will be able to wrest a destiny or fortune (*Schicksal*) from their situation only if the determination, which is to say the situation as such, creates "within itself" (*in sich selbst*) a possibility of resonance, or response (*Widerhalls*), to this determination (31–32). The possibility of resonance or response is self-created; that is, the German people come to understand and choose their determination as that which they have been given to choose. This possibility is what Heidegger means by his characterization of the German people as the metaphysical people. Since philosophy, as an essential form of spiritual life, must reach and raise the fundamental metaphysical question, the German people stand in an essential relation to this question. The self-creating spiritual possibility, as we may call it, requires the people to have a creative understanding of its tradition (32). "All this entails," Heidegger writes, that "this people as historical [*geschichtliches*] moves itself and thus the history of the West out of the middle of its future happening [*aus der Mitte ihres künftigen Geschehens*] and into the originary realm [*ursprünglichen Bereich*] of the powers of Being." That is, the present, the age of spiritual decline, leads to a future happening from which the German people can remove itself and in so doing, redirect the West as well. In recovering the proper motion of its own historical Dasein, the German people contribute to the recovery of the proper motion of the historical Dasein of Europe. "If the great decision [*die grosse Entscheidung*] concerning Europe," Heidegger goes on, "is not to fall onto the path of annihilation, it can only fall into the unfolding [*Entfaltung*] of *new spiritual* historical forces [*neuer geschichtlich geistiger Krafte*] from the middle." I agree with Derrida's remark on the significance of the emphasis on "spiritual" (*geistiger*). The word is italicized "both to mark that the fundamental determination of the relation to Being occurs there, and to ward off the possibility of a politics other than that *of spirit*."[9] To this I would add that "middle" plays a double role here, for it designates both (1) the future happening of the German people and Europe, which is reached in and as the decline of the West, and the successively more essential middles, Europe, Germany, and (2) the metaphysical determination of the German people, from which the movement into the originary realms of Being can be unfolded, a theme which Lyotard calls Heidegger's "geophilosophy."[10]

The fourth response turns back on and clarifies its governing question. When we ask: "How does it stand with Being?" we engage in the retrieval (*wieder-holen*) of the "inception of our historical-spiritual Dasein [*Anfang unseres geschichtlich-geistigen Dasein*] in order to transform it into an other inception [*anderen Anfang*]." Retrieval is never an exercise in nostalgia and is certainly not, in Heidegger, a moment in the economy of conservatism. The "other inception" or "other beginning" is a possibility correlate with the transition from philosophy to "thinking" and makes an early appearance here. Such a retrieval and transformation is the "decisive form [*massgebende Form*] of history, because it begins in the fundamental happening [*Grundgeschenis*]." Here, as in BT, Heidegger explains that retrieval is not the mere imitation of what is past and known. Rather, the inception must be "begun again *originarily* [*ursprünglicher*] with all the strangeness [*Befremd-lichen*], darkness [*Dunkeln*], insecurity [*Ungesicherten*] that attend a true inception."

Nietzsche's word that "Being" is a vapor and a fallacy is the true answer to the question of how it stands with Being (32). While Heidegger recognizes that for Nietzsche "Being" is a "delusion that should never have come about," he acknowledges the truth of Nietzsche's account as an assessment of what "Being" in fact means to us today. The questioning Heidegger follows brings us into the "landscape" (*Landschaft*) in which we must dwell, that is, into the situation in which we already *are* if our "historical Dasein" is to recover its "rootedness" (*Bodenständigkeit*). The word "Being" is no longer meaningful because we have fallen away (*herausgefallen*) from what it says (33). We ask about Being because "everything, if we merely take hold of it, dissolves like a tatter of cloud in the sunlight" and because "truths have never fallen into any people's lap." Because his project in BT, an "attempt to bring Being to speak itself," differs essentially from the search for universal concepts which academic philosophy continues to regard as "ontology," Heidegger remarks that these two kinds of inquiry "should not bear the same name" (33–34).

The questions "How does it stand with Being?" and "What is the meaning of Being?" are not asked in order to produce an ontology but rather involve something "wholly other" (*ganz Andere*): "to restore man's historical Dasein—and that always includes our own future, in the totality of the history allotted to us in the power to open up Being which has originarily for himself" (34). While the question of how it stands with Being is preliminary, this does not mean that it can be considered "before and outside" the fundamental metaphysical question and then somehow discarded. Rather, the preliminary question is the "blazing hearth fire" (*glähende Herdfeuer*), the "hearth" of all questioning (34–35). For Heidegger it is necessary to arrive at the "decisive fundamental standpoint" (*entschiedene Grundstellung*) and "essential attitude" (*wesentliche Haltung*) for asking the preliminary question (35). "That is why," Heidegger says, "we have related the question of Being to the destiny of Europe, where the destiny of the earth is being decided—while our own historical Dasein proves to be the middle for Europe itself." The question can now be formulated as: "Is Being a mere word and its meaning a vapor, or does what is designated by the word 'Being' hold within it the spiritual destiny ↔ fortune [*geistige Schicksal*] of the West?"

A comparison of this formulation with its earlier version is revealing. First, the quotation marks around the first and only appearance of "Being" in the earlier version are absent in the first appearance but present in the second appearance of "Being" in this formulation. The earlier formulation asks a question about the word or concept "Being," while the later formulation does not ask only about this. The phrase from Nietzsche—"a mere word and its meaning a vapor"—which Heidegger takes over as his ongoing characterization of how it stands with Being, is carried over unchanged. What is added in the later version is the qualification "what is designated by the word 'Being.'" This modification lifts the referent of the word "Being" out of the traditional ontology Heidegger has put behind and below him. Heidegger suspends and questions the word and concept "Being" while employing it. Clearly what is important is what is designated by "Being." It is *this*, rather than any traditional concept, that holds within it the spiritual destiny of the West, and it is Heidegger's task to recognize this fact.

The question, Heidegger recognizes, may seem at first to be related only very indirectly to the "decisive historical question of the earth" (35). What seems even more unlikely—Heidegger admits that the question may sound "noisy and exaggerated"—is that the "basic position and attitude of our questioning might be directly determined by the history of the spirit on the earth [*Geschichte des Geistes der Erde*]." Even Manheim's seemingly harmless interpolation of "human" before "spirit" must be avoided if we are to trace Heidegger's politics of the spirit, for we cannot simply take for granted that spirit is only or even essentially human. The relationship between the history of the spirit and the condition of our questioning simply stands (*dieser Zusammenhang besteht*). Heidegger must then show that the asking of the question is an integral element in the "historical decision-question" (*geschichtlichen Entscheidungsfrage*).

Heidegger introduces an anticipated "essential insight in the form of an assertion" to carry out his demonstration (35–36). The preliminary and the fundamental questions, he claims, are "historical questions through and through." Metaphysics and philosophy do not become historical sciences by virtue of the fact that these questions are historical. What may be called received opinion holds that historical science is concerned with the temporal, while philosophy "investigates the timeless." Now we have already seen that Heidegger disagrees fundamentally with such a characterization of philosophy. It is more difficult to determine the status of the following sentence: "Philosophy is historical only insofar as it—like every work of the spirit—realizes itself in the course of time." (*Philosophie ist nur insofern geschichtlich als sie wie jedes Werk des Geistes im Ablauf der Zeit sich verwirklicht.*) If received opinion holds only that philosophical questions have a history, this view "cannot characterize metaphysics, but merely expresses something obvious." Philosophy for Heidegger, however, is never some sort of timeless thinking, only realized in time, but he certainly agrees that philosophy is an essential form of spirit. As we shall see, what is ultimately at issue is the question of what the "realization" of philosophy can mean. To return to Heidegger's criticism of received opinion, the claim that metaphysics and philosophy are historical is either "meaningless and superfluous" or "impossible" because philosophy and the historical sciences are incompatible sorts of science. Against this conclusion Heidegger advances two basic points of his thinking. First, metaphysics and philosophy are not sciences and cannot be made sciences simply because their questioning is historical. Second, historical science, like any science, and unlike philosophy, cannot establish by itself, but must rather presuppose, an essential relation to its subject (36). As Heidegger had long argued, historical science can never produce its own "historical relation to history" but can only illuminate a relation already supplied to it and "ground it in knowledge." Such knowledge is inherently political, for it is an "absolute necessity for the historical Dasein of a wise people [*eines wissenden Volkes*]" and thus is neither an "advantage" nor a "disadvantage." "Because it is only in philosophy," Heidegger writes, "—*as distinguished from all science*—that essential relations to the realm of what is take shape, this relation *can*, indeed *must*, for us today be a fundamentally historical one."

To clarify his claim that metaphysical questioning is essentially historical, Heidegger explains that history is neither the purely past nor the purely contemporary, for neither of these is history understood in terms of "happening." This understanding is "for us" (*heisst uns*), that is, for the Germans and not merely the authorial plural. As "happening" (*Geschehen*), history is "an acting and being acted upon which pass through the *present*, which are determined from out of the future, and which take over the past. It is precisely the present that vanishes in happening." In our asking, the fundamental question of metaphysics is historical because it opens up the "happening of human Dasein" in its relations to what is as such and as a whole—"opens it up to unasked possibilities, futures, and at the same time binds it back [*zurückbindet*] to its past inception, so sharpening it and giving it weight in its present." Our Dasein is called to its history in this questioning, "summoned" (*angerufen*) in the "full sense of the word" to a "decision" (37). We are not summoned to our history after our questioning, for this sequence might suggest that the process is a matter of drawing "moralist-worldview-related applications" (*moralisch-weltansschaulichen Nutzanwendung*) from a situation. Rather, "the standpoint and attitude of questioning is itself historical, standing and maintaining itself in the happening, asking out of and for it."

The "essential insight" is required to show why the historical asking of the question of Being is itself an essential part of the "world history on the earth." "We have said," Heidegger reminds us, that "out of and around the earth, happens a darkening of the World [*Weltverdüsterung*]." As we have seen, in its first appearance, the darkening of the world is subsumed under the heading of the "spiritual decline" of the earth. Here it is raised to a thematic level, and several of the symptoms of spiritual decline listed after it are now presented as "essential happenings" (*wesentlichen Geschehnisse*) of it. These are "the flight of the gods, the destruction of the earth, the transformation of men into a mass, the pre-eminence of the mediocre." This last happening replaces and specifies "the hatred and suspicion of everything free and creative."

The "world" Heidegger speaks of as "darkening" is "always world of spirit" (*immer geistige Welt*).[11] The darkening is always *within* spirit and is not an opposition of spirit and alterity. Indeed, all of the elements Heidegger identifies, whether they belong conventionally to spirit or body, to philosophy or geopolitics, belong to spirit. "World" in its technical philosophical sense, intelligibility, as it has been treated throughout Heidegger's work, is evidently world of spirit. This teaching inscribes politics in world, and one could hardly imagine a deeper inscription of politics for Heidegger than this. The darkening of world means the "deprivation of spirit" (*Entmachtung des Geistes*), the elements of which include its "dissolution, consumption, repression, and misinterpretation" (*Auflosung, Auszehrung, Verdrangung, und Miss-*

deutung). To understand the deprivation of spirit is to recognize that all of these elements can *only* be exhibitions of spirit. Heidegger proposes to explain the deprivation of spirit from only *"one* perspective," that of misinterpretation of spirit. We are reminded of Europe's position between Russia and America, which are, Heidegger repeats, "metaphysically the same." There is a crucial addition to this formula. Metaphysical sameness is now the sameness of Russia and America in their "world character" (*Weltcharakter*) and their "relation to spirit" (*Verhältnis zum Geist*).

The situation of Europe is made worse by the fact that the deprivation of spirit originated in Europe and was determined in particular by the spiritual condition (*geistigen Läge*) of the first half of the nineteenth century, the time of the "collapse" (*Zusammenbruch*) of German idealism. This "collapse" is a "protective shield" (*Schutzschild*) which conceals the "dawning spiritlessness" (*anbrechende Geistlosigkeit*) and the "defense [*Abwehr*] against all originary questioning [*ursprünglichen Fragens*] into and [our] bonds with grounds." Heidegger then recharacterizes this situation fundamentally. German idealism did not collapse; instead, "the age was no longer strong enough to stand up to the greatness [*Grosse*], breadth [*Weite*], and originariness [*Ursprünglichkeit*] of that spiritual world." That is, the age was unable "truly to realize" (*wahrhaft zu verwirklichen*) German idealism, a task which most emphatically does not mean the application of the "propositions and insights" (*Sätze und Einsichten*) of academic philosophers.[12]

III

To illuminate Heidegger's understanding of German idealism and thus to clarify what it means to realize a philosophy, I turn to his lecture course on Schelling's *Treatise on the Essence of Human Freedom*, given in the summer semester, 1936. Heidegger's interpretation of Schelling begins with politics; Schelling's treatise is inscribed in the condition of Prussia under Napoleon in 1809, who "oppressed and abused Germany" (ST 1). In 1808, in their conversation in Erfurt, Napoleon had said to Goethe that tragedies "belonged to a darker period. What do we want with fate now? Politics is fate." The year in which Schelling's treatise appeared, however, is also the year in which Prussia began to regain its strength and spirit. Heidegger calls a distinguished roll: Fichte, Baron von Stein, Scharnhorst, Schleiermacher, Wilhelm von

Humboldt, Kleist, Hegel, and Hardenberg were all in agreement that they wanted the new Prussian state to be a " 'state of intelligence,' that is, of the Spirit" (2). "The profound untruth of those words that Napoleon had spoken to Goethe in Erfurt was soon to come to light: Politics is fate. No, Spirit is fate and fate is Spirit." Heidegger turns to Schelling's treatise because the "essence of Spirit, however, is freedom." Hegel, Hölderlin, and Schelling each shaped the German spirit, he explains, but "the transformation of that spirit into a historical force has not yet come about." In a passage omitted from both the first German printing and the English translation of the lectures, Heidegger characterizes Mussolini and Hitler as leaders who have introduced "contrary movements concerning the political shape of the nation and of the people" against nihilism but who are "again in different ways essentially limited by Nietzsche" (G42 40–41) A philosophico-political problem of immense importance governs Heidegger's Schelling interpretation.

Heidegger claims that Schelling's lengthy silence, from 1809 until his death in 1854, was the result of his "manner of questioning," a problem which links him with Nietzsche (ST 3). Neither Schelling nor Nietzsche could reach an "inner center in the standpoint of philosophy" in his time. This "breakdown of great thinkers" is not a failure but rather the "sign of the advent of something completely different, the heat lightning of a new beginning." "Whoever really knew the reason for this breakdown," Heidegger continues, "and could conquer it intelligently would have to become the founder of the new beginning of Western philosophy." Although Heidegger maintains a discreet silence, it is impossible for one to fail to complete the thought contained in this sentence, for has not Heidegger just explained the reason for the breakdowns of Schelling and Nietzsche? And for one who agrees that Heidegger has conquered, or can conquer the problem, is not Heidegger the very founder to whom he refers?

In understanding the "essence of human freedom" for Schelling, Heidegger seeks to bring into knowledge the "innermost center of philosophy," into which we "place ourselves knowingly"; this allows us to reach an "understanding of the philosophy of German idealism as a whole in terms of its moving forces." Schelling is the boldest thinker in German idealism because his thinking drove German idealism "from within right past its own fundamental position" and toward the present age, which has a "very definite stamp of its own and that means a direction and a manner of its historical domination over existence" (4,

22).[13] Nietzsche, and not Schelling, is able to recognize this stamp as nihilism (22–23). It is German idealism, and not the present age, that requires and is determined by conditions that predispose it to develop a "system of freedom." By "today," Heidegger means "the whole transitional age from the nineteenth to the twentieth century and at the same time this transition in its whole European expansion," which encompasses politics. Heidegger identifies six conditions for the system-building of German idealism, all of which are intimately related to modern science, and therewith, I must add, to political modernity (29–33). These are (1) the predominance of the mathematical, (2) the elevation of certainty over truth, as exhibited in the search for certain foundations for knowledge, (3) the ego as truly knowable, (4) the resulting understanding of self-certainty as the criterion for truth and therewith the modern understanding of the meaning of Being, (5) the decline of the power of the church and the consequent change in the Christian experience of Being, and (6) the liberation of humanity in all areas of existence, which appears as the will to take charge of Being. System-building thus depends upon a crucial change in human existence. It is this change that makes Schelling's treatise a work in which "a new, essential impulse enters philosophy's fundamental question of Being" (98). Schelling's philosophy exhibits a distinctive attunement to the present epoch. Modern liberation is served by system-building: "The will to a freely forming and knowing *control* over beings as a whole projects for itself the structure of Being as this will" (34). To this projection, the course of German idealism from Kant to Hegel adds the notion that knowledge must be absolute, that philosophy is absolute infinite cognition (35, 44–47).

Later Heidegger explains the limits of Schelling's philosophy and therewith the limits of German idealism (ST 160–64). Regardless of the location of the system in the divine understanding, God remains above the system, which means that the system, as incoherent, ultimately fails to *be* a system. As a result, Schelling cannot include within the system an adequate understanding of ground and thus cannot comprehend relations between ground and understanding except by falling back unwittingly into the categories inherited from the tradition. Schelling cannot sufficiently transform the tradition, a failure which inadvertently shows the difficulties inherent but unthought in and of the inception of Western philosophy. His thinking shows that a second, other inception requires a complete deconstruction of the first inception. For Schelling, like Kant, freedom is ultimately unintelligible. The source of this aporia is the failure of modernity to provide an account of human being, a failure which is elevated to the status of a principle in Kant.

Elsewhere, Heidegger explains the larger significance of German idealism: "Where the last trace of the concealing of Being vanishes, namely in the absolute self-knowing of absolute spirit in the metaphysics of German idealism, the revealing of beings respective of their Being, that is, metaphysics, is complete and philosophy at an end" (PR 65). The failure of the age to live up to German idealism is the failure of the age to attune itself to the end of philosophy.

Even with his failures, Schelling experienced human being as something more than an object of scientific observation "which we then drape with little everyday feelings" (164). Human being is experienced, Heidegger writes, in the insight into the "abysses and heights of Being, in regard to the terrible element of the godhead, the life-dread of all creatures, the sadness of all created creators, the malice of evil and the will of love." As the boldest German idealist, Schelling exhibits the significance of human beings in and for the spiritual world of German idealism: "God is not debased to the level of man," Heidegger writes, "but on the contrary, man is experienced in what drives him beyond himself in terms of those necessities by which he is established as that other. The 'normal man' of all ages will never recognize what it is to be that other because it means to him the absolute disruption of existence. Man—that other—he alone must be the one through whom the God can reveal himself at all, if he reveals himself."

With the failure of the age to realize German idealism, "Dasein began to slide into a world which lacked," Heidegger writes, "that depth out of which the essential [*Wesentliche*] always comes to the human and comes back to the human, so compelling him to superiority [*Überlegenheit*] and making him act in conformity with a rank" (IM 37–38). Here we find Heidegger's understanding of what the realization of philosophy means. To act in conformity with a rank is to act in conformity with the essential, that which addresses itself as spirit to philosophy, and to which philosophy is the essential response of spirit. That the realization of philosophy cannot be severed from the situation of an age and thus from its history and politics I believe to be taught in the following passage from the Schelling lecture: "In the history of man, essential things are never overcome by turning one's back and apparently freeing oneself in mere forgetfulness. For what is essential comes back again and again. The only question is whether an age is ready and strong enough for it" (ST 4).

The descent of Dasein into a world without essential depth, however, continued: "All things sank to the same level, a surface resembling a blind mirror that no longer reflects, that casts nothing back" (IM 38). The "prevailing dimension" is now that of "extension and number," a theme Heidegger treats at greater length in his lecture course on Kant in the winter semester, 1935/36 (WT 66–96), and in such addresses as "The Age of the World Picture" (1938) (QCT 118–20). In *Beiträge* Heidegger links modern gigantism to quantity with the claim that gigantism is an expression of the "emptiness of the forgetting of Being" in which "the quantitative becomes quality" and "rules all beings" (G65 137). In the Nazi organization of "strength through joy" (*Kraft durch Freude*) is exhibited the degree of "organized commonness"—the totality of the *Volk* is supposed to share common experiences, typical of the present era in which the "greatest nihilism" is apparent (138). The "pure setting-in-motion" of beings is a mark of the age as well (139). Today the appearance of the human has two symptoms—the "breakout" or "revolt" of the masses (*Der Aufbruch ins Massenhafte*) and an inner emptiness or boredom, presented here as the correlate of the rule of quantity (121).

The result is a change in the meaning of intelligence, which no longer means a "wealth of talent, lavishly spent, and the command of forces [*Beherrschung der Krafte*]," but rather only "what could be learned by everyone, the practice of a routine, always associated with a certain amount of sweat and a certain amount of show" (IM 38). This change is exhibited in America and Russia as a "boundless etcetera of indifference and always-the-sameness—so much so that the quantity took on a quality of its own." In America and Russia the "domination of a cross section of the indifferent mass" is no longer accidental but has become an "assault of suchness" (*Andrangen von Solchem*)—I suggest that something like the "average everydayness" described in BT conveys Heidegger's sense here—that "aggressively destroys all rank and every world-creating impulse of the spirit, and calls it a lie." Heidegger calls this "assault of otherness" or "thatness" (*Andrang von Jenem*) the "demonic" in the "sense of destructive malignity" (*zerstörerisch Bosartigen*).

Now since everything Heidegger has said has been said of the world of spirit, it is imperative that we must understand the demonic under the heading of spirit as well. This requires us to turn again to the Schelling lectures. For Heidegger, the "new, essential impulse [that] enters philosophy's fundamental question of Being" with Schelling's philosophy of freedom is exhibited in Schelling's "metaphysics of evil," which "itself determines the new beginning in metaphysics. The question of the possibility and reality of evil brings about a transformation of the question of Being" (ST 97–98). What governs Heidegger's account of Schelling's understanding of evil is the movement of thinking, as Heidegger understands it, toward a denial of the reality of evil from the sense that evil is the absence of something—its nonexistence (ST 101). Heidegger writes: "The question of evil and thus the question of freedom somehow have to do essentially with the question of the being of the nonexistent. Regarded in terms of the principle of the system in general, that is, of the question of Being, that means that the question of the nature of Being is at the same time the question of the nature of the not and nothingness. The reason this is so can only lie in the nature of Being itself." I agree with Wayne Froman's interpretation of this passage as marking Heidegger's transformation of Schelling's question of the reality of evil into the question of the reality of nothingness, which is to say, a transformation that has the effect of leaving evil behind as it reaches toward the more fundamental level of the question of Being.[14] It should be compared with Heidegger's transformation of "good" in BT (BT 435, 131–32, 332–42). We must now see precisely what direction this movement takes.

Heidegger explains Schelling's teaching that the separability of the principles of self-will and universal will in man is the condition for the possibility of evil (ST 139–46). Self-will is spiritual; it can put itself in the place of universal will and can will to be the ground of the whole, to put itself above all else and thus to determine the unity of the principles of self-will and universal will in terms of itself. For Heidegger this means that human beings can stand in the "jointure of Being" (i.e., the ontological difference) such that they "dispose over this jointure and its joining in a quite definite way" (142). Thus, only human beings can sink "beneath the animal," unlike the animal, since the animal cannot have self-knowledge. Now this does not mean that human finitude is itself evil; rather, it is finitude "elevated to the dominance of self-will," which can only be a spiritual elevation (145). Thus, "evil belongs in the realm of domination of spirit and history." Schelling equates evil with sin, an identification possible, as Heidegger had argued in PT, only in terms of Christian thinking.

In Schelling, evil is related to individuation (146–52). The movement of striving-for-itself is the desire for separation or individuation in the creature that prefigures evil. In nature this is exhibited as exaggeration, deformation, a tendency to dissolution. In spirit and in history, this movement appears as discord, a common theme in German idealism. Heidegger identifies the diremption of the unhappy consciousness in Hegel's *Phenomenology of Spirit* as in part, at least, a variation on this theme (150). In "histories of spirit" it is "not a matter of a supposedly arbitrary and inaccurate adjustment of so-called facts, but of the opening of essential, that is, possible, historical regions and their extensions." That is, the historical constructions of German idealism are political, for the opening of a possible historical region is and must be political. Schelling's metaphysics of evil is, after all, a failure; another, better response to the new impulse that enters philosophy is possible. The metaphysics of evil, then, *does not* open up a possible historical region; its replacement by Heidegger's teaching may not suffer from this defect.

Evil is realized in and as a decision in which the essence of human freedom as self-determination—the basic teaching of German idealism—is realized (152–56). Heidegger's understanding of the philosophy of freedom claims to be deeper than that philosophy's understanding of itself. His understanding must include a characterization of the ground from which decision and its decidedness emerge from undecidedness. Decision and decidedness are the same, since idealist freedom as self-determination is self-necessitation. Thus, the essence of a human being is the unity of existence and ground in him which is determined by eternity: "since it is the essence of man as an actual individual, determined in the eternal determination of itself to itself. Every man's own essence is each time his own eternal deed. Thence comes that uncanny and at the same time friendly feeling that we have always been what we are, that we are nothing but the unveiling of things long since decided" (153–54).

In man evil or good involves the appearing of both; with each comes the other (156–58). Evil appears as the hunger of self-craving which, to maintain itself and dominate, must transcend itself. This movement is not simply negative. Indeed, it fills us with terror precisely because it is necessarily spiritual. Thus, the "self-craving of malice mirrors that

110

originary ground in God." Similarly, the form of good as a way of decidedness must exhibit evil, which belongs to the highest examples of decision, such as enthusiasm, heroism, and faith.

If we turn to LH, we find the more comprehensive teaching within which the appearance of good and evil is inscribed. There, after telling us that thinking "never creates the house of Being," Heidegger explains that it "conducts historical eksistence, that is, the *humanitas* of *homo humanus,* into the realm of the upsurgence [*Aufgangs*] of the healing [*Heilen*]" (LH 237). Then he writes: "With healing, evil appears all the more in the lighting of Being. The essence of evil does not consist in the mere baseness of human action, but rather in the malice of rage. Both of these, however, healing and the raging, can essentially occur only in Being, insofar as Being itself is what is contested. In it is concealed the essential provenance [*Wesensherkunft*] of nihilation [*Nichtens*]." Nihilation is not subjective negation but, rather, belongs to Being (237–38). Da-sein, then, "nihilates inasmuch as it belongs to the essence of Being as that essence in which the human ek-sists. Being nihilates—as Being" (238). This nihilating is what Heidegger has called the nothing; then: "Hence because it thinks Being, thinking thinks the nothing. To healing Being first grants ascent into grace; to raging its compulsion to malignancy." This says as plainly as possible that Being is indifferent between grace and malignancy. If Schelling's metaphysics of evil gives way to the question of Being, we are entitled to ask, as Manfred Frings has asked: "Is there room for evil in Heidegger's philosophy or not?"[15] An affirmative answer is possible; the teaching of IM from which I moved to the Schelling lectures makes that clear. Moreover, the "demonism" Heidegger identifies there is clearly political, for it is "identical with the increasing helplessness and uncertainty of Europe against it and within itself" (IM 38).

I suggest that for Heidegger, Schelling's teaching on evil, however suggestive, remains mired in the ontotheology that pervades German idealism (ST 50–51). This means that Heidegger can accept that teaching as an index of the more fundamental issue his own thinking has already reached.[16] I want to conclude this chapter with one final look at the Schelling lectures. In his own preparation for his study of Schelling, Heidegger makes clear that this study, like so much else in his thinking, is and must be concerned with nihilism. About nihilism he writes: "It belongs to the inmost essence of nihilism that it can be overcome only when more and more deeply known, thus never through deciding one day to close one's eyes to it. Therefore, reflection and ever more keen reflection! Knowledge, ever more unswerving knowledge. A knowledge which is not good and bearable for everyone, but is inevitable for those who have essential things to do in all areas of human activity" (23). Such knowledge, we may say, is, and must be, situated beyond good and evil, and therewith so must the action necessarily related to it.

4 | Properly Human Work

All that is great is singular, but this singular has its own
manner of constancy, that is, historically transformed and
altered recurrence. Singular here does not mean present at
one time and then gone at another, but rather: having been,
and therefore in the constant possibility of a transformed
development of essence, and consequently inexhaustibly
disclosed in appropriation always anew, and becoming more
powerful.

(G39 144–45)

THE ESSENCE OF the German university is "self-governance" (*Selbst-verwaltung*), but Heidegger raises the question of whether the demands imposed by the claim to self-governance have been rightly understood. In order to carry out its mission, the university must govern itself, which requires it to know, articulate, and defend its essence. We must know "who we ourselves are," a necessity which requires the "most constant and unsparing *self-examination* [*Selbstbesinnung*]" (RA 470). For Heidegger, the question of *who* we are is crucial, for with it one asks about the temporal particularity or Dasein of the questioner, which is distinguished absolutely from such notions as subjectivity, personality, ego, biological nature, and the like (BT 67–71, 150–53; HCT 236–50). The question of who we are, as a philosophical question, a question about Dasein, is necessarily a question about the site or place of the questioner as well (G65 48–54). The ground of questioning lies in the strength of self-assertion (*Selbstbehauptung*) (RA 470–71). The essence of the German university must be understood for it to be willed, and hence for the body of teachers and students to assert itself. It is now clear that "the self-assertion of the German university is the originary [*ursprünglich*], shared will to its essence" (RA 471). "Grounded in science, by means of science [*Wissenschaft*]," the German university "educates and disciplines the leaders and guardians of the fate of the German people."[1] Heidegger then states the principle of what I shall call his "political" science: "The will to the essence of the German university is the will to science as will to the spiritual historical mission [*geschichtlichen geistigen Auftrag*] of the German people, a people that knows itself in its state." For Heidegger, "science and German destiny must come to power in this will to essence" together. The condition for the conjunction of science and German fate is stringent: ". . . if, and *only* if, we—this body of teachers and students—*on the one hand* expose science to its innermost necessity and, *on the other hand,* are equal to the German fate in its most extreme distress."

The articulation of the university as a community under suitable spiritual leadership provides the institutional form for the realization of the essence of science. Heidegger presents the results of his reflections on science in the address, which is not, and cannot be, a philosophic inquiry into science. He is concerned with the political sense or significance of science; the legitimacy of this understanding cannot be established in the address. Heidegger dismisses recent or contemporary views of science. In refusing to continue the debate about the "self-sufficiency and lack of presuppositions on an all too up-to-date science," we recover the possibility of experiencing science in its "innermost necessity."

The first requirement for a proper understanding of science is to recognize that there is no unconditional necessity for science to be, in the first place. Rather, "we," the university, must understand that if there is to be science "*for* us and *through* us," there are conditions for its existence (RA 471). In other words, science is a way of our being. "We" are a transcendental condition for science. In BT the "existential conception of science" is reached through an analysis of the conditions of Dasein's Being necessary for science as a way of Dasein's existing (BT 408–15). We have seen this understanding at work in Heidegger's earliest reflections on science. The thesis of the rectoral address that science is a possibility grounded in "us" restates one of Heidegger's fundamental teachings. Put briefly, science emerges from or is a fundamental modification of the circumspective concern which operates in relationships within the context of equipment and which is guided by the intelligibility of the present equipmental totality and its public environment (410). Circumspection makes the ready-to-hand present

114

in a manner which accomplishes its transformation into the present-at-hand (412). The derivation of present-at-hand from ready-to-hand is not a derivation of "theory" from "praxis," for praxis has its theoretical element, and theory has its praxis (409). In theorizing, we look at the ready-to-hand thing *as* present-to-hand, thus employing a determinate understanding of Being in terms of which the environmental context of the ready-to-hand, including its equipmental character and its place, is methodically overlooked. To the extent that the understanding of Being as present-at-hand is decisive for an area, the more secure will be the status of that area as a science (413). Thus, mathematical physics is correctly understood as a coherent way in which nature is projected mathematically, which depends upon an a priori projection of the state of Being of entities *as* the objects of mathematical physics (414). While the projective or thematizing activity of science, which objectifies entities, is the result of a transformation within the conduct of Dasein, it is characterized by its own kind of making present, in which the discovering characteristic of science is based on a resoluteness by which Dasein projects itself toward its possibility for Being-in-the-truth (414–15). Since Being-in-the-truth is a way in which Dasein may exist, "science has its source in authentic existence" (415). Authentic existence is essentially historical, which suggests that science is also historical, and we have seen that the political is inscribed in the historical.

The rectoral address inscribes the existential and therewith the historical and political understanding of science in the necessity of a recovery of the origin of science. The condition for science to be *for* and *through* us is that we must place ourselves under the power of the "*beginning* of our spiritual-historical Dasein" in and with the "break out" (*Aufbruch*) of Greek philosophy. To understand the task of the *German* university it is necessary to begin with the *Greeks*. We are led to the question of the nature and significance of the connections between the German people and their situation, which is the occasion for Heidegger's political engagement, and the Western tradition or the West simply, itself understood from the Greeks. In "The Rectorate" Heidegger writes that the renewal of the German people, which he had believed was a possibility of National Socialism, "would allow it to discover its historical vocation in the Western world" (R 483). The teaching on science, or "its preservation of the tradition that has handed down to us the beginning of our Western way of knowing in the Greek world," is in keeping with "our responsibility as part of the Western world" (R 487). The first-person plurals "we" and "our" refer to the body of teachers and students, the German university, and the Germans, joined to the rebellion of Greek philosophy.

In this chapter I examine the comportments of those bodies—teachers and students within the university and the students in their threefold joining of labor, military, and knowledge "service"—whose actions are conditions for the recovery of science. Central to my account is Heidegger's teaching on work. In the following chapter I shall turn directly to science and its shifting roles in Heidegger's thinking.

I

The body of *teachers* must "actually advance to the most extreme posts of danger in constant uncertainty" (RA 475). If from its "steadfastness—in essential nearness to the hard-pressing insistence of all things—arises a communal questioning [*gemeinsame Fragen*] and a communally attuned saying [*gemeinschaftlich gestimmte Sagen*], then it will gain the strength to lead." Germany's student body does not have to be awakened, for already "on the march," it seeks suitable leaders. A will to the essence of the university emerges from the resoluteness of German students to be equal to the "German fate in its most extreme distress." Heidegger cites the Student Law of May 1, 1933, as evidence that the German student body has for the first time determined its own essence. In giving itself its own law, it exhibits the highest freedom.[2] Conventional academic freedom, the banishing of which Heidegger welcomes, appears as a negative freedom from concern. Indifference, arbitrariness, and lack of restraint are its features. Nearly forty years later Heidegger would still "stand behind" this criticism, for the academic freedom he rejects is "freedom *from* taking the trouble to reflect and meditate that scientific studies demand" (Sp 269). The thinking truly required in and by scientific studies is *political;* it is concerned with the present situation. "Academic freedom" is the liberal's name for indifference to the essential and hostility to the spiritual.[3]

The "bond and service" of the German student unfolds from the truth of the concept of freedom exhibited in the Student Law (RA 476). Heidegger identifies three bonds: the labor service (*Arbeitsdienst*), military service (*Wehrdienst*), and knowledge service (*Wissenschaftsdienst*), which are "equally necessary and of equal rank," since they issue from the three bonds—"*by* the people, *to* the destiny of the state, *in* a spir-

116

itual mission"—which are "equally originary to the German essence" (477). I must note here a common interpretation of the three services as an echo of the classification of classes and souls of citizens in Plato's *Republic*.[4] This does not strike me as especially illuminating. Heidegger's threefold division is a classification of functions performed or modes of comportment presented as possible and necessary for *one* "body"—the students; Socrates' classification identifies parts of the soul, each of which is presented as dominant in the members of a specific part of the city. For the Socratic teaching to bear more than a vague resemblance to that of Heidegger, those who proved suitable for training in philosophy would have to be capable of serving as artisans as well as soldiers.

"Labor service" is one of the principal themes of Heidegger's political speeches and requires a close examination. In the rectoral address "labor" is the first bond; it binds the student body to the community of the people (*Volksgemeinschaft*) and "obligates to help carry the burden and to participate actively in the troubles, endeavors, and skills of all its estates and members" (476). Several of Heidegger's speeches while rector are concerned with labor or work and its nature and role in Nazi Germany. While there is doubtless an element of compromise in the articles and addresses of 1933–34, the ease with which Heidegger adapted to the Nazi idiom and appropriated the phrases and slogans of the Nazi effort to appeal to German workers and labor organizations suggests that something more than opportunism is involved. Heidegger's political utterances on work are rooted in and sustained by his philosophical teaching on work. Some students of Heidegger's thinking fail to see this connection. Lacoue-Labarthe, for example, understands the theme of work as a "relatively minor and subordinate one in Heidegger's thinking; if not, it would not have fallen out of that thinking so quickly (it was one of the rare philosophical concessions to the programmatic themes of National Socialism, and therefore to the times . . .)."[5] He goes on to argue that nothing in Heidegger's philosophy "prefigures the type of ontology of labour" which appears in these utterances and which "last only for the period of [Heidegger's] commitment *stricto sensu* to Nazism."[6] Because Lacoue-Labarthe is insufficiently attentive to the political dimension of Heidegger's philosophy, he does not see what he regards as an instance of "rare philosophical concessions" is rather an example of Heidegger's political rhetoric, his teaching which addresses his times in a manner he judges appropriate to those times. Heidegger was neither merely duped by, nor was he simply a true believer in, the Nazi doctrine of labor. That doctrine exhibits in its way the present conditions for thinking. Heidegger's attempt to think from these conditions includes—indeed, must include—reflections on work. His own understanding of work provides the setting for his assimilation of the Nazi rhetoric, which is inscribed in, and does not dominate, his own rhetoric.

Heidegger's discourse on work is, and must be, a response to the ways in which the present is stamped, to what is "thrown toward" us to think (OWA 75). Thus, "work" is situated epochally, and its phenomenology is necessarily historical. This, however, cannot be all, for there lies beneath Heidegger's teaching on work, taken up into it and transformed, the Aristotelian conception of properly human work, the *ergon tou anthrōpou* (*Nicomachean Ethics* 1097b22). To put the matter with appropriate bluntness, the revolution brought about by National Socialism brings with it the opportunity for the transformation of work along what can still, without misunderstanding, be called lines of authenticity. My aim is to reveal how "work" is situated in a number of texts in order to show at least some of the manifold developments from it. Lines of thinking Heidegger develops *from* work, or which inscribe work in a significant way, exhibit the multiple roles work plays.

Let us look first at some of the speeches made during 1933–34. "Work" as a theme is correlated with both an emphasis on the radical transformations that have already affected German Dasein as well as those yet to come, and with the distinctive role and responsibility of students. With National Socialism comes the necessity of a new thinking commensurate with the revolutionary nature of the change brought about by National Socialism. The students are faced, as Heidegger explains in his "German Students" speech, with the fact that "the National Socialist revolution rings in the total collapse of our German Dasein" (NH 135). German students must become "those who are always ready, those who are hardened, those who never cease developing. Your will to know," Heidegger tells the students, "seeks contact with the essential, the simple, the great. You are restless to seek out what assails you, what presses hard against you, what engages you from afar. Be harsh and authentic in your needs" (150). As Heidegger apparently explained in his course in the summer of 1933, "The Fundamental Questions of Philosophy," the "student youth seized the importance of the historical moment that the German people experienced in the space of a few weeks."[7] "What," Heidegger asks, "was in the process of becoming? The German people found itself and also found at its head a great leading [*Führung*]" (131–32). The leading with which Heidegger is concerned is that of the *students* and *not* Hitler. The students have helped the German people to find itself. "Now returned to itself," the people "created its own state," enabling it to become a nation that "accepted the destiny of its people," "conquered its spiritual mission," and "forged its history" (132). German youth "has today begun to march" to encourage this "vast movement with distant repercussions moving toward the difficult dawning of a still obscure future." In responding to its vocation, German youth is "moved by the will to find a discipline and an education that will bring it to maturity and strength so that it can assume the role of spiritual and political guide." This political pedagogy will be guarded for a future generation and "will be invested by the people at the determined moment for the state, in the midst of the peoples of the world." Heidegger goes on to write: "Every grand and authentic leading is moved by the force of a fundamentally hidden determination [*Bestimmung*]." The will of such leading "finally, will be nothing other than the political and spiritual mission of a people. It is the knowledge relating to this mission that is to be wakened, rooted in the heart and will of the people and of each and all that constitute it."

The struggle in and for which studying must become a "venture" and not a "shelter" "brings about the *complete transformation of our German Dasein*" (NH 150). This change is not simply identical with the National Socialist revolution, although it is necessarily rooted in it. Certainly Heidegger anticipates a lengthy process, which places rigorous demands on German students: "Whoever does not endure the struggle, remains left behind. The new courage must accustom itself to steadiness, because the struggle for the educational places of the leaders will last a long time. It gets fought *from* [my emphasis] the forces of the New Reich which the *Volk*-Chancellor Hitler will bring to reality. A hard stock [*Geschlecht*] without thought for itself must be equal to it; this stock lives from constant testing and for the goal which it assigns for itself" (75).

National Socialism, then, has not yet created a suitable place, or one may well say, a suitable rank, for educational leaders. The "forces of the New Reich" are the ground and not the completion of the transformation to which Heidegger summons the students. Here, as in all other

"Nazi" utterances of Heidegger with which I am familiar, there is no suggestion that National Socialism understands, or is by itself capable of understanding, its own significance. There is, I think, ample textual evidence for Pöggeler's claim that the rectoral address and the 1933–34 political speeches exhibit Heidegger's understanding of his task to "lead the leader" (*den Führer führen*).[8]

In an address to workers, Heidegger characterizes work as every "regulated deed and act" done with responsibility to the individual, the group, and the state, which therefore serves the people (NH 202, cf. 156–58). To follow Hitler is to will the growth of the German people in its unity as a "work people" and its "duration and greatness as a work state." Obligatory work service, in Heidegger's view, "affords a basic experience of toughness, of closeness to earth and tools, of the rigor and severity of the most simply physical work, and thereby of what is most essential within the group" (180–81). The basic experience of daily activity as ruled by the discipline of work brings about purification, solidarity, responsibility, and comradeship.

The awakened youth of Germany are engaged in work service that prepares a "complete restamping" (*Umprägung*) of German existence which transcends differences between intellectual work and other forms of work by showing that all human work is intellectual, since it exhibits the experience of commitment, decision, and resolve which brings "*freedom*, that is to say, brings *spirit*" (180). It is a "cultured man's" prejudice that only "spiritual creators" work, for "every work is *spiritual as work*" (181). Intellectual work, spiritual work—which is to say, properly human work—"leads us more deeply and sympathetically into the imperious necessity felt by a people" and is "more knowingly and immediately hemmed in by the harsh dangers of human existence." Unemployed workers learned from Heidegger that urbanization had brought them to their present crisis, beset by dehumanization and class conflict (200). Against the Marxist doctrine of irreconcilable class struggle, and in agreement with the Nazi position on labor, Heidegger asserts, in sentences remarkable for their fusion of his own philosophical idiom with the Nazi line, that "there is only a single German living class [*Lebensstand*]. That is rooted in the supporting ground of the *Volk* and in the *worker's class* [*Arbeitstand*] freely articulated in the historical will of the state, whose stamping [*Prägung*] becomes pre-formed in the movement of the National Socialist German *Workers'* Party" (181).

Through the political education courses he established for workers, Heidegger sought to create a "living bridge" between students and workers (199, cf. 204, 22–23, 40, 167). The possibility for this bridge lies in the fact that "our whole German reality has been changed by the National Socialist state, with the consequence that our whole manner of thinking and seeing and our concept ought to change" (199). With National Socialism comes the necessity of a new thinking commensurate with the revolutionary nature of the change National Socialism has brought in the conditions of work, which is to say, of action.

As an illustration of the conjunction of Heidegger's technical and political teachings, I note that in his addresses on work service Heidegger assimilates knowledge of science to the knowledge of workers with a simple version of an argument that appears in various works between 1928 and 1951. The knowledge of science "is not distinguished in its essence from that of the farmer, the lumberjack, the miners, the craftsman," for knowledge means "knowing one's way around the world in which we are placed communally and individually" (201). Knowledge means as well "to be growing in resolve and performance of the task given each us respectively whether this task is now ordering the fields, felling the trees, mining, questioning the laws of nature, or placing history out in the power of fate." Finally, knowledge means "to be master of the situation in which we are put."

An early version of this idea appears in Heidegger's interpretation of *sophia* as knowing one's way around (MFL 11).[9] In his 1943 lectures on Heraclitus, he claims that *sophia* had the same signification as *technē* and designates know-how, while in the 1951 essay "Logos," know-how is joined to destiny, a play on two senses of the German *geschickt:* "skillful" and "sent," employed to render *sophon* (G55 247; EGT 68). The result is that practical knowledge, know-how, is understood as a response to what is "sent" by destiny.[10] This understanding, however, is already present in Heidegger's remarks to workers in 1934. We may ask if and how this understanding of science as know-how, or the assimilation of science to work, is compatible with the teaching that science stands exposed to crisis. The vertical assimilation of work to science ennobles work and exhibits the work-character of science. The common denominator of science and work seems to be authenticity, which is to say that both science and work stand exposed to the uncertainty of the totality of what is.

II

In BT a "work" is "that which is to be produced at the time; and this is accordingly ready-to-hand too" (99). "Work-world" is the intelligibility within which something produced is located. Heidegger reaches "work" and the "work-world" in his explication of Dasein's manifold dispersions into ways of Being-in (*In-Sein*), which in turn is governed by the larger task of explaining that and how Dasein is Being-in-the-world. Much of Heidegger's account of work contributes to his explication of "world," which is to say of intelligibility. Thus, the emphasis is on the work-*world* rather than the *work*-world. Indeed, if we follow Heidegger strictly, there is no *one* work-world, but rather a manifold of work-worlds, which requires us to qualify his numerous discussions which include some reference to "the" work-world, understanding them as "always already" inscribing a determinate work-world in his analysis. As he explains, when we "go to work," we do not "push out from the 'nothing' " and find equipment in isolation; rather, "in laying hold of an item of equipment, we come back to it from whatever work-world [*Werk-welt*] has already been disclosed" (BT 403–4).

"Knowing" is not the initial or decisive encounter we have with beings. Our everyday Being-in-the-world *is* our "dealings" (*Umgangs*) in the world and with beings encountered in the world in which what is closest to us is the "kind of concern which manipulates things and puts them to use" (95). It is unnecessary for us to "put ourselves into a position" to make such concern accessible, for everyday Dasein already *is* in this way (96). We fail to recognize this or understand its significance adequately unless we put aside our tendency to interpret or theorize beings as "things" with some property such as materiality attached to them or as things "invested with value." Here the larger issue, which Heidegger had recognized in his early lectures, is the nature of the Being of "value," which must be clarified in order to make sense of the notion of investing things with value.

Heidegger invokes the Greek *pragmata*—that with which one has to do in "one's concernful dealings" (*praxis*)—as in some way evidently preferable to "Things" (96–97). "Equipment" (*Zeug*) names the "pragmatic" character of *pragmata* by showing that there is necessarily "something in-order-to," a structure in which there is an assignment or reference (*Verweisung*) of "something to something" (*von etwas auf etwas*) (97). The Greeks, however, left this pragmatic character ontologically obscure and thought of *pragmata* as "mere Things." In HCT Heidegger explains that while Greek philosophy experienced the world as *pragmata*, "as the *wherewith of having-to-do*," the world "did not become ontologically understood in this sense, but rather in the widest sense as a thing of nature" (HCT 185). In his appropriation of the Greek designation, Heidegger shows that both "we" and the Greeks have made tacit ontological assumptions. While Dasein "was known to antiquity" as "authentic [*eigentliche*] action, as *praxis*," antiquity lacked an adequate understanding of *praxis* (MFL 183). As we shall see, Heidegger later claims to exhibit what antiquity did not and could not articulate fully concerning *praxis*.

"Equipment" is never intelligible in the singular; the condition for something to be "this equipment" is a "totality of equipment." In turn, equipment is always "something in-order-to . . ." ("*etwas um-zu . . .*") (BT 97). In the structure of an in-order-to is an "assignment" or "reference" of something to something. Thus, Heidegger says, equipment *is* "in terms of." It shows itself only in and as part of a totality of equipment and thus not as an "occurring Thing" (98). The Being of equipment is its readiness-to-hand which makes it usable. Readiness-to-hand cannot be discovered by looking at the appearance of things. Heidegger's point is to argue against the priority of "theorizing" understood as the primary or even as the sole form of "sight." "Circumspection" (*Umsicht*) is the sight which guides our use of equipment and from which equipment acquires its "thingly" character. Accordingly, "practical" comportment is not "atheoretical" in the sense of "sightless" (99). Now in order for what is ready-to-hand to be such authentically, it must "withdraw" (*zurückzuziehen*), which is to say that it cannot be that with which we initially concern ourselves. The sight which guides comportment depends upon the presence of equipment as an absence. The withdrawal of equipment is its proper motion. What our dealings "dwell" with is not primarily equipment but *work*. It is work that bears the "referential totality" (*Verweisungsganzheit*) within which equipment is encountered, which is to say that it is work that furnishes the intelligibility of equipment.

As a world into which concern has fallen, the work-world is "not thematically perceived, not thought, not known, and it is just this which grounds the possibility of an originary [*ursprüngliche*] reality" (HCT 193). In bringing what is not thought to thought, Heidegger takes the decisive step toward realizing this originary reality, for it is the absence of thematization that conditions both Heidegger's account and the actualizing of the originary. Such a reality could be only a transformed work-world, and it is precisely this transformation, in my view, that Heidegger projects upon the Nazi doctrine of labor.

The priority of the work-world appears in and as its appresentation of the wider environment in which we find beings ready-to-hand, with such handiness as the immediately available, and the extant as the always-already-there. All such distinctions in the environing world, which itself can be articulated as my own world, the public world, the world as nature, are not separate, juxtaposed regions but are present on the basis of an "exchange of presence" (HCT 194). That is, something of concern to us, placed under our care, allows us to encounter what is around it; it is a locus of orientation and action. The presencing of what is present is the condition for our encounters with the various aspects of the environing world (cf. BPP 293–94).

The work is the "toward-which" of tools and has the kind of Being possessed by equipment (BT 99). It is the usability of the work that allows us to encounter that for which it is usable. The work is a use of something; it has a "whereof," such as its dependence upon and thus its assignment in terms of specific materials (100). This dependence furnishes access to nature, which is discovered in the use of equipment. At this point I must mention an interpretive issue that arises concerning not only the role of nature in BT but Heidegger's thinking in general during the 1920s. The teaching that begins, including nature, are encountered initially and primarily as ready-to-hand, and that other modes of encounter are distinguished and derived from this, has been called Heidegger's "instrumentalism," and scholars debate the issue of whether or with what consequences BT presents an "instrumentalist ontology."[11] The short way with this problem is to label it as based on the misunderstanding of BT as propounding an ontology. If BT does not present any ontology, but rather challenges ontology by raising the question of the meaning of Being, it can hardly present an instrumentalist ontology. Moreover, even if the thesis of the primacy of the work-world suffices to allow us to call Heidegger's account "instrumentalist," his argument is not that Being is to be understood instrumentally but rather that Dasein's way of Being is best explicated by attending to its actions. Finally, Heidegger himself rejects this interpretive claim explicitly (G29/30 263).

To return to the textual issue of access to nature, the "whereof" of work issues in a *conditional* access to nature; it is the "Nature we find in natural products," for example, the animals from which hides are taken to make leather or the wood and iron from which a hammer is made. Heidegger is clear that nature is not understood here as what is present-at-hand nor as the " 'power' of Nature." Certainly nature as the object of scientific study is not presented in this way (HCT 193). Moreover, if we leave behind this conditional access to nature and thereby discover nature as "pure presence-at-hand," Heidegger tells us that the nature which " 'stirs and strives,' which assails us and enthralls us as landscape, remains hidden. The botanist's plants are not the flowers of the hedge-row; the 'source' which the geographer establishes for a river is not the 'springhead in the dale.' " While it is the case that beings can be discovered as nature only in "some definite mode" of Dasein's Being-in-the-world and that nature does not make worldhood intelligible (BT 93–94), nature as hidden is neither treated thematically in BT, nor is it dismissed as unreal. That is, it is nature as *discovered* that appears in the existential analytic and not nature as treated thematically.

In addition to its references "toward-which" and "whereof," the work has an assignment, "under simple craft conditions," "to the person who is to use it or wear it" (100). It is "cut to his figure; he 'is' there along with it as the work emerges." In the case of mass-produced goods, there remains an assignment, but it is "indefinite, and points to the random, the average." In the 1925 account, Heidegger explains that the reference of such goods is "quite generic; [they] have an indeterminacy, an arbitrariness, but they nevertheless have a reference to indeterminate others" (HCT 192). Such a reference is an example of appresentation.[12] In appresenting the world *of* users and consumers, the work-world appresents *them*. Moreover, "my *own environing world* is appresented as at the same time entering into a *public world*. More accurately, this public world is always already there with the work to be provided; because of it we encounter the work-world in a salient way." In BT Heidegger tells us, without the intervening process of appresentation, that in and with work we encounter entities with Dasein's kind of Being. It is along with these that we encounter the world in which they live, which is our world. "Any work with which one concerns oneself is ready-to-hand not only in the domestic world of the workshop," Heidegger writes, "but also in the *public world*" (BT 100). This conclusion inscribes work in the domain of the political.

III

The apparent priority of "simple craft conditions" suggests that for Heidegger handiwork and handicraft production occupy a position superior to that of mass or machine production. If this is the case, it is argued, I think correctly, that Heidegger stands with the *völkisch* antiindustrial and antimodern supporters of National Socialism and shares with them a radically mistaken understanding of it which he later corrects when he comes to recognize that the Nazis had not set out to repeal modernity. Certainly Heidegger differs decisively on this point from such technological enthusiasts of the Right as Ernst Jünger.[13] I simply want here to shift the focus from the immediate political resonance of Heidegger's remarks on handicraft production to what I see as their larger sense, which lies in his understanding of the relation between handicraft and thinking. From the vantage point thus reached, we may in turn clarify that part of Heidegger's teaching on work that is concerned with and criticizes Marxism.

Thinking, like handicraft, must be rooted, located in a determinate site. In "Why I Stay in the Provinces" (1934), his explanation of his refusal to accept a university appointment in Berlin, Heidegger calls the mountainous setting of his ski hut his "work-world" (*Arbeitswelt*) (G13 9). His openness and attunement to experiences of weather and the seasons happens only when his own Dasein "stands in its *work*" (10): "Work *first opens* a space for this mountain reality. The going-on of work remains implanted in the happening of landscape." Thinking resembles the work of the peasants and is similarly rooted. "The effort of molding something into language [*sprachlichen Prägung*]," Heidegger writes, "is like the resistance of the towering firs against the storm" (10). Such philosophical work is not like "the aloof studies of some eccentric" but instead "belongs right here in the midst of the peasants' work." He goes on: "When the young farmboy drags his heavy sled up the slope and guides it, piled high with beech logs, down the dangerous descent to his house, when the herdsman, lost in thought and slow of step, drives his cattle up the slope, when the farmer in his shed gets the countless shingles ready for his roof, my work is of the same sort. It is intimately rooted in and related to the life of the peasants." The "inner belonging [*Zugehörigkeit*] of my own work to the Black Forest and its people," he asserts, "comes from a centuries-long and irreplaceable rootedness in the Alemannian-Swabian soil" (10–11; cf. Sp 277).

In his wartime lecture course on Parmenides, Heidegger asserts an essential relation between the hand and human being: "Through the hand happens prayer and murder, greetings and thanks, the oath and the wink, but also the 'work' of the hand, the 'handiwork' and the implement. No animal has a hand, and never does there arise a hand from a paw or a claw or a talon. Even the despairing hand is never . . . a 'talon,' with which the human 'grasps.' Only from and with the word has the hand arisen. Human beings do not 'have' hands, but instead the hand has in it the essence of the human, because the word as the essential realm of the hand is the essential basis of the human" (G54 118–19). There is rather more here than just an analogy between thinking and grasping.[14] Indeed, Heidegger's examples here are precisely *not* those of philosophers concerned with questions of knowledge, but rather with questions that concern the affairs of everyday life. Inscribed here is the radical disjunction of human and animal as well. The most difficult thought here is that of the word. Later, in OWL, Heidegger finds that "the word, the saying, has no being" (OWL 87). That is, "word," like "is," does not "belong among things." Here I do not need to attempt to explicate Heidegger's instancing of "it gives" / "there is" (*es gibt*) except to note that "word" as he understands it "reveals itself as what is properly worthy of thought, but for whose definition all standards are still lacking in every way" (88). This is a "simple ungraspable situation [*ungreifbare Sachverhalt*]." Now I think that Bruns is on the right track when he writes that the word "gives, but not of itself. Itself it withholds as in a paratactic tactic." Bruns adds that the word "gives, rather than is, roughly in the way that things thing and worlds world."[15] If "word" is the "essential basis of the human," then we see that there is, or must be, a sense in which the human is also ungraspable, and if this basis is *as* the hand, then the hand, so to speak, does not and cannot grasp itself. This line of thinking restates the teaching according to which the human, but never the animal, is characterized by Dasein, as we may now name the movement and location of the hand. What is shown is the spiritual character of properly human work, to which must be added, I think, the rooted character of such work.

That Heidegger may have something like this in mind is evidenced, I think, by his discussion later in the Parmenides lecture, when he sets the fivefold constellation Being/Word/Reading/Hand/Writing over against technology, exemplified by the typewriter (124–30). The development of the technology of printing points toward the replacement of the human writer by writing machines. In Heidegger's view, the mechanization of writing produces a "cloud" (*Wolke*) that obscures the relation between word and hand, which together in writing correspond with *logos*, which he reminds us in an inceptive name of Being.

In WCT Heidegger suggests that thinking may be "something like building a cabinet. At any rate, it is a handi-work [*Handwerk*]" (WCT 16). "Work" refers here to the strength and skill of our hands. The hand is not rightly understood in terms of the human body as an organism; its "essence can never be determined, or explained by its being an organ which can grasp. Apes, too, have organs that can grasp, but they do not have hands." The hand is "infinitely different" from the grasping organs of animals, different, according to Heidegger, "by an abyss of essence [*Abgrund des Wesens*]." The work of the hand, he explains, allows it to grasp, catch, push, and pull, but also to reach, extend, receive, and welcome. All of this involves not only things, however, for the hand

> extends itself, and receives its own welcome in the hands of others. The hand holds. The hand carries. The hand designs and signs, presumably because man is a sign. Two hands fold into one, a gesture meant to carry man into the great oneness. The hand is all this, and this is the true handicraft. Everything is rooted here that is commonly known as handicraft, and commonly we go no further. But the hand's gestures run everywhere through language, in their most perfect purity precisely when man speaks by being silent. And only when man speaks, does he think—not the other way around as metaphysics still believes. Every motion of the hand in every one of its works carries itself through the element of thinking, every bearing of the hand bears itself in that element. All the work of the hand is rooted in thinking. Therefore, thinking itself is man's simplest, and for that reason hardest handiwork, if it would be accomplished at its proper time. (16–17)

There is nothing in Heidegger's writings thus far available that can rightly be called a thematic treatment of Marx and Marxism. Instead, Marx and Marxism appear at several crucial points in lines of thinking as exhibitions of the ruling principle of the present epoch, as instances of *Gestell*. In the Parmenides lecture, for example, the remarks about technology cited above provide the context for Heidegger's observations about the significance of Bolshevism and thus of the Soviet Union: Lenin's word that "Bolshevism is Soviet power + electrification" means that Bolshevism "is the 'organic,' i.e., calculatively organized (and as +) thrusting together of the unconditioned power of the party with fully realized technologization" (G54 127). What the "bourgeois world" fails to understand is that in "'Leninism,' as Stalin calls this metaphysics, has been realized a *metaphysical leap forward*, from which in a certain way first becomes comprehensible the metaphysical passion of today's Russian for technology, from which he brings to power the techno-logical world." Since we have already seen in IM that "metaphysically" America and Russia are the same, we are not surprised to find that elsewhere Heidegger calls Bolshevism a "variety of Americanism," asserting that "the latter is the genuinely dangerous form of the measureless, because it arises in the form of bourgeois democracy and is mixed with Christendom, and all of this in an atmosphere of decisive historylessness" (G53 86–87). Heidegger recognizes, in other words, the greater power of the combination of bourgeois democracy and Christendom. Leninism is a "metaphysical leap forward" in the sense that it, in Heidegger's view, allows the "calculative" aspect of technology to become visible.

Now the place and rank of Marxism can hardly be what Marxists understand it to be.[16] When Heidegger writes that "the Marxist vision [*Anschauung*] of history [*Geschichte*] is superior to any other historiography [*Historie*]" in LH, he has most assuredly not adopted anything like dialectical materialism; on this point Schürmann, who finds this passage "rather puzzling," is correct (LH 219).[17] The puzzle is solved by the preceding sentences: "What Marx recognized in an essential and significant sense, though derived from Hegel, as the alienation [*Entfremdung*] of man has its roots in the homelessness [*Heimatlosigkeit*] of modern man. This homelessness is specifically evoked from the *Geschick* of Being in the form of metaphysics, and through it [metaphysics] is simultaneously entrenched and covered up as homelessness." Marxism cannot think this *Geschick* "Being-historically" (*seinsgeschichtlich*), as Heidegger puts it just before he explains Marx's indebtedness to Hegel. This is a crucial limitation, for homelessness is "coming to be a world-destiny [*Weltschicksal*]." Nonetheless, the Marxist understanding of history as the history of production does reach an "essential [*wesentliche*] dimension of history." Elsewhere Heidegger explains that for Marx all change in the world—and here I suggest that we read "world" in Heidegger's sense—is change in the relations of production (*Produktionsverhaltnissen*) (G15 352). Production, in turn, is exhibited in praxis, understood as the production of man through his own "self-stamping," a teaching which Heidegger regards as a "theoretical representation of man" derived, as the theory of alienation is, from Hegel. The "modern metaphysical essence of labor" is foreshadowed in Hegel's *Phenomenology of Spirit*, Heidegger explains, "as the self-establishing process of unconditioned production [*unbedingten Herstellung*], which is the objectification of the actual through man experienced as subjectivity" (LH 220).

For Heidegger, Marx's teaching fails to comprehend its own relation to the history of metaphysics and therewith to the history of Being. There is a straightforward and simple formulation of this point in an interview with Richard Wisser. Heidegger explains that "the question of the demand for world change leads us back" to Marx's teaching in his *Theses on Feuerbach* that "philosophers have only *interpreted* the world differently; what matters is to *change* it" (MHUD 82). He goes on to explain that when "this statement is cited *and* when it is followed, it is overlooked that changing the world presupposes a change in the *conception* of the world. A conception of the world can only be won by adequately *interpreting* the world." Thus, "Marx's demand for a 'change' is based on a very definite interpretation of the world, and therefore this statement is proved to be without foundation. It gives the impression that it speaks decisively against philosophy, whereas the second half of the statement presupposes, unspoken, a demand for philosophy." Heidegger emphasizes that "for Marx it has been *decided in advance* that man and only man (and nothing besides) is the issue. Whence has this been decided? By whom? By what right? By what authority?—These questions can be answered only by going back to the history of metaphysics" (VS 132).

How does Marx understand the human essence? In LH Heidegger writes that "Marx demands that 'man's humanity' [*menschliche Mensch*]," which he finds in "society," be "recognized and acknowledged" (LH 200). His program is one of humanism, by which Heidegger means a "concern that man become free for his humanity and find his worth in it" (201). Thus understood, Marxism, Christianity, and Sartrean existentialism are all humanisms, for they "all agree in this, that the *humanitas* of *homo humanus* is determined with regard to an already established interpretation of nature, history, world and the ground of the world, that is, of beings as a whole" (201–2). Any understanding of the essence of the human that fails to inquire into the truth of Being is metaphysical, and every humanism "is either grounded in a metaphysics or is itself made to be the ground of one" (202). More specifically, every humanism from the first humanism, which for Heidegger is that of republican Rome, regards the essence of the human as *animal rationale,* which "is not false" but is "conditioned by metaphysics." Heidegger then reminds us that the "essential provenance" (*Wesensherkunft*) of metaphysics "became questionable" (*fragwürdig*) in BT. With this development, then, must come questioning into humanism.

The humanistic understanding of man as rational animal reaches beyond animality as conventionally understood. The crucial question, which humanism cannot ask, is whether "the essence of the human lies inceptively and most decisively in the dimension of *animalitas* at all" (203). For Heidegger "in principle we still think of *homo animalis*" when we posit *anima* as *anima sive mens,* soul as mind, and this as "subject, person, or spirit," for it is this "positing" (*Setzen*) that is metaphysics. Metaphysics, then, ignores and fails to think the essence of the human in its origin, which is the "essential provenance that is always the essential future of historical mankind [*geschichtliche Menschentum*]" (203–4). With the appearance of "historical mankind," we see now, if any further evidence is needed, that the political sense of humanism, and of Heidegger's criticism of it, has never been far from these reflections. "Metaphysics," he writes, "thinks of the human on the basis of *animalitas* and does not think toward his *humanitas*" (204). We have already seen how this distinction is employed. *Humanitas* is comprehended in its radical separation from animality, thought in terms of Dasein. What is distinctively human has never yet been thought adequately.

As he explains in one of the Nietzsche lectures, humanism results when *logos* is taken as "the basic determination of the world-totality [*Weltganzen*]" (N1 369). In turn this decision brings together "the supreme humanization [*Vermenschung*] of beings in one with the extreme naturalization [*Vernatürlichung*] of man" (380). Noting the apparent "allusion to the young Marx" in Heidegger's formulation, Schürmann is again puzzled, "since the notions of 'nature,' 'planet,' 'globe,' retain a strong, if only occasional, romantic overtone in Heidegger himself."[18] Now Heidegger is not reproaching Marx for romanticism, nor does he understand his own use of the words Schürmann instances as romantic. Rather, Marx's thesis is an example of *logos* understood humanistically.

With the inception of metaphysics, *logos* comes to belong to and define the essence of man; while *zoion logon echon* is not *simply animal rationale, logos* thus understood loses its originary relation to *phusis*.[19]

"One must be clear about what it means," Heidegger says in his 1931 course on Aristotle's *Metaphysics* Theta, 1–3, "that man has a relation to the works which he produces. Hence, in a certain book, *Being and Time,* the talk is of dealings with equipment; not in order to correct Marx or to set up a new national economy, especially from a primitive understanding of the world" (G33 137). To be sure, this last comment is a response by Heidegger to criticisms of his supposed "primitivism."[20] What is equally important is that Heidegger recalls Marx to us; his noncorrection of Marx moves us to think unavoidably of his massive correction of Marx.

IV

I return to the rectoral address and its account of the services. Military service binds the German student body to the "honor and destiny of the nation in the midst of other peoples" (RA 476). This service requires the "readiness, secured by knowledge and skill, and tightened by discipline, to give all." It must be noted that Heidegger is silent here about more concrete issues of war and peace. The bond from which military service issues is characterized as a bond to the destiny of the state, which suggests that for Heidegger there is indeed a sense in which this destiny is not intelligible apart from consideration of military service.

The knowledge service receives the longest and most complex treatment of any of the *Bindungen* in the rectoral address. Here the student body is bound to the "spiritual mission" of the German people. Heidegger projects his understanding of the essence of science onto the German people that "shapes its fate by placing its history into the openness of the overwhelming power of all the world-shaping powers of human Dasein and by ever renewing the battle for its spiritual world. Thus exposed to the most extreme questionableness of its own Dasein, this people wills to be a spiritual people." While the German people demand leaders and guardians who possess the "strictest clarity of the highest, widest, and richest knowledge," students "who at an early age have dared to act as men" and will the future destiny of the nation "force themselves, from the very ground of their being, to serve this knowledge" (476–77). The students, Heidegger explains, will not allow knowledge service to remain mere professional specialization, since those who lead the people must themselves be trained by those who understand that the knowledge the people require concerning its Dasein is not the "settled taking note of essences and values in themselves; it is the most severe endangerment of human Dasein in the midst of the overwhelming power of what is" (477). It is the "very questionableness of Being" that "compels the people to work and fight and forces it into its state, to which the professions belong." The people, then, are held out into what is, but it is not clear that or how they understand what compels them.

The knowledge (*Wissen*) students require cannot be limited to knowing the "present political situation of the people, a knowledge admittedly indispensable but not decisive" (NH 132). "The knowledge relating to the political and spiritual mission of the German people," Heidegger writes, "is a knowledge tied to its future." This knowledge is nothing like "prophetic knowledge," which "would sap, would strangle, all action," but is rather the "demanding knowledge of what is necessary, before everything merely possible and taking precedence over everything else, so that a people can raise themselves to the spiritual grandeur that is theirs." The actions, the way of being, of those who seek knowledge—and Heidegger must surely have faculty in mind as well as students—have epochal significance, for they lead to the question of the identity of the German people: "Be exigent, go to war, venerate—these three things together constitute that single great anguish that must drive us to become our own destiny. We are, to the extent that we demand, that we go to battle, that we venerate, that we continue in that direction. We are, to the extent that we seek ourselves. And we seek ourselves to the extent that we question who we are. Who is this people, what is their history, and what is the process at the depth of their being?" (132–33). This question itself is a "spiritual commitment [*Einsatz*] at the highest level, an essential questioning," reflection upon which allows Heidegger to articulate the relation between the German people and philosophy—indeed the decisive sense, I believe, of his political thinking: "With such questioning, we live our destiny, we expose ourselves to the obscure necessity of our history. This questioning through which a people lives its destiny, affirms it in the face of danger and threat, exposes it to risk, which is the grandeur of its mission—this questioning is its philosophizing, its philosophy. Philosophy is the questioning of the law and structure of our being. We want to make of philosophy a reality to the extent that we ask the question. We initiate this question to the extent that we risk ourselves on the fundamental question of philosophy" (133).

We are brought to the decisive difference between Heidegger's National Socialism and that of the National Socialists themselves. The movement of the German present, its dangers and opportunities, call, in Heidegger's view, for a response which confronts, embraces, and endures in the holding out of German Dasein into what is. To the extent that the German people become, or can become, a philosophical people, to the extent that philosophy is or can be realized in, even as, the German people, radical openness to the questionability of what is must be achieved and maintained. Nothing could have been further from the agendas of National Socialism than such openness and radicalism.

After his assertion that the three bonds and their correlative services are *"equally originary* to the German essence," Heidegger clarifies the principles of his political science. Heidegger may be said to agree with the Nazi doctrine that science is not and should not be neutral. Science is to serve the people, but Heidegger and his Nazi critics disagree on what is required to grasp the interests of the people and thus disagree on the nature of political science. The Nazi position is external to science and calls for political criteria to shape science. For Heidegger, the relation is internal, since science is necessarily already linked to the people or their destiny. Science is inherently an element in the constellation of the present epoch. The neutrality claimed for science by liberalism or humanism is illusory because it pretends to stand above history. Thus only "engaged knowledge about the people and knowledge about the destiny of the state that keeps itself in readiness," joined with knowledge about the "spiritual mission" of the people, create the "full essence of science, whose realization is our task" when we submit to the command of the "beginning of our spiritual-historical [*geistig-geschichtlich*] Dasein" (RA 477). Moreover, this idea of science obligates us to "make our questioning in the midst of the historical-spiritual [*geschicht-lich-geistig*] world of the people simple and essential," for it is only thus that the objectivity of science can "discover its nature and limit." The reversals here of *geistig* and *geschichtlich* are not accidental. In the first sentence, *geistig-geschichtlich* characterizes Dasein's *spiritual* submission to the command of the beginning, while

134

geschichtlich-geistig emphasizes the *historical* character of the spiritual world of the people. Questioning, then, is to be inscribed in and takes its place as the essence of the spiritual world of the people. Heidegger writes: "Such an original concept of science carries the obligation not only of 'objectivity' [*Sachlichkeit*] but again and above all of the essentiality and simplicity of questioning at the center of the historical-spiritual world [*geschichtlich-geistigen Welt*] of the people." It is only from this site—the joining of questioning and the center of the world of the people—that objectivity "can establish itself, that is, find its character and limits."

The "objectivity" of science is conditioned by the installation of questioning as the essential principle, which is to say the political principle of the people. Now since questioning is necessarily an exhibition of epochality, as a political principle it brings the motion of presencing and the deconstruction of any metaphysical first into politics. This is to say that the German people, as a people who knows itself in its state, is to stand in the open or exposed position of fundamental uncertainty, of the questionability of what is. It is not unreasonable to characterize Heidegger's teaching as one of Enlightenment, for in standing open to the questionability of what is, in placing questioning at the center of the historical world of the people, the people are freed from the illusions of contemporary doctrines of knowing and strengthened to confront the distress of the age. Heidegger's Enlightenment, however, holds its ground in the "self-concealing totality of what is," recognizing its own finitude. It is an Enlightenment predicated on the limits of illumination and the necessity of the surrounding darkness.

The "simplicity" of questioning is the absence of abstraction, of the theoretical. Questioning exhibits the simple when it remains close to the matter for thinking. I glance ahead to Heidegger's wartime lecture on Heraclitus to suggest the sense of "simplicity." What is sought in, by, and for thinking is what is direct and imageless. The beginning of thinking is an "initiating soundless word," and thinking "sees Being itself, imageless, in its inceptively simple essence as an organizing process (*Fügung*]" (G55 27, 146). The Greeks can teach us how to listen or co-respond to pure emerging; we must "listen inceptively" and "put aside personal opinions and to think what is inceptive about incipient thinking really as if we were 'initiates,' and that is to say, with simplicity." The installation of simplicity at the center of the historical-spiritual world of the people shows us that the people, or their historical-spiritual world, can become philosophical, that is, scientific, in the proper sense of the word.

When the bodies of teachers and students are and remain seized by this concept of science, their organization must also change. The condition for the faculty of the German university to *become* a faculty—one is tempted to say, an authentic faculty—is its rootedness in the essence of science. Thus grounded, the faculty becomes capable of "spiritual legislation, able to shape those powers of Dasein that press *it* hard into the *one* spiritual world of the people" (RA 478). Spiritual legislation is a shaping in response to what presses it and not, as some critics of Heidegger suggest, an independent activity of an academic mandarinate. An academic speciality becomes what it is when it overcomes the vitiating effects of contemporary professionalism. When faculties and specialities raise "the essential and simple questions" of their sciences, they are already "encompassed by the *same* final necessities and pressing concerns, inseparable from the Dasein of people and state." The site of the fundamental questions of the sciences proves to be the site of the Dasein of people and state. Questioning, as the essence of science, is connected as well to the specific action of the present situation, which is to say, National Socialism. Science and politics are fused. While the reorganization these tasks require is unlikely to be completed in the current or the coming semester—the Greeks took three centuries just to put the question of what knowledge is "upon the right basis and on a secure path"—Heidegger knows that the German university "will only take shape and come to power" when the three services "coalesce originarilly and become *one* formative force."

Having initially identified and distinguished the services and their significance, Heidegger then turns to their internal articulation (479). The teaching body needs to awaken to what is required to gain knowledge of the essence of science. The student body must rise to "the highest clarity and discipline of knowing" and "integrate its engaged understanding of the people and its state, which is itself a kind of science, into the essence of science." The wills of the teaching body and the student body "must confront one another, ready for *struggle* [*Kampf*]. All faculties of will and thought, all strengths of the heart and all skills of the body, must be unfolded *through* struggle, heightened *in* struggle, and preserved *as* struggle."

In "The Rectorate," Heidegger explains that the "attitude that governs" the rectoral address is "oriented toward 'struggle'" and that if "what is essential in this reflection returns to the Greek *epistēmē*" and hence to *alētheia,* then "battle" is thought in the sense of Heraclitus's understanding of *polemos* (R 488). The name of Heraclitus does not appear in the address, and *Kampf* exhibits the mutual inscription of Heidegger's teaching and the Nazi idiom. Heidegger's explanation of his choice of words, however, cannot be dismissed as merely an apologetic.[21] Heraclitean *polemos* has the sense of *eris,* or "strife," understood as "confrontation that sets those who confront one another apart, so that in such setting-apart, the essential being of those who thus confront one another exposes itself, one to the other, and thus shows itself and comes to appearance," which on Heidegger's understanding of the Greek sense of appearance then "enters into what is unconcealed and true." Heidegger characterizes struggle as "reciprocal recognition that exposes itself to what is essential," which accounts, he says, for the emphasis in the rectoral address on "being-exposed" (*Aufgesetzheit*). A passage from "The Origin of the Work of Art" sheds additional light on Heidegger's understanding of *polemos* as *Auseinandersetzung:* "In essential striving . . . the opponents raise each other into the self-assertion of their natures. Self-assertion of nature, however, is never a rigid insistence upon some contingent state, but surrender to the concealed originality of the source of one's own being. In the struggle, each opponent carries the other beyond itself. Thus the striving becomes ever more intense as striving, and more authentically what it is. The more the struggle overdoes itself on its own part, the more inflexibly do the opponents let themselves go into the intimacy of simple belonging to one another" (PLT 49).

The movement of *polemos* is one of Heidegger's most basic themes. It is *how* one becomes what one is. As Heidegger explains in ". . . poetically man dwells . . . ," the "same" is never understood correctly as the "equal" (PLT 218). The equal, in the sense of the identical, moves toward an absence of difference, while the same designates the belonging together, in and as *polemos,* of what differs. Thus, to think the "same" is to think "difference." As we shall see in later chapters, the economy of *polemos* figures crucially in Heidegger's explorations of Hölderlin's poetry in his attempt to understand the situation and task of the Germans. Heidegger explains further that *polemos* is not to be understood in terms of war and the warlike (R 489). We may say that war and the warlike are to be understood instead in terms of *polemos,* which has the sense of to show and to produce, or, as Heidegger interprets the Greek saying, "to make-it-stand-out in open view." In IM he explains that Heraclitean *polemos* is the conflict that prevailed prior to the emergence of the divine and the human. This conflict is the "originary struggle, for it gives rise to the contenders as such," projecting "what had hitherto been unheard of, unsaid and unthought" (IM 51). "Creators, poets, thinkers, [and] statesmen" establish "the barrier of their work" against chaos, and "in their work they capture the world thus opened up." *Phusis* first "comes to stand" with the works of "world-building," which is "history in the authentic sense." However, as Heidegger makes clear, *phusis,* understood as a designation for what "emerges and endures" of itself, *governs* the deeds of creators, poets, thinkers, and statesmen, since, as we have already seen in the rectoral address, knowing has always been delivered up to and falls before fate (IM 14; cf. VS 69).

The university chooses the "knowing struggle of those who question" and agrees with Clausewitz: "I take leave of the frivolous hope of salvation by the hand of accident" (RA 479).[22] Heidegger then states the condition for the success of the "struggle community" (*Kampfgemeinschaft*): "teachers and students [must] arrange their Dasein more simply, more unsparingly, and more frugally than all their fellow Germans." The teaching concerning struggle is inscribed in the relations between leading and following, each of which, we recall, is fundamentally spiritual. Heidegger establishes a requirement for leading: "All leading must grant the body of followers its own strength." Then he describes the decisive feature of following: "All following, however, bears resistance within itself." Spiritual leading is conditioned by this essential characteristic of following, for Heidegger's statement that the "essential opposition of leading and following must not be obscured, let alone eliminated," makes sense only if he is understood as holding that leaders are unwise or mistaken in attempting to eliminate such opposition. "Struggle alone" holds the opposition of leading and following open. It implants the mood "which lets self-limiting self-affirmation empower resolute self-examination to genuine self-governance."

5 The Teaching on Science

It is the truth of Being that dispenses the hold for all conduct.
(LH 238)

THE RELATION BETWEEN science and philosophy is stated in the rectoral address as follows: "All science is philosophy, whether it knows and wills it or not. All science remains bound to that beginning of philosophy. From it, it draws the strength of its essence, supposing that it still remains equal to this beginning" (RA 471–72). The assertion that science *is* philosophy compresses greatly Heidegger's reflections on the natures of philosophy and science and on their relations, and it is essential for us to comprehend Heidegger's understanding of science if we are to comprehend his understanding of politics.[1] In this chapter I shall examine first a number of texts which are concerned with the nature of science and of its relation to philosophy. Then I shall turn to the discussion of science in the rectoral address, which is followed by an examination of the action of decision called for in the address. Finally, I consider what I believe to be one of the most important statements of Heidegger's understanding of science, thoroughly inscribed in his *Auseinandersetzung* with National Socialism, in *Beiträge*.

Throughout his work, Heidegger always teaches that science is dependent upon a prior projection or understanding of Being and that science cannot understand its own conditions, which is to say that it cannot understand itself and that it cannot raise or even acknowledge the question of Being and remain science. In BT, as in its predecessors, phenomenology is the science of the Being of entities, which means that it is "universal phenomenological ontology or science" (BT 58–62). Thus, philosophy is a science, a position which appears as well in BPP (BPP 11). Philosophy as a science is separated from other sciences with the argument that the nonphilosophical or positive sciences have as their theme beings which are posited in advance (13).

The more nuanced account offered later in section 22 clarifies nonphilosophical sciences in the course of showing that philosophy as a science is grounded in the essential nature of Dasein. The distinction between Being and beings is latent in Dasein and indeed existence, taken in its technical Heideggerian sense, is "to be in the performance of this distinction" (319). The temporalizing of temporality is the condition for the temporalizations of the distinction between Being and beings, which is to say that it is the condition for our recognition and investigation of the distinction. When it is recognized explicitly, the distinction is the ontological difference. The accomplishment of the ontological difference is a basic comportment of Dasein which makes philosophy possible (319–20). Both philosophical and nonphilosophical sciences are grounded in Dasein. As cognition, science is the unveiling and thus the exhibition of the truth of something. As a mode of Dasein's existence, science is cognizing for the sake of truth, which requires the objectification of what has already been given *as* unveiled (320). Philosophy and the positive sciences differ in the ways in which they objectify what is unveiled. The latter project an ontological constitution of the region of beings with which they are concerned but do not attempt genuine ontological inquiry. Rather, they maintain a pre-ontological relationship to, or employ without reflection, a pre-ontological understanding of Being (321–22; cf. PT 6–7).

Science is a freeing of beings such that they can be examined "objectively," where "objectivity" is already projected (BT 415). Thus, science requires a preparation of its object which allows it to be determined as real, where "real" has the sense of "present." In his Kant course of 1927/28, Heidegger says that the "struggle" in and of science "is directed to the being itself and solely in order to free it from its hiddenness and precisely thereby to help it into what is proper to it, that is, to let it be the being which it is in itself" (G25 26).

Dasein's finitude conditions the proper action of science. As early as 1928, Heidegger insists that this finitude cannot be effaced by technology. In its transcendence, Dasein is beyond beings such that it experiences them "in their resistance against which transcending Dasein is powerless" (MFL 215). This "essential" or "metaphysical" powerlessness "cannot be removed by reference to the domination of nature, to technology, which rages about in the 'world' today like an unchained beast"; indeed, mastery of nature is, paradoxically, the "real proof of the powerlessness of Dasein, which can attain freedom only in its history" (215).

While Heidegger never deviates from his teaching that science is a way of Dasein's Being, he acknowledges in BT—and therefore projects this limitation of his account back into BT's predecessors—that "a fully adequate existential interpretation of science cannot be carried out until *the meaning of Being and the 'connection' between Being and truth* have been *clarified* in terms of the temporality of existence" (BT 357). The clarification Heidegger achieves is his understanding of the history of Being, of epochality. Thus, what one might call his existential-projective understanding of science, science as a way of Dasein's Being in which beings are projected in terms of the mathematical and the utilitarian, is itself understood in terms of the ruling principles of the present epoch. The result is that Heidegger inscribes science in a wider horizon and comes to emphasize its subordination to its epoch.

The subjectivity fundamental to modern science has its origins in the political and religious freedom of modernity. In Descartes— although its antecedents appear in the methodological problematic of medieval philosophy—that which is as a *subiectum*, a particular being, is a *hupo-keimenon*, something "lying before from out of itself," which is *also* taken as a ground; it is what "simultaneously lies at the foundation of its own fixed qualities and changing circumstances" (AWP 147–50; cf. WT 96–119). As "a ground lying at the foundation," the subject's superiority—it is "preeminent because it is in an essential respect unconditional"—comes from our claim to a "self-supported, unshakable foundation of truth, in the sense of certainty." This claim in turn is grounded in man's self-emancipation from "obligation to Christian revelational truth and Church doctrine" to self-legislation: "Through this liberation, the essence of freedom, that is, being bound by something obligatory, is posited anew" (148). Common to all modern determinations of the obligatory is liberation from the certainty of salvation, which must be a "freeing *to* a certainty in which man makes secure for himself the true as the known of his own knowing." Human beings must guarantee the certainty of the knowable themselves. Thus, the subject is ground of freedom, its activity is thinking as representing, which as calculating, makes secure. Representing is transformed from "self-concealing"—and we hardly need reminders of the importance of the relation of concealing and unconcealing in Heidegger's understanding of Greek thinking—to "assault" (= objectification, mastering). What Heidegger has explained is the historical condition for the making effective of what was concealed within and thus is intelligible as a possibility of Greek knowing (SR 157–58). It is a possibility which contains a profound danger, for "the peculiar unchaining of the demand for the supplying of ground threatens all homeyness [*Heimische*] of man and robs him of every ground and basis for a rootedness" (PR 30).

The projection characteristic of modern science is "the mathematical," the significance of which in and for the development of modern science from ancient science figures prominently in his course "Basic Questions of Metaphysics" of 1935/36 (WT). What has attracted comparatively little attention is his presentation of the connection between philosophical and scientific questioning on the one hand and the political question on the other, which precedes and governs Heidegger's archaeology of the historical ground of Kant's *Critique of Pure Reason*. Put briefly, there is always a "direct transition and entrance" to science and thus to scientific questioning *from* everyday "representations, beliefs, and thinking" (WT 1–2). In contrast, philosophy must accomplish its shift of attitude with a "jolt" (*Rück*). Whether elementary or difficult, scientific questioning is carried out on the same plane as everyday thinking. Philosophical questioning "executes a continuous shifting of standpoint and level." The question "what is a thing?"—with which the Kant interpretation is concerned—is a useless question, for there is literally nothing that can be started with it (3–4). A brief reflection on occurrences of "thing" in everyday language shows its multiple senses and accomplishes the transition to philosophy with Kant's "thing-in-itself" (4–7). In a further clarification, the question is shown to be about conditions, and in asking what conditions the thing, we are seeking the unconditioned (7–10). In asking for the unconditioned, philosophy distinguishes itself from science, in and for which this question does not and cannot properly arise. Such inquiry is "presumptuous" (*amassend*), for philosophy seeks to know what science cannot know (9). This "presumption" (*Anmassung*) is "the kind found in every essential decision [*Entscheidung*]." What must be decided is whether we want to know "those things with which one can start to do nothing" (10). If we do not ask the question, we can remain as we are, since in asking it, we do not become better "overnight" at whatever we do. What we *can* become in and through such asking is "different" (*andere*). Heidegger then explains what is truly at issue: "*With our question, we want neither to replace the sciences nor to reform them.* On the other hand, we want to participate in the preparation of a decision; the decision: Is science the measure of knowledge, or is there a knowledge in which the ground and limit of science and thus its genuine effectiveness are determined? Is this genuine knowledge necessary for a historical people [*geschichtliches Volk*], or is it dispensable or replaceable by something else?"

Such decisions are worked out by "creating situations and taking positions in which the decision is unavoidable, in which it becomes the most essential decision when one does not make it but rather avoids it." The knowledge sought in philosophical questioning is neither better nor worse than that sought by science but is "completely different" (*ganz andere*), both from science and from what is called a world-view. Only philosophical questioning can ask whether it is itself necessary for a historical—which is to say, a political—people. Science cannot determine its own political significance.

Science, in Heidegger's view, was displaced by technology. In his 1930 course on the essence of human freedom, Heidegger sounds what will become a familiar warning. The condition of modern science is "catastrophic," for as technology in the service of industry, it covers over fundamental questions (G31 142). According to a lecture course given in 1937/38, philosophy is useless, while science is useful. One who struggles with philosophical questions will appear "always and necessarily strange" (G45 4): "'Science' is the denial of all knowing of the truth. To suppose that today 'science' is persecuted is a fundamental error: never has it gone better for 'science' than today, and it will go better still for it than up till now," Heidegger writes. "But no knowing one will envy the 'scientist'—the most wretched slave of the most recent time." The scientist submits himself to the animal's craving for security, while the thinker submits himself to what is worthy of thinking—Being. Indeed, "the taking back [*Rücknahme*] of 'science' into question-worthiness is the disintegration [*Auflösung*] of modern 'science.'" In the German sentence there is a parenthetical reference to the rectoral address; the political sense of its understanding of science is inscribed in the present lecture. This is to say that in the rectoral address modern science yields to ancient science, that is, to philosophy.

Philosophy or philosophical science projects Being upon the temporal horizon of its intelligibility—the "basic act" of philosophy—which makes the objectification of Being possible (BPP 323). The fundamental uncertainty exhibited in philosophy or philosophical science as the necessity of thinking truth and untruth together is related essentially to the historical character of philosophy. Thus, in the history of philosophy, "faulty interpretations" are not "mere defects of thought." Rather they "have their reason and their necessity in Dasein's own historical existence" (321–22; cf. G25 24–28, 32–36). The projection of philosophy is necessarily "ontical projection." Apart from such projection into the ontic, the realm of beings, philosophy flies free without sobriety. Philosophy, then, is rooted in and projects itself onto or into the ontic, which is to say, onto or into beings (19–20; cf. BT 31–35). Its truths and untruths will be projected as well. If the ontic includes the political, we may say that philosophy is necessarily rooted in and projects itself upon the political as well, a teaching of the rectoral address prepared for in and by some of Heidegger's most technical and fundamental lines of thinking.

In the last of his Marburg lectures (MFL), Heidegger proposes to understand the nature of philosophy "from historicity," which is to say from the "unity of the temporality of the philosophizing factical Dasein itself," a clarification which abolishes the conventional distinction between historical and systematic understandings of philosophy and reiterates a familiar theme from Heidegger's early works (MFL 8–9; cf. BT 453). The "recollection from historicity" is required, he continues, even if there were no history of philosophy, for "it would still be necessary to go back and take up the tradition in which every human Dasein stands, whether it has a developed historical consciousness or not, and whether or not what it has to recollect is expressly called 'philosophy' " (9). Heidegger announces here his intention to broaden the scope of his inquiry well beyond the philosophical tradition as traditionally understood to an as yet unnamed tradition within which philosophy is *one* element. Given this wider compass, it is not surprising that he declines to explain the nature of philosophy by distinguishing it from the nonphilosophical sciences. He turns instead to Aristotle's understanding of philosophy, not because he wants simply to agree with, or to urge agreement with, Aristotle but because "in ancient thought, basic philosophical problems are intelligible in their elemental originality." Ancient philosophy, as a beginning, contains possibilities undeveloped and hidden, which is to say that it has an "elemental originality" or "originariness" absent from contemporary philosophy. In this respect, ancient philosophy "corresponds to the *present necessity* of bringing problems back to simplicity; only in this way can they be given their full sharpness."

According to Heidegger, Aristotle's understanding of philosophy as the most noble type of science, in its twofold concern with knowledge of Being and knowledge of the "overwhelming," exemplified by the heavens, prefigures the notions of existence and thrownness in BT (11). Genuine philosophy—the highest science— must be sought anew continuously and cannot become a possession. Accordingly, the *sophia* loved by the philosopher, while it "denotes the possibility of the correct conceptual understanding of what is essential," is also a matter of "the outstanding free disposition over knowing what one is about" (11; cf. *Nicomachean Ethics* 1141a12). The genuine philosopher's existence, unlike that of the sophist, has been deeply moved by the seriousness of fundamental questioning, which is to say by the question of Being (12–13). Philosophers have been concerned with the question of the human because the striving to understand Being is constitutive of human Dasein. Thus, the question of Being, rightly understood, is the question of the human. For this reason the "struggle over Being" among philosophers takes place on the "battlefield" of human Dasein (15–16). The site of the struggle, however, is misunderstood if it is grasped in terms of psychology, anthropology, characterology, ethics, or sociology. Indeed, when issues within such areas are mistaken for the fundamental question, we see that the question has not been raised correctly. Heidegger asks: "What is easier than, in a comfortable and interesting way, to interest a human being in human beings, to enumerate for him his complexes, potentials, standpoints, one-sidedness, and failings, and to say this is philosophy?" (17). He distinguishes between the "sophistical sense" of the human being and the fundamental question about human being, to which this sense is completely irrelevant. Instead, "human Dasein gains depth only if it succeeds for itself, in its own existence, in first throwing itself beyond itself—to its limits. Only from the height of this high projection does it glimpse its true depths." While philosophy is "the most radical, universal, and rigorous conceptual knowledge," it is exhibited "solely in the loyalty the philosophizing individual has to himself." Thus, "only he can philosophize who is already resolved to grant free dignity to Dasein in its radical and universal-essential possibilities, which alone makes it suitable for withstanding the remaining uncertainty and gaping discord, while at the same time remaining untouched by all the idle talk of the day" (17–18).

To the extent that there is a philosophical world-view, it is not a product of philosophy but "resides rather in the philosophizing itself" (18). The rigorous conceptual knowledge of philosophy "is grasped in its genuine content only when in such knowledge the whole of existence is seized by the root after which philosophy searches—in and by *freedom.*" Philosophy, Heidegger explains in a supplement to the lectures, is more "originary" (*ursprünglich*) than any science or world-view (221). In philosophizing, we attempt to "exist from ground," and it is the "freedom toward ground" characteristic of the human being that allows us in philosophizing to transform "each and every thing in ourselves and to ourselves."

In the presentation of freedom and its relation to ground in ER (1929), Heidegger explains that freedom makes the governing of a world and the "worlding" of Dasein possible. This exhibition of the happening of Dasein in man is the condition for the derivative sense of freedom as causality which is to be found in Kant (ER 103–5). More important, freedom is the origin of reasons or grounds, or freedom for grounds. Heidegger clarifies this understanding by distinguishing freedom from any determinate way of grounding. Freedom is the "abyss" (*Ab-grund*), the groundlessness, of Dasein. As such, it provides Dasein with possibilities which "gape open before its finite choice, that is, its destiny" (127, 129). Heidegger makes clear, however, that the power of freedom extends neither to Dasein's thrownness nor to the fact that transcendence, as freedom for grounds, "comes about as a primordial happening." Thus, the essence of Dasein's finitude "discloses itself as *freedom for grounds*" (131). In this same text, philosophy itself is characterized as a finite enterprise (11). While the sciences occupy an intermediate stage between the pre-ontological understanding of Being and philosophical or ontological inquiry, which takes the meaning of Being as problematic, their essential lack of ontological concepts prevents them from providing an account of the constitution of Being (25).

A similar analysis appears in "What Is Metaphysics?" (1929). In the more dramatic existential idiom, the original oneness of beings arises in the "clear night of the Nothing of anxiety," and the Nothing brings Dasein before beings. Thus, Heidegger characterizes Dasein as "being held out into the Nothing" (WM 105). The disclosure of the Nothing is the condition for selfhood and freedom—indeed, for Dasein's relation to beings. This means that the nihilation or activity of the Nothing occurs within Being as a necessary element in the unfolding of beings (106). Heidegger identifies Dasein's condition of being held out into the Nothing, which surpasses beings, with transcendence, which brings reflection to metaphysics, understood as inquiry beyond beings. Heidegger explains that Dasein's transcendence is not something we can will, which is to say that our finitude prevents us from "bringing ourselves originally before the Nothing through our own determination or will" (108). Now if it is the case that our present-day existence is determined by science, which is the initial claim of the lecture, then science, like any other way of Dasein's being, must be held out into the Nothing. It is only because the "nothing is manifest in the ground of Dasein" that the "total strangeness of beings" can overwhelm us and evoke the wonder which is the condition for scientific inquiry (111). If the movement of going beyond beings takes place in the essence of Dasein, and if that movement is identified as metaphysics, then metaphysics is the "basic occurrence" of Dasein. Heidegger cites Plato: "For by nature, my friend, man's mind dwells in philosophy" (*Phaedrus* 279a). As Dasein opens to the Nothing which is the ground of its transcendence, it reaches its limits. Since the site of metaphysics is the "groundless ground" of Dasein, it "stands in closest proximity to the constantly lurking possibility of deepest error," and it is for this reason that philosophy cannot be measured by the idea of science (WM 112). Philosophy is a whole which necessarily encompasses both truth and error; science cannot afford this degree of wholeness.

I

Heidegger proposes to recover for "*our* Dasein" two distinguishing properties of the "original Greek essence of science" (RA 472). We do not know from the address if there are other distinguishing properties. It is evident that Heidegger's intention is neither antiquarian nor academic. He turns to the Greek beginning, as he always had, out of "our" needs, from the present situation. The first property is the relation between knowing (or science or philosophy) and fate. In Aeschylus's *Prometheus*, Heidegger finds a line which "expresses the essence of knowing"—"*technē d' anankēs asthenestera makrō:* Knowing, however, is much weaker than necessity" (line 514). I note that this thought is not characterized as being limited to Aeschylus or indeed to the Greeks. Heidegger's explanation is that "all knowing about things has already been delivered up to overpowering fortune and fails before it." This thought is put less dramatically in "On the Origin of the Work of Art" as: "Thinking corresponds to a truth of beings that has already happened" (PLT 80). This happening is the site in which our possibilities are inscribed, for our way of being always follows historical ways of presencing (G55 377).

As we have seen, from very nearly the beginning of his thinking, Heidegger had understood the task of explicating any human situation in terms of a "how" which itself was necessarily historical (G9 29–31). Moreover, a historically enacted situation required a historically enacted understanding for its comprehension. As Heidegger puts it in one of his lecture courses on Schelling: "We philosophize only when the position of our human being becomes the real need of the question about Being as a whole. Since, however, our human being is historical, it remains so in philosophizing, too. That means the more originally we begin our philosophical question, the more inwardly we grow in the binding force of our history" (ST 12). I remind the reader that in WT what Heidegger still calls "metaphysical" questioning consists of a residuum of positions taken by Dasein and that with its chosen level of questioning "a people always posits for itself the degree of its being" (WT 49–52, 43–44). The task this insight into the essentially historical character of philosophy sets for Heidegger in the rectoral address is to identify precisely what truth has already happened that has delivered knowing to its fate or fortune. We have already seen that the happening of Nietzsche's truth that God is dead delivers knowing to its fate in the present.

In two extraordinary sentences in the rectoral address Heidegger presents the consequences of this situation: "Just because of this, knowing must develop its highest defiance; called forth by such defiance, all the power of the hiddenness of what is must first arise for knowing really to fail. Just in this way, what is opens itself in its unfathomable inalterability and lends knowing its truth" (RA 472).

These sentences deserve close attention. The thought they contain is first that knowing has always been delivered up to and fails before fate/fortune. The failure of knowing before *Schicksal* exhibits the embeddedness of knowing in its plural deliverances. Second, knowing must develop its highest defiance. We recall the *Aufbruch* of Greek philosophy and thus of Western humanity, standing up to the totality of what is. Third, the power of the hiddenness of what is arises as response to this defiance. Fourth, all of the power of the hiddenness of what is must arise for "knowing really to fail." Fifth, in and through this setting-apart or conflict, "what is opens itself in its unfathomable inalterability and lends knowing its truth." These last two points are especially important, for they show that knowing necessarily fails and that its truth, which is imparted to it by what is, is limited, which is to say that it is epochal. When we remind ourselves that Heidegger's two sentences occur in a political address, we are led to the thought that self-assertion, which requires knowing, must itself share in the failure of knowing before fate as well as in the opportunities of fortune. The finitude which marks all knowing—indeed, which marks knowing more essentially than it marks anything else—must also characterize self-assertion. When Western humanity comes to stand up to the totality of what is, it reaches a limit or measure of finitude. In asking about the conditions of the possibility reaching an understanding of Being, Heidegger agrees with Plato that we want "to do nothing but bring ourselves out of the cave into the light, but in all sobriety and in the complete disenchantment of purely objective inquiry" (BPP 284). In the wartime course on Parmenides, he writes that *phronēsis*, in the myth of Er, "*means Philosophy* and the word says: having an eye for the essential" (G54 178; cf. IM 107). In the wartime course on Heraclitus, Heidegger explains that "philosophy" is the ancient name for thinking. The Greek *philia tōn sophōn* has the sense of "friendship for what destines" (*das Zu-denkende*) (G55 3). In having an eye for the essential and friendship for what destines, philosophy never loses its complete disenchantment. It would seem that if "science" carries the same meaning as "philosophy," then the German university, grounded in the essence of science, proposes to provide spiritual leadership and contribute to the spiritual mission of the German people by bringing to its tasks the disenchantment inseparable from an insight into the essential, that which destines. As we have seen in the previous chapter, Heidegger seems to have taught that the German people can—indeed must—become philosophical or be shaped by philosophy.

To return to the rectoral address, Heidegger insists that the "creative impotence of knowing" expressed in Prometheus's utterance is *not* correctly understood in terms of the "theoretical attitude," for such a knowing "based purely on itself" has rather "forgotten its own essence." Greek *theōria*, contrary to the traditional view, is precisely *not* "contemplative behavior," for "theory" is pursued by them not for its own sake "but only in the passion to remain close to and hard pressed by what is as such." *Theōria* is the "highest mode of *energeia*, of man's 'being-at-work,'" which makes theory the "highest realization of genuine practice" (RA 472–73). The second property of the Greek essence of science is the relation of this practice to politics. Unlike a point of view Heidegger does not name but which we may as well call liberalism, the Greeks do not regard science as a "'cultural good,'" but the innermost determining center of their entire *volklich*-state Dasein [*des ganzen volklich-staatlichen Daseins*]" (473). They do not regard it as "a mere means of bringing the unconscious to consciousness, but the power that hones and embraces Dasein in its entirely." Greek science is inherently political, while modern science is not.

The rectoral address's definition of science follows: "Science is the questioning holding of one's ground in the midst of the ever self-concealing totality of what is" (RA 473). In the next sentence Heidegger reiterates his understanding of knowing as weaker than necessity, when he writes: "This active perseverance knows, as it perseveres, about its impotence before fate." While this understanding exhibits the "original essence of science," Heidegger is aware that science has been changed by both the "Christian-theological interpretation of the world" that followed antiquity and the later "mathematical-technological thinking of the modern age," both of which "have separated science both in time and its concerns from its beginning." If "this originary Greek science is something great," Heidegger writes, "then the inception [*Anfang*] of this great thing remains what is *greatest* about it." Indeed, if the greatness of the inception of science did not endure, the essence of science could not be "emptied out and used up" as it is today. I translate *Anfang* here as "inception" and not "beginning," for Heidegger is concerned here with the emergence of the essence of science in terms of which its significance may be understood and not primarily its historical beginning. Thus Heidegger can write: "The inception still *is*. It does not lie *behind us,* as something that was long ago, but stands *before* us." Accordingly, it "has invaded our future. There it awaits us, a distant command bidding us catch up with its greatness." Two closely related, and perhaps inseparable, results follow if we "submit resolutely to this distant command to recapture the greatness of the origin." Science can become the "innermost necessity of our Dasein" and "must become the fundamental happening of our spiritual-volkisch Dasein [*unseres geistig-volklichen Daseins*]" (473–74). What has occurred and what continues to await us is the inception. What a knowing recovery seeks in and through the inception is the originary.

The "awed perseverance of the Greeks in the face of what is, transforms itself into the completely unguarded exposure [*ungesetzen Ausgesetzsein*] to the hidden and uncertain, that is, the questionable" (474). Heidegger returns to the Greeks to recover their "awed perseverance" and to reach the beginning of what has changed decisively in the present. "Questioning" has replaced "science" in the address. Questioning is no longer merely a preliminary step toward knowledge but is rather the "highest form of knowing." As such, questioning destroys the division of the sciences, returning them, and thus exposing science "once again to the fertility and blessing bestowed by all the world-shaping powers of human-historical Dasein." Heidegger provides what is evidently a *partial* list of these powers: "nature, history, language; people, custom, state; poetry, thought, faith; disease, madness, death; law, economy, technology." Since science is and can only be a way of our Dasein, it is exposed *necessarily* to the ways in which Dasein "worlds." No explanation is offered, nor is it even acknowledged in the address, or for that matter, anywhere else in Heidegger's writings as far as I am aware, that the powers of Dasein are grouped into five collections, each with three members. There is no obvious ranking either among or within these groupings. These powers of Dasein are ways in which Dasein is, or can be. In a speculative vein, I note that the list is bounded by "nature" and "technology," at the greatest distances from each other.

The first group—nature, history, language—consists of topics we may without hesitation consider essential or fundamental themes in Heidegger's thinking. The second group—people, custom, state—consists of topics never thematized by Heidegger. "People" is one of the names of collective, historical Dasein. "Custom" directs our attention to tradition and rootedness. Heidegger is very nearly silent about "state." The third group—poetry, thought, faith—contains the names of two governing themes that emerge in and from Heidegger's thinking in the 1930s ("poetry," "thought"), and which have an undeniable political sense. (Heidegger's references to the Germans as a people of poets and thinkers abound in the Hölderlin lectures and in the wartime lectures on the pre-Socratics.) While "faith," the third member of this group, is a less prominent theme, it is nonetheless visible in both early and later writings. The fourth group—disease, madness, death—includes one topic ("disease") about which Heidegger says relatively little, another ("madness") which plays a greater role, and one topic ("death"), the importance of which in and for his thinking is virtually impossible to overestimate. Finally, the fifth group—law, economy, technology—contains two topics seldom mentioned ("law," "economy") and one topic ("technology") of overwhelming significance in Heidegger's thinking. If this last group is understood as associated with or belonging to the present epoch, then the extremes of the list might stand in the relation of permanent to transient—if Heidegger allowed for "nature" to be permanent. The first group might also be thought under the label "originary," to designate the theme to which thinking can turn only by first thinking the elements of the present epoch, and in terms of which that epoch is intelligible. In any case, the powers of Dasein are themselves delivered up to fortune, for we have seen that world-building can be understood only in terms of its conditions, and its conditions are themselves are necessarily historical. By inscribing "world" in the rectoral address, Heidegger fuses his technical and his political teaching.

Now we learn that if we will the essence of science, "understood as the *questioning unguarded holding of one's ground in the midst of the uncertainty of the totality of what is,* this will to essence will create for our people its world, a world of the innermost and most extreme danger, that is, its truly *spiritual* world [*eine wahrhaft geistig Welt*]" (RA 474). The will to science as questioning creates a world which is spiritual to the extent that it is a world of danger. We next learn what spirit is *not:* "empty sagacity," "the gratuitous game of joking," the "unlimited work of analysis of the understanding, nor even the reason of the world." Rather, spirit is "originarily attuned, knowing resoluteness [*ursprünglich gestimmte wissende Entschlossenheit*] toward the essence of Being." With this remarkable sentence, Heidegger inscribes spirit in the relation between resolve and the question of Being, indeed in the existential analytic in its entirety. The question of Being is thereby cast in the light of politics.

The spiritual world (*geistige Welt*) of a people is not the "superstructure of a culture" or an "armory stuffed with useful facts and values" (RA 474–75). Spirit is detached from "culture"; it is the "power that most deeply preserves the people's strengths, which are tied to earth and blood; and as such it is the power that most deeply moves and most profoundly shakes its Dasein" (RA 475). Here is a further inscription of "world" into the idiom of earth and blood, and therewith, as many interpreters have noted, into the idiom of National Socialism, although a careful reading shows that it is only *in and as* a spiritual world that the strengths rooted in earth and blood can be preserved: "Only a spiritual world gives the people the assurance of greatness. For it necessitates that the constant decision between the will to greatness and a letting things happen that means decline [*des Verfalls*] will be the law presiding over the march that our people has begun into its future history" (RA 475).

II

Heidegger asks: "Do we, or do we not, will the essence of the German university?" (RA 479). We have already considered what is at stake in this question. The failure or deliverance of the West depends upon whether or not "we, as a historical-spiritual people, still and once again will ourselves" (480). "Every individual *participates* in this decision," Heidegger writes, "even he, and indeed especially he, who evades it."

The historical is the futural, and the origin is the "most futural," for it is at once constantly withdrawing and furthest ahead, both reserving itself from thought and reserving itself for thought (G45 82). Since the origin "holds sway beyond all its consequents and prior to them," it cannot properly be said to lie behind but rather "comes before us, toward us, in a mysterious turning" (G55 43). Accordingly, we cannot find the origin of Western thinking "by calculating backward through historical comparisons. We will find the inception only by thinking forward through historical experience" (80). The retrieval of the essence of science follows the same path that Dasein follows in BT: a continual coming of Dasein to itself in and through the structure of temporality. Heidegger makes clear that retrieval has nothing to do with any literal repetition. It is rather "*handing down explicitly . . .* , going back into the possibilities of the Dasein that has-been-there" and does not bind the present to the past (BT 437–38). In returning to the *Greek* beginning, we return to the determinants of our spiritual-historical Dasein. In other words, just as the future, in making possible

Dasein's potentiality to exist, exhibits its own finitude, which is to say, its determinant character (377–79), the essence of science, as exhibited in Greek thinking and coming to us from our future, brings us to the specific conditions of science, which exhibit its possibility. Heidegger's rejection of the notion that science is always or timelessly possible is based on his understanding of science as a constituent of the specific historical path which begins with the Greeks and extends to our present. We cannot retrieve this origin except by a "*transformation* of the direction of our view, the standards, and the claims—a transformation which is also nothing else than the leap into a more original and simpler road of essential happenings of the history of Western thought a history we *ourselves are*" (G45 188). Heidegger explains that we err in understanding the essence of a thing as something invariant, atemporal, or general (60). Instead, the essence of something is brought forth, which is to say that it is temporal (81–96).

In retrieving the essence of science, we move into its historical character as an event and in standing in it, stand exposed to that to which science itself is exposed. Our relation to what is essential, moreover, has its origin in the essential, a relation "wherein historical man becomes free" (G51 6). In the experience of *Wesung* we seize the ground as what arrives for and claims us, which requires experience of the origin which is futural, since it has determined what is to come (2–3, 12, 15). *Wesung* is a coinage employed to characterize essences temporally; "essencing" is a possible translation (cf. G65 317–18).[2] In lectures in 1937/38 Heidegger says: "We speak of the experience of *Wesung* and mean by this the knowing, voluntary, attuned *moving into* [*Einfahren*] *Wesung*, to stand in it and to stand it" (G45 202). Now what may not be clear from such passages is that the originary, in determining what is to come in the futural mode, marks the beginning of the West in and as the (Greek) site where Being becomes "worthy of thought" (EGT 76) *and* the subsequent working out or completion of what begins in and with the Greeks (IM 150). This movement does not amount to a mere recovery of the substance or content of Greek thought. As Heidegger writes, "Our thinking today is charged with the task of thinking what the Greeks have thought in an even more Greek manner," which is to say, in even greater responsiveness to the originary (OWL 39).

The essence of science or knowing to which Heidegger directs his audience in the rectoral address belongs to the inception, and not to the originary. The Greek understanding of the essence of knowing is grounded in the decision in and through which the origin was decided. The notion of "decision" hovers over the rectoral address, but Heidegger's understanding of "decision" would seem at first to leave nothing to decide. Christopher Fynsk argues that Heidegger "pretends to put before his public a *choice* regarding science and the historical way of existence that it defines" when the alternative Heidegger presents is a "false one," since "the decision must *have taken* place" if it is to be "first posed as a possibility."[3] Before we accept or reject this criticism, we must look more closely at "decision." For Heidegger, history has the sense of "the event of a decision [*Entscheidung*] of the essence of truth" (G51 21). This decision establishes both the way that beings presence within the epoch marked by the decision and the way in which humanity stands within the epoch. We are set into and thus situated within a determinant context in which Being conditions the appearance of beings in terms of or as intelligible within that context. Heidegger explains that we must come to recognize this situation as one of inescapability which is nonetheless the location in and from which our historical essence can be decided (82–83, 89). "Decision" in its essential sense does not mean some arbitrary choice but rather names the separation or differentiation of Being, unconcealment, appearance, and Nonbeing into which we are situated and to which the Greek thinkers responded, beginning the history of the West (IM 93). When Dasein wills the decision, it resolves itself as finite (IM 148–49; cf. G51 89). The self-affirmation called for in the rectoral address is inscribed in the larger text of finitude. Heidegger emphasizes the limits and thus the true nature of spirit's self-affirmation in the address.

One of the clearest explanations of Heidegger's understanding of decision appears in his 1936 Schelling course. In his account of the idealist understanding of freedom, Heidegger notes that for idealism, freedom is self-determination, which is to say self-necessitation, which gives to our essence the character of an eternal deed. "Thence comes," Heidegger writes, "that uncanny and at the same time friendly feeling that we have always been what we are, that we are nothing but the unveiling of things long since decided" (ST 153–54). Given this understanding of necessity, freedom is "capable only when it positions its decisions beforehand as decidedness in order for all enactments to become necessary in terms of it. True freedom in the sense of the most originary self-determination is found only where a choice is no longer possible and no longer necessary" (154). Originary willing—that is, a decision for decidedness—is genuine self-knowledge. Accordingly, such decidedness "no longer needs a choice because it is grounded in essential knowledge." The necessity "by which or as which freedom is determined" is "that self-overreaching as self-grasping which originates in the original essence of human being. The most futural element of all decidedness of human being in its individuality is what is most past" (155). Thus, human freedom can only be our deciding originally "for the necessity of [our] essence," a decision which was not made at some time "but falls as a decision to temporality. Thus where temporality truly presences, in the moment, where past and future come together in the present, where man's complete essence flashes before him as this his own, man experiences the fact that he must always already have been who he is, as he who has determined himself for this." Only some, rarely, reach this self-knowledge:

> And when they do, only as "often" as this moment of the innermost essential look is a moment, that is, most intensified historicity. That means that decidedness does not contract one's own being to an empty point of mere staring at one's ego, but decidedness of one's own being is only what it is as resoluteness. By this we mean standing within the openness of the truth of history, the perdurance which carries out what it must carry out, unattainable and prior to all calculation and reckoning. In the moment of deciding we are as in no other experience of self, protected from the vanity of self-overestimation and the self-righteousness of self-depreciation. For in the decidedness of our own being, we experience the fact that no one attains the height of what is his best as little as he attains the abyss of what is his evil, but that he is placed in this Between in order to wrest his truth from it which is in itself necessary but, precisely for this reason, historical. It stands beyond the distinctions of a truth for everyone and a truth for "special individuals." Only a wrested truth is truth.

Here it is evident that Heidegger inscribes his understanding of freedom as articulated in such texts as ET and his 1930 lecture course *Vom Wesen der menschlichen Freiheit* (On the essence of human freedom) (G31) in his exploration of *alētheia*. This means that freedom is understood not as anything like a property or power of human beings but rather, as a condition for the manifestation of the truth of Being, is "in its essence more originary than man" (G31 133). In ET we learn that freedom is neither "mere absence of constraint with respect to what we can or cannot do" nor "mere readiness for what is required and necessary" (ET 128). More fundamental than "positive" or "negative" freedom is "engagement in the disclosure [*Entbergung*] of beings as such." In this engagement "through which the openness of the open [*die Offenheit des Offenen*], that is, the 'Da,' is what it is," disclosure is "preserved" (*verwahrt*). Thus, "existence" in its distinctive Heideggerian sense ("ek-sistence") "is exposure (*Aus-setzung*—more literally, 'being set out into') to the disclosedness of beings as such." It is clear that "human caprice [*Belieben*] does not have freedom at its disposal"; rather, "freedom, ek-sistent, disclosive Dasein, possesses man—so originarily [*ursprünglich*] that only *it* secures for humanity that distinctive relatedness to beings as a whole in their totality which first founds all history" (129). Since "only ek-sistent man is historical," this understanding of freedom is inscribed in Heidegger's political thinking. As Heidegger puts it in the 1930 lecture course: "Human freedom henceforth no longer means freedom as the property of man, but inversely, *man as a possibility of freedom.* Human freedom is freedom inasmuch as it appears in man, takes him upon itself, thus making him possible" (G31 135).[4]

The human, then, is the "site" (*Stätte*) and "occasion" (*Gelegenheit*) of freedom. Now since freedom, "understood as letting beings be [*Seinlassen des Seienden*]," exhibits the essence of truth, understood as "disclosure of beings through which an openness essentially unfolds," truth "is in essence freedom," and freedom has "already attuned [*abgestimmt*] all comportment to beings as a whole" (ET 129–31). This "attuning letting-be of beings" (*stimmende Seinlassen von Seienden*) brings human comportment into an accord unintelligible to "everyday calculations and preoccupations" (131–32). Heidegger makes clear that such accord "cannot be understood on the basis of the beings opened up in any given case, whether they belong to nature or to history"; rather, the "as a whole," the way in which the openedness of beings opens, "coincides for the most part with what is most fleeting and most unconsidered" (132).

The concealing of beings is what brings into accord, because "letting be always lets beings be in a particular comportment," which means that it discloses and conceals. The movement of concealing necessarily inscribes untruth in truth (132–33). Indeed, untruth, the concealment of beings as a whole, is "older" than "every openedness of this or that being" as well as "letting-be itself which in disclosing already holds concealed and comports itself toward concealing" (132).

The "concealing of what is concealed as a whole," the "mystery" (*Geheimnis*), is precisely what "preserves" letting-be. In letting-be, which is at once disclosing and concealing, "concealing appears as what is first of all concealed," which means that Da-sein, as exsisting, "preserves the first and broadest undisclosedness, untruth proper" (133). Heidegger's point here is that the untruth exhibited in Dasein necessarily "points to the still unexperienced domain of the truth of Being." This teaching governs what follows: "As letting beings be, freedom is in itself the resolutely [*entschlossene*], that is, *not* self-closing [*sich nicht verschliessende*], *Verhältnis*." If *Verhältnis* is translated as "bearing," following Krell, the movement character of freedom, which Heidegger then says grounds comportment and gives it "directedness toward beings and disclosure of them" and conceals itself, "letting a forgottenness [*Vergessenheit*] of the mystery take precedence and disappearing in it," is emphasized (133–34). As Krell puts it, *entschlossen* "signifies just the opposite of that kind of 'resolve' in which one makes up his mind in such fashion as to close off all other possibilities: it is rather a kind of keeping *unclosed*" (133 n.). If *Verhältnis* is rendered as "matrix of relationships," following Richardson, what one might call the possibility character or perhaps the site-character of freedom is emphasized. As Richardson puts it, "The Open must be conceived as a matrix of relationships [*Verhältnis*] which constitute the sphere of potentialities of There-being, one of which potentialities is exploited when an actual contact takes place. This is the sense of the metaphor that the encounter takes place *in* the Open."[5] There is a political resonance here as well, for when we take our bearings from what is "readily available and controllable, even where first and last things are concerned," when we get our direction in our attempt to "extend, change, newly assimilate, or secure the openedness of the beings pertaining to the most various domains of [our] activity and interest" from "the sphere of readily available intentions and needs," we do not "let the concealing of what is concealed rule" (*Nichtwaltenlassen der Verbergung des Verborgenen*) (134). The forgottenness of the mystery of Dasein does not remove it but gives its "own presence [*Gegenwart*] to the apparent disappearance of what is forgotten." That is, the seeming absence of the mystery "leaves historical man in the sphere of what is readily available to him, leaves him to his own resources." On the basis of "the latest needs and aims," and "by means of proposing and planning," humanity (*Menschentum*) "replenishes" and "fills out" its world. In the German text "world" ("*Welt*") is enclosed in quotation marks; is world to be understood in a deficient sense when it is encountered thus by humanity? It is from such needs and aims that man takes his "standards" (*Masse*), "forgetting beings as a whole," and "continually supplies himself with new standards, yet without considering either the ground for taking up standards or the essence of what gives the standard." Man, then, "goes wrong as regards the essential genuineness [*Wesens-Echtheit*] of his standards," understanding himself "as subject, to be the standard for all beings" (135). The "bearing" or "matrix of relationships"—again, *Verhältnis*—supports both Dasein's "insistence," its holding fast to what is available, and its ek-sistence.

Since we flee from the mystery, the concealing of what is concealed, we move toward what is available and thus necessarily err (134–35). Thus, errancy (*Irre*) "belongs to the inner constitution of the Da-sein into which historical man is admitted [*Eingelassen*]. Errancy is the free space for that turning in which insistent ek-sistence adroitly forgets and mistakes itself constantly anew" (135–36). As the "essential counter-essence [*Gegenwesen*] to the inceptive essence of truth," errancy is the site for "error" (*Irrtums*), which is the "kingdom" (*Königtum*) or "dominion" (*Herrschaft*) of the history of those entanglements in which all kinds of erring get "interwoven" (136). The "errancy in which any part of historical humanity must proceed for its course to be errant," Heidegger writes, "is essentially connected with the openness of Dasein." Errancy, in leading us astray, however, also brings to light the possibility that "by experiencing errancy itself and by not mistaking the mystery of Dasein," man "*not* let himself be led astray." Both the "oppression" (*Bedrängnis*) inherent in being led astray and the mystery of Dasein place us in the "need of being constrained" (*Not der Nötigkeit*)—that is, this condition of being constrained engenders need (136–37). The proper motion of Dasein is its "turning into need" as it moves between the "rule" (*Walten*) of mystery and the oppression of errancy. It is thus only from Dasein that the "disclosure of necessity and, as a result, the possible transposition [*Versetzung*] [of Dasein] into the inevitable [*Unumgängliche*]" (137). Finally, it is only because freedom itself "originates from the inceptive essence of truth, the rule of the mystery in errancy," that it can be the essence of truth.

III

In the rectoral address Heidegger seeks to endow modern science, dispirited science, with the essential character of Greek, and thus Western, philosophy or science. In 1945 he writes that "the case of the rectorate 1933/34 would seem to be a sign of the metaphysical state of the essence of science, a science that can no longer be influenced by attempts at its renewal, nor delayed in its essential transformation into pure technology," a realization exhibited in such works as "The Age of the World Picture" (R 497–98). This is an acknowledgment of the failure of Heidegger's reinspiriting of science. It also registers Heidegger's assessment of "metaphysics"; the essence of science is metaphysical, constituted by metaphysics. *Beiträge* contains a decisive working out of the reasons for this failure joined to criticisms of National Socialism as an exhibition of modernity.[6] I shall examine the discussion of modern science found in that work's second part, concerned with "intimation" (*Anklang*) (145–58). Indeed, Vietta notes that an alternative title for the discussion of intimation in connection with the forgetting of Being by science is "modern science" (*neuzeitliche Wissenschaft*).[7]

It is necessary to supply enough of the larger context of *Beiträge* to orient its treatment of modern science. I shall follow some of the important lines of thinking in the introductory part of the work in order to present Heidegger's understanding of his task.[8] We shall see that he eventually reaches the political, which has a bearing on the work's teaching on science. The title "Contributions to Philosophy" appears to promise what in fact Heidegger will not and cannot provide: a " 'scientific' 'contribution' toward the 'progress' " of philosophy (3). Among many other things, *Beiträge* is a massive objection to the very idea of scientific philosophy. It is an "attempt" (*Versuch*) to think from the most originary fundamental positioning in the question of the truth of Being, a "future thinking"—which is to say, in the manner of Nietzsche, both a *future* thinking and a thinking *of* the future—understood as a process "through which the as yet hidden realm of the becoming of the essencing [*Wesung*] of Being passes and so is first illuminated and reached in its ownmost event-character [*Ereignischarakter*]." Here, as in many writings of the 1930s and 1940s, Heidegger employs an archaic spelling of *Sein* as *Seyn*. In the 1949 edition of ET he explains that *Seyn* names the "difference that holds sway between Being (*Sein*) and beings (*Seiendem*)," that is, the ontological difference as such (ET 140)—

although the English translation of that work fails to distinguish between *Seyn* and *Sein*. Truth as "sheltering that lightens," which is to say the movement of "concealing withdrawal" (*verbergenden Entzugs*), the "lighting" (*Lichtung*) called *alētheia*, is the "basic characteristic" (*Grundzug*) of Being. With this device Heidegger wants to distinguish his concern from any determinate traditional ontology. Thus, *seyns-geschichtliche Denken* conveys the sense of Being, historically understood, along with the distinctive sort of thinking attuned to and conditioned by it.

The movement of questioning in the *Beiträge* follows a path into an other inception that brings its passage into the open of history (*Geschichte*) and grounds it as a "long sojourn" (*langen Aufenthalt*) before that inception (G65 4). The saying of philosophy is *as* the *Wesung des Seyns* (5). In passing to an other inception, there must be a projection (*Entwurf*): "the grounding opening of the time-play-spaces [*Zeit-Spiel-Raumes*] of the truth of Being," that is, epochality. This is to say that thinking understands the "projection of the truth of Being as *historical* reflection" that exhibits itself "as the condition of its own deciding." The question of Being, asked in this manner, is the "fundamental question" (*Grundfrage*), distinguished from the conventionally philosophical question about beings, the "leading question" (*Leitfrage*) (6–7). The thinking Heidegger attempts stands in the first happening of the truth of Being, which brings the "unquestioned essence" to word. In knowing this, such "transitional" (*übergänglichen*) thinking understands the first inception *as* first and overcome *as* inception.

The "unmastered groundplan" of the historicity of the transition itself is named by the basic words of the *Beiträge:* "intimation," "interplay," "leap," "founding," "the futural," and "the last god" (*Anklang, Zuspiel, Sprung, Gründung, Zukünftigen, der letze Gott*). It is only in this way that "the inceptive thinking 'of *Ereignis*' can become said. Whatever is said here is asked and thought in the 'interplay' of the first inception and that other one; asked and thought on the basis of the 'intimation' of Being in the needy state to which Being has abandoned us; asked and thought for the sake of the 'leap' into Being and in order to 'found' the truth of Being; asked and thought as a preparation for 'the futural,' 'of the last god' " (7). "This thinking saying," Heidegger writes, "is a *pointing out* [*Weisung*]"; it is not and cannot be a "command" (*Befehl*) or a "teaching" (*Lehre*). Rather it is a free sheltering of the truth of Being in its necessity, which is to say, a way of being, a kind of comportment. There is inevitably "danger" (*Gefahr*) inherent in the happening of the essencing of Being, for the human becomes "weak" (*unkräftig*) toward Da-sein; the "unchained" (*entfesselte*) violence of madness can overpower "under the illusion of the 'great' " (8).

The difficulty of this thinking is evident, for Heidegger writes: "No one understands what 'I' think here: from the truth of Being (and from the essencing of truth) the Da-sein allows itself to spring." His claim, then, is that his thinking does not merely discuss, but exhibits, the transition he thinks. In this thinking, history is truly exhibited in its "superabundant movement" (*Überschwung*) into the future (9). *Ereignis* is reached solely *from* the question of the truth of Being (10). The fulfillment, the completion, of beginning must be originary; thus, the question resembles the setting apart with first beginning. Both require a leap. "Only in an unmediated over-leaping of the 'historical,' " Heidegger writes, "does history [*Geschichte*] *become.*" (10). Inscribing himself ever more deeply in this thinking, he writes: "The question of 'meaning,' that is, the site in 'Being and Time' of the question of the founding of the projection-domain, put concisely, the *truth of Being* is and remains *my* question and is mine *alone.*"

In the present age a "complete absence of questioning" prevails, and the "need of needlessness" remains unrecognized (11). Still, the problem persists: "the bringing back of beings out of the truth of Being." Accordingly, the question of the meaning of Being is the "question of all questions," for in the "fulfillment of its unfolding the essence of 'meaning' is determined," which is to say that it is opened as questioning. "The question of Being," then, "is *the* leap in Being that man as the seeker of Being enacts, insofar as he is a *thinking creating worker* [*denkerisch Schaffender*]." While the "lesser" (*Wenigen*) question "from time to time," the "rare" (*Seltenen*), with the "highest courage," think and say the "nobility [*Adel*] of Being in its singularity." That thinking in this exalted sense is action is made clear: "Thinking into the other beginning is in its ownmost manner originary-historical; it is itself the ordering ordinance [*fügende Verfügung*] concerning the essence of Being." There is as well the inherent limit of thinking along with a necessity for daring: "A projection of the essencing of Being as *Ereignis* must become bold [*gewagt*], *since* we do *not* know the arrangement of our history. The power of the essencing of this unknown in its self-concealing of the ground is beyond our experience." The seeking of such questioning, then, lies in an abyss, a thought that governs Heidegger's claim that because the decision between "historicity" (*Geschichtlichkeit*) and "historylessness" (*Geschichtslosigkeit*) falls, questioning is necessary; this is "loneliness in its greatest hour" (13).

A further clarification of Being follows. Heidegger explains that it is not an "earliest" (*Früheres*) standing for and in itself, but instead *Ereignis* is the "time-spacelike contemporaneity [*zeitraumliche Gleichzeitigkeit*] for Being and beings." Such a formulation, however, is nothing like a traditional philosophical proposition, and there can be no "evidence" or "results" connected with it in any traditional sense. Heidegger is emphatic that he will not begin with any "moralistic-existential sense" of philosophical knowledge, but rather with a "dasein measuring" (*daseinmasssig*) orientation, a declaration that asserts the distance of his thinking from the normative preoccupations of the tradition (14). That is, "the relation to Being and thus always to the truth of Being changes itself in the manner of a displacing [*Verrückung*] in Da-sein itself." In an other inception, "questioning about the truth of Being" requires a leap into the "Between" (*Zwischen*), which is not a chiasmus "between Being (Beingness) and beings" as a relation of priority, but rather as contemporaneity.

The "fundamental determinant of thinking into an other inception" is named as "the frightening" (*Erschrecken*) and "the restraint" (*Verhaltenheit*), both of which are "the presentiment" (*Ahnung*), and as "the reticence" (*Scheu*). I pass by Heidegger's further discussion of these determinants (15–16) to reach a crucial formulation which distinguishes the first inception from an other inception: "in the first inception: the astounding [*Er-staunen*); in an other beginning: the foreboding [*Er-ahnen*]" (20). "The presentiment" (*Ahnen*) is a crucial thought. It also appears in one of the reflections on Hölderlin, where the poet's knowing of the holy, from the holy having been drawn them into its compass, is called "the presentiment" (G4 62). There is another appearance on the final page of the *Nietzsche* volumes, where it marks the impossibility of measuring the epochal time spans granted by *Ereignis* and therewith, as I believe Schürmann rightly argues, signals the impossibility of asserting, once one thinks history in Heidegger's manner, any version of the theses that "reason supremely rules the world; still less that reason comes to itself in and through history, that reason recognizes in history its own aspiration to complete self-possession" (NII 490; cf. EPh 83).[9] "The presentiment" places the "inceptive urgency" in Dasein and is "in its horror [Schrecken] and inspiriting [*Begeisterung*]" what the "trembling of Being intones [*an-stimmt*] and pre-determines [*be-stimmt*] in *Da*-sein as Da-*sein*" (G65 22). That is, the presentiment is the preunderstanding or pre-having of what is to be understood.

The "exertion" (*Anstrengung*) of thinking called for by Heidegger's task separates his thinking from that of his contemporaries, who "seek refuge in 'new' doctrines and supply the staple of traditional school philosophy with hitherto unknown decor by dressing it up in the mantle of 'politics' and 'racism'" (18–19). Later he explains that the "the ascending predominance of the 'metaphysics' of Richard Wagner and [Houston Stewart] Chamberlain" conceals Nietzsche's creative exhibition of the end of metaphysics (174).

World-views fail to comprehend the forgetting of Being; from their transcendences they cannot understand the need for this forgetting, for they have, as it were, made men transparent, obscuring the mystery by means of their seemingly opposed, but at bottom indistinguishable, clarifications. It is from the need of the forgetting of Being that grounding of truth of Being is necessary for the grounding of Dasein (28): "This necessity enacts itself in the standing of all historical human-Being in a completely ruling decision." Paraphrased, the alternatives are whether we will have sufficient strength to belong to the truth of Being and out of and for this belonging to bring beings to be in the truth of Being, or whether we begin on the beginning of the "last man" (*letzten Menschen*), which is to say, in "animality" (*Tierheit*) and a refusal of the last god. The difficulty in thinking an other beginning is that there is and must be a "struggle" for a measure. There is in this movement a "great transformation," an "essential turning over" (*Um-schlag*): "Only a few always stand in the hell of these lightnings."

The struggle for measure is carried on in an age of world-views, which Heidegger distinguishes as always from philosophy (36–37). A world-view "aligns experience in a determinate track [*Bahn*] and within its own circle," thus removing the possibility of essential questioning, while philosophy opens experience. Unlike philosophy, which is "always an inception and requires its own overcoming," a world-view is "always an end." The genesis of world-view philosophy lies, as Heidegger had argued in the 1920s, in the responses to scientific philosophy in the nineteenth century articulated in the idioms of "culture," "values," and "ideals" (37–38). The resulting "arbitrariness"

(*Beliebigkeit*) of opinions is exemplified in the "liberal" (*liberalen*) world-view, which is "dogmatic [*Rechthaberische*] in the sense that it requires that everybody be left to his own opinion" (38). "But this arbitrariness," Heidegger writes, "is the slavery of 'contingency' [*Zufälligen*]." The "genuine matter" (*eigenste Sache*) of philosophy is forgotten as philosophy divides into "disciplines" such as epistemology and ontology and its "old leading question," the question of Being, is forgotten as philosophy becomes a "cultural good." The age of world-views is the age of "world-building," "a growth of modernity, a *consequence* [*Folge*] of modern metaphysics." A world-view is always an organizing principle of "machination" and rule (38–39). In Heidegger's view, the "rule" (*Herrschaft*) of the church exemplifies the nature of rule by a world-view, which exhibits itself in and as a "total" organization of action and thinking, which appears as well in the "total political belief" of the present, which we must read as a reference to National Socialism (40–41). While these world-views seem to be in conflict with one another, "their struggle is not creative struggle but rather 'propaganda' and 'apologetic'" (41). "Machination" (*Machenschaft*) rules the age; everything is experienced as calculable and manipulable (126–34). The disenchantment of Enlightenment has reached its end-stage and is being replaced by the enchantment, the "bewitchment" (*Behexung*) of technology (124). The gigantism of technology is a mark of "darkening of the world and destruction of the earth" (119). Machination conditions the "lived experience" (*Erlebnis*) of the present age and furnishes the dominant modes of thinking for its comprehension (128–34). Culture is now merely decoration, for machination names the "rule of power and its legacies" (131). Thus, machination exhibits the "emptiness of the forgetting of Being" in which the "quantitative becomes quality . . . and rules over all beings" (137).

Just before the teaching on science Heidegger characterizes "total mobilization" as a "consequence" (*Folge*) of the "originary abandonment of Being" (*der ursprünglichen Seinsverlassenheit*) (143). It is the "pure setting-in-motion" (*das reine In-Bewegungsetzen*) of beings. Heidegger asks, "For what" are the masses mobilized and put into service? That a "new stamp [*Schlag*] of men" is forced into existence cannot be the "end" (*Ziel*) of this happening. Rather, this "end-setting" can only emerge out of the inception (*Anfang*), which leads Heidegger to ask: "What is inception?" This question governs the teaching on science in that this teaching, in the form of twenty-four propositions (*Satze*) on science, shows that and why science is precluded from answering it.

Today "science" can only be modern science. Medieval and ancient science are not recognizable now as "science." Given this condition, science cannot be "knowledge" in the sense of grounding essential truth. It is rather a "derivative foundation" (*abgeleitete Einrichtung*), for it takes its bearings from established domains of truth regarded as beyond questioning, such as "nature," "history," and "right" (145). "Scientific recognition" of something is conditional on truth as established for some known region (*Gebiet*) of beings, for it depends upon beings lying *as* a region. Since a region is a "posit" (*ein positum*), each science is, or becomes, therefore a "positive" science. There cannot be "science" as such, for "science" is only "a formal title," comprehending only individual sciences. Accordingly, specialization is a necessary development of the character of a science (145–46). This means that each science projects an ongoing clarification of its own conditions (146). Such clarification amounts to an ongoing reworking of the science in which hindsight plays a prominent part. The foundation of a science completes itself as a "connection of explanations" (*Erklärungszusammenhangs*) through its inquiries, themselves arranged to provide this connection, which is the "cohesion" (*Bindung*) of science, its "rigor" (*Strenge*). The "unfolding of the rigor" of a science completes itself in "method" in and through which categories such as the statistical, the causal, the historic, and the like are deployed (146–48). What is decisive in a science is not the question of the essential character of the things with which it is concerned but the manner of proceeding it calls for (147–48). For Heidegger this trait is also linked to the utilitarian character of science, exhibited in its emphasis on "results" (148). Science receives its "confirmation" (*Bestätigung*) from its results; whether it is as "cultural value," "service to the people," or "political science" "makes *in essence no difference.*" "Only a thoroughly modern [i.e., 'liberal'] science can be '*völkische* science,'" Heidegger writes, because only modern or liberal science can be completely neutral, can permit itself to serve any end, as shown in the "materialism and technicism in Bolshevism, employment in four-year plans, political education" (148–49). Modern science is thus "international" (149). Its "'liberal' essence and its 'ideal of objectivity'" suit it for any "political-*völkischen* 'alignment.'" Science becomes harmonious with world-view to such an extent that a discourse concerning a

" 'crisis' of science"—and surely Husserl is meant here—is "only chatter [*Geschwätz*]."[10]

I turn to Heidegger's treatment of the university as the site of scientific research and teaching. It is now, in the absence of a decision, merely "cultural decoration," available for "culture-political propaganda," and can no longer bear the essence of "universitas," since it is overflowing with its "political-*völkische* commission" (155–56). Philosophy, understood here as "thinking reflection from the truth and thus the question-worthiness of Being," is "without place" [*keinen Ort*] in the university (156). Hope can no longer be placed in science, for its future lies with the total rule of nihilism as an exhibition of the withdrawal of Being, which Heidegger calls the "end-stage" (*Endzustand*) of the history of Being. Scientific "progress" becomes the "exploitation and using of the earth, the breeding and training of men," which brings us to an "unimaginable condition" today and goes on without end (156–57). "Only the blind and the foolish," Heidegger writes, "can speak today of an 'end' of science." Indeed, science "drives" (*betreibt*) the security of its position to a "complete needlessness in knowledge" and "remains on that account at all times the 'most modern' (*das 'Modernste'*) in the age of absolute questionlessness (*Fraglosigkeit*)" (cf. 187). The "hidden end" (*verborgene Ziel*) to which the utilitarian successes of science "hasten" (*zueilt*) is "the condition of absolute boredom [*volligen Langeweile*] in the circling around of its own acquisitions," to a time when such boredom can no longer be hidden. There will then remain enough "knowing power" (*Wissenkraft*) to horrify and to uncover the "gaping Being-abandoned of beings." This "great horror" (*grosse Einsetzen*) can come "only from the essential, standing already in another *inception* of knowing, never out of impotence and naked helplessness" (158). Such knowing is "urgency in the question-worthiness of Being, that guards its own dignity, that seldom enough gives itself away in the weighing-out [*Verweigerung*]" of beings "as the hidden eventuation of the passing by of the decision concerning the arrival and the flight of the gods in beings." Heidegger asks the decisive question which suspends this line of thinking before us as governing his further reflections on science: whether "another history of Being" grounds this insight into the movement toward the inception of another "age."

Science is displaced from its political role in Heidegger's deepening reflections, which trace a descent into conditions. The reinspiriting of science was to have been accomplished by the inscription of philosophy in it. With this possibility lost, the modern of way of life grounded in and shaped by science yields to the force of technology, against which modern science is ultimately powerless. Recovery of the founding power of science cannot take place; a different and more fundamental founding power is required.

6 | Politics at/of the Inception: Plato and the Polis

> The beginning of Western thought is not the same as its origin.
> The beginning is, rather, the veil that conceals the origin—
> indeed an unavoidable veil. If that is the situation, then
> oblivion shows itself in a different light. The origin keeps
> itself concealed in the beginning.
>
> (WCT 15)

> The open place in the midst of beings, the clearing, is never a
> rigid stage with a permanently raised curtain on which the
> play of Being runs its unchanging course.
>
> (PLT 54)

THE RECTORAL ADDRESS concludes with a line from the *Republic* (497d9): "*ta . . . megala pant' episphalē*," which Heidegger translates as "All that is great stands in the storm" (*Alles Grosse steht im Sturm*) (RA 480). It is only when "we carry within ourselves that profound and far-reaching thoughtfulness that gave ancient Greek wisdom" that we "fully understand the splendor and greatness of the setting out" of the decision by which the German people wills itself, something already decided by the "young and the youngest strength of the people."

The passage is found in the response of Socrates to Adeimantus's charge that even the best of philosophers are useless to the city and hence unsuitable to rule it. Socrates claims that the people of the city have misunderstood genuine philosophers, that the city itself, like a sophist, corrupts potential philosophers, and that imperfect imposters have filled the positions left by these corrupted potential philosophers. In these circumstances, genuine philosophers withdraw from public life. Adeimantus remarks that the withdrawal of the genuine philosopher to a private life that can be lived free of injustice is no small accomplishment. Socrates replies that this accomplishment is also not the greatest, for in a regime suitable for his rule, the philosopher "will grow more and save the common things along with the private" (497a4–5). Adeimantus then asks which existing regime Socrates thinks is suitable. In his reply, Socrates explains that no regime is suitable except the best regime. Adeimantus's next question is whether this regime is the same as the regime discussed earlier. In his affirmative answer, Socrates reminds Adeimantus that there must be present in this city something with the same understanding of the regime which Adeimantus had as its lawgiver. While Adeimantus believes that this point had been made sufficiently plain, Socrates disagrees, for Adeimantus has shown that the proof of this point would be long and hard. Something else remains to be shown which is difficult. Then comes the passage used in Heidegger's speech. Adeimantus asks: "What is it?" Socrates replies: "How a city can take philosophy in hand without being destroyed? For surely all great things carry with them the risk of a fall, and, really as the saying goes, fine things are hard." The second sentence translates *ta gar de megala panta episphalē, kai to legomenon ta kala to onti chalepa.* Heidegger cites the words of Socrates and not the Greek saying. Has he subsumed these words under the heading of "ancient wisdom" and thereby effaced Socrates as the speaker, not to say Plato as the writer, of these words? "Sturm" translates the Greek *episphalē,* establishing a contemporary resonance too obvious to be accidental.[1] The beginning of Socrates' demonstration is his proposal that philosophy should not be taken up by the young, as is the current practice, but rather by those in their maturity. While Adeimantus agrees, he doubts that others will, beginning with Thrasymachus. Socrates, however, knows that Thrasymachus will not disagree, for he and Thrasymachus have become friends and were not previously enemies (498c9–d1). We do not hear which arguments may have persuaded Thrasymachus; the agreement between Socrates and Thrasymachus that preceded these arguments must be inferred.[2] The rhetoric of Thrasymachus appears to be necessary if Socrates is to persuade the people to accept the rule of philosophers. We are left with the possibility that Heidegger's rhetoric resembles that of Thrasymachus. In other words, Heidegger leads us to the question of whether or how the German people may take philosophy or science in hand without being destroyed. It is necessary for the German people, or at least for the

170

German university, to turn to the Greek beginning and to Plato to catch sight of and make its own the properties of Greek knowing.

In this chapter I am concerned with Heidegger's interpretation of Plato and with his understanding of the Greek *polis*, two lines of thinking closely related to each other. Some scholars characterize Heidegger as a political Platonist or quasi-Platonist, as a thinker who adds yet another chapter to the history of the error or delusion that philosophers are somehow better suited to rule than anyone else.[3] The conjunction of Heidegger's supposed political Platonism with that of National Socialism shows the dangers of this mistake. Heidegger's reflections on the *polis* are inscribed in the history of "the tyranny of Greece over Germany"; as one interpreter puts it, "the modern state is seen in the image of the Greek *polis*."[4] Other scholars argue that Heidegger is ignorant of, gives insufficient attention to, or is perversely wrong about the place of politics in Plato, reading him according to modern conventions, that is, anachronistically, as an epistemologist and ontologist, insensitive to the philosophical importance of Platonic dialogue.[5] If the two interpretations are combined, Heidegger appears as a Platonist with a defective understanding of Plato. In the first part of this chapter I organize my commentary around "Plato's Doctrine of Truth" (PLW), drawn from a lecture course Heidegger gave at Freiburg in 1931/32, written as an essay in 1940, and published in 1942.[6] While most commentators on this work concentrate on Heidegger's claim that the allegory of the cave in Plato's *Republic* exhibits a turn or transformation in the meaning of "truth" from *alētheia* as unconcealment to adequation or "correctness" (*orthotēs*) as correspondence between propositional speech and beings (PLW 230–31), I am concerned with his account of Platonic *paideia*, which allows us to see that his interpretation of Plato has a political sense insufficiently recognized. Plato's *paideia* is deficient because it is grounded on his understanding of Being as *idea*, which is in turn inadequately attuned to, or is ultimately incorrect about, the way beings are, which is to say for Heidegger that it is incorrect about Being.

Heidegger's interpretation of Plato, however, is an account of the *consequences* of Plato and is reduced to a caricature if it is understood only as "criticism."[7] I shall mention only the most important of Heidegger's points. "The stamping [*Gepräge*] of the essence of truth as correctness of representing an assertion," Heidegger writes, "becomes measure-giving for the totality of Western thinking" (PLW 232). When

Plato understands the *idea* of the good as conditional for beings and their appearance, "the decisive step for all metaphysics is taken through which the a priori character of Being at the same time receives the distinction of being a condition" (N4 169). "Being" is understood as if it were a determinate "being"; the ontological difference is not recognized, and Being necessarily remains unthought in metaphysics (207). Metaphysics, in turn, is the historical site for the unfolding of nihilism, which begins in and with Plato and is completed in and with the reign of technology in our present epoch in and as which metaphysics is completed (204–5; QCT 62, 67; EPh 80). As we shall see, humanism also begins with Plato's understanding of Being as *idea.*

A word is in order about the relation of "Plato" and "Platonism" for Heidegger. While he distinguishes them, remarking that Platonism is "struck with naked terror" at the prospect of uncovering what lies behind Plato's philosophy, he also argues that Platonism is a possibility of Plato actualized in and as the metaphysical tradition (WCT 184, 57, 67).[8] "Platonism" pervades the West; ontology as such, all Christian and un-Christian metaphysics, all theories of value and meaning, the very idea of "ideas" in the epistemological tradition, positivism, biologism, philosophies of life, world-views, Nietzsche (G65 218–19). Heidegger agrees with Nietzsche that Christianity is Platonism for the people, a thesis he had long made his own (BPP 118; IM 89–90). Plato's thinking, however, is a response to the "claim" (*Anspruch*) of Being (EPh 4; G54 184; G55 78–89; WCT 57, 67). Since Being as *phusis* is experienced as "emerging appearing," its interpretation as *idea* is necessary; the interpretive possibility actualized in and as Platonic thinking displaces emerging with appearing. The motion of *phusis* is replaced by the stasis of the visible: "The crux of the matter is not that *phusis* should have been characterized as *idea* but that the *idea* should have become the sole and decisive interpretation of *phusis*" (IM 152). It is from our own age, however, that we have the condition for the recollection (*Erinnerung*) in and through the beginning of metaphysics as a possibility intelligible as decidable, as itself a condition for "another beginning" (PLW 237; IM 39). At the very least, we must keep in mind that Heidegger's focus in PLW is Plato's "doctrine" (*Lehre*) of truth, the necessarily unsaid "turn" (*Wandel*) or "shift" (*Wendung*) in the "determination of the essence of truth," something that happens and is registered in Plato's texts and that is not simply the opinion of an erring philosopher (PLW 203). His thinking "follows the shift in the essence of truth, which shift becomes the history of metaphysics, that in Nietzsche's thinking has begun its unconditional completion" (237). Thus, his doctrine of truth remains "historically 'present' [*geschicht-liche 'Gegenwart'*]" and is not merely an accomplishment of past thought.

In turning to Heidegger's understanding of the *polis*, I note that he criticizes Nazi appropriations of Greek antiquity. In his 1942 lectures on Hölderlin, he ridicules Nazi claims that the Greeks anticipated National Socialism and that the *polis* was a forerunner of the new order (G53 98). On the basis of dubious "research results" which amount to crude manipulations of ancient texts and sources, Nazi scholars would have "one believe that the Greeks would already all have been National Socialists." This absurdity springs from a retrospective determination that "naturally" understands the *polis* from contemporary notions of "the political." Today we think about the "political" in the same manner as we think when we understand "logic" as the essence of the Greek *logos* or "ethics" as the essence of the Greek *ethos*. What must be retrieved is the sense the *polis* had in Greek thinking, which cannot be reached by means of a definition (99). What was thought by Plato and Aristotle, for example, when they thought the essence of the *polis*? Given the present-day meaning of "the political," Heidegger writes, "the *polis* did not let itself be determined 'politically.' The *polis* and precisely it is then no 'political' concept." If we are interested in Heidegger's understanding of the *polis*, we must put aside the assumption that we—or for that matter, any Greek thinkers—possess a correct understanding against which Heidegger's interpretation may be compared. We must be prepared to consider the possibility that the *polis* has not been properly understood before Heidegger. The principal texts for Heidegger's account of the *polis* are IM and wartime lectures on Hölderlin (G53) and on Parmenides and Heraclitus (G54; G55). Finally, I shall examine Heidegger's interpretation of the myth of Er in the *Republic* as an exhibition of the "last saying" of the Greeks on the theme of *alētheia*. Plato is invoked here for what is said in and through the myth of Er and not for his own teaching. The *polis* is the site measured by the gods; caring for the gods is the essential concern of political men. For Heidegger this originary sense of the political differs essentially from that available today because we—and especially the Germans—live in an age from which the gods have fled.

I

The overcoming of Platonism calls for inquiry into the experiential and conceptual basis of the understanding of Being as *idea* (G65 220–21). In PLW Heidegger draws attention to the importance of "image" (*Bild* translates *eikōn*) in the allegory of the cave (PLW 213–15). Socrates asks Glaucon to *make* and *see* an image or images and the cave-dwellers and the released prisoner encounter images (*Republic* 514a). As some interpreters have recognized, Heidegger criticizes Socrates' turn to images.[9] A brief look at a line of argument in BPP will clarify this point. There Heidegger's reflection on Plato are located within his effort to show that temporality is conditional for both preontological and ontological understandings of beings and Being (BPP 274–302). Either sort of understanding requires that Being must be projected upon something because each must be given somehow prior to any thematic inquiry, in and for which that upon which the given is projected must itself be unveiled in a projection (281–82). Plato's image-making is related to his failure to proceed "in all sobriety and in the complete disenchantment of purely objective inquiry," for Heidegger argues that inquiry into the conditionality of understanding allows the possibility of comprehending this conditionality "without an image," allying himself with both Kant's criticism of "enthusiasm" (*Schwärmerei*) in philosophy, exemplified by Plato, and his endorsement of the need in philosophy for "sobriety and real work" (285–86, 328–30). Presumably "real work" can dispense with images. As Heidegger puts it in a discussion of Heraclitus, the latter's thinking, responding to what claims it, "sees Being itself, imageless [*bildlos*], in its inceptively simple essence as an organizing joining [*Fügung*]" (G55 146).[10] Platonic images stand in the way of a retrieval of such responsive thinking.

An intelligible image is or shows an exterior or appearance (*Aussehen*) (PLW 214). The appearance (*eidos, idea*) of a being is the way in which a being presents itself. The looks of beings allow us to perceive beings *as* beings, that is, as self-presenting beings. What is visible in the cave resembles what is visible outside of it, since the illumination furnished by the fire in the cave resembles the illumination furnished by the sun outside of it in that both provide images. The things seen are images of the *ideas*. The sun, which makes *ideas* manifest, is itself the image for the *idea* of *ideas,* the *idea* of the good, which Socrates explains is "beyond Being" (*epekeina tēs ousias*); one who acts with "discernment" (*Einsicht*) in one's private or public conduct must have it in view (215, 229).

Plato's attempt to get "beyond Being" is an effort to get "to the light from which and in which [Being] itself comes into the brightness" (BPP 282–83). He fails to understand, however, that the *epekeina* is a projection grounded in Dasein's transcendence (BPP 298–302; MFL 166–68; cf. BT 291–92). Like any genuine philosopher, Plato recognizes the experiences indicative of transcendence, but he is mistaken in locating "beyond" in a *huperouranios topos* (MFL 181–82; cf. BPP 300). Classical *noēsis,* "intuition," is modeled on seeing, which for Heidegger is an untenable restriction to a single, privileged sensory analogy that results in a mistaken conceptualization of transcendence "along the lines of looking," for Being is understood as analogous to something seen (N4 167; MFL 183). Transcendence, then, is misunderstood as an epistemological issue. Heidegger understands transcendence as ontological, which means that it cannot be reduced to any activity—theoretical, aesthetic, or "instrumental-utilitarian." This last point returns us to PLW; the *idea* of the good as conferring unconcealment and conditioning both beings and knowing makes beings and Being appear only as the "useful" (*tauglich*); beings are intelligible in terms of their calculable properties, or even man's "mastery" (*Mächtigkeit*) of them (PLW 227–29; N4 169; ER 93–94). Moreover, to the extent that the Platonic *idea* of the good, in serving as ground, resembles the modern principle of sufficient reason, it, like that principle, is intrinsically related to "preference" (MFL 109–17). The question, then, is not simply whether the condition of the visibility of beings must be an *idea* of any sort, but whether this *idea* must be an *idea* of the good. What is at issue is made clear by Seth Benardete, who notes that Socrates says that the defectiveness of his own opinion of the good would be "unknown to him unless something made the satisfying not satisfying" and that the "something is the divination of the good."[11] All human beings may well desire "the real thing" in the case of the good (505d 5–10), but from this it may be that nothing can be said to show that this desire can be satisfied. The stability extended by the *idea* of the good to the *ideas* and thus to beings is, or at least Plato is unable to show that it is not, an all-too-human prejudice.

Heidegger explains the conditioning role of Platonic *ideas* in one of the Nietzsche lectures. Because *alētheia* is thought as *noein* in Parmenides and Heraclitus, there is a predisposition to understand what is a priori in terms of the temporal structure of perception (N4 170–71). The *idea* is placed in a temporal sequence, making it first, *proteron*, and, not accidentally, ready for God's thought; metaphysics and theology depend upon the notion of a highest being (PLW 235–36). *Nous* becomes, then, a property of man, of human nature, correlated with truth as correctness. Our perception of what is present, however, names the movement of presencing ↔ absencing only fleetingly (WCT 209; EGT 99–100). Because the structure of precedence and subsequence is determined by perception, which is limited to the realm of opinion, one cannot think "place" (*topos*) clearly as what Being exhibits (EGT 100). When Being as *phusis* is "more essentially thought," it requires no sequential structure "by which one can decide about its before and after, its previous and subsequent; because it is in itself a proceeding into its lighting; as going forth it is the foregoing; it is what essentially unfolds of itself into the lighting and what through the lighting first comes toward man" (N4 171).[12] *Idea,* in contrast, is a "*determinate interpretation*" (*bestimmte Auslegung*) of Being (167).

The passage of the former prisoner from the cave into the daylight and back is crucial for Heidegger's discussion of the abodes and stages (*Aufenthalte und Lagen*) men occupy inside and outside of the cave. Just as one who leaves the cave must accustom his eyes to the light, so one who returns to it must accustom his eyes to darkness (PLW 216). Heidegger notes Socrates' remarks that the eyes can suffer from a "twofold confusion" (*zweifache Verwirrungen*) which has a "twofold source" (*zweifache Gründen*) (518a2). Until his eyes are acclimated, it is difficult even for one who has returned from the contemplation of divine things to human things to tell if a man who seems confused has come from the daylight into the dark or from greater darkness to greater brightness. What is visible is a confusion which exhibits indifference with regard to the distinction between ascent and descent. Ascent and descent are symmetrical in a way to which Plato, as Heidegger interprets him, would seem to be insufficiently attentive. The released prisoner, while he sees the light, does not dwell permanently in it.

Plato calls the acclimation of man's essence *paideia*, which names the movement of man from the cave into the light and what is learned in this movement (216–17). As the "turning around of the whole man in his essence," *paideia* is essentially a transition (*Übergang*) from *apaideusia* (absence of education) into *paideia*. "Given this transition-character *as* transition," Heidegger writes, "*paideia* stays constantly related to *apaideusia*" (217). *Paideia* is not something that can simply be completed. *Paideia* and *apaideusia* belong together, for each is its other's possibility. The instability of each exhibits its finite character. The movement of the soul up or down in the allegory of the cave is a transition across determinate joinings of this relation.

Paideia, Heidegger notes, is not easily translated. He draws attention to its radical character and the need to rethink the German *Bildung* as a translation, which requires a return to the originary naming power (*Nennkraft*) of the German word and the need to set aside its nineteenth-century meanings.[13] *Bildung* has a twofold meaning, or put more literally, " '*Bildung*' says a two-fold" ("*Bildung*" *sagt ein Zweifaches*). It is a forming in the sense of an "unfolding stamping" (*entfaltenden Prägung*). At the same time stamping stamps out of a "pregrasped measure" (*vorgreifenden Anmessung*), intelligible as a "standard look" (*massgebenden Anblick*) which amounts to a "pre-image" (*Vor-bild*). Thus, the stamping of *Bildung* is carried out *as* and *by means of* an image. "Image" as such, in turn, must itself be conditioned by some determinate understanding of Being. This requirement inscribes Heidegger's understanding of epochality in his account of the *Republic*, because the Greek understanding of Being as presence stems from the primacy of production for the Greeks and thus the primacy of what is as what is present (BPP 99–108). As he puts it in 1931, "the basic concepts of philosophy," the concepts of Plato and Aristotle, have their origins in production (G33 137; cf. PLT 168).

Apaideusia is the absence of the transitive and reflexive stamping, or the absence of image and imaging. If Platonic *paideia* is the forming of the soul as and by means of images, then it must exhibit the character of images as unstable and finite couplings of moments of unconcealment ↔ concealment. Plato's inattention to the importance of the prisoner's return to the cave would appear to be related to his inattention to the finite character of education, which is to say his misunderstanding of what Socrates will call elsewhere the true political art (*Gorgias* 521d). Must one thinker who can recognize this deficiency in another possess the true political art himself? We are drawn irresistably to this question, whether or not we can answer it.

Plato claims "defensively" (*Abwehrend*) that *paideia* is not an accomplishment of a naked intelligence in an unprepared soul, nor is it a passive filling of the soul as a container. The purest education catches and converts (*verwandelt*) the soul against itself. To show that Plato's *paideia* requires images Heidegger cites the beginning of book 6 of the *Republic*, where Socrates tells Glaucon to produce a view, an image (*Anblick*), of the essence of education and its want which belongs to our human Being in its ground (PLW 217–18). In order to understand Platonic *Bildung*, it is necessary to understand the turn in the essence of truth in Plato's thinking (218). The order of inquiry here suggests the priority of *paideia* or *Bildung* over "truth," and thus the priority of the political over the epistemological in Heidegger's account.

An essential relation (*Wesensbezug*) governs education—conditioning its fundamental makeup (*Grundegefüge*)—and truth: "This relation consists in the deed." The question becomes: "What fits 'education' and 'truth' together in an originary essential unity [*ursprüngliche Wesenseinheit*]?" *Paideia* names the movement of the whole human being as an "acclimating displacement [*eingewöhnenden Versetzung*] out of the region of what is proximally encountered into another realm in which beings themselves appear." This displacement is possible only when what was "evident [*Offenkundige*] to human beings up to now and the manner, the way in which it was evident, becomes otherwise." That is, the way in which "unconcealment" (*Unverborgenheit* translates *alētheia*) takes place, as well as the place thus taken, has changed. Heidegger warns us that what is at issue here is more than a matter of words but is rather what the Greeks thought was joined in the essential unity of "education" and "truth" (219). What was thought is conditioned by, and reflexively conceals, the "deed" Heidegger has mentioned. Put concisely, unconcealment "continually overcomes a concealment of what is concealed." The unconcealed must be "wrested" (*entrissen*) from concealment (223). Exhibited in the alpha-privative (*a-lētheia*) is the Greek understanding of "truth" as removed or stolen from concealment: "Truth is thus a transient theft [*Entringung jeweils*] in the mode of revealing [*Entbergung*]." The story of the cave shows that the uncovering of the concealed from concealment is a struggle of life and death. "Privation, the laborious wresting away of the unconcealed," Heidegger says, "belongs to the essence of truth" (224). The cave-dweller lives in the performance of the uncovering of beings, in letting beings be, which is to say in comportment which encompasses both truth and untruth as concealing and errancy. Plato or Socrates, then, fails to recognize the place of human conduct, of action, in the happening of truth. The deed in and through which truth and education are joined remains obscured.

Plato's understanding of the essence of unconcealment is shown in his account of the movement of the released prisoner from and then back to the cave (219–20). The unconcealed in its unconcealment is "what in the dwelling region [*Aufenhaltsbezirk*] of men is always the open of that-which-comes-to-presence [*das offen Anwesende ist*]." The ascent and descent of the cave-dweller traverses a series of four abodes, each of which exhibits a stage in and of unconcealment and thus a kind of "truth" (219–24). Within each stage, *alēthēs*, the unconcealed, "must one way or another be considered and named" (219). What is more unconcealed is more true, which means that *paideia* traces the movement of the soul from what is least unconcealed to what is most unconcealed. In the first abode, the cave, unconcealment occurs as the shadows cast upon the wall of the cave, a mode of unconcealment intelligible only from beyond its domain. In the second abode, the released prisoner is dazzled by the light of the fire in the cave and finds the shadows to be even more unconcealed or truthful than the originals of which they are images, a recognition available only later (219–20). This abode and stage teach that unconcealment is understood in terms of the appearance of and as the exterior of a thing; it is the site of the experience that engenders the notion of *ideas* (220). The exterior of a shadow *as* exterior, however, cannot be distinguished from the exterior of a being. In the third abode the prisoner is forced out of the cave and into the sunlight (221–22). What is most unconcealed (*Unverborgenste*) emerges as the ground of unconcealment of what appears (221). The liberated prisoner becomes accustomed to "fixing his view upon the fixed boundaries of things affixed in their forms," and acting accordingly (222). Mimesis orders Platonic politics (cf. N1 169–78).

Paideia as a turning around (*Umwendung*) is a determinate turning toward the most unconcealed upon which authentic *Bildung* depends: "The essence of '*Bildung*' is grounded in the essence of 'truth.'" Thus, the relation of truth and errancy conditions the relation of *paideia* and *apaideusia*. Again, Heidegger draws attention to *paideia* as a process which is always threatened by its other, for the want of education calls for a "standing overcoming" (*ständige Überwindung*). He is emphatic that the story does not end with the description of the highest step beyond the cave, for in the fourth and final stage the former prisoner, now identified as the "liberator" (*Befreier*), returns to it as the fourth and final abode. He "cannot find his way around in the cave anymore" and "comes into danger [*Gefahr*] of succumbing . . . to the demand ordinary 'reality' makes to be the only reality" (222–23). It is crucial to Heidegger's interpretation that this danger be genuine. Errancy is necessary; as Heidegger says elsewhere, it "belongs to the inner constitution of the Da-sein into which historical man is admitted" (ET 135–36).

I turn now to some further remarks on the consequences of Plato's doctrine. As Heidegger puts it elsewhere, in Plato and Aristotle beings win the *gigantomachia,* the struggle between Being and beings, for Being is now understood as the highest or first being (G33 24, 43–44; cf. EPh 9–10). As he explains in his wartime Parmenides lectures, in and with the philosophical tradition's understanding of truth and falsehood, *alētheia* is opposed to *pseudos,* to falsehood in the sense of incorrectness, which displaces the inceptive Greek senses of unconcealing and concealing (G54 24–56). The translation of *alētheia* as *veritas* is related to the political-moral economy of ancient Rome, and therewith, Heidegger makes clear, to the manifold successors to Rome: medieval Christianity, modernity, Nietzsche, and—I agree with William V. Spanos on this point—National Socialism (57–72).[14]

The Latin *falsum* has the sense of "bringing to a fall" or "downfall," which is "only a subsequent effect [*Wesensfolge*] within the essential domain [*Wesensbereiches*] of dissembling and concealing which makes up the essence of *psuedos*" (58).[15] "*Imperium*" and the "imperial" constitute the "essential domain" decisive for the "experiential domain" (*Erfahrungsbereich*) in, from, and for which "bringing to a fall" acquires its status as the designation for the counter-essence of "what the Greeks experience as *alēthēs,* the 'unconcealing' and the 'unconcealed.'" The experience of *imperium* is that of "command," of the taking over of a territory, which is ruled by commandment. "Command," then, is the "essential ground of sovereignty" (*Wesensgrund der Herrschaft*) and, moreover, describes the characteristic actions of the god of the Old Testament and the gods of Rome, but not those of Greece (59). In a further specification, "command" determines Roman law and right, *ius* and *iustum*; *iustitia* "has a wholly other [*ganz anderen*] essential ground than that of *dike,* which arises from *alētheia.*" "Being-superior" (*Obensein*) belongs to "command" and is the "constant surmounting [*Überhöhung*] of others, who are thereby the inferiors [*Unteren*]." Surmounting requires the power to "oversee" (*übersehen*), which means, therefore, to "dominate" (*beherrschen*) (59–60). The "overseeing" of imperium requires constant "action," by which en-

180

emies or rivals will be brought to fall through "'direct' attack" (*Ansturm*) or "subterfuge" (*Hintergehen*) or "trick," which, "not accidentally," is an "English" word (60). Those who fall are not destroyed but rather "raised up" (*aufgerichtet*) within the boundaries established by those who rule; this "fixing" (*Abstecken*) is Roman peace. Indeed, the greatness of the imperial, Heidegger writes, lies in the subterfuge by which it secures its dominion. The expansion of early Rome through treaties and treachery shows this (60–61).

The "Romanizing" of the Greeks conditions not only all subsequent understanding of them in the history of the West but also the historical and metaphysical *Auseinandersetzung* of the modern world and antiquity. Even Nietzsche's metaphysics, as a modern attempt to recover antiquity, is conditioned by Rome and thus is ultimately "unGreek." The Roman experience of beings, encountered under the "Roman stamp" (*der Romisch Prägung*), reaches into Christianity and hence to the medieval and modern ages (64–72; cf. EPh 13). "Romanization in the essential sense of the Greco-Roman historical domain," Heidegger writes, must be understood as a "change in the essence of truth and Being"; it is an "authentic event [*Ereignis*] in history" (63). The transformations of *alētheia* and *pseudos* as correlates with the imperial experience mark an epochal boundary. "The imperial as a mode of Being of historical collectivities [*Menschentums*]," Heidegger explains, is not the ground for the essential change of *alētheia* into truth as correctness but is rather a following of the enfolding of truth into the meaning of correctness (62–63). Heidegger makes clear that there is something "make-shift" (*Notbehelf*) in the phrase "change in the essence of truth," which does not speak clearly enough of the way "in which it unfolds itself and history 'is' (*wie sie selbst west und die Geschichte 'ist'*]" (63). This process exhibits the inner connection of the coherent modes of action which ground Western history, and is not to be understood causally.

What was lost with the transformations of *alētheia* into adequation, into rectitude as conformity to the given, located in the intellect, was the sense of "holding something to be what it is" *within* the domain of unconcealment (PLW 232; G54 73–74). For Nietzsche, who thinks "in the time of the inceptive completion of the modern age," truth is characterized in aphorism 493 in *The Will to Power* as "the kind of error without which a "certain kind of life could not live. The value for *life* is ultimately decisive." With Nietzsche's understanding of truth as a kind of error, a way of thinking is reached in which the real, understood in terms of becoming, falsifies itself. There is in Nietzsche's thinking, then, the possibility of giving up the notion of the essence of truth as correctness of assertion. Heidegger says that Nietzsche's concept of truth is the last reflection of the change of truth from unconcealment of beings to correctness of seeing, which is based on the determination of the Being of beings as *idea.*

Prefigured here as well is Heidegger's interpretation of Nietzsche as having failed to "twist free" of Platonism (N1 148–210). Nietzsche's sensuous inversion of Platonism fails to change the "ordering *structure* of Western thinking" because as an inversion it remains Platonism (210). Put briefly, Nietzsche understands art and creativity as an exhibition of the body. What begins in and with Plato and Platonism as an understanding of Being as *idea* and of knowing as the conforming of some higher attribute of human beings—"reason," "mind," or an equivalent—to the ideas culminates in and as the triumph of the body, of animality. Truth is understood as conditioned by "life," which means that the schematizing activity of the mind, thus conditioned, is determined more fundamentally by nature understood as "chaos" (N1 214–20; N3 68–76, 77–83). The doctrine of eternal return, thought in these contexts, is intended to oppose a "humanization" of the world, but the deeper dependence of thought on the needs of life, of the body, ensures the failure of this opposition (N2 77–83; N3 84–89). The operations of the Kantian schematism, calculation, and the law of contradiction, to name the most important instances of thought, amount to commands, which is to say, exhibitions of will to power, itself in turn an exhibition of the body, of animality (N3 90–127, 155–56, 193–200). Finally, overman exhibits the triumph of the body, and Nietzschean politics, politics in the "grand style," is intelligible as the politics of the body (N3 212–32). Platonism, if not Plato, begins with the *ideas* and ends with animality, for both overman and last man are animals differing only in the degree of will to power they are.

Humanism begins, Heidegger argues, when correct seeing is the model for *paideia;* the beginning of metaphysics is the beginning of humanism (PLW 236–37). Humanism is coeval with the beginning, unfolding, and the end of metaphysics, in which man steps back from his position among beings without on that account becoming the highest being. Heidegger explains that "man" is variously the human race, humanity, an individual, community, a people, or a group of peoples

(*Menschentum, Menschkeit, Einzeln, Gemeinschaft, Volk, Völkergruppe*). That is, any of these can be and has been understood "humanistically"; it is possible to deploy a humanism for any or all of them. From the metaphysical basis of humanism, man is understood as a rational animal, impelled toward the liberation of his possibilities, the certainty of his determination, and the protection of his life: "This happens as the stamping of his 'moral' conduct, as salvation of his immortal soul, as unfolding of his creative powers, as development of his reason, as cultivation of his personality, as awakening of common sense, as training of his body, or as an appropriate coupling of some or all of these 'humanities' " (236). "A metaphysically determined circle," Heidegger writes, "always comes to pass around man, more or less approximating his course." In the epoch of the completion of metaphysics, humanism or anthropology is pressed to its uttermost limit and is at the same time an "unconditional [*unbedingten*] 'position.' " We may characterize humanism as the refusal of the metaphysical tradition to recognize epochality; its action is domination, and the distinctive feature of disclosure in modernity is "the fanatical" (*das Fanatische*) (G54 112).[16]

According to Heidegger, *alētheia*, however unrecognized, however transformed, remains the condition for all later understandings of truth. The change in the essence of truth exhibited in Plato's thinking "is current as the slowly accommodated and yet still undisplaced fundamental reality ruling everything in the rolling on of world history up to the most recent modernity" (PLW 237; cf. G65 208–24). As a consequence of the shift in the essence of truth that rules everything, historical man himself dwells in a "standing decision" (*stehenden Entscheidung*) concerning the essence of truth as correctness, and thus in a decision for humanism as well. The story of the cave tells the story of an essential happening in the history of "Western-stamped humanity." In and from this decision man thinks the meaning of the essence of truth as the correctness of representations of beings according to "ideas" and estimates (*schätzt*) all reality in terms of "values." What is decisive is not "which ideas and which values" should prevail but rather the genuine status of ideas and values.

The "inceptive" (*anfängliche*) essence of truth can, however, be remembered. "Unconcealment unveils itself in this remembrance [*Errinerung*]," Heidegger writes, "as the distinctive feature [*Grundzug*] of beings itself." An addition from 1947 identifies *Grundzug* as "Being" (*Seyn*). "Remembrance of the inceptive essence of truth," he goes on, "must think this essence inceptively [*anfänglicher*]" (238). Thus far, unconcealment continues to be understood in Plato's sense, "under the yoke of the *idea*" (238). Accordingly, all attempts to recover unconcealment by means of any kind of "subjectivity" such as "reason," "spirit," "thinking," "logos," are untenable, for what is required is clarification of the "unconceived essence of unconcealment." What must be recovered is the "positive" sense of the "privative" essence of *alētheia*, which is experienced, but not articulated, by the Greeks. The condition for this recovery is the "need [*Not*] not only for beings in their Being but for Being itself (i.e., the difference) to become question-worthy." Heidegger's final word brings us back to the present: "Because this need is at hand, the inceptive essence of truth moves in its concealed inception." Another addition from 1947 explains that this need is the need of needlessness; the forgetting of Being has been forgotten, and our distress is measured by this absence.

II

The account of the *polis* in IM is reached by means of a line of thinking for which the question of the meaning of Being must become "explicitly what it is, namely a reflection on the source of our hidden history," since the question of how it stands with Being—an inherently political formulation—"must itself remain within the history of Being if it is, in turn, to unfold and preserve its own historical import" (IM 77). The first move in Heidegger's retrieval identifies what is distinguished from Being, its "others" (*Anderes*): Being and—becoming, appearance, thinking, the ought—distinctions that (1) belong originally to Being and trace the subsequent history of Being (80); (2) are at bottom the same determination: "enduring presence" (*ständige Anwesenheit*): *on* as *ousia*" (169). Being as enduring presence comes from the "determination which dominates our historical Dasein by virtue of its great beginning among the Greeks"; (3) are grounded on "*one* originary distinction [*ursprüngliche Scheidung*], whose intimacy and originary breaking up [*ursprüngliches Auseinandertreten*] sustains history, the difference between Being and beings" (170). The ontological difference is not something thinking has to initiate but is rather to be re-enacted (*nachvollziehen*), for it has already been accomplished (*ist vollzogen*) "out of the necessity of the inception [*Anfang*] in which we stand" (170–71). The ontological difference exhibits itself as a temporal difference, a process of temporal differentiating. An "originary perspective [*ursprünglichen Blickbahn*] must be reached if Being in "its originary differentiation [*seiner ursprünglichen Unterscheidung*] between Being and beings is to be disclosed (171); (4) are of decisive significance for politics because they "permeate all knowledge, action, and discourse even where they are not specifically mentioned or not in these words" and "must be developed into a fundamental experience of our future historical Dasein" (80). Since "the concept of Being that has been accepted up until now does not suffice to name everything that is," Heidegger's call for a new experience of Being "from the ground up and in the total breadth of its possible essence" is massively political, for this experience is required "if we are to set our historical Dasein to work *as* historical" (170).

The second move brings us to the Greeks, for the only way in which the greatness of the inception can be preserved is in and through a "thinking retrieval" (*denkende Wiederholung*) of its "originary originariness" (*ursprünglicher Ursprünglichkeit*) (160). What is a stake, Heidegger tells us, is nothing less than an "arising determination of being-human [*Menschseins*] from the opening of the essence of Being [*phusis*]" (171). The great age of the Greeks was a "single creative self-assertion amid the confused, intricate struggle between the powers Being and appearance," the "originary power" of the "unity and conflict" of which is exhibited in the final choral ode of *Oedipus Rex* (90–91). The action of the play is the conflict between appearance (concealment, distortion) and unconcealment (Being). "Step by step," Heidegger says, Oedipus "must move into unconcealment, which in the end he can bear only by putting out his own eyes, that is, by removing himself from all light, by letting the cloak of night fall round him, and, blind, crying out to the people to open all doors in order that a man may be made manifest to them as what he is" (90). Oedipus is not simply a man who meets his downfall but must be seen as the "form [*Gestalt*] of Greek Dasein, in which ventures forth its basic passion in the broadest and wildest way, the passion for the disclosure of Being [*Seinsenthüllung*], that is, the struggle for Being itself." Heidegger appropriates Hölderlin's line from his late poem "In lovely blueness . . .": "Perhaps King Oedipus has an eye too many" to characterize the "fundamental condition [*Grundbedingung*] for all great question and knowing and also their own metaphysical ground. The knowledge and the science of the Greeks were this passion" (90–91). Heidegger also makes this line stand for Hölderlin himself and thereby, as Christopher Fynsk rightly observes, "marks Hölderlin as a witness to the modern German historical destiny" (G4 47).[17] Since appearance not only distorts the appearing being but also distorts itself in showing itself as Being, Heidegger agrees with the traditional view that appearance deceives (92; cf. 49–50, 53). Deception is "only one among the modes according to which man moves in the interwoven threefold world [*verschrankten Dreiwelt*] of Being, unconcealment, and appearance" (92). This is the space (*Raum*) of *error* that opens in the "interwovenness" of Being, unconcealment, and appearance and is the site for the basic words of Greek thinking, whose "originary force" (*ursprüngliche Schlagkraft*) stems from their indexical character (95). Heidegger turns, then, from *Oedipus Rex* to Heraclitus and Parmenides.

Heidegger's aim in retrieving the inception is deconstructive and reconstructive, that is, political: the "great and long venture of demolishing [*abzutragen*] a world that has grown old [*eine altegewordene Welt*] and of rebuilding it truly [*wahrhaft*] new" (106).[18] In Heraclitus *logos* is the "steady gathering, the intrinsic togetherness of what is," or Being, which means that *kata ton logon tonde*—"according to the *logos*"—has the same sense as *kata phusin*—"according to emergence," or Being, which means that his injunction to listen to the *logos* is call to the "collectedness [*Gesammeltheit*] of beings itself" (110, 109). *Eon*, Being, is thus *xunon*, "collected presence" (*gesammelt Anwesen*) (110). Against the traditional understanding of *xunon* as "universal," Heidegger emphasizes that the collecting and holding together of beings in and by *logos* is characterized by *polemos*, which brings us to the political. Heraclitus says that the *nomos* of the *polis* is a *xunon*, what "constitutes or puts together, the inner structure [*innere Gefüge*] of the *polis*, . . . not something that hovers over all and touches none, but the originary unifying unity of what strives to set itself apart [*ursprünglichen einigende Einheit des Auseinanderstrebenden*]." *Polemos* is inscribed in *nomos*. "True speaking and hearing" occur only if they are directed toward Being, and those who do not truly speak and hear "cannot bring their Dasein to stand in the Being of beings" (111). Those who *can* do this are the "poets and thinkers"; the rest stagger amid beings, for Being is hidden from them (111–12). The gathering of *logos*, that is, Being as *logos*, is not a mere aggregating in which everything is equally valuable (or valueless). "Rank and ruling [*Rang, Herrschaft*]," Heidegger writes, "belong to Being" (112). When Heraclitus characterizes the many as dogs and donkeys, he exhibits a "comportment" (*Haltung*) essential to Greek Dasein. To the extent that Greek Dasein was attuned to the exhibition of Being in and as the gathering of *logos*, rank and ruling correspond to Being's disclosure. Heidegger remarks that concern with the *polis* today—which to some extent he deems excessive—must remember rank and ruling, without which it is "insignificant and sentimental."[19] Since "what has the higher rank is the stronger," the *logos* is not available in the same way to everyone. While the harmony "that is mere compromise, destruction of tension, flattening" is visible, the stronger harmony, Heraclitus says, is hidden, which means that Being "does not show itself as one pleases" and that "the true is not for every man but only for the strong."

Parmenides thinks the unity of *logos* and *phusis*, and thus sheds light on their separation, by showing that and how man belongs to Being (116–21). "To apprehend" (*vernehmen*) and "apprehension" (*Vernehmung*), *noein*, *nous* in Parmenides, name the essence of man's being as belonging to Being as the "receptive bringing-to-stand of the intrinsically permanent that manifests itself," as the "accepting apprehension of what shows itself" (117–18). Apprehension is a "happening [*Geschehen*] in which man first happens [*geschehend*] as a being in history, appears, that is (in a literal sense) comes into Being" (119). Indeed, so far is apprehension from being anything like a property man has that Heidegger can say that apprehension is the "happening that has man" (*Geschehnis, das den Menschen hat*). What is accomplished (*vollzieht*) is the "knowing appearance of man as historical Being (guardian of Being)," which defines the essence of man in and for the West and exhibits an "essential characterization of Being." "In the togetherness of Being and being-human," Heidegger writes, "their separation comes to light." The originary origin (*Ursprung*) of this separation is lost unless its inception (*Anfang*), covered over by the tradition's distinction between Being and thinking, is recovered. We now learn why this distinction is of such significance. It is in the opposition of Being and thinking that man encounters Being, a "happening [*Geschehnis*] which is the knowing appearance of man as the historical [*als des geschichtlich*]," itself the condition for the traditional definition of man as *zōion logon echōn*, the rational animal. All variations on this definition stand as obstacles in the path of genuine inquiry into the question of man, itself now paralyzed with all "measures and comportments" (*Masstäbe und Haltungen*) confused (120).

What is exhibited in Parmenides' saying—but not what is simply intended by Parmenides—traditionally and misleadingly translated as "thinking and Being are the same" is "a definition of the essence of man from out of the essence of Being itself" (121).[20] For further illumination it is necessary to inquire into "Greek Dasein." The separation between gods and men in *polemos*, which sets apart, is crucial for the showing of gods and men as they are. Accordingly, our understanding of man is not reached by "learned definitions" but rather by grasping man's efforts to project beings into "limit and form," when he creates original poetry or "builds poetically." While the poetic and the philosophical have not yet separated in Parmenides and Heraclitus, the *thinking* in poetic thinking has priority and follows its own direction. Poetic thinking belongs together with the "thinking poetry" of tragedy "in which the Being and Dasein of the Greeks was most genuinely created" (122).

Since the definition of Parmenides—the "decisive determination" (*entscheidende Bestimmung*) of man's being—is "strange and hard to approach directly," Heidegger seeks "help and counsel by consulting the poetic project of being-human among the Greeks" through an interpretation of the first chorus from Sophocles' *Antigone* (lines 332–75) (123).[21] Heidegger is not concerned with literature or philology; he seeks the intrinsic meaning of the poem, "that which sustains the edifice of words and rises above it" (125). What sustains the poem and towers above it "bursts upon us like a triple assault [*Ansturm*], shattering at the very outset all everyday standards of questioning and definitions" (125). In the first two verses of the choral ode, "There is much that is uncanny, but nothing / that surpasses man in uncanniness," Sophocles presents the Greek view of the Being of man. Man is characterized as *to deinotaton*—the "uncanniest of the uncanny—"a designation which encompasses the "extreme limits and abrupt abysses" of man's being, which only "poetic insight" can disclose.[22] Elsewhere Heidegger characterizes *deinon* as the fundamental word of the choral ode (G53 76). *Deinon* refers to both the "overpowering power" (*überwältigenden Waltens*) of Being, both mighty and able to "hold its overpowering power in check," and the powerful in the sense of "one who uses power" against the overpowering and thus exhibits "power" as the basic character of his action and Dasein. (IM 126).

The thought here is that the "activity of power" (*Gewalttätigkeit*) of human beings is the correlate of the power of disclosure of Being. Haar is correct when he notes that a translation of *Gewalt* as "power," rather than "violence"—chosen by both the English and French translators of IM—preserves the coherence of Heidegger's teaching, yet the matter is not this simple.[23] Heidegger *does* write of *Gewalt-tätigkeit* that its essential sense (*wesenhaften Sinn*) must be distinguished from its "conventional meaning" (*gewöhnliche Bedeutung*) of "simple brutality and the arbitrary." The latter meaning belongs to a realm, Heidegger writes, in which the "measure of Dasein" derives from "agreed upon compromise and mutual aid," from which such action must appear as "disturbance and wrong-doing" (*Störung und Verletzung*). The Dasein of man's activity of power, of the Greek project of being-human, is set over against the Dasein from which "violence" acquires its conventional meaning. The essential sense of violence is found in man's use of power against the overpowering. Being is *deinon*, the overpowering, and man is *deinon*, first because he stands within the overpowering, and second, because he "gathers the power and brings it to manifestness." Since the translation of *deinon* as "uncanny" (*unheimlich*) exhibits the "highest limit and link" (*hochsten Steigerung und Verkoppelung*) of man's Being, it must show the essence of his Being decisively (126–27). Heidegger understands the uncanny as "that which casts us out of the "familiar" or "homely" (*Heimlichen*) (127), a view which he distinguishes from any derivation of the uncanny from the impression the powerful may make on us and which is a deliverance of our "states of feeling." Indeed, the uncanny both gives and is the ground for human beings (G53 83–91). Man is uncanny in that he both lives in the midst of what keeps him from making himself at home and, as the violent one, departs from the familiar limits within which he dwells and moves in the direction of the "uncanny in the sense of the overpowering" (IM 127). To say that man is *to deinotaton* is not to impute a property to him; Heidegger does not read Sophocles as a proto-metaphysician. Rather, "uncanniest of all" is the "basic trait [*Grundzug*] of the human essence [*Menschenwesens*] within which all other traits must find their place." Thus, *to deinotaton* gives the "authentic Greek definition of man." "We get down to the happening of uncanniness fully," Heidegger writes, "only when we experience the power of appearance and the struggle with it in its essential belonging-together [*Wesenszugehö rigkeit*] with Dasein."

The second passage, the second assault, Heidegger finds in line 360 of the choral ode, *pantoporos aporos ep' ouden erchetai*, which he renders as *Überall hinausfahrend unterwegs, erfahrungsslos ohne Ausweg kommt er zum Nichts.* In English: "Journeying underway everywhere, without experience, without passage, he comes to nothingness." The essential words, in Heidegger's view, are *pantoporos aporos.* In making himself a path (*poros*) or venturing into "all realms of Being," man is "flung out of all paths [*pantoporos*]" and is therefore without a path (*aporos.*)[24] In this condition, man shows his surpassing uncanniness. He tries, or puts to the test (*versucht*), the "totality of beings in their uncanniness" and as the violent one strives beyond his home (128). As without passage on all paths, man is finally the most uncanny because he is "cast out of every relation to the familiar and befallen by *atē*, ruin, catastrophe."

A few remarks are in order concerning the discussion of *Antigone* in the 1942 lectures devoted to Hölderlin's "The Ister." Heidegger explains that in the choral ode *deinon* is determined by "Being-homey" and its correlate, "Being-unhomey" (*Heimischseins, Unheimischseins*) —these are ways in which one can *be,* ways of Dasein's Being, modalizations of Dasein's Being-in-the-world in BT (G53 74, 76–83). He turns to Antigone herself and his account supplements, but does not reject or replace, the interpretation in IM. Antigone takes into herself what has been given—a destiny "against which one exerts oneself in vain" (122–23). In this, however, she does *not,* at least for Heidegger, follow a path antithetical to that of "man" in the choral ode.[25] The "arrogance" with which the strangest or uncanny one, "Being-unhomey," may attempt to force from beings an "escape and abode" is conditioned by its source in the "forgottenness of the hearth [*hestia*], of Being," a forgottenness it can break through "remembrance of Being and from belongingness to the hearth" (128–29). Thus, in her appropriation of death and Nothing, Antigone knows herself as belonging to Being (147). Heidegger invokes the last line of Hölderlin's "In lovely blueness . . .": "Life is death, and death is a kind of life." In the domain of Greek truth as exhibited in the tragedy of Antigone, we see that Being itself is named as the ground of "Being-homey." The "counterplay" (*Gegenspiel*) of the tragedy is not that of "religion" versus "the state," but rather the inner conflict of the *deinon* insofar as this conflict comes to language. This is to say that the way of being that is belonging to the hearth and the way of being belonging to the most uncanny are internally related. This is why Heidegger can write that "Antigone herself," then, "*is* the poem of becoming-homey [*Heimischwerden*] in Being-unhomey" (151). What Sophocles poetizes is the becoming-homey of men, which is "poetry-

worthy" (*Dichtungswürdige*) in the highest sense (152). The choral ode
stands in an inner relation to Antigone and therewith to the center of
tragic poetry, a relation that opens to Hölderlin and therewith to the
"site and wandering of historical man."

With the third passage, Heidegger finds in line 370 the phrase
hupsipolis apolis, "above the *polis*, devoid of *polis*," which completes
the uncovering of the poem's intrinsic meaning (128).[26] This phrase
points to the *polis* as the "crossing-place" (*Kreuzungsstelle*) of the multiple paths man takes into all realms of what is. The *polis* is the "ground
and site [*Grund und Ort*] of man's Dasein itself." I reproduce the entire
passage that follows, divided into what seem to me to be its articulations, with commentary (128):

> The polis is the place, the there, wherein and as which Da-sein is as
> historical. The polis is the historical site [*Geschichtsstätte*], the there, *in*
> which, *out of* which, and *for* which history happens [*Geschichte geschieht*].

The polis is a historical site in two senses; it is historically located,
and it is the site of the happening of history. This second sense, in turn,
is modified in three ways: *in, out of,* and *for* which history happens.
"In" names the place of historical happening and thereby both differentiates it from any other candidate for this status and indicates that
historical happening is *within* the polis. "Out of" names the polis as the
source *from which* historical happening emerges. "For" which names
the polis as what is in turn affected by historical happening; it is that for
the sake of which, to employ a formula from BT, history happens.

The elements of the polis, what belong to it, are named.

> To this historical site [*Geschichtsstätte*] belong the gods, the temples, the
> priests, the festivals, the games, the poets, the thinkers, the ruler, the
> council of elders, the assembly of the people, the army, and the fleet. All
> this does not first belong to the polis, does not become political by entering
> into a relation with a statesman and a general and the business of the state.

These are items in a list about which the text makes no claim for
completeness, although they are referred to collectively. The gods are
named first; the army and the fleet last. One possible internal articulation of the list is as follows: the gods, the temples, the priests, the
festivals, the games (the gods and what pertains to them); the poets,
the thinkers (those who exhibit and respond to what is); the ruler, the
council of elders, the assembly of the people, the army and the fleet

(political things as conventionally understood). What makes all of them political is not to be understood conventionally, for that sense of the political must be distinguished from the essence of the political:

> Rather, what is named is political [*das Gennante ist politisch*], that is, at the site of history [*an der Geschichtsstätte*), provided there be, for example, poets *alone,* but then really poets, priests *alone,* but then really priests, rulers *alone,* but then really rulers. Be, but this means: as violent men to use power [*Gewalttätige Gewalt*], to become high-ranking [*Hochrangende*] in historical Being [*geschichtlichen Sein*] as creators [*Schaffende*], as men of action [*Täter*].

The essential meaning of the political is explained, first with a repetition of the earlier definition—the political means a location "at the site of history"—and then with disclosure of the core meaning, which is conditional for this location. Poets, priests, and rulers—clearly identified as *examples*—must "really" (*wirklich*) be poets, priests, and rulers. "Be" (*Sind*) is a term of distinction, for it designates those who exhibit the essence of man's Being, which we recall is the basic trait with encompasses all other traits.[27]

> High-ranking in the historical place, they become at the same time *apolis,* without city and place, lonely, strange, and alien, without issue amid beings in their totality [*des Seienden im Ganzen*], at the same time without statute and limit, without structure and order, because they themselves as creators must first create all this.

The polis is the condition for *apolis.* It is only because the polis is the intersection of all paths that such men can be thrown out of all paths. The last sentence is misinterpreted if it is read simply as praise of founders, or worse, an implicit legitimizing of Hitler. I repeat a point made earlier in another context. The thought governing this passage is that *phusis,* issuing as *alētheia,* is exhibited in the "originary struggle" (*ursprünglicher Kampf*), *polemos,* the "ruling strife" (*waltender Streit*) in and through which "position and order and rank," and "cleavages, intervals, distances, and joints"—that is to say, "world"—takes place (51). *Polemos* "first projects and develops what had hitherto been unheard of [*Un-erhörte*], unsaid [*Un-gesagte*] and unthought [*Un-gedachte*]." The "creators, poets, thinkers, statesmen" are those who set the "barrier of their work" against the "overpowering power" of the *polemos* and "capture the world thus opened up"; in their works *phusis* "comes to stand in presencing" (*im Anwesendenzum Stand*) "This world-becoming [*Weltwerden*]," Heidegger writes, "is authentic history [*eigentliche Geschichte*]."

III

The Parmenides course is concerned with the transformations in *alētheia* exhibited in the history of metaphysics. In his account, Heidegger explains why the nature of the polis is misunderstood by moderns and finds in the myth of Er which concludes Plato's *Republic* the "last saying" of the Greeks on *alētheia*. The courses on Parmenides and Heraclitus reflect on what we may call the "first saying" of the Greeks. Although I am concerned primarily with the Parmenides lectures here, a brief characterization of the aims of the lecture courses is in order.[28]

In the Parmenides course Heidegger explores *alētheia* through reflections on four "indices" (*Weisungen*)—"paths," one might say—to, of, and in *alētheia*. As a matter for thinking, *alētheia* is not a Greek word, much less anything like a "concept" in ancient philosophy. It is rather a name for the movement of unconcealing and concealing. From the outset, in other words, Heidegger's intention is not philological; *that* controversy is tangential to his undertaking.[29] The indices are "crossing over" into *alētheia*, and not "translating" it, strife in *alētheia*—the emergence of "false" as the "counteressence" of "true" and "truth," a chapter in the history of Being that I have already shown is abundantly political. Openness, the sitedness of the motion of unconcealing and concealing, is the thematic environment in which the myth of Er and the essence of the polis are examined. Here Heidegger's own teaching, articulated in such themes as lighting, clearing, and freedom, brings to the study of *alētheia* thinking unavailable to the Greeks.

The Heraclitus lectures thematize *polemos, logos,* and *phusis;* they are concerned with the "inception of Western thinking," as the topic of the third lecture is characterized. There *alētheia* will eventually be understood as an "uncovering into unconcealment" that is the essence of *phusis* (G55 173). Their political dimension is of the utmost importance, for they are also concerned with the correlates of *phusis* and therewith of action. These lectures are the principal source to which we must turn to explore what Heidegger means when he speaks of thinking and acting *kata phusin.*

Both sets of lectures are political in a more topical sense, for they both contain remarks concerning events or the significance of events in

the war. These remarks have their places in the structure and movement of Heidegger's thinking concerning the Greeks—and the Germans, for the events of the war are understood from the standpoint of a
concern with and defense of the historical mission of the Germans.

The treatise *Being and Time* is an index (*Hinweis*) of *Ereignis*, showing that Being itself has sent an inceptive experience (*anfänglichere
Erfahrung*) to Western *Menschentum* (G54 114). This collectivity is
identified quite clearly as the *German* people. The originary (*ursprüng-
lichere*) inception can come to pass only as the first inception (*erste
Anfang*) in a Western historical people of poets and thinkers. With a
"self-springing up of consciousness of their mission" (*Sendungsbe-
wusstsein*), the people, having come up against the experience of chaos,
will no longer need Heidegger's lines as they take their position in the
destiny of the West and of the world. Indeed, "when it comes to 'victory'
[*Siegen*], this historical people has already won and is unconquerable
[*unbesiegbar*] so long as it remains the people of poets and thinkers that
it is in its essence, so long as it does not fall victim to the ever-pressing
and thus fearful threat of straying from, and thereby misunderstanding,
its essence." While this lecture course was being given, the German
offensive against the Soviet Union stalled at Stalingrad and collapsed
in January 1943. Nonetheless, Heidegger writes in the Heraclitus lectures: "The Germans, and they alone, can save the West for its history"
(G55 108). A few pages later: "The planet is in flames. Only from the
Germans can there come a world-historical reflection—if, that is, they
find and preserve 'the German essence'" (123).[30]

Both lectures begin with a goddess; the gods are seldom far from the
lines of thinking deployed in the texts. The Parmenides lectures begins
with Aletheia; the Heraclitus lecture with Artemis. As preparation for
his reflections, Heidegger emphasizes that the Greek thinkers cannot
be understood as primitives, protoscientists, mystics, and the like (G54
1–23; G55 5–43). Against religious and theological interpretations of
Heraclitus, he writes: "There is no Greek religion at all," for "the word
religio and its matter are romish essences" (G55 13). Since there is no
Greek religion, moreover, there can be no "Greek theology." Discourse
about the gods, then, is radically other than what the tradition has
understood it to be.

Heidegger recounts two stories about Heraclitus (G55 6–13). From
Aristotle comes the story in which Heraclitus says that in his stove, too,
there are gods (*De partibus animalium* 645a17). From Diogenes Laer-

tius comes the story in which Heraclitus, playing a game with children in the temple of Artemis, asks bystanders whether it is better to play children's games or to care about the polis (9.3). Heraclitus the thinker dwells, Heidegger says, at an intersection of the familiar, the canny, and the uncanny (7–9). What is uncanny: the gods "reach into" the stove. We shall see in the Parmenides lectures that the gods also "look into" the polis. The domain of the thinker is one of *eris*, strife; the thinker dwells in the nearness of strife (9). In both stories it is also evident that the thinker dwells near the gods (10–11). In the first story, the word of the thinker is inviting, encouraging, while in the second story it is not. This is because in the second story, Heraclitus seems to care nothing for the polis (11). Heidegger dismisses the modern view of such a thinker as "unpolitical," as limited to his own "private existence" (11–12). When "thought Greekly" (*griechisch gedacht*), the care of the gods is the highest care, in which is the true care of the polis. The thinker, who cares about the gods, is the "authentic 'political' man [*eigentlich 'politisch' Mensch*]," truly concerned with the polis (12). The lectures contain a setting-apart of the true from the false senses of the political.

At the beginning of his account of the myth of Er (130–82), Heidegger explains that the history of the Greeks, the way in which they stand open to, or undergo, history, is exhibited in the event of forgetting. That is, the Greeks dwell in the site governed by the relation of *lēthē* and *alētheia,* which lies beneath their saying and thinking. "In Plato's thinking," Heidegger says, "the Greeks complete themselves" (131). The inceptive sense of "truth" is found in *lēthē* as the counteressence (*Gegenwesen*) of *alētheia.* The inceptive saying of the Greeks takes the form of myth, within which the movement of withdrawing concealment, of *lēthē* within and against, yet always with, *alētheia* can be heard. The relation *lēthē* ↔ *alētheia,* then, is more fundamental than, because it conditions the polis as, the site of the happening of history.

The "thinking saying" (*denkende Sagen*) gives itself, in the completion of Greek thinking, in the thinking of Plato, in the form of the dialogue (131–32). Plato's dialogue concerning the polis has nothing to do with a theory of the state; neither the Roman *res publica* nor the modern state (*neuzeitlichen Staat*) are genuine equivalents of the polis, nor is the *politeia* of the dialogue a "constitution" (*Verfassung*) in any modern sense or a utopia, without a site (*u-topos*) (132). What is discerned through reflection on the myth of Er is the essence of the polis, exhibited in and as its *politeia.* In thinking what the polis as such is, the thinker says what and how the polis unfolds or essences (*west*), but the *politeia* of the polis is "not unambiguous" (*nicht eindeutig*) (140). As the site in which insight into the truth of Being happens, the polis encompasses the motion of unconcealing and concealing. It is precisely the opposite of a utopia, "namely the metaphysically determined site of the essence of the polis. Plato's *Politeia* is a recollection in essentiality [*Wesenhafte*] and not a plan in facticity [*Faktische*]" (141). As the "essential site of historical men," the polis is the temporal "where" wherein men are as *zōion logon echōn,* where history is gathered. The Greeks exhibit the gathering and safeguarding (*Sammlung und Verwahrung*) of *alētheia.* The thoughtless (*gedankenlose*) activity of "historical research" (*historischen Forschung*) fails to recover what is essential in the Greeks, producing instead only a historical mush (*Brei*). Thus, neither Christian understandings of God nor modern atheism can be a starting point for understanding the Greeks (162–68). Indeed, in a strict sense "atheism" is not a philosophical position at all but is rather the loss of the gods which takes place with the decline of the Greek world (166–67). Its use in other contexts is ultimately incoherent.

Tragedy articulates the "decline" of the Greeks and is not to be understood from positions such as that of Spengler, who understands "cultures" as if they were biological processes (168). Heidegger understands the "decline" of the Greeks as an exhibition of the forgetting of inception, which is a "happening of the essential decision of the essence of truth" that governs forgetting, and is necessitated by the relation of *lēthē* and *alētheia.* Heidegger's account of the polis precedes and governs his interpretation of the myth of Er, which is to say that he understands the polis apart from the myth constructed by Socrates. The passage offers an account of the original of which the myth of Er is an image. It restates, by refining, the teaching of IM on the polis (IM 128).

> What is the polis? When we bring an essential insight into the Greek experience of the essence of Being and truth—an essential insight that illuminates everything—then the word itself gives us the right indication. Polis is the *polos,* the pole, the place around which, in a peculiar way, revolves everything which appeared to the Greeks in beings. The pole is the place around which all beings turn and precisely in such a way that in the domain of this place beings show their turning and their condition. As this place, the pole lets beings appear in their Being and show the totality

of their condition. The pole neither makes nor creates beings in their Being, but as the pole it is the site of the unconcealedness of beings as a whole. The polis is the essence of the site, so we speak of the sitedness of the historical dwelling of Greek humanity. Because the polis always let the whole of beings come forward in the unconcealedness of its involvement in some way or another, the polis is essentially related to the Being of beings. Between polis and Being an inceptive [*anfänglicher*] relation rules. (132–33; cf. G53 100–101).

As the site of the motion of *lēthē* and *alētheia*, of the strife in *alētheia*, the polis is the inceptive ground (*anfängliche Grund*) of what Jacob Burckhardt was the first to recognize as the horror (*Furchtbarkeit*), the shocking (*Grauenhafte*), the disastrous (*Unheil*) heard by the Greeks (133–34). This is the condition of men in their ascent and downfall (*Aufstieg und Absturz*) in their historical site of essencing named by Sophocles, as we have already seen, with the words *hupsipolis apolis*, projecting high above the site and deprived of it (134). From the ground of the struggle in the essence of *alētheia*, and thus out of the relation of polis and *alētheia*, comes the possibility and necessity of tragedy itself. It is only *Greek* tragedy that is made possible and necessary, for it is only the essence of the Greek experience of Being that can be the inception of tragedy. The darkness in *alētheia*—or perhaps we should say more precisely the darkness accompanying the movement of withdrawl, of *lēthē*—makes possible tragedy as its response.

IV

The myth of the cave and the myth of Er figure *alētheia* and *lēthē* respectively (135–40). The polis as the site of essencing of historical man is necessarily a location of the violence of un-essencing, where disaster is heard (135). The movements of the unconcealing and concealing of beings as such in their totality compose what Heidegger calls *Zugefügt*, the joining, or putting into position of beings (136–37). In his interpretation of the Anaximander fragment, Heidegger understands the presencing of beings as the occurrence of the while as transition (*Übergang*) between unconcealing and unconcealing (EGT 41–42). The location of presencing is between the "twofold absence" of approach and withdrawal, that is, in a joining (*Füge*), which is Heidegger's translation of *dikē*. In the Parmenides lectures, *Fug, dikē* names the positioning or emplacing of beings and men in the historical site of the polis (G54 137). *Dikē* names the "joining organizing [*das fügende Gefüge*] which compels adaptation and compliance"; it exhibits *deinon* as the overpowering and is the correlate of *technē* as the exhibition of *deinon* as violence (IM 134–35). The relation *dikē : adikia* as the struggle between the rule which governs the transit of beings in the juncture and the resistance of beings as their perseverance in presencing is inscribed in the *Republic's* thematic of justice, *dikaiosuné*. That is, the movement of men into, and their dwelling within, what is genuinely or ultimately appropriate for them is *Fugsamkeit*, pliancy, which is Heidegger's rendering of *dikaiosunē*. What is sought in the *Republic*, then, is the way in which such pliancy as a way of being for man can be reached. I go, I believe, only slightly beyond the letter of Heidegger's text, in saying that what is required for the teaching of pliancy is a measure for man's sojourn in the polis. This measure is provided in and by Plato's account of the course of life as a *periodos thanatophoros*, a "death-gravid passage," after which men transit the time-space (*Zeitraum*) and begin life anew (G54 138). The horizon of the polis, its measure, is the teaching of the myth of Er.

As a temporal site, the polis is historically from the earth, the "here" (*enthade*) (143). It is the site of the "course of life" (*Lebenslauf*), of the passage men make from concealment to unconcealment and back to unconcealment, from "here" to "there," *enthade* to *ekei*, from life to death and back to life. Men must pass over, as Er does, to the *topos daimonios*, the "daimonic place." The movement of souls from the polis to the *topos daimonios* and back also traverses the relation between *lēthē* and *alētheia*. Or perhaps we should say that the passage along the *periodos* simply *is* the performance of the identity within difference of unconcealment and concealment.

The daimonic is the *Un-Geheur*, the "uncanny," the vast, uncommon, unfamiliar, but *not* the "monstrous"; it is really the nearest of the near, *phusis* itself (150). "For the Greeks," he reminds us, "the astonishing is the simple, the plain [fact] of Being itself." What the Greeks show, but do not and cannot think, what is exhibited in the myth of Er, is that the uncanny conditions the "canny," the beings that presence. Thus, Heidegger writes of the "uncanny in the canny" (*des Un-geheuren in das Geheure*). *To daimonion* is the "essence and essential ground of the uncanny. It is that which proffers itself to the canny and comes to presence in it" (151). The movement of the daimonic is the movement of *phusis.* Accordingly, the daimonic, the dark radically other, has nothing to do with any notion of an evil spirit or spirits. Heidegger associates *daimonion* with *daiō,* "to look, to offer something to be seen" (152–55). For the Greeks the gods look and reach into the polis toward the unconcealed there, movements which must be gathered in and by looking, in which the uncanny becomes more familiar and can be represented as it is in myth (154). The Greeks are superior to the moderns in their sense of the nature and significance of the look, although it is precisely the look, the "tranquil light of openness," that is distorted by *hubris,* which Heidegger translates as "mismeasurement" (*Vermessenheit*) (160; G55 326–27). The "gods," then, "those who gaze into the unconcealed and who, thus gazing, signal," are the same as the Daimones (161; cf. G55 8). If we go on to read this account so that "gods" and Daimones give way to "Being," then it is evident, in Manfred Frings's words, that "man is constantly 'looked at' by the openness of Being. Being's look comes to man, it is not a 'subjective' activity. Being's look is nothing human, but belongs to the essence of Being in its appearing and unconcealing."[31]

The uncanny becomes "canny," for as the gathering of the uncanny look and the gods' reaching into the polis become increasingly familiar to men, the gods themselves are given human or animal forms as in mythology (161–62). This is the origin of what moderns call anthropomorphism, but for Heidegger the importance of this transformation lies in what it shows about our relation to the uncanny in the emergence of Being: the canny is conditioned by the uncanny. Heidegger remarks that the Enlightenment never understood any of this correctly, mistaking mythology for a cultural product and thereby ignoring the conditioning role of the uncanny. The inscription of the gods into the "ordering of presencing" (*Anwesenheit*), found in poetic thinking, Heidegger writes elsewhere, is "the ground and the base of the polis as the essence-state in history determined from the Holy" (G4 88). In this way "the polis determines 'the political,'" a determination that "can never be decided from the polis itself concerning its ground and grounding." That is, the political in its genuine sense remains related to the gods, although it is impossible to understand this fully from the standpoint *of* the polis.

The *daimonion* shines in myth as word and "word-having" (*Worthaben*), which is to say, as the foundation of man's being (170–73). Plato and Aristotle understand the essence of man in terms of *eudai-*

monia, misunderstood in the "roman-christian" interpretation as beatitude and then as "happiness" (*Glückseligkeit*). *Eudaimonia* means, rather, that the "*eu*-appearance and estimable look of the *daimonion* rules in accordance with measure." The "socratic-platonic discourse" concerning the *daimonion* exhibits, then, the inner determination of man (174). It is this, unconcealed, that is said in saying, the uncanny said in myth. It is also the meaning of the title of Plato's dialogue concerning the essence of the polis presented as *daimonios topos,* that is, the *myth* of Er. Thus it is that *topos* is the "Greekish" (*grieschisch*) site, the essence of which is the "particular where" to which those beings that must have a site belong. In its Greek sense this site is never completely familiar, never completely canny. As the site of the motion of *alētheia* and *lēthē,* it is uncanny as well. The topology of the uncanny would be a discourse in principle incapable of complete transparency and thus in closest correspondence to that which it brings to speech.

The site of the myth is the subterranean and the supraterranean where the uncanny dwells (175). Heidegger is concerned primarily with the plain of forgetfulness which is traversed by the souls of the dead after they have chosen their next lives and have undergone the operations of the Fates to inscribe their choices in ordinary human time (620d6–621b7). In his translation, the *to tēs lēthēs pedion,* "the field of forgetfulness," is the field of "withdrawing concealment in the sense of forgetting" (*entziehenden Verbergung im Sinne der Vergessung*). On this plain can be found the demonic of the afterlife in its utmost (*aussersten*) and highest sense. Heidegger emphasizes that this barren field is devoid of all that grows naturally on the earth (621a3f), which is to say that it is opposed to *phusis* (176). *Lēthē,* then, allows no *phuein* and shines as the counteressence (*Gegenwesen*) of *phusis.* Our conventional understandings of *phusis* as "nature" and of *lēthē* as a psychological process of forgetting make this part of the myth unintelligible. If, in contrast, *phusis* names emergence, the presencing of beings, then *lēthē* prevents (*verwehrt*) the revealing of beings and the canny; it names the movement of withdrawal in which withdrawing withdraws itself. Withdrawing, then, is pure forgetting. As the counteressence of *phusis,* it is sheer withdrawing, as *phusis* is sheer presencing. The field as a site remains empty (*leer*) and is as such the most uncanny. However, the emptiness (*Leere*) is here what remains and presences. "The emptiness of the site," Heidegger says, "is the look [*Blick*] that looks into and fills itself." The "singular exclusiveness" (*eigentümlichen Ausschliesslichkeit*) of this site makes it the location of the demonic.

The wandering souls must stop and make their camp by the river, the essence of which is *lēthē* and which is called *amelēs* (621a4ff.), which Heidegger translates as *Ohnesorge*, "without care" (176–77). Heidegger thus inscribes his own understanding of care (*Sorge*) as the structure of Dasein's Being in the characterization of the river in the myth (cf. BT 236–38). The care which the river does not have is distinguished from any mere concern with troubles or the external condition of the world and men (G54 177). Care in its proper sense in the myth is care as linked intrinsically with *alētheia*, with the unconcealment of beings. "Care," Heidegger says, "belongs to the *Ereignis* of the essencing of revealing and concealing." The absence of care (*Sorglosigkeit*) is also understood ontologically here, from its account in BT (BT 237). The water of the river cannot be contained in any vessel, and the river itself can have no bed. The river is rather pure flow or flux with no structure, which means that it knows nothing of and cares nothing for the unconcealment of beings (G54 177). The absence of care understood in its proper sense in the myth is indifference to *alētheia*, given the rule of *lēthē*. Both care and carelessness are located in the realm of the demonic. Heidegger's insistence on this point exhibits his emphasis on the uncanny as inextricably linked not only to the relation of *alētheia* and *lēthē* but to the location of Greek humanity and the polis in a site which it bounds.

All of the souls must drink the water of the river, but some, saved by insight (*phronēsis*), drink only the right measure, while others drink to excess (621a7f.) (178). The souls forget all they have seen and undergone, and they forget the forgetting as well. Heidegger's gloss makes explicit the relation between *phronēsis* and philosophy intimated in much of his work:

> Phronesis means here the insight [*Einsicht*] of that in-seeing [*Ein-sehens*], which has a sight into what is authentically seeable and unconcealed. The seeing meant here is the looking of the gaze into the essence, that is, of "philosophy." *Phronēsis* means here the same as philosophy, and the title says: to have sight for what is essential. Philosophy is man's look into the look of Being that is coming toward him. Thus, for the Greeks, philosophy has sense of saving what shines, of preserving the self-shining [*Sichzeigende*] *as* the self-shining. Accordingly, philosophy in its original sense has

nothing to do with general conceptualizing. Rather, philosophy is the self-speaking-being of Being itself [*das Angesprochensein vom Sein selbts*]. (179)

Those without philosophy are without insight. They have drunk more than the measure. Although they belong to a people of poets and thinkers, such people are nonetheless care-less and thought-less. In these times, Heidegger adds, the ministry of propaganda characterizes the Germans rightly as no longer a people of poets and thinkers but rather of corn and oil.

Heidegger continues his account of philosophy by characterizing it as attentiveness to the claim of Being on man, which is before all else the care of Being rather than *Bildung* and knowing. Philosophy is not the totality of philosophical opinions about Being. Indeed, it is possible for one to be overflowing or soaked with the claim of Being without knowing it or thinking in accord with it. A knowledge and precision of consciousness and words belongs freely to truly *thinking* thinking (*denkenden Denke*) which exceeds the demands of scientific exactitude. Such thinking remains after the Greek thinker's experience of the shining of the unconcealed before the concealing in the sense of the concealed withdrawal, which is the originary experience in thinking (179–80). The thinker must drink the right measure of water from the river. Seeing, as the essential glimpses of authentic thinking, is not produced from itself but is, as habitual seeing and seeing ahead, a reversal of a mistake, that is, the reversal of drinking to excess (180). Heidegger concludes this paragraph with a question: "How does it stand with those who not only drink more than the measure but who always drink only this water?" Such a one could not dwell on earth as a man, for unconcealment would not take place for him; "complete, measureless oblivion . . . would exclude the least ground of the essence of man, because such oblivion would allow no disclosure and would deny unconcealedness its essential foundation" (183).

Plato leaves the relation between the field and *lēthē* undetermined; Heidegger articulates the relation (180–81). What is at issue here is whether and how any relation of priority obtains between the two. The field and its field-character (*Feldcharakter*) belong to *lēthē*, but the field and *lēthē* are not divided from each other. That is, *lēthē* itself is field. Although Heidegger does not use the device of parataxis here, the sense of his analysis, I think, can be summarized in the relation field :

lēthē. Withdrawing concealment is not simply given in a field but rather enfolds as the Where (*Wo*) of beings. To understand unconcealment, then, calls for an understanding of the location of and for unconcealment which recognizes the intrinsic withdrawing concealment found at this location. Thus the field of *lēthē* is given for thinking. The field together with the other sites composes the *topos daimonios*, a "daimonische Ortschaft."

The myth of Er articulates the Greek experience of the gods as the reaching of the uncanny into the familiar, of the demonic into the polis. The account of the demonic leads to an understanding of the essence of the gods. Withdrawing concealment is the condition for the preservation of *alētheia*, which we fail to recognize adequately because of the distance (*Ferne*) between the Greek gods and ourselves. Moreover, this distance is itself a happening (*Ereignis*) of our history. We stand, Heidegger says, in the danger posed for our understanding of the relation of concealment and unconcealment by a "literary way" of understanding the Greeks, found in books, addresses, and feuilletons written from the perspective of the history of religion or culture. The way to the gods is through the word, "but the word cannot be 'literature.'" The everydayness of the divine is the basis for the "Dionysian" understanding of the Greeks found in Nietzsche, but his perspective, as we have already seen for Heidegger, shares the defects of the uncritical biologism of the late nineteenth century (182). Heidegger concludes his discussion by reminding us that the condition for the preservation of *alētheia* lies in the withdrawing concealment of *lēthē*, which attunes man to unconcealment. Apart from the uncanny, *alētheia* is unintelligible. In Plato's myth the field of *lēthē* is the final location, the condition of all conditions, from which the wandering soul rises to earth. The uncanny belongs essentially to the emergence and appearance of Being and is not an addition (cf. OTB 71). This is why *alētheia* and *lēthē* seem godlike, *theion*. Now we understand why *alētheia* is for Parmenides Aletheia, the goddess. This is not merely poetry, as philology maintains, but is instead the "naming of the site of Being, where the thinker as thinker stands" (188). It is not available to us now.

The conclusion of the lectures returns us to our present time (240–43). For the Greeks, as exhibited in Parmenides, the essence of truth is a goddess; *thea* is *alētheia* (240–41). The final question, however, is, "What is truth for us?" (241). Parmenides' answer cannot be our answer; because we do not know who we are, "we know it not" (*Wir wissen es nicht*). Perhaps this "twofold nescience [*Unwissenheit*] concerning truth and ourselves is one and the same," Heidegger writes. This situation is "already good," for thinking, which is "not knowing" (*kein Wissen*), happens in the nearness of Being that is most distant. We do not know the essence of truth but are thereby able to experience what conditions the question-worthiness of the question: "The condition is that we thinkingly [*Denkende*] become." Heidegger emphasizes that these reflections belong together from "*an* insight," for our thinking the essence of truth is needed precisely because we "walk on the utmost edge of beings in their totality." Thus, we know that "a moment of history is near," a "singularity" (*Einzigkeit*) that "determines itself" from the "standing of the beingly [*seienden*] world and our own history." What is at stake is more than but, I note, does not include the "Being and Nonbeing" of "our historical people," of a "'european' 'culture.'" Before these is the necessity for an "inceptive decision" about Being and Nonbeing "in the truth of their essence." Another reminder of what is at stake: "How can beings become free in their essence when the essence of Being is undecided, unquestioned and therewith forgotten?" There is no "constancy [*Beständigkeit*] of beings without the truth of Being," and without both this truth and the Being and essence of truth there remains the decision about the Being and Nonbeing of beings without the openness of freedom" (241–42).

History "sends" (*schickt*) beings "always again and always only in the destiny of goings-under [*Unterganges*] in long-lasting concealments [*Verbergungen*]" (243). Heidegger names the West—the *Abendland*—from the way in which *Geschick* rules: the "goings-under," the "declines," the "evening (*Abend*) of the inceptive risings." The land of this "history in its time-space" is the "evening-land" (*Abend-Land*) after an inceptive (i.e., after a "being-historical [*seinsgeschichtlichen*]) sense of this word." "The evening-landish [*abendländische*] saying says the inception," Heidegger writes, "that is, the concealing essence of the truth of Being." This word "guards the belongingness of Western humanity [*Menschentums*] to the house domain of the goddess Aletheia." Heidegger has named the way in which our time belongs to Aletheia, but there remains the question of whether or how another way of belonging is possible. For this question it is necessary to turn to Hölderlin.

7 Poetic Dwelling: Homeland

> The age for which the ground fails to come, hangs in the
> abyss. Assuming that a turn still remains open for this
> destitute time at all, it can come some day only if the world
> turns about fundamentally—and that now means,
> unequivocally: if it turns away from the abyss. In the age of
> the world's night, the abyss of the world must be experienced
> and endured. But for this it is necessary that there be those
> who reach into the abyss.
>
> "What Are Poets For?" (PLT 92)

IN THE "BREAK-OUT" (*Aufbruch*) of Greek philosophy, "Western man
[*abendländische Mensch*] first raises himself up from his nationality
[*Volkstum*] and, by virtue of his language, against the *totality of what is*
[*auf gegen das Seiende im Ganzen*], which he questions and conceives
as the being that it is" (RA 471–72). Western man stands up from a
"nationality," a determinate people. Thus, the break-out of Greek philosophy means first that it is from *this* nationality that Western man
arises and second that it is from a *nationality* that this activity springs.[1]
This thought is continued in the *Beiträge*. While it is simplistic to hold
that the great inception of Western philosophy is the philosophy of the
"Greek people," and the "great end" of Western philosophy is "German
idealism" and "Nietzsche" (i.e., philosophy of the "German people"),
the issue is to determine precisely how philosophy and "the people"
are linked (G65 42). What must be asked: "Through what does a people
become a people? . . . What is a people? . . . What are we ourselves?"
Before these questions all "platonizing ways of thinking" break down.
For Heidegger "reflection on the folklike [*Volkhafte*] is an essential
passage," for "a higher rank of Being will be attained if a '*völkisches*
principle,' as determinative for historical Da-sein is mastered and

brought into play." The people "first becomes a people" when it "comes into its ownmost [*Einzigsten*]" and returns to its beginning (43). Philosophy indeed shapes a people, "grounds that people historically in its Da-sein and determines it guardianship of the truth of Being." "This people is in its origin and determination," he writes, "only according to the singular occurrence [*Einzigkeit*] of Being, whose truth it must ground in a singular place in a singular moment" (97). Rejecting all understandings of "the people" grounded in world-views, the "essence of the people can be understood only from Da-sein," that is, from the site from which the people is intelligible (G65 319; cf. 25, 134, 139, 142). While the "essence of the people" is its "voice," this voice "speaks seldom and only in the few, if it can be brought to sound."

In this final chapter I shall turn to Heidegger's encounter with Hölderlin, the poet of "German destiny," the "voice of the [German] people" as Homer was of the Greeks (G39 134). "As the poet of poets," Heidegger writes, "Hölderlin has a singular historical position and mission [*Stellung und Sendung*] . . . [he] is the poet of the future Germans and the only one" (220–21).[2] At the outset it is essential to understand that Heidegger's reflections on Hölderlin's poetry are not "interpretations" or "readings" in any conventional literary sense. They are, rather, as the title of one of the collections of them has it, *Erläuterungen*—"elucidations," in the dictionary definition—"soundings" of the poems in and through which Heidegger registers their evocations.[3] The *Erläuterungen*, to be sure, "arise from a necessity of thinking" and belong to a "discourse of thinking with poetizing" (G4 7; cf. G50 136–45), but they are "observations" (*Ammerkungen*) from the "danger, the truth of Hölderlin's poetizing," belonging to Heidegger's intention to "create a space and site [*Raum und Ort*] for our historical Dasein," where "our" names the German Dasein (G53 1–2; G39 213). Indeed, the first person plural in the Hölderlin lectures and essays is, alongside anything else it might be, almost always a reference to the Germans. What many interpreters criticize as Heidegger's "misreadings" of Hölderlin (and other poets) I want to characterize as *political* readings; in my view such readings are integral to Heidegger's reflections on the relations of poetry and thinking.[4] "Hölderlin" names, among other matters, the political pedagogy, the *paideia*, of the Germans, a path I shall trace in Heidegger's texts.

Heidegger's choice of Hölderlin is a "historical decision" (*geschichtliche Entscheidung*) with three essential grounds (G39 214): (1) as the "poet of poets," he thinks and poetizes the "essence of poetry," which can never be gathered properly under any sort of "universal concept" (G4 33–34; G39 221; G53 34); (2) he is the poet of the Germans (G39 214, 220); (3) since he is the thus-far hidden and powerful poet of poets and poet of the Germans, he must become what he already truly is, a "power [*Macht*] in the history of our people."[5] "To contribute to this task," Heidegger writes, "is 'politics' in the highest and authentic sense" (*im höchsten und eigentlichen Sinne*), so that "who effects [*erwirkt*] something here has no necessity to speak about 'politics'" (G39 214). Politics thought and brought about in and through Hölderlin, the most genuine German politics, is a politics that no longer belongs to everyday chatter; as essential politics, it is great politics.

"Hölderlin" names the present age, with "Nietzsche," surpassing him. Our historical site makes it essential to arrive at an appropriate understanding of Hölderlin," for "we stand before a decision between the end," Heidegger writes, "and another beginning," and what falls into this domain is our *"preparation or unpreparation* for the future," which has nothing to do with optimism or pessimism (G45 124). The domain "first opens itself," he goes on, *"when* it unfolds itself according to its originariness [*Ursprünglichkeit*]" from our "lostness" (*Verlorenheit*) in "machination and busyness" and our "entanglement" (*Verfängnis*) in the self-understanding of the present. We are brought to Nietzsche and Hölderlin because we stand in the domain of the end of the first inception of Western history in which they belong together (G45 125–27; cf. G52 84). Hölderlin is understood as the poet of the fatherland, but this role is misinterpreted when he is regarded as a folk hero, or in "Christian" terms, or as a poet situated between classicism and Romanticism, thereby to be discussed along with Klopstock, Herder, Goethe, Schiller, and Kleist. When Hölderlin sings of the "Fatherland," he is not singing of "noisy patriotism" (G39 120). Indeed, "our fatherland Germany," Heidegger writes, is, as Hölderlin poetized it in "Germanien," "forbidden most of all, removed from everyday haste and busy noise," that is, a mystery inaccessible to the vulgar (4). Heidegger does not seek a "cheap timely relevance" for the poet, nor does he wish to adapt him to the present, but rather to "bring us and those after us under the measure [*Mass*] of the poet." Hölderlin exhibits an authentic response to and bearing up under what is in the present epoch, as distinguished from "christian-moralistic-psychological" (*christlich-moralisch-psychologisch*) thinking (G45 175). Moreover, the inner relation between the Greeks and the Germans has nothing to do with humanism (G53 155; LH 219). Hölderlin is the pivotal figure of the present age because, although he suffered the need of the age and was shattered by it, as were Kierkegaard and Nietzsche, he alone allows truth to appear as the Holy, even in the age of the death of God (G65 204). "In the age of the world's night, the abyss of the world must be experienced and endured," Heidegger writes, "but for this it is necessary that there be those who reach into the abyss" (PLT 92). Hölderlin is the "most futural" (*Zukünftigste*) poet because he hears from the greatest distance (G65 401). He must be understood as having "already overcome the time-space-less work [*zeit-raum-loses Werk*] of our historical circumstance" and "having grounded the inception of an other history, a history commencing with the struggle and decision regarding the advent or flight of the gods" (G39 1).

Two other invocations of "Hölderlin" indicate his political role. In OWA art is "in its essence" originary; it is a way in which truth happens, becoming historical and thus ingredient in the "historical Dasein of a people" (PLT 77–78). "We" ask the question concerning the essence of art "in order to be able to ask more authentically [*eigentlicher*] whether art is or is not an origin in our historical Dasein, whether and under what conditions it can and must be an origin." With its reference to *our* historical Dasein, the question about art is shown to be a political question. What the movement questioning provides is the "preliminary and therefore indispensable preparation for the becoming of art" by preparing "space for the work," a "site for sojourning" (*dem Werk den Raum Ortschaft, Ortschaft des Aufenhaltes*) (PLT 86, 79, 78). What "is decided" (*entscheidet sich*) is *whether* "art can be an origin" and thus a "leap forward" (*Vorsprung*), or whether it will *remain* a mere "appearance of culture." Heidegger's fundamental political question then appears in one of its variants: "Are we in our historical Dasein at the origin? Do we know, which means do we give heed to, the essence [*Wesen*] of the origin? Or, in our relation to art, do we still merely make appeals to a cultivated acquaintance with the past?" This "either-or and its decision" is marked by an "infallible sign" named by Hölderlin, "the poet, whose work still confronts the Germans as a test to be stood."

In LH, Heidegger inscribes Hölderlin in his own criticisms of the defective understandings of action found in existentialism and Marxism with the claim that unlike these teachings that belong entirely to modern metaphysics—indeed, unlike any humanism—the poet "thought the destiny of man's essence more inceptively [*anfänglicher*] than 'humanism' could" (LH 201–3; cf. G39 47–51; G53 67–68). Metaphysics and humanism fail to understand the true rank of man's *humanitas* because they cannot understand that and how man is thrown from Being into its truth, and thus decided by and in the movement of "presencing" and "absencing" (*an- und abwesen*) in response to the sheer "there is" / "it gives" (*es gibt*), the "self-giving into the open, along with the open region itself," that is Being, and that "rules as the *Geschick* of Being" (LH 214–15). Although *Geschick* is exhibited in "the words of essential thinkers," even Hegel's subsumption of history into his philosophical system is inferior to Hölderlin's inceptive thinking, which thinks the history of Being to which it belongs as "recollection [*Andenken*] of this history that unfolds of itself." In so doing, Hölderlin outstrips Hegel, for while the thinker sought the ground of modernity, the poet sought to break through that ground and thus go beyond modernity (G15 287). Standing beyond Nietzsche's reversal of metaphysics, which could not furnish a solution to modern homelessness, Hölderlin's poetizing "first determines a new time. It is the time of the gods that have fled and of the god that is coming. It is the time of need [*dürftiger Zeit*] because it lies under a double lack [*Mangel*] and double Not [*Nicht*]. The no-more [*Nichtmehr*] of the fleeing gods and the not-yet [*Nochnicht*] of the coming gods" (G4 47). Hölderlin "poetically invents the Germans," for he comes from and is their future (G39 220, 225); the decision concerning the flight or the coming of the gods belongs to the Germans.

The deepest political dimension of Heidegger's engagement with Hölderlin is drawn from a letter written by Hölderlin to Casimir Ulrich Böhlendorff in December of 1801 in which the poet explains the relation between the Germans and the Greeks through a reflection on the relation between the essential characteristic or quality of a people, its "own" (*Eigene*), and that people's "foreign" (*Fremde*). Cited in a number of texts, including the Hölderlin readings and the Nietzsche lectures, taken up and disseminated across an immense range of reflections, this relation is fundamental in Heidegger's political thinking.[6]

Hölderlin writes:

> We learn nothing with more difficulty than to freely use the national. And, I believe that it is precisely the clarity of presentation that is so originarily natural to as as is for the Greeks the fire from heaven. . . . For exactly that

reason they will have to be surpassed in beautiful passion . . . rather than in that Homeric presence of mind and talent for presentation . . . in the progress of education the truly national will become the ever less attractive. Hence the Greeks are less master of the sacred pathos, because to them it was inborn, whereas they excel in their talent for presentation. . . . With us it is the reverse. Hence it is also so dangerous to deduce the rules of art for oneself exclusively from Greek excellence. I have labored long over this and know by now that, with the exception of what must be the highest for the Greeks and for us—namely, the living relationship and destiny—we must not share anything identical with them.

Yet what is familiar must be learned as well as what is alien. This is why the Greeks are so indispensable for us. It is only that we will not follow them in our own, national [spirit] since, as I said, the *free use of what is one's own* is the most difficult.

The foreign of the Greeks is clarity of representation; its ownmost is heavenly fire. The foreign of the Germans is heavenly fire; its ownmost is clarity of representation. In the relation of "own" and "foreign," Heidegger's attention is devoted to "own." What is a people's "own" may be understood as having, or being, a movement articulated as its own lack; an "own" is incomplete, yet, to borrow language from BT, is a coming toward itself and thus a becoming what it already is. The temporal structure of the relation of "own" and "foreign" is one of projection and retrieval. In projecting its lack onto the "foreign," the "own" retrieves itself authentically. Its being is a being-possible, which inscribes in it the relation of resolution and finitude. The task of becoming what it already is cannot be completed. If we must think of these movements as mimetic, then they imitate the movement of unconcealing and concealing. The articulation of that movement is that concealing is the condition for unconcealing—*lēthē* in *alētheia*—and unconcealing of necessity conceals concealing, which in turn lets concealing exhibit as absence. An "own" is always coming to stand in its site; while it is self-founding, it is self-limiting, as any "authentic" Heideggerian founding must be. What is sought, as the poet says, is the "free use of what is one's own." Freeing and use must become determinate in and at and as a *time; kairos,* as Heidegger had spoken of it in the 1920s, is inscribed here, which means that to know one's "own," one must have an insight into what is, an understanding of a historical site. The task of the German people is its historical mission, hence, its political mission. While this movement is intelligible in and as poetry, the sense of limit, the compound movement of presencing ↔ absencing that is integral to the as-structure, means that nothing like full discursive intelligibility is to be sought in poetry. The power of poetry, or of authentic poetry, is made possible by Being: "Being permits poetry to emerge, in order to find itself in an originary [*ursprünglich*] way within it and hence in a closed manner to open itself up as a mystery [*Geheimnis*]" (G39 237).

BT was intended to show "time as a first name for the projective realm of the truth of Being. 'Time' as the ecstatic Between (time-space) [*Zeit-Raum*], not the wherein of beings, but the opening of Being itself" (ST 189); "thinking the most difficult thought of philosophy means thinking Being as time" (N1 20). I invoke these texts to situate Heidegger's task in thinking German identity; "we" must be determined from the horizon of the question of time (G39 49–59). What must be thought together is the time of the poet and the "originary time of the peoples" (*ursprüngliche Zeit der Völker*) (49). When and what is the time of the German people, as articulated in Hölderlin? Is it, Heidegger asks, 1801, 1934, 1980, or no year at all? We "do not know our own authentic historical time. The world-hour [*Weltstunde*] of our people is hidden from us. We do not know who we are, when we ask our authentic timely question concerning our Being" (50). The time of the people is thought from the line from "As on a holiday . . .": "Now breaks the day! / And my word for what I saw shall be the Holy." Heidegger asks: "When is this 'Now'" of the poet, the time determined in and through his word that the "Now" names the coming of the Holy (G4 75–76)? It is this coming alone that "declares the 'time' in which it is 'time,' the history that sets essential decisions" (76). It is a time that can never be dated or measured in years or centuries, for the time that can be measured thus is not truly "history," not *Geschichte*. Such time is at best a foreground, a "reconnaisance" (*Erkundung*): "History is seldom" (*Geschichte ist selten*). "History is only then," Heidegger writes, "as the essence of truth becomes inceptively decided [*anfänglich entscheiden wird*]." In an addition made in 1941, Heidegger replaces *Wesen der Wahrheit* in this sentence with *das Seyn selbst*. That is, history in its genuine or highest sense is *as* an inceptive decision concerning Being.

Because the German people have not yet heard, much less heeded, the poet's message, they must be "carried back" (*einrücken*) into and to stand within the "domain of power of poetry" (*im Machtbereich der Dichtung stehen*) (G39 4, 19). What *we* do with a poem—our everyday diminishing of it as something ready to hand, as something belonging to a "bourgeois book of rules" (*Bürgerlichen Gesetzbuch*)—must give way to the rule of the poem and poetry over us. Such rule is exemplified in Heidegger's reading of "Homecoming." The title names a *German* homecoming; Heidegger notes that in a revision the poet replaced "But the best, the discovery . . ." with "But the treasure, all that is German . . . is reserved" (G4 14). The hidden is German; the "ownmost" (*Eigenste*) of home has been prepared, given to those who "dwell in the land of their birth." It is the "sending of a dispensation" (*das Geschick einer Schickung*), or as we now say the word: "history" (*Geschichte*). While given, it is not given completely; it is held back as well and as such is the reserved (*Gesparte*).[7] It is the sought-after (*Gesuchte*) because those who, in Hölderlin's words, "are beset with care in the fatherland" are not yet ready to have the ownmost, "all that is German, as their possession [*Eigentum*]." "Homecoming," then can be defined more precisely as "the people of the country becoming at home in the still-withheld essence of home." The political problem, then, is how to find, in order to know, "what is ownmost and best," not in home as such but in the German home. Indeed, the dwelling place of the action of the poem is more precisely the "Swabian homeland," which "must be that very site of nearness to the origin [*der Ort der Nähe zum Ursprung*]" (22). Heidegger identifies the rank and significance of the homeland, writing that "the ownmost and best in the homeland consists only in being just this nearness to origin—and nothing else besides" (23). Indeed, "loyalty [*Treue*] to the origin is innate in the homeland," which is why "one only forsakes the site of the near when he must. . . . Homecoming is the return into the nearness of origin."

In his interpretation of the choral ode from *Antigone* Heidegger tells us that the second strophe, in naming man, names as a part of the "overpowering power"—"language, understanding, sentiment, passion, building"—which rule within and which he, "as the being that he himself is, must take upon himself" (IM 131). The "uncanniness of these powers," Heidegger writes, "resides in their seeming familiarity," but they "yield themselves directly to man only in their nonessence, so driving and holding him out of his essence," which brings him to "regard what is fundamentally more remote and overpowering than sea and earth as closest of all to him." In his belief that he "invented" or even "could have invented" language, man exhibits the distance between himself and his own essence. Heidegger asks: "How could man ever have invented what rules him from the ground, which first enables him to *be* a man?" "In accordance with its historical, history-opening essence," he writes, "man's Being is *logos,* the gathering and apprehending of the Being of beings: the happening [*Geschehnis*] of the most uncanny in whom through violence the overpowering comes and is made to stand" (143). With man's "break out [*Aufbruch*] into Being happens his self-finding in the word, in language." The "origin" (*Ursprung*) of language is and remains a mystery, which means that it "can only have arisen [*angefangen haben*] from the overpowering and uncanny in the breakout of man into Being." "In this breakout," Heidegger writes, "language as the word-becoming [*Wortwerden*] of Being was poetry. Language is the originary poetry [*Urdichtung*] in which a people speaks Being" (144). "Reciprocally" (*Umgekehrt*), Heidegger then writes, "the great poetry through which a people enters into history begins the shaping [*Gestaltung*] of its language" (cf. G39 74, 76). In and through the poetry of Homer, language was "exhibited [*offenbar*] to the Dasein of the Greeks as breakout into Being, as opening shaping of beings." I remind the reader of Heidegger's characterization of the poetic thinking and the thinking poetry of the Greeks, and of the "thoughtful-poetic" character of all great philosophy (IM 121–22; N2 73; EGT 19). Language and poetry have for Heidegger an essentially political dimension; they form and exhibit the historical Dasein of a people and therewith exhibit the way in which Being comes to stand. Thinking and poetizing are "historical action" (*geschichtliches Handeln*); they are now understood as "culture," and "culture" in turn as the "recreation-and-edification business" in the "American" manner (G52 27). What is shown, when thought fittingly, is: "Here a most singular space opens itself for historical action," not mere "deeds" and "effects," but "to *be*," action which is "poetizing and thinking."[8]

"Language," moreover, is always specific (*jeweilige*); it is *a* language in which a people is born and in which it lives historically, in which it is "nurtured and dwells" (G13 156). Language and "home" (*Heimat*) belong together, for language, in its ruling and speaking the essence of home, is the language of home; "language is language as mother-tongue [*Muttersprache*]" and, more fundamentally, as dialect, as *Mundart,* a mode or way of the mouth related to the earth, "part of the earth's flow and growth in which we mortals flourish, and from which we receive the soundness of our roots" (156, OWL 98). When the joining of language and home is lost, as it is in and with the "universal reasoning and binding world-language" of human "planning and machination," human beings are "speechless" (*sprachlos*) and "homeless" (*heimatlos*) (G13 155–57). Indeed, rather than "Language and Home," Heidegger finally writes: "Language as Home" (180). As Heidegger puts it in a reflection on the "metaphysical site of Hölderlin's poetry," mother earth is a land, "das deutsche Land" (G39 288). To this it is necessary to add a crucial point: If the essence of language withholds itself, and if, in consequence, "such withholding belongs to the very nature of language" (OWL 81), then alterity, darkness, is necessarily inscribed in "home," in the particular, in the people, in the nationality.

I have not forgotten Heidegger's own claim in LH that "homeland" is "thought here in an essential sense," "Being-historically" (*seinsgeschichtlich*), and not "patriotically or nationalistically" (LH 217). He goes on to write that "every nationalism is metaphysically an anthropologism, and as such subjectivism," which is his assessment of "internationalism" as well (LH 221; cf. G54 203–7). In "Homecoming," Hölderlin, "concerned that his 'countrymen' find their essence," does not call for "an egoism of his people" (LH 218). Instead, he seeks their essence "in the context of a belongingness to the destiny of the West," which in turn is not thought as Occident or Europe, "but rather world-historically out of nearness to the origin" (*Ursprung*). The teaching is summarized: "'German' is not spoken to the world so that the world might be reformed through the German essence; rather, it is spoken to the Germans so that from a fateful belongingness to the peoples [*Völkern*] they might become world-historical along with them. The homeland of this historical dwelling is nearness to Being."[9]

Here Heidegger assists those scholars who would dilute the claims made concerning Hölderlin and the Germans, but I think no such dilution is possible. Even if the Germans are merely exemplary for the West, we cannot forget it is the *Germans,* and not the English, the French, or any other people, who have this possibility. On this point Fynsk remarks: "The origin sought by the poets is not German and not Greek; it exists in relation to, but is not identical with, the historically defined, 'natural' home of a people."[10]

To be sure, but it remains the case that thinking the origin is possible only in and through thinking a people and homeland. What is at issue, in other words, is precisely the relation between the origin and the "natural" home of the people. The "liberal" questions of whether Heidegger has read, and is therefore able to rank, all of the greatest poets, or whether each people has been, so to speak, equally formed by its originary poetry, are also irrelevant, for Heidegger's ranking is never presented as a comparison of this sort.[11] It is in and from Hölderlin's access to the inception of the West that there can come the possibility that the history of the West "opens itself to the few other great inceptions [weingen anderen grossen Anfängen]" (G4 178). This is not a gesture in the direction of universalism; it is in and through thinking the German essence and the German task that the poet exhibited the access Heidegger presents as the condition for such an opening. Even where he seems to retract his claim on behalf of the Germans, he advances it as well. "German" in quotation marks, as Heidegger has it in LH, cannot be detached completely from the "German" in which Hölderlin poetizes, and which—along with Greek and, later, superior to it—is the "most powerful" and "most spiritual" of languages (IM 47; OWL 162–64).

Poetry has nothing whatever to do with the mere joining of words; rather, in coming into the power of poetry, we are ruled by the "saying" (Sagen) of words (G39 23). Sagen is "not a name for human speaking"; rather, as the "essential Being of language," it is "showing," "a projecting of the clearing in which announcement is made of what it is that beings come into the Open as" (OWL 47, 123; PLT 73). Saying, moreover, in opening up the Being of beings, preserves the emergence and withdrawal of phusis (IM 144).[12] Indeed, "we do not have language; rather, language has us, in the ordinary and correct sense" (G39 23). We understand who we are in the happening of discourse, itself exhibited in poetic saying. The question of who "we" are is asked in the "vortex" (Wirbel) of language (42–49). A "saying" more fundamental than discourse is exhibited in Hölderlin's poetry; "this joining of language is itself a vortex that tears us away from any place whatsoever" (45). From Hölderlin we learn that man is the discourse of all that is, that he is "the meaning of the earth" and that through his Dasein "all beings first arise, close themselves off, prosper and fail, and turn back again into the origin [Ursprung]" (60–61). The authentic projection of the essence of man among beings, and particularly in nature, comes from the mission or calling (Beruf) of poets into the historical Dasein of men. The poetic word, the word of language—indeed language as such—is "the most dangerous good (der Güter Gefahrlichstes), for it is the ground of the highest danger for the Dasein of men. The manifestation of beings happens in language; the "originary unveiling" (ur-

sprüngliche Enthüllung) itself, appearance, which means that "through language man is the witness of Being [*Zeuge des Seyns*]" (62). Apart from language there can be no manifestation of Being and thus neither nonbeing nor the void of Nothing, for "only where language is, does world rule," which means that only where there is language "is there the highest danger, *the* danger as such, that is, the menace [*Bedrohung*] of Being as such through nonbeing. Language is not only dangerous, in that it brings men into danger, rather it is the most dangerous, the danger of dangers, as it first creates and alone maintains the possibility of the Being-menace [*Seynsbedrohung*]." Since man *is* in language, he is of necessity brought into this danger of his destruction. "As the most dangerous," Heidegger writes, "language is double-edged and ambiguous" (*Zweischneidigste und Zweideutigste*). It places us in the domains of the highest achievements and the greatest decadence. This is why poets, who dare the "venture with language," take the greatest risk (PLT 133). The poet faces a special danger, for "the highest pleasure of the first founding saying is at the same time the deepest pain of loss; the first born are sacrificed," a necessity to which Heidegger makes two references in the interpretation of "Germanien" (G39 63, 146).[13] Such risks cannot be avoided, for "the danger of language is its *most originary essential determination [ursprünglichste Wesensbestimmung]*" (64). What the poets provide can never, moreover, be simply "conservative," for "poetic projection comes from Nothing in this respect, that it never takes its gift from the ordinary and the traditional" (PLT 76).

I emphasize the danger in and of language because it is essential to recognize the human, all too human, inclination to read into Heidegger's talk of rootedness, attunement to Being, and releasement a doctrine of harmony and pastoral rootedness plainly at variance with the Heraclitean strife integral to his way of thinking.[14] Rootedness is inscribed in the movement that calls for a setting-apart with the foreign (G53 156). This motion is always characterized as struggle, *Streit*, *polemos*. The "originary struggle" (*ursprüngliche Streit*) in Being is the movement of Being/Not-Being (*Seyn oder Nichtseyn*) in the "essence of Being itself" (G65 264–65). It is this to which we may become attuned and which is given to thinking; Being plays through us and has set us into our "there" (G51 68).

Accordingly, it is also a mistake to draw "liberal" conclusions from Heidegger's retrieval of Hölderlin's "We are a discourse [*Gespräch*]," which he glosses with "We are a happening of language [*Sprachge-*

schehnis]" (G39 68–69). The discourse we are is nothing like a Habermasian "ideal speech situation," and it cannot ground anything like a political order legitimized by the communicative rationality said to inhere in everyday praxis. Nor is there any hint that in such discourse we register our deliberations concerning what is just and what is advantageous, to revert to an older formulation. The poet articulates the fundamental character of historical Dasein, which for Heidegger shows that language exhibits the originary essence of man's historical Being (67–68). Indeed, it is pointless to try to separate the essence of language and the essence of man, since for man "the originary presencing of man's Being is language itself" (*das ursprüngliche Wesen seines Seyns ist die Sprache selbst*) (68). Language happens in discourse, "and this happening is truly its Being [*Seyn*]." The "happening of language" is "timely" (*zeitlich*) in Heidegger's distinctive sense. It is "the inception and ground of the authentically historical time of men." Indeed, discourse in its happening *is* "first time and history" (69–70). Poetry is the "inceptive" (*anfängliche*) discourse, which means, in the words from Hölderlin's "In lovely blueness . . ." which Heidegger makes his own, that ". . . poetically, dwells / Man on this earth" (70). "Only after 'ravenous time' [*reissende Zeit*] has been riven into present, past, and future," Heidegger writes, "does the possibility arise of agreeing on something permanent. We have been a single discourse since the time when 'time is.' Ever since time arose, we have existed historically. Both—Being-a-single-discourse [*ein Gesprächsein*] and Being-historically [*Geschichtlichsein*]—are alike ancient; they belong together and are the same" (G4 39–40). "Our Being happens as discourse" in which "the gods address us, placing us under their claim, *bringing us to language,* whether and how we are, how we answer, recalling or refusing to them our Being" (G39 70). In this happening of our Being, we bring beings to language, for it is "only where language happens" that Being and Nonbeing open, and "we ourselves are this opening and closing."

As a discourse, we are "held out into" (*ausgesetzt*) self-opening beings because Being "encounters and determines us," a condition that exhibits us as "history" and not "nature" (G39 72). A political sounding of this teaching follows. Our "capacity to hear" does not create a "relation between one and another as a community [*Gemeinschaft*] but only as a society [*Gesellschaft*]," for "originary [*ursprünglicher*] community . . . *is* through the previous binding of *each one* in what overwhelmingly binds and determines each one"; indeed this condition is what "community as such is," thus inscribing here BT's teaching on Dasein's resolute retrieval of itself in the people. Heidegger's example is the comradeship of soldiers at the front, itself made possible by the nearness of death (72–73). Does this mean that comradeship springs from anxiety? (73) The answer is "no" for a Philistine (*Spiessbürger*) for whom anxiety is suffering the "helpless quaking" of a "thoughtless cowardice," and "yes" when anxiety is understood in terms of the metaphysical "nearness of the unconditioned" that requires the highest "independence [*Selbständigkeit*] and preparedness [*Bereitschaft*]." Comradeship is not possible, he writes, when we do not compel the power in our Dasein to take on our death as a free offering.

The relation of this reflection to the topic of Heidegger's text lies in his claim that our capacity to hear is conditioned by how we are held out into the nearness and distance of the essences of things. The parallel, then, is between the happening of this process in and as language and the happening of our being held out into the nearness or neighborhood of death. The happening of language is the "originary establishment [*Stiftung*] of Being." Experiencing the essential power of things here, we come back into ourselves; we come and "*are* with and for one another—of self, and to be sure, in the strong sense of the words 'of self.'" Discourse, then, must be understood as the "fundamental happening of being held out [*Aufgesetzheit*] into beings." "Therewith," Heidegger says with finality, "the possibility of a misunderstanding of the site is removed." The larger political sense of this teaching is that the people, bound into its own determination, becomes what it truly is.

There is a political *Auseinandersetzung* carried out against conventional understandings of poetry, including Nazi views. In order to reach the underlying experience of poetry, Heidegger must first reject such notions as doctrines of the "poetic soul"; explanations from "depth psychology"; theories of poetic types, such as the lyrical and the dramatic; "individualistic" and "collectivistic" understandings of expressions of experience (*Ausdruck von Erlebnissen*), as in theories of a "mass soul" (*Massenseele*); or with Spengler, of "culture soul" (*Kulturseele*); or with Alfred Rosenberg, of "racial soul" or "folk soul" (*Rassenseele, Volksseele*); or of world-views (G39 26, 22, 27–29). The rise, the height, and the fall of historical Dasein is related to poetry (20–24). It is necessary to recover the power of poetry, for it is only as the poet himself becomes both the "master and servant" (*Herr und Knecht*) of poetry through "battle" (*Kampf*) that the "space of poetry" (*Raum der Dichtung*) can be opened (23).

Heidegger rejects pointedly the claims of the Nazi poet E. G. Kolbenheyer, who in his 1932 work *Lebenswert und Lebenswirkung der Dichtkunst in einem Volke* (Life-value and life-effect of poetic art in a people) claimed that poetry is a biologically necessary function of the people. All such views have their essential ground in the "way of being of man" (*Seinsart des Menschen*) in the nineteenth century and in modernity as such (27–28). Such standpoints are the products of worldviews, philosophies of culture, and the like which are themselves grounded on the "liberalist" (*liberalistisch*) position for which poetry is an expression of experience (28). Even a dog, Heidegger remarks, is capable of expressing its experience. This understanding of expression, indeed this "manner of thinking" (*Denkweise*), is itself the essential way of being, the "enactment [*Vollzug*] of 'liberal' man." Hölderlin's poetry is not a cultural product but must be understood in terms of the flight of the gods and the condition in which our historical Dasein is thereby placed (99, 93–97). Poetic works are intelligible as products or expressions of culture only "where historical Dasein stands under the rule of what is today called 'Liberalism.'" As Heidegger explains, "The Greeks had no time for culture" and it is only in "small times" (*kleine Zeiten*) to which the whole of Dasein descends as a legacy that the cultivation of the true, the good, and the beautiful are placed in the hands of appropriate ministries (99). Even a Nazi poetics, as we may call Kolbenheyer's teaching, belongs to "culture" and "liberalism." Heidegger opens a cleft between his own teaching and that of National Socialism which assimilates the latter to the more encompassing domain of "liberalism." National Socialism, then, becomes a symptom of, and not the solution for, the crisis of the age.

I

In his discussion of "Germanien," Heidegger speaks of the "originary belonging together" (*ursprünglichen Zugehörigkeit*) of poetry and language; poetry is a fundamental joining, and language is a fundamental happening, of historical Dasein in which Dasein's openness to danger is exhibited (G39 76–77). The "decision of the world-time of our people comes to discourse" in and as poetry. The "site" (*Ort*), the "there" ("*da*") from which the poet speaks, is the "determination which de-termines" (*be-stimmt*) the ground and soil, the space from and in which poetic saying establishes Being (79). The fundamental determination opens the world that "in poetic Saying receives the stamping of Being [*Gepräge des Seyns*]." In order for us to "seize" (*begreiffen*) the essence of this determination and thus the essence of human historical Dasein, it is necessary to understand the fundamental determination (*Grundstimmung*) of the poem, which is "mourning" (*Trauern*) (78–104). A later series of propositions from Heidegger's course "The Rhine" explains what mourning does (223). As a *Grundstimmung*, it:

1 . . . carries us away to the limits of beings and places us into relation with the gods, whether as a turning toward or a turning away.
2 . . . draws us out of, and at the same time, in the rapture, draws us into the mutual relations with earth and homeland. The *Grundstimmung* is always a carrying-away (*entrückend*) and a carrying-back (*einrückend*) above all.
3 As such, it opens beings as a whole as a thoroughly charged domain, as the unity of a world.
4 [It] thus delivers our Dasein over to being, so that (Being) must accept it, bear it up, and give it shape.

Mourning is the attunement appropriate for a time marked by the absence, the flight of the gods, an absence not disproven by the existence of Christianity (80). The flight of the gods must become an experience of Dasein, which must be "pushed" (*stossen*) into its fundamental determination. This is what the poet "establishes in the historical Dasein of our people." The poet, then, marks the essential time of the people, whose historical Dasein must become what it already and truly is.

The naming of the gods is a calling (*Rufen*) that lets what is distant remain distant; the calling is what locates the distant *as* distant (81). The calling is "the differentiating [*Austragen*] of a conflict between the self-opening of readiness and the withholding of fulfillment." This conflict is pain, suffering (*Schmerz, Leiden*); the calling is the lamentation (*Klagen*); together these are the fundamental determination of "Germania." "Mourning" is not an affect or property of man, god, or anything else but is rather the name of the site in which all are given together originarily (81–83). This is to say that mourning is not "of the soul" (*Seelisches*) but is rather "something spiritual" (*etwas Geistiges*) (83). Men and other beings are set into this determination in relations neither subjective nor objective; rather, they are "dis-placed" (*ver-setz*) (89–90). Hölderlin calls such poetic mourning "holy" (82, 87). Holy mourning is not a mood of the poet but rather a mourning with earth and homeland (87–89). "Homeland" is neither as birthplace nor landscape, but rather "as the power of the earth" (*als die Macht der Erde*), from which historical Dasein "dwells poetically" (88). Mourning is thus the appropriate exhibition of the attunement of Hölderlin's poetry with the absence, the "missingness" (*Fehl*) of the gods (93–97). It is a fundamentally *political* determination, for it inscribes spirit and historical Dasein in what is fitting for our present condition and shows itself as a "pressing as a readiness," for "those past as such press us, approach us as the already pressing" (103).

The "homey" (*Heimische*) earth, Heidegger explains, is not a "naked, externally bounded space," or natural territory, but is brought up or prepared as the home for the gods (104–5). Indeed, it is through this preparation that earth first *becomes* home, and "it can fall back into a simple dwelling place. . . . The becoming of the home does not occur through mere settlement." When earth enters into the play of concealment ↔ unconcealment, the play is history—"the great play [*Spiel*] that the gods play with . . . a people" (105). Here Heidegger cites Heraclitus's fragment B 52, which he translates as "Worldtime [*Weltzeit*] is a child at play, setting board-pieces here and there; to such a child belongs dominion [*Herrschaft*] [over Being]." As Heidegger puts the matter later: "The question remains whether and how we, hearing the movements of this play, play along and accommodate ourselves to the play" (PR 113). The earth, as opened to the gods, is a homeland for men. But it is torn open "in the storm [*Sturm*] of the gods, into its grounds and abysses." "Man, who 'poetically dwells upon the earth,'" Heidegger writes, "and he alone, belongs as well to the abyss that the earth carries" (G39 106). The abyss is experienced from the flight of the gods, which brings us to the happening of time in which "the shadows of those who are past visit us anew, come toward us, are futural" (108, 107–9). The joint happening of past and future is originary time, and the "temporalizing of this time is the fundamental happening [*Grundgeschenis*] of the attunement in which poetry grounds itself" (109). With recognition of this grounding, we reach the present moment, thought as it is in BT, as the conjunction of the past and a projection into the future.

The relation between the Greeks and the Germans is the theme of Heidegger's reading of "Germanien" as the site of German Dasein in the horizon of the thinking of Heraclitus (113–37). Heidegger's focus is the nature of German "intimacy" (*Innigkeit*), to be thought from reflection on the "historical Being of the people," which is "reserved in mystery" and to which Hölderlin's poem is the "gate" (120–23). Thus understood, the " 'Fatherland' is Being itself, that of the ground from the history of a people as carried and joined dasein-ishly [*daseienden*]: the historicity [*Geschichtlichkeit*] of its history." Heidegger explains that fatherland is not an abstraction or idea as such, but rather "sees the poet in its originary sense historically" (121). In Heraclitus, there is thought the setting-apart, the originary *polemos*, of gods as gods, and men as men, a thinking of conflict and harmony correlate with the poetry of Hölderlin (123–29). Against any tendency to soften Heraclitus's teaching that *dikē* is *eris*, Heidegger says: "No! Originarily and holding itself in its essence, right [*Recht*] first forms and guards itself, becoming true in strife [*Streit*]" (126).

The power of Heraclitus is inscribed in German thinking, exemplified by Meister Eckhart, Hölderlin, Hegel, and Nietzsche (133–34).[15] The name of Heraclitus, then, does not stand for an ancient, forgotten Greek philosopher but names the thinking of "allworldly humanity in itself" (*Allerweltsmenschheit an sich*). Thus, it is the name of "an original power [*Urmacht*] of Western-Germanic historical Dasein" in its first *Auseinandersetzung* with the "Asiatic" (134). The "new inceptive need of our historical Dasein" is inscribed in the "metaphysical need of the West" (134–37). The original *Auseinandersetzung* marked by Heraclitus is exhibited in the happening of questioning, which effects a "historical spiritual space" (*geschichtlich geistigen Raum*). Now the neediness (*Notigung*) of need must come out of the need of historical Dasein, but the forgetting of this need is exhibited in Hölderlin's poetry. The site of the inner movement of poetic saying, the vortex, is said in "Mnemosyne," where Hölderlin writes (135):

> A sign we are, without meaning
> Without pain we are and we have almost
> Lost our speech in a foreign land.

This means for Heidegger that Dasein has become alien to its own historical essence, its "sending and its differentiating" (*der Sendung und dem Austrag*) (cf. WCT 10–12). Dasein without strength, without pain, and without meaning is therefore without "the basic form of knowledge of spirit" (*die Grundform des Wissens des Geistes*). "Where there is no determining opening in the cleft of Being," Heidegger writes, there is no need which "obliges naming and saying," which shows in turn our near loss. "Foreign" (*Fremde*) stands over against the "national," "our own," the "German." In this condition we are a sign of the absence of the gods. The poet stands in this site of "metaphysical need," and there must rule in him the "highest intimacy of the belonging to Being of his own people." Here, as always in Heidegger, the fundamental determination has nothing to do with feelings, with experiences of fullness, nor yet with any traditional concept of spirit with which the void can be overcome (G39 139). From this determination, there is the possibility in which the Germans are carried away (*entrücken*) to new gods or carried back (*einrücken*) to earth and homeland (140). When the manifestness of beings is opened up, there is the possibility of world. In the constellation of carrying away / carrying back, the opening power of the fundamental determination determines our Dasein, bringing it to stand in its site (141). Poetic saying, then, transforms the mood of "horror" (*Schrecken*) which characterizes the German people into "holy affliction, mourning but prepared." The fundamental determination is the manner in which Dasein is held out into the midst of beings in their totality. This manner cannot be in any sense neutral; rather, it has, and must have, the character of care (*Sorge*). Heidegger distinguishes the situation from anything intelligible in terms of modern subjectivity and makes clear that its determination has nothing whatever to do with introspection or psychology (142–43). Moreover, in the happening of its being held out into the midst of beings, Dasein is not alone; it is with "the Dasein Other" (*das Dasein Anderer*), and only is, as it is, "in Being-with with the Other" (*im Mitsein mit den Anderen*) (143). This repetition of a basic teaching of BT (cf. BT 154–56) is then altered, for Dasein is essentially "Being-with-one-another, for-and-against-one-another" (*Miteinandersein, Für-und-Gegeneinander-sein*). In world thus opened up in and as *polemos*, Dasein finds its ground and the ranges (*Bereiche*) of its "decisions and actions" (*Entscheidungen und Haltungen*). As a fundamental character of Dasein, "Being-with-one-another" exhibits Dasein's historical character and is thus bound into the power of history and joined to it.

There is a more fundamental account of "intimacy" in "The Rhine" lectures to which I shall now turn. "Being lets poetry originate," Heidegger writes, "in order to find itself originarily [*ursprünglich*] in poetry and thus to concealingly reveal itself in poetry as the mystery" (237). This relation is clarified in Heidegger's reflections on the riddle of the "purely-originated origin" (*Reinentsprungen Ursprung*) and the origin of poetry (239–61). In poetry "sound" and "meaning" (*Klang, Sinn*) have not yet been completely separated (239–40). As Heidegger will write later: "It is just as much a property of language to sound and ring and vibrate, to hover and tremble, as it is for what is spoken to have a meaning" (OWL 98). The unity in and of the opposition of originary and originated is the "purely originated," an "un-nameable relation" exhibited in and by poetry (G39 240–41). The "purely originated" is explained as follows (241): "In that which springs purely from its origin must the origin, as well as the having-arisen [*Entsprungensein*]," he writes, "unfold in the serenity of their determining powers." To the extent that these, "according to their essence, enter into conflict against themselves, they must unfold as more pure in highest hostility [*höchsten Feindseligkeit*]." However, "because hostility as bliss [*Seligkeit*] constitutes the *unity* of Being, this unity must also gain the highest purity [*höchste Reinheit*] and better: retain [*behalten*]."

"Intimacy" is the "originary unity" of the power of the purely originated (248–50). Hölderlin's "the Holy," as "intimacy itself," is thus the "originary unity" that "unifies and holds apart the originated [*Entsprungene*] in the hostility of its essential powers [*Wesenmächte*]" (249). Hölderlin names the Greeks the "intimate people" (*das innige Volk*). "Intimacy" cannot be brought to conceptual clarity, for it happens or presences (*west*) as "mystery" (*Geheimnis*) (250). Thus, "mystery is only where intimacy rules." The poet brings himself to stand in and holds the mystery which has come to stand in him. Thus, "Being itself, the hostility of the conflicting powers, in which happens the hostility concerning the gods and the earth, men and everything that is made, comes to a decision" (251). This means that "poetry, as the institution of Being, is the grounding opening of intimacy."

In Heidegger's account of the fundamental determination as the "truth of the people," we reach a crucial element of the political teaching of his interpretation of "Germania," for here is where the philosopher speaks of three examples of creative violence: poetry, thinking, and state-creating (143–44). "The truth of the people," Heidegger writes, "is the particular manifestation of Being in its totality" (144). This truth is that out of which the people wills itself as historical. The fundamental determination and thus the truth of the Dasein of the people is "originally established" by the poet, "comprehended and ordered as Being, and thereby first exposed, by the thinker, and Being thus comprehended is placed in the first and last seriousness of what is—that is, in de-terminate historical truth [*be-stimmte geschichtliche Wahrheit*]—so that the people is thereby brought to itself as people. This occurs through the creation by the state-founder of the state that is appropriate to its essence." Earlier Heidegger identifies the poet, thinker, and state-creator (*Staatsschöpfer*) as "those who authentically found and justify the historical existence of a people" (51–52). The historical being of the people is founded by the poet, made known by the thinker, and actualized by the political founder. The powers of poetry, thought, and state-creating, "working in the ages of un-folding history, are not calculable, forward and backward," Heidegger explains. "They can work for a long time unrecognized," Heidegger explains, "without bridges, next to one another, and still for one an-other" (144).

It is not self-evident that the "state-founder" here is Hitler, and I shall suggest some reasons why Hitler is *not* meant.[16] Hölderlin is the site of the German historical Dasein, where its highest need is framed and where its decision lies (146). In his poetizing struggle to transform the "fundamental tonality" of the people, the poet revives (*Erwecken*) the "holy affliction," mourning, that is the fundamental determination of the people (146–47). In "Sophocles," Hölderlin shows that it is in mourning that joy is exhibited (148): "Many have tried in vain to say the joyous joyously / Here it finally speaks to me, here in mourning it utter itself." The relation of joy and mourning, "resonating thus in opposing strife," Heidegger says, is the character of the fundamental determination. Thus, the "poet experiences poetically a creative down-fall of the hitherto existing truth of Being, that is, in the dissolution he is captivated and carried away by the youthful and the new powers" (150). A comment: National Socialism and Hitler do not exhibit the fundamental determination of the Germans. They have been antici-pated and surpassed by Hölderlin; the state-founding of which Heideg-ger speaks is precisely what has *not* happened (cf. 254).

The phrase "the true and only Führer" (*wahre und je einzige Führer*) appears in the reading of "The Rhine" (210). There Heidegger is con-cerned with the "halfgods" (*Halbgötter*) in Hölderlin's river-poems. The context in which the incendiary phrase appears is Heidegger's instancing of "The Only One" to claim that in that poem Christ is precisely *not* meant (209–10). We cannot indeed speak today of Christ as Führer, Heidegger argues, for he is clearly not, unlike the "true and only Führer," a halfgod; church and creed proclaim him infinite. "*Führersein*," writes Heidegger, "is a *Schicksal* and hence finite Being [*endliches Seyn*]." The true rank of Führer is intimated; distinguished from the Christian—and I am tempted to say—"bad" infinite, and elevated above the simply human, *Führersein* names a leadership only the poet provides.

It is necessary to turn to Heidegger's reflections in "The Rhine" for a closer look at the role of the poet in the founding of historical Dasein, that is, in the political founding of the people. Heidegger's aim is to clarify the place of the poet between gods and men, in the space of the "between essence" (*Zwischenwesen*) occupied in Hölderlin's river-poems by the "halfgods." In thinking the halfgod, the poet enters the "difference" (*Unterschied*) between gods and men, questioning it in a thinking that "founds and breaks open [*stiftet und bricht auf*] the entire domain of Being [*den Bereich des Seyns*]" (167). The halfgod (and the Rhine in the poem) is thought and poetized as a "destiny" (*Schicksaal*) (171–72).

"Destiny" has several senses. It is as "an attuned dominating power" (*bestimmte herrschende Macht*), a "mode of Being" (*eine Weise des Seins*), and a "distinctively determined being of the kind of Being [*jeweils bestimmtes Seiendes von der Art dieses Seyns*] that stands under such power." Neither "fate" nor "fatality," an "Asiatic" view Hölderlin overcomes, *Schicksaal* gets its proper sense from Dasein's fundamental experience of death, obviously an inscription here of the crucial thematic of BT (173–76).[17] Moreover, *Schicksaal* is an "essentially German" (*wesentliche deutsche*) word which must be learned as a name of essential Being in its true German fullness (*wahren deutschen Gehalt*), which is to say, "seldom" (*selten*) (173).

I abridge Heidegger's reflections on the river-poems to the following: The turbulent flow of the river, its force, generates within it an opposition that, in bringing it into self-founding self-limiting, binding it to its origin and freeing it for its destiny, enacts its own limits. It is not surprising that "thrownness" (*Geworfenheit*) is inscribed here (175). As Heidegger explains this point, for example, in his reading of "The Ister," the river makes the land, flux makes stability (G53 182–84; cf. G39 230). Similarly, the poet opens the "time-space" of the dwelling of the people (183). The poet is an enigmatic sign (184–89). "When Hölderlin poetizes the essence of poetry," Heidegger writes, "he must think the essence of half-gods" (173). Finally: "The sign, the halfgod, the river, the poet, all these name poetically the one and only ground of the becoming-homey of historical men and its establishment through the poet" (192; cf. G39 181–84).

"The Rhine" begins and ends with Dionysus. The final words of the poem, ". . . and back again comes / Primeval confusion" show the "Being of night, the rule the darkening violence and frenzy—the Reich of Dionysus and his priests." Hölderlin sings the relation between Dionysus and the poets in lines Heidegger cites from the end of the seventh strophe of "Bread and Wine," in which "they" refers to the poets (G39 191):

> But they are, you say, like the wine god's
> holy priests,
> Who roamed from land to land in holy night.

"We know," Heidegger says that the "last, and at the same time futural, preparatory Western interpretation of Being by Nietzsche also names Dionysus." We also know, I must add, Heidegger's interpretation of Nietzsche which exhibits the epochal character of Nietzsche's teaching.

The poet hears the suffering of the river as a clamor and rage to become an origin, but mortals flee this origin, turning to world (196–203). The poet hears the river as well prior to its breaking free and is therefore close to the gods who are located at the origin but, as a mortal himself, must hear this from the world in which he lives. What he hears is shown and articulated in his word, through which a destiny and world are given, but the poet, as the voice of the people, also turns back to the origin. The poet's hearing brings suffering (201). He hears, but cannot *will* to hear, the origin, which comes to stand in his hearing. Such hearing is suffering, and indeed, suffering "is the Being of the demigod." The poet experiences "destiny as suffering" (*Schicksal als Leiden*). What is heard is the "originary origin" (*ursprüngliche Ursprung*), which brings itself to stand in the poet's hearing. This "placing" (*stellt*) or the origin *by* itself is authentic happening, *is* "is" (*überhaupt* "*ist*"). Such hearing brings what is heard into the "sound of words" (*den Klang des Wortes*) and is therefore the condition for the possibility of the discourse that is the fundamental characteristic (*Grundzug*) of our Dasein (201–2). While the poet tries to hear the origin in its innerness as the mystery, Heidegger makes clear that this never really happens successfully. Poetry is "more a covering than an uncovering saying, and thus is everything other than a discursive narration and description" (203). Thus, poetry, even the poetry of Hölderlin, is not foundational in the sense Heidegger has disowned. It is not a substitute for a metaphysical first, for the seeing of the halfgod—and the poet—is not an "unbinding [*unverbindfliches*] looking or retrospection," but rather the "accomplishment of an originary binding [*Vollzug einer ursprünglichen Bindung*]" (267). Such binding, itself "grounded in the originary," is riven by a "fault" (*Fehl*); it urges "boldness [*Verwegenheit*] in order to will the preservation [*Wahrung*] of the originary." The halfgods have an "eye too many; an eye for the originary." The poetic founding of people and state takes place in and through action in which the "highest questionworthiness of Being" opens in our history (269–70). The tragic is thus decisive for the political.

The saying of *Schicksal* in the language of a people is decisive; "Only a historical people is truly a people" (284). In turn, the "historical" (*Geschichtlich*) is only "if it happens out of the ground of the middle of Being, if the Between [*Zwischen*] is there [*da*], if the halfgods, the creators, bring about [*erwirken*] the happening as history." A historical people, in turn, "is as a people only a community [*Gemeinschaft*]," and the community is as historical only if "those others as others venture and differentiate their Being-other [*jene Anderen als die Anderen ihr Andersseins wagen und austragen*]." Radical alterity is necessary, then, in the creation of people and state.

In an essay on the requirements for mutual understanding between the French and the Germans, written in 1937, Heidegger applies this teaching (G13 15–16). The condition for "authentic understanding among peoples" is a "creative reciprocal discussion" which brings awareness "concerning historically shared past and present conditions," awareness of which brings a people "back to its ownmost," which it "grasps with increased clarity and resoluteness." A people's ownmost, Heidegger explains, "is its creativity, through which it grows into its historical mission and so first comes to itself." The mission of the "historically cultured peoples" in the present time is the "rescue of the West" (*Rettung des Abendlandes*), which for Heidegger means "the originary, newly creating justification of its past and future history," and not the "simple maintenance of what is already present to hand." The reciprocal understanding of people identifies for each people its "ownmost task," which is "to know how to give oneself the necessity of this rescue." This knowledge comes from both the "experience of need, which arises with the innermost meance of the West, and from the power for an enlightening projection [*Entwurf*] of the highest possibilities of Western Dasein [*abendländischen Daseins*]." "Just as the menace of the West drives toward a full uprooting and general disorder," Heidegger writes, "so, on the contrary, the will to the renewal from the ground up must be led through the final resolutions," which in turn must be prepared for by "authentic philosophical knowledge"—"the anticipatory opening through knowledge of the consistently hidden essence of things" (18). "Ruling knowledge [*herrschaftliche Wissen*] rises to a new height and clarity. It prepares the way for the first time for a transformation of the peoples which is often invisible" (19).[18]

II

For Heidegger the "originary origin of speech as the grounding essence of human Dasein remains a mystery" (G39 75). Against the claim that animals have some capacity for language, Heidegger advances the teaching concerning the decisive difference between animal and man we have already examined in a previous chapter. The animal does not speak because there is nothing that can be given to it, nothing that is appropriate for it. It cannot be in language as man is and must remain in its benumbedness. The nearness and distance between animal and man becomes a question when we think the "authentic speechlessness of nature in its totality" (76). Thought more closely, the apparent distinction between the speechlessness of nature and the speaking of men belongs to natural science, for it is in poetry that the "fundamental happening of the historical Daseins of men toward nature" is exhibited. Natural science, for all its exactness, "leaves us in the lurch" because it " 'de-natures' Nature." We may say that "nature" in whatever sense is most significant for human things is exhibited better in poetry, or in Hölderlin's poetry, than in science. "Poetry," as Heidegger understands it, takes over from "science" as the mode of comportment in which man is held out into what is, in which the Dasein in man, and the German Dasein, is brought into its appropriate site. "Science" names this possibility when Heidegger calls for its inspiriting through a retrieval of its origin, which amounts to its assimilation to philosophy.[19] As we have seen, however, science finally takes its place as a constituent of the present epoch. Ultimately it no longer exhibits the inception but rather its inscription in the age of nihilism. There is, I think, another political limitation of science. Science, even in the age of the *Gestell*, retains something of its supposed universality. The issue may be put more pointedly. Science cannot ask, let alone answer, the question of the *German* essence.

In supposing nature exists "for itself" and is "colored with myth" by man, we do not experience "what is as what is" (G4 21). What is to be understood from "Wie wenn am Feiertage . . ." (As on a holiday . . .) is "nature, the mighty, beautiful as a god" (*Die mächtige, die gottlich-schöne Natur*) (49). For Heidegger it is no accident that the poem, composed in 1800, was ignored until 1910, for during that interval the "open rebellion [*der offene Aufruhr*] of modern world-history" has begun, and with it has come the domination of technology, both of which developments make a recovery of Hölderlin possible and necessary (51; cf. QCT 28–33).

Because nature is "divinely beautiful" and "wonderously all-present," it embraces the poets. "This bringing-in" (*Einbezug*), Heidegger writes, "sets the poets into the basic features of their essence. This setting-into is education" (54). Nature comes "in the appearance of absencing" (*in den Schein Abwesenden*), which is conditioned by the presence of nature "in the heavenly gods, in the earth and its growths, in peoples and their history." In lines from "As on a Holiday . . .":

> So when she seems to be sleeping at times of the year
> Up in the sky or among plants or the peoples,
> The poets' faces likewise are sad,
> They seem to be alone, but are always divining.

Nature's first lesson, then, is taught as its apparent absence, which is articulated temporally, which is to say, historically—and, one must say, politically. Heidegger explains that " 'the Year' means here the year of 'seasons of the year' as well as 'the years of the peoples,' the world-ages [*Weltalter*]." The divining of the poets is attuned to this absence, for, as the last line of the second strophe says, "For divining too she herself is at rest" (55). Nature's rest, however, is not a "cessation of movement" (*das Aufhören der Bewegung*). Heidegger explains that rest is rather the "self-gathering" (*Sichsammeln*) of the contrary motion of the inception and its coming. This coming is the "presencing" and thus the "essence" of nature's "all-presencing" (*Allgegenwärtigen*).

"Nature" here is not part of the familiar oppositions between nature and art, spirit, history, supernature, or the unnatural (55–56; cf. PLT 101–3). Rather, it is "the opening of the Open, the lighting of that clearing in which anything can appear in the first place, can posit itself in its contour, can show itself in its 'outlook' and thus be present as always this or that." Heidegger writes that Hölderlin "poetizes in the word '*Natur*' an other [*ein Anderes*] that stands yet in concealed relation to what was once called '*phusis*'" (57). In thinking or attempting to think this other, Heidegger aims for what the Greeks could not think with the name *phusis* (cf. Phy 221–22; G55 32, 54, 82, 104, 108, 123, 142).[20] Hölderlin's nature is "what is not only above everything 'elemental' and everything human, but even above the gods." Heidegger then cites the third strophe from "As on a Holiday . . .":

> Now breaks the day! I yearned for it and saw it come.
> And my word for what I saw shall be the Holy.
> For she, she herself, who is older than the ages
> And higher than the gods of West and East,
> For nature has awakened with the clang of a warrior's arms.
> And from aether on high to abyss below
> By fixed law as once from Holy chaos born,
> She feels herself new inspiration [*Begeisterung*]
> The All-creative again.

Heidegger explains: "Here 'nature' becomes the name for that which is *above* the gods and 'older than the ages' in which beings always come to be. 'Nature' becomes the word for 'Being': Being is prior to all beings, for they owe what they are to Being. And the gods likewise: to the degree that they *are,* and however they are, they too all stand *under* 'Being.'" While nature "retains all in its openness and illumination," it "seems at times to sleep," and the light has "in mourning, retired into itself" (G4 57). "Self-closing, mourning is impenetrable and appears as darkness," Heidegger writes. However, the night is "resting anticipation of the day." According to Heidegger, the "day" which breaks in the first line of the third strophe is "the coming of leading, resting, anticipating Nature," and the twilight is "Nature itself in coming." The "call of Nature" has its correlate in the word of the poet as the "pure call" (*das reine Rufen*) (57–58). In saying what is given necessarily to say, the poet is compelled to name Nature as the Holy, as Hölderlin says in the last three lines of the fifth strophe of *Am Quell der Donau* (At the source of the Danube):

We name you, under a Holy compulsion we
Now name you Nature, and new, as from a bath
From you emerge all that's divinely born.

In speaking of "the Holy" as he has spoken of "nature," Hölderlin names nature "the Holy" and, in so doing, "overcomes" (*überwunden*) what the name "nature" designates in "As upon a Holiday . . ." (58). "This overcoming," Heidegger writes, "is the following and sign of an inceptively commencing saying [*anfänglicher anhebenden Sagens*]." With this word—the Holy—there is an awakening of nature "with a clash of poetic words," for the word divides essence from unessence (*Unwesen*) and thus binds them together in strife. "The word is a weapon" (*Das Wort ist Waffe*), Heidegger writes, as Hölderlin explains in "At the Source of the Danube," where the "weapon of words," as the sanctuary of the Holy, guards the Holy. But it is still necessary to explain why the Holy must be the word of the poets.

The answer is to be found in thinking the sense in which nature is older than the ages and above the gods of West and East, which will bring us to Heidegger's teaching on "spirit" (59). Nature is "older than any times that are allotted to men and people and things" but is neither a metaphysical "supratemporal" nor the "Christian-conceived 'eternity.'" Indeed, as the "wondrous all-presence" (*die wunderbar Allegegenwärtig*), nature is "more temporal [*zeitiger*] than the 'times,'" for nature "grants beforehand for all actual things the Lighting, whose Open first of all enables what an actual thing is to appear." "The Bright"—holy nature—in Hölderlin's "Mother Earth," opens the clearing and is the "highest," standing above the "peaks of time" (G39 52); God and the gods, the poet shows, are "nothing but time," an insight which for Heidegger shows the superiority of Hölderlin's understanding of temporality to that of Hegel (54–55). Nature, then, is above or before all actual things, including the gods, but is not such as some "separated region of reality." Rather, it is the site within which the gods can appear. The "holiness" of the Holy does not stem from any connection with a god, for "the Holy is not Holy because it is godlike," Heidegger writes; "rather the godlike is godlike because it is in its manner 'Holy'" (G4 59). Hölderlin names the Holy from "chaos"; for as the "essence of nature," which itself is engendered from chaos, the Holy is "Holy chaos." When "nature" thus understood has vanished, there is no site for the gods.

Heidegger then turns to the last four lines of the third strophe of "As on a Holiday . . ." (59–60):

> And from aether on high to abyss below
> By fixed law as once from Holy chaos born,
> She feels herself new inspiration [*Begeisterung*]
> The All-creative again.

The crucial word here is *Begeisterung*, "inspiration," which fills all-presencing nature, renewing it as the "all-creative," marking it as awakening to itself (60). In letting all be seen from its own reality in its shining, light illuminates as allowing everything to stand in its own "outline and measure" (*Umriss und Mass*). The differentiating of each thing in its own essence and its shining "is all a shining of illuminating spirit." After the colon Heidegger writes: "*be-geistert.*" While this might be translated as "in-spired," I suggest "in-spirited," for what nature does is to instill or install *Geist*. Thus, we learn that nature "in-spirits all as the all-presencing, all renewing." "It itself," Heidegger writes, "is 'the inspiriting.' In-spiriting can be only as 'spirit' is. [*Begeistern kann sie nur, weil sie 'der Geist' ist*]." He goes on to explain that "spirit rules as the sober but daring setting-apart, that places all that comes-to-presence [*Anwesende*] in its presencing [*seiner Anwesung*] into its well-separated boundaries [*wohlgeschiedenen Grenzen*] and articulative wholeness [*Gefüge*]. Such setting apart is essential thinking." Spirit is the "unifying unity" in and through which the setting-apart and gathering-together of thinking takes place. It is in thinking the "common spirit" (*gemeinsame Geist*).

Heidegger discusses spirit in his 1942 course "The Ister," the 1943 course "Andenken" (Remembrance), and in the earlier Trakl essay. In the 1942 lectures the teaching on spirit is reached from a joining of the choral ode from Sophocles' *Antigone* and Hölderlin's river-poems (G53 153–56; cf. G52 71–73) that follows a massive exploration of the choral ode (G53 63–172). The river-poems and the choral ode say the Same (152). There is a "poetic-historical dialogue" between Hölderlin and Sophocles; they say the Same and thus say difference, where difference means that the Greeks and the Germans must become who they are in different ways, under different, yet the same, conditions.

Hölderlin's letter to Böhlendorff is not, Heidegger emphasizes, a "contribution to a future aesthetic of German 'literature'" but is instead a "reflection on what is to be poetized essentially [*was das wesen-*

haft Zu-Dichtende ist]" (154): "the becoming-homey [*Heimischwerden*] of the historical humanity of the Germans within Western history." We are "first experiencing the essence of history in its true law," and thus we "become caught by the need of historicity." Heidegger explains the "historicity of a collectivity [*Menschentums*]": "Being-unhomey" (*Unheimischseins*) conditions the "Being-homey" (*Heimischseins*) of "becoming-homey," a conditioning that can only be determined and said poetically, as Hölderlin has been the first German poet to do. The task facing "historical man" is spelled out: "The law of Being-homey as a becoming-homey consists of the fact that historical man at the beginning of his history is not versed in the homey (156)." Moreover, Heidegger writes, man "must be come unhomey toward the latter in order to learn by departing from the homey toward the foreign about the appropriation of what is his own, and he first becomes homey only in the return from the foreign." "The historical spirit of history of a collectivity" must allow itself to be foreign to itself "in order to find itself in a setting-apart with it, what for the return to the hearth is a *Schickliche*," which I suggest here can mean "what is suitable." There is a skeptical breath drawn here: "Provided that history is nothing other than such a return to the hearth." In this return a "historical people" takes up its "*natural* condition," "when the natural becomes historical (as its) history" (G4 88). The way in which the people dwells on the earth that is correlative with this relation is found in Hölderlin's lines from "In Lovely Blueness . . .": "Full of merit, yet poetically, man / Dwells on this earth" (89).

The question of "historically grounding spirit" is explored from lines from a version of Hölderlin's "Bread and Wine" not published until 1933 (G53 156–70; G4 89–90):

> For spirit is not at home
> In the inception, not at the source. It is consumed by the homeland.
> Colony spirit loves, and bold forgetting.
> Our flowers enchant and the shadows of our woods
> He who consumes himself. He would be almost ash the besouler.[21]

From this fragment, "what poetry, what history, what truth is, and what most importantly 'is' will be experienced as 'Being'" (157).

Hölderlin's poetizing of "Geist," while indebted to German idealism, is an "overcoming and turning away" (*Überwindung und Abkehr*) from metaphysical senses of "Geist" (157–58). German idealism understands "spirit" as subjective, objective, and absolute spirit, as the unconditioned; as Absolute, spirit "conditions and determines" (*bedingt und bestimmt*) all beings and, gathering in and as thinking itself, exhibits its self-grounding, its home. "Only when spirit thinks itself as itself," Heidegger writes, "is it truly spirit. And its thinking is not only heard, but rather has the distinction [*Auszeichnung*] itself to *be*. Thinking itself 'is' in a superior [*ausgezeichneten*] sense." The thoughts of spirit are those which gather into a community, a point Heidegger makes with a line from Hölderlin's poem "As on a Holiday . . ." (159): "The thoughts of the communal spirit they are" (*Des gemeinsamen Geistes Gedanken sind*). In the poem this line refers back to the final line of the previous strophe: "The all-alive, all-animating powers of the gods." *These* powers are exhibited, situated, in three locations: in "song" grown from the soil, in "storms that are in the air," and in "others," the poets. The poets, as responsive founders, exhibit the movement of spirit, for poetic remembrance is a self-enacting speech act that is also a self-enacting (i.e., foundationless), political founding (G4 65–67, 148–49). In that founding the gods are joined into the "order of presencing" (*Anwesenheit*) in and through the "rigor of poetic thinking" (G4 87–88). Attunement to spirit—orientation of Dasein toward what is sent—is attunement to conditionality, and this is the correction of German idealism exhibited in Hölderlin (G53 159).[22] It is only to the extent that a historical people is and has a history that it can make history, for what becomes, what is fitting, exhibits in man what spirit thinks (*denkt*) and destines (*zudenkt*). The lack of these relations to and in history is a loss (*Verlieren*) of historical being.

The poet as "besouler" (*Beseeler*) can exhibit the homey because his *Mut* ("courage," "heart," or, "spiritedness") is the site for the reception of divine fire; he is turned toward the "cooling clarification of the fires from heaven," a formula that joins the ownmosts of the Germans and the Greeks (159–60, 166–67). The political significance of the poet is made evident: "Hölderlin speaks in these fragments historically-poetically [*geschichtlich dichterisch*] for the unique [*einzige*] history of the Germans from the law of Being-unhomey as the law of becoming-homey" (168). We know this freely, Heidegger says, only when we truly understand what Hölderlin says at the beginning of "The Ister": "Now come, fire!" The Germans must remain in "danger and weakness" (*Gefahr und Schwäche*) as the condition for them to "mount and furnish" (*Einfassen und Einrichten*) a place for the heavenly fire to bring itself to stand (169). Essential to this role is Hölderlin's account of the difference between the Greeks and Germans in his "Remarks on 'Antigone.'" For us, the immediacy of the relation between the word of tragic representation and the "sensuous body" for the Greeks transforms itself into a relation between this word and the "more spiritual body"; thus, "it is the main tendency in the modes of representation of our time"—Heidegger glosses this: "the time of the Germans"—"to designate something, to possess a skill [*Geschik*], since the destinylessness [*Schicksaallose*], the *dysmoron,* is our weakness" (169–70). It is, however, a possibility that the Germans may surpass the Greeks; they may build a "guest-house" for the gods, to receive the heavenly fire when the Greeks can no longer build appropriate temples (155).

Even Hölderlin could not sing directly of the fatherland, after all, because he could not name the god; in the poet's words in "Homecoming," ". . . Holy names are wanting" (G4 26–27). For Heidegger this phrase becomes a motto for our time, for our present condition as the "destitute time of the world's night" marked by a "want of god" ("want" translates *Fehl,* which can also be rendered as "lack" or, in Hofstadter's translation, "default") so severe that it cannot be seen as a want (PLT 91–93). Hölderlin's experience "does not deny that the Christian relationship with God lives on in individuals and in the churches; still less does it assess this relationship negatively." What must be understood here is that the Christian God is separated decisively from what Heidegger understands as the decisive activity of a god. Thus, the want of god means "that no god any longer, visibly and unequivocally, gathers men and things unto himself, and from such gathering, joins world history and the sojourn of men in it" (91). "More troubling" is that the "radiance of the godhead" (*Glanz der Gottheit*) has "become extinguished in world history." The lack of god is the condition for the absence of ground, which means the absence of "soil for striking root and standing," and the "age, for which the ground fails to come, hangs in the abyss" (92). If a "turn" (*Wende*) away from the abyss remains possible, the abyss must be "experienced and endured," "but for this it is necessary that there be those who reach [*reichen*] into the abyss." The "turning of the age" is not brought about by a god, old or new, for men have not yet prepared an "abode" for him, nor could there be such an abode "if a divine radiance did not first begin to shine in everything that is." The gods can return only at the "right time" (*richtiger Zeit*), when "there has been a turn among men in the right place [*rechten Ort*], in the right way [*rechten Art*]." Heidegger's political thinking attempts to promote such a turn.

Although we do not know whether we have reached the greatest distress, the midnight of the world's night, or whether, despite "the immeasurable need, despite all suffering, despite nameless sorow, despite the growing and spreading peacelessness, despite the mounting confusion," we have not, the world's night must be thought as a "destiny" (*Geschick*) (93). Thus, in his essay ("Der Fehl Heiliger Namen") (The lack of holy names) (1974), Heidegger writes that if the present age of technology could experience Enframing as the determinate way in which unconcealing ↔ concealing happens today, distinguished by its concealing of this motion itself, our Dasein "would be allotted participation in the open region of the saving" (WHN 264; cf. QCT 27–40). There is a turn for "mortals" (*Sterblichen*) when they "find their way into their own essence" (*Wesen*); "they reach into the abyss sooner than the heavenly," for they "remain closer to that absence [*Abwesen*] because they are touched by presence [*Anwesen*], the ancient name of Being" (PLT 93). "But because presence conceals itself as the same time," Heidegger writes, "it is itself already absence. Thus the abyss holds and marks [*merkt*] everything." A mortal who reaches into the abyss "sooner than [other] mortals and otherwise than they" experiences the "characteristic marks" (*Merkmale*) "recorded" (or, "remarked," *vermerkt*) by the abyss; for the poet these are the "traces" (*Spuren*) of the "fugitive" (*entflohenen*) gods, in which he traces "the way toward the turning" for "kindred mortals" in his singing (93–94). The "ether" (*Äther*) is the godhead, "in which alone the gods are gods"; the "element" of the ether "within which even the godhead itself presences [*west*]" is the holy, which is the "trace" of the fugitive gods, itself traced in the poet's singing (94). Heidegger explains that this is why "the poet in the time of the world's night utters the holy" and why in Hölderlin "the world's night is the holy night." In a formulation which joins Hölderlin and the Greeks, Heidegger writes that only the poet's kind of understanding, which in poeticizing allows the "pure appeal" of the "presencing" (*Anwesen*) of "withdrawal and denial" to reach him, allows him "to endure distress, namely that inceptive urgency out of which the urgency of the want of Holy names first arises," which is the "oblivion of Being, that is, the self-concealing [*Lethe*] of the uniqueness of Being as presencing." The oblivion of Being names the *Geschick* of the clearing (*Lichtung*) of Being, *alētheia*, which must, as we have already seen, withhold itself from thought. This withdrawal "happened at the inception of Western thought *as* this inception and has since then characterized succeeding epochs of the history of Being up to the contemporary technological age in such fashion that the oblivion of Being without knowing it adheres to the destiny of the clearing as its principle" (WHN 265–66).

"Since the flight of the gods," Heidegger writes, "the earth is pathless. Neither can man find the way, nor do the gods immediately show it" (G39 224). In the motion allegorized in the river-poems, however, "land and earth secure limit and shape [*Grenze und Gestalt*], and become a homeland to men and thereby the truth to the people." Now Heidegger's thinking concerning the gods and their flight has nothing to do, he maintains, with the ontotheological transcendence found both in Christianity and ostensibly "counter-Christian" (*gegenchristliche*) world-views such as transcendent conceptions of the *Volk* (G65 24–26). Such "transcendence," thought as "idea," "value," or "meaning," intelligible in "culture," whether as "*völkische* ideas and Christianity," "*völkische* ideas and cultural politics [*Kulturpolitik*]," or "Christianity and culture," separately or in combination, are all world-views and as such, expressions of "liberalism" (25). They all must be measured by the forgetting of Being. Rather than conventional "transcendence," Heidegger writes of the Between, characterized as the Open, together with man as its "grounder and preserver," standing and remaining in the truth of Being (26). *Ereignis*, the theme of the *Beiträge*, is the Between as related to the "passings-by" (*Vorbeigangs*) of gods and the history of human beings (27). The three elements—*Ereignis*, these "passings-by," and human history—are not identical; rather, the difficult thought here is that the passing gods may give an opening or access to human beings, an "eventuating" (*ereignende*) happening of the grounding of Dasein and of the consequent bringing back by Dasein of beings to the truth of Being. Put in more propositional terms, human beings think and act in a way freed of any and all epochal principles. It is from the need disclosed and concealed in the forgetting of Being that the grounding of the truth of Being is necessarily the grounding of Dasein (28). "This necessity enacts itself in the standing of all historical human-Being in a completely ruling decision" whether man will have the strength to belong to the truth of Being and out of and for this belonging to bring beings to be in the truth of Being, or whether man begins to become the "last man," grounded, as we have seen, in "ani-

mality" (*Tierheit*), and thus refuses the "last god." Da-sein, hyphenated
to emphasize sitedness, is the "Between between [*Zwischen zwischen*]
men (as grounded historically) and the gods (in their history) (311).
Now the significance of the gods, or of a site for them, can be ascer-
tained in connection with Heidegger's decisive teaching on the identity
of a people. "A people is only a people," he writes, "if it receives
its history through the discovery of its god, through the god, which,
through history, compels it in a direction and so places it back in
being" (398). The "few" or the "one" who can speak for the people and
who seek the god "even apparently must oppose the still insufficiently
folklike 'folk' [*volkhafte 'Volk'*]" (319, 399). Thus, "the essence of the
people is grounded in the historicity of those listening to themselves on
the basis of the relation of belonging to the god" (399). This teaching is
found in reflections on the "last god," emblematic of an other inception,
and not a new foundation; that is, a "god" compliant with finitude, the
"last end" or "essential end" "demanded from the inception and not
brought to it from without" (409–10). With this god in its singularity all
"theisms" fall, and its "beckoning" opens to an "other inception" as a
possibility of "our history" (411). "This god," Heidegger writes, "will
set up the simplest, but furthest contradictions over his people as the
paths over which they wander outward in order to find its essence again
and to exhaust the moment of its history" (399).

As thought in *Beiträge*, "the people" are, or must become, Hölderlinian "mortals," and it is necessary to turn to several texts in which
Heidegger speaks of the fourfold (*das Geviert*) to understand the significance of this identity. The fourfold is a way of naming sitedness as such,
thought from Hölderlin, which is to say, thought without a foundation,
without a metaphysical first. A brief resume of the path which leads to
the fourfold is in order. In "Building Dwelling Thinking," Heidegger
presents "building" (*bauen*) as dwelling (PLT 146–47). In turn, "to be
human means: to be on the earth as a mortal [*Sterblicher*], to dwell"
(147)—and "the poetic is the basic capacity for human dwelling" (228).
Thus understood, building includes cultivation and construction, activities which take over "building," the real sense of which is "re-
tracted" (*zurücknimmt*) by language, which thereby shows the "originariness" (*Ürsprungliche*) of "dwelling" (148). Dwelling is not inaction
but rather has its own proper motion, that of bringing to peace, which
for Heidegger means as well freedom and "sparing" (*Schonen*); in
dwelling we free things to be what they are (148–49). The site of

dwelling is on the earth, which means as well under the sky (*Himmel*); taken together, "on the earth" and "under the sky" mean "remaining before the gods" and include a "belonging to men's being with one another." The fourfold—earth/sky/mortals/gods—belongs together "out of an originary oneness" (*aus einer ursprünglichen Einheit*) (149).

A "thing" is, presences, as a gathering (*Versammlung*) of the fourfold (153). In "The Thing," the "thinging" of a thing "gathers the fourfold's stay, its while," into the thing, a self-limiting motion Heidegger calls a "gathering-appropriating staying of the fourfold" (*versammelnd-ereignenden Verweilen des Gevierts*) (173–74). In Old High German "thing" means "anything that in any way bears upon men, concerns them, and that accordingly is a matter for discourse" (174). While this sense attaches to the Latin *res*, from the Greek *eirō*, the Latin *causa*, the Romance *la cosa*, French *la chose*, English "thing," it is not thought, for the Romans took the *realitas* of *res* from the metaphysically thought Greek *on*, which means that gathering hardens into what is merely present. (176–77).

None of the four is privileged, for each is always already implicated in the others; as Heidegger says in connection with each of the four, "we give no thought to the onefold [*Einfalt*] of the four" (149–50). As Heidegger explains in "The Thing," each of the four "mirrors" (*spiegelt*) the others and "reflects itself in its own way into its own, within the onefold of the Four" (179). This is an "appropriate mirroring" (*ereignende Spiegeln*) in which none of the four exhibits mere likeness. Rather, "each of the four plays to each of the others." Such mirroring "sets each of the four free into its own, but it binds these free ones into the onefold of their essential being toward one another." Mirroring is the "play" in which none "insists on its own separate particularity. Rather, each is expropriated [*enteignet*], within their mutual appropriation, into its own being. This expropriative appropriating [*enteignende Vereignen*] is the mirror-play [*Spiegel-Spiel*] of the Four," also known as "world," which cannot be explained in any more grounded or deeper way (179–80; cf. 199–200). The "fouring" (*Vierung*) presences as "worlding of world" (*Welten von Welt*) (180). "The mirror-play of world is the round dance of appropriating"; as Heidegger explains in "Language," "world" thus understood is distinguished decisively from "world" as thought in and by metaphysics (201).

Gathering and the fourfold are not to be explained in any more foundational (i.e., metaphysical) way; in particular, the fourfold is not a new set of ontological categories. I agree with Reiner Schürmann that what is shown in this account is Heidegger's sense of the "fragmentation of the originary," on his view that the originary is "irreducibly manifold" and that the use of "fourfold" "stresses the plurification of *hen*"; in his words, "Presencing has lost its center."[23] Heidegger's account of the unity of the fourfold as fouring detaches the fourfold and its unity from metaphysical discourse. The fouring, presencing as appropriating mirror-play, the worlding of world, happens as ringing, as a round dance (PLT 180). The four are called "nestling, malleable, pliant, compliant, nimble" (*schmiegsam, schmiedbar, geschmeidig, fügsam, leicht*)—in Old German *ring* and *gering:* "Out of the ringing mirror-play the thinging of the thing takes place." Our response, in which "we let ourselves be concerned by the thing's worlding being . . . [and] called by the thing as the thing," retrieves one of Heidegger's earliest and latest thoughts. "In the strict sense of the word [the English translator interpolates "German" before "word"], we are the *Be-Dingten*," that is, the conditioned. "We have left behind us the presumption of all unconditioned-ness." This advance in our *paideia* is a step back from thinking that explains to "recollective thinking" (*andenkendede Denken*), which is no mere shift of attitude (181). The fourfold intimates an other inception.

In "The Turning" this teaching is inscribed in the crisis of the present age, in which Enframing is the way Being presences and which comes to light as danger (QCT 41). Governed by Hölderlin's lines in "Patmos"—"But where danger is, grows / The saving power also"— Heidegger's thought here is that the presencing of Being as its own oblivion is both danger and saving power. Coming to light as danger, this motion is the clearing and lighting of the clearing, the site, of Being (44). The "lightning-flash" of the truth of Being is both "flash" and "glance" (*blitzen = blicken*) (44–45). The glancing both "retrieves that which it catches sight of and brings back into the brightness of its own looking" and "in its giving of light, simultaneously keeps safe the concealed darkness of its origin as the unlighted. The in-turning [*Einkehr*] that is the lightning-flash of the truth of Being is the entering, flashing glance [*Einblick*]." The truth of Being is as worlding of world; when "oblivion turns about" and "world turns in," there is the "in-flashing" (*Einblitz*) of "world into the injurious neglect of the thing" that belongs to Enframing. The flash *is* "insight into that which is" (46–47). When Enframing is thus illuminated as danger, it is as saving power. This is why Enframing is "no blind destiny in the sense of a completely ordained fate" (47). Thus, human beings "are caught sight of" when their essence is struck by the flashing of Being, a thought irresistibly suggesting of the way in which the gods look into the *polis*. In his corresponding to the claim of this insight, which is a renunciation of self-will, man is "gathered into his own, that he, within the safeguarded element of world, may, as the mortal, look out toward the god." The god, in turn, is a being and thus conditioned by way Being presences, "which brings itself disclosingly to pass out of the worlding of world." "Whether the god lives or remains dead is not decided by the religiosity of men and even less by the theological aspirations of philosophy and natural science. Whether or not God is God comes disclosingly to pass from out of and within the constellation of Being" (49).

I return to the Hölderlin lectures for the final example of Heidegger's political teaching in this section. The law of history thought through Hölderlin is not a logic of history but is more fundamental than any such logic (G53 179). When it is forgotten, mankind (*Menschentum*) falls into the "unhistorical" (*Ungeschichtliche*). The unhistorical is the "breaking down" (*Abbruch*) of history into a "completely other essence as the historyless" (*ganz anderen Wesens als das Geschichtslose*). That Heidegger intends a political sense for this teaching is evident in the passage that follows. "Historyless is nature," he writes, "unhistorical and catastrophic" as is "Americanism," which has its ground in an "unessence" (*Unwesen*) that is its essence. This pronouncement completes a thought found earlier in the lecture, in a "retrieval" in which the sitedness of historical man, as exhibited in *Antigone* and Hölderlin's river-poems, is contrasted with the understandings of space and time, and therewith of the human situation, offered in and by the tradition of metaphysics (65–69). The tradition culminates in the triumph of machine technology, which Heidegger explains is incorrectly understood as "materialistic" (66). It is rather "spirit" and is "as this a decision concerning the actuality of the actual," the spiritual effects of which necessarily remain with us (66–67). It is possible and necessary, however, for *us* to think the "singularity of origin," and for this undertaking, Hölderlin's law of history is essential (67). Hölderlin thought this issue more profoundly than Romanticism or Nietzsche and thus reaches an inner relation between the Greeks and the Germans that eluded his successors (67–68). After this, Heidegger remarks, on the entry of the United States into the war, that the "anglo-saxonish world of America is resolved to annihilate [*vernichten*] Europe," and thus the "home [*Heimat*], and the inception [*Anfang*] of the West." "The inceptive," however, is "indestructible." America's entry into "this planetary war is not an entry into history; rather, it is already the last American act of America's historylessness [*Geschichtslosigkeit*] and self-destruction [*Selbstverwüstung*]. This act is a renunciation [*Absage*] of the inceptive [*Anfängliche*] and a decision for the inceptionless [*Anfanglose*]." There can be no stronger Heideggerian condemnation than this.

III

Spirit is flame, according to Heidegger's reflection on Trakl (OWL 181). In the final part of this chapter I attempt a more directly "political" reading of the later Trakl essay than is found in Derrida's influential account.[24] Heidegger's aim in the essay is to "situate the site" (*Ort zu erörtern*) of Trakl's "poetic saying" (*Sagen*), which is created from a single poem, a "singleness" (*Einzigen*) to which he is committed (160). This single poem is "unspoken" in the poet's poems and is nowhere spoken as a whole, yet it is from the whole (*Ganzen*) that each poem is said. "From the site of the poem there arises the wave [*Woge*]," Heidegger writes, "that in each instance moves his saying as a poetizing." The wave lets the "movement of saying" flow back to its "ever more hidden origin [*Ursprung*]." The recursive motion of poetic saying traces the motion of unconcealing ↔ concealing; each poem, which requires clarification, is a compound of this latter motion. Heidegger's dialogue with Trakl is a dialogue of thinking with poetry and is distinguished from an "authentic" (*eigentliche*) dialogue—"the poetic dialogue between poets." The aim of Heidegger's dialogue is political; it seeks to "call for the *essence* of language, so that mortals may learn again to dwell within language" (161). As an instance of Heidegger's political thinking, the situating of the site of Trakl's poetry is a retrieval, and the structure of his undertaking here is that of the Hölderlin readings.

The first clarification is decisive; from one of Trakl's poems Heidegger takes the line "Something strange is the soul on the earth" and distinguishes this condition fundamentally from the "common notion," beginning with Plato, that the earthly is "the perishing" or "transitory" (*Vergänglichen*) and the soul the "imperishable" (*Unvergängliche*), belonging to the "suprasensuous" (*Übersinnlichen*) (161–62). If the soul appears in the "sensuous" (*Sinnlichen*), it does so only as *verschlagen*, as "cast away" or having "lost its place"; "on earth" the soul does not have the "right cast" (*rechten Schlag*). *Schlag, schlagen,* and *Geschlecht* play through the Trakl essay.[25] *Schlagen* means to strike, hit, beat, stroke; a *Schlag* is a blow, hit, or stroke. Since *schlagen* can also mean to coin or stamp, a *Schlag* can be a specific coinage or type, a cast or stamp, and as such *schlagen* is the root of *Geschlecht*—human beings with a common ancestry, a stock or kind, humankind, a generation that dies to be replaced by another. *Geschlechters* are members of a *Geschlecht*, male and female human beings, and *Geschlecht* is a root for a family of words naming aspects of sexuality. Thus, *Geschlechters* names a "how" of human beings, a way human beings are—*as Geschlechters.* In the passage under discussion we learn that the site of the soul and the location of the site are thematic; the *soul* is stamped (given an identity), *stamped* (within limits), and stamped *as* . . . (something conditional, determinate). Thus, we learn that there is or may be a fitting stamping, as well as a stamping unfitting for the soul. Behind the figure of *Schlag* is *epochal* stamping, for it is in and from the stamping named by "Plato" that the stamp or cast of the soul on earth is not "right." Is another, better stamp possible?

Heidegger registers the rupture with "Plato" and the tradition by distinguishing what is "strange" for them, from the proper understanding of "strange" in Trakl's poem. Heidegger reads Trakl's "fremd" as the Old High German (*althochdeutsch*) "fram," which means "forward to somewhere else, underway toward . . . , onward to the encounter with what is kept in store for it," a movement toward its "determination" (*Bestimmung*), "already following the call that calls it on the way into its own [*Eigenes*]," a call already sited "on the earth" (162–63). The relation of "own" and "foreign," the principal motive of the Hölderlin readings, is condensed here into a drop of etymology. Moreover, the determination and call that portends the proper siting of the soul on the earth is, and must be, said in *German.*

The soul seeks the earth "so that she may poetically build and dwell upon it, and thus may be able to save the earth *as* earth, fulfilling the essence of the soul" (163). Thus characterized, the soul's seeking is excluded from any traditional understanding of transcendence and is inscribed in Heideggerian transcendence, which means that it transcends, that is, moves essentially, *toward* earth and thus toward finitude. It cannot lose its strangeness; it is "always underway [*Un-*

terwegs]" and is "called to go under [*Untergang*]" into "peace and silence" (163–64). The movement of the soul is into the "twilight" (*Dämmerung*), which Heidegger notes, belongs both to night and morning (164). In Trakl's poem, the "blue" of the sky *dämmert* "spiritually" (*geistlich*). *Dämmern* can mean "to dawn," but in order to convey the dual sense Heidegger intends, one must transform "twilight" into a verb, which can be done if "twi-" is taken as in Old English, in which it can mean "half," thus "half-lighting." "Twilight" encompasses both the day and the year; their movement is half-lighted spiritually, at once sheltered and illuminated, both of which are spiritual *actions*. The year is crucial, for in Trakl's poetry the recurrence of "so quiet" (*so leise*) marks the slow slipping away of the seasons, a quiet in which rings "the music of [the stranger's] spiritual years [*geistlichen Jahre*]" as he follows the paths (*Pfade*) into the twilight (164–65). I remind the reader of the "year of the people" in Heidegger's reading of Hölderlin's "Germanien"; *this* year is sheltered by spiritual night.[26] It is also worth noting that "paths" is plural; what is to be recalled (*gedenken*) is not a one (165). For Heidegger those who follow the stranger are named in Trakl's poetry by "blue wild game" (*blaues Wild*), that is, a kind of animal whose color is that of the night.

The "sheaf of blueness" of night, Heidegger writes, "gathers the depth of the holy in the depths of its bond. The holy shines out of the blueness, even while veiling itself in the dark of that blueness. The holy withholds in withdrawing. The holy bestows its arrival by reserving itself in its withholding withdrawal." Heidegger has inscribed "the holy" in Trakl's poetizing; its movement we have already followed in the Hölderlin readings. Here the dark shelters "clarity" (*Helle*), which is the "blueness" of the poem, and which is "originarily" the "tone that calls out of the shelter of stillness, and thus lightens itself [*sich lichtet*]." The thought here blends the resounding, the ringing, of blueness and the shining of its darkness. The holy is never brought to full discursive clarity, but its withholding withdrawal is both heard and seen.

When the "animal face" of Trakl's poem encounters the holy in its self-shining self-veiling, it "freezes" (*erstarrt*), looking toward the holy and retracting into gentleness, which "transforms [*verwandelt*] [its] discord by absorbing the wounding and searing wildness into appeased pain" (166). Its looking "says: entering into silence," the power of the "rock" to gather the "soothing power" of pain, which "stills" us "into the essential [*Wesenhafte*]." In the earlier Trakl reading: "Pain rends. It is the rift [*Riss*]" that tears and separates, yet gathers (OWL 204). It is "the joining [*Fügende*] in the dividing-gathering rending. . . . Pain joins the rift of the dif-ference (*Unter-Scheides*). Pain is the dif-ference itself." "Still" names a motion, explicated when Heidegger says: "To keep in repose is to still" (OWL 206). "Stilling," then, is a compound of motion and rest, which we know in Heidegger is always self-restraining motion as well. Heidegger goes on to say in OWL that the difference "stills the thing, as thing, into world," calling "world and thing into the middle of their intimacy," a "gathering calling" he calls "the pealing." "Language," he writes, "speaks as the peal of stillness" (207). In speaking thus, language sounds the proper motion of Dasein.

The identity of the "animal" is made clear when Heidegger explains that, in the poem, "it is called upon to think"; its animality remains "undetermined," not yet gathered into the "home of its veiled essence" (166–67). It is man, the rational animal, as thought by Nietzsche at the end of "Western-European metaphysics," which struggles, perhaps in vain, to accomplish this determination. Heidegger's invoking of "Nietzsche" here marks a setting-apart from Western metaphysics of Trakl's tracing of the journey of those who "would think of the stranger and wander with him to the one home [*Einheimische*] of human essence" (167). This movement of the wanderers into a death which is without decay leaves behind the decaying of "previous" (*bisherige*) man, an echo of Heidegger's decisive separation of Dasein and world from animality. And yet, this "human form" (*Menschengestalt*) has a *soul*, albeit one that "does not stand in the wind of the holy" and thus is "without course" (*ohne Fahrt*) (168).

Those who follow the stranger and go under, who *have* a course, must themselves "become strangers and solitary," exposed to the cool glance of "spiritual night" and, distinguished once again, parted "from loved ones" who to them are "others," from the "cast" (*Schlag*) of the "decomposed form" (*verwesten Gestalt*) of man (170). Heidegger explains that "our language" names the "human essence" (*Menschenwesen*) "stamped out of a single cast" (*aus einem Schlag geprägte*) and "cast away into this cast," "Geschlecht." "Mankind [*Menschengeschlecht*] in the sense of humanity" means "as *Geschlechter* in the senses of stock, tribe, family, and all these in turn stamped in the twofold of the *Geschlechter*." The poet names the "'decomposing' kind" ("*verwesende*"

Geschlecht) as the "decomposed form" of man, "removed from its kind of essence and therewith a 'displaced' (*'entsetzt'*) *Geschlecht.*"

"By what," Heidegger asks, "is this *Geschlecht* struck, that is, cursed?"

> The Greek word for curse is *plēgē*, the German word *Schlag*. The curse of the decomposing *Geschlecht* consists in the fact that this ancient *Geschlecht* has been dispersed [*auseinandergeschlagen ist*] in the discord of *Geschlechter*. Within such discord each of the *Geschlechter* seeks the unchecked tumult of individualized and utter savagery. Not the twofold [*Zwiefache*] as such, but discord [*Zwietracht*], is the curse. From the tumult of blind savagery, discord casts the *Geschlecht* into abscission and imprisons it in unchecked individuation. So ravaged, so severed in twain, the "fallen *Geschlecht*" can on its own no longer find its way into the right *Schlag*. It can find its way only as that *Geschlecht* whose twofold wanders forth out of discord into the gentleness of an innocent twofold [*einfältigen Zweifalt*]. That *Geschlecht* is "foreign" [*ein Fremdes*], and it follows the stranger.[27]

Note that the dispersion of *Geschlecht* into *Geschlechter* must not be read too narrowly, for more is thought here than the division of male and female human beings; rather, that distinction figures all distinctions marked by discord. The inceptive dispersion, as one might call it, displaces the *Geschlecht* of human beings, giving it the wrong stamp or cast; displaced into the Western site of the thinking animal, human *Geschlecht* traces the path I have already followed in Heidegger's interpretation of Plato—what begins in Plato with human beings oriented toward the *ideas* ends in Nietzsche with animality divided into last man and overman.

The wandering soul of the stranger is "set apart" (*geschieden*) to "yonder" ("Jener"), which Heidegger explains, in a sentence omitted from the English translation, is, in the "old language," "ener," which means "other" ("andere") (US 46). The stranger, then, is the "other to the others," to the "decomposing *Geschlecht*," which I think should be taken broadly as Western humanity, stamped by the inception of the West, and thus by any epochal stamping (171). He is "the apart" (*Abgeschiedene*), a depersonalized name, registered as such when Heidegger asks "to where" (*Wohin*) is "one such" who "assumes the essence of the strange," a "strange being" (*ein Fremdes*) called? The stranger is called to "go under" (*Untergang*), "to lose itself [*Sich-verlieren*] in the spiritual [*geistliche*] twilight of the blue." He "happens [*geschieht*] out of the decline toward the spiritual year," and although this decline must move through the "destructiveness" (*Zerstörende*) of winter, it is not "annihilated" (*Vernichtung*), the "self-losing" (*Sichverlierende*)—a further depersonalizing of the stranger—is a disappearance into the "November destruction" which is a slipping through it, a move toward and into "evening" (*Abend*) (171–72). "Evening," Heidegger explains, "consummates a change [*Wechsel*]"; it "inclines to the spiritual," making the appearances of what the poets say and the thinkers try to grasp in thought look differently (172). It is also the case, I think, that "Abend" retains its role as the prefix of "Abendland," the *German West*, or the West as German. The descent into evening is a going under into the "beginning" (*Beginn*) of the stranger's wanderings, to the "site" (*Ort*) where "everything has come together in another way, where everything is sheltered and preserved for an other ascent [*ein anderen Aufgang*]." The site now reached must be named.

"Apartness" (*Abgeschiedenheit*) is the site of Trakl's poetizing; Heidegger's teaching on spirit illuminates this site, for apartness is "spiritual" (172, 177). "Apartness" in the Trakl reading must be distinguished from the "parting" (*Abschied*) against and obstructing of the path into the Open carried out by technological man (PLT 115–16). To understand apartness, it is necessary to follow the stranger's path, asking: "Who is the departed one? What is the landscape of his paths?" (OWL 172). Because his paths through the blue are illuminated by the cool moonlight, Heidegger calls these paths, after Trakl, "lunar paths of the departed" (*mondenen Pfade der Abgeschiedenen*) (173). The departed, the stranger, has died into another kind of life, that of the "madman" (*Wahn-sinnige*), whose mind is *not* filled with "the delusional" (*Unsinniges*). In another sentence omitted in the English translation, Heidegger again invokes the authority of Old High German to tell us that "mad" ("Wahn") was originally *wana,* meaning "without" ("ohne") (US 49); the madman is "without the sense of the others," for "he is of another mind [*anderen Sinnes*]" (173). In yet another sentence omitted in the English translation, Heidegger cites the "originary" (*ursprünglich*) meaning of the Old High German "sennan"—"to journey toward, to strive to . . . to take the direction of [*eine Richtung einschlagen*]," from the "Indogermanic roots *sent* and *set,*" which mean "way" (*Weg*).

The apartness of the madman lies in his having taken another direction, from which "his madness may be called 'gentle' [*sanfter*], for he pursues a greater stillness" (173). In Trakl's poetizing the stranger is also the boy who died young, thus, early, "shrouded in that childhood which preserves in greater stillness [*stiller*] all the burning and searing [*Brennende und Sengende*] of the wilderness" (174). His is the "dark shape of coolness" that walks before the wanderer because his "blue voice retrives [*zurückholt*] the forgotten and *fortells* [*vorsagt*] it." The temporal structure of retrieval, fundamental for Heideggerian politics, is inscribed in the going under of the stranger, the boy named Elis in Trakl's poem, into the evening. Heidegger joins Trakl's Elis and Nietzsche's Zarathustra, each differentiated from his creator, as alike in their "forms" (*Gestalten*) and in the beginnings of their journeys as descents. Elis "goes down into the primeval earliness [*uralte Frühe*] that is older than the older, decomposing *Geschlecht;* older because it is more mindful [*sinnender*], more mindful because it is more still, more still because it has itself a greater stilling power." The boyishness of Elis is the "appearance of his stiller childhood," which I read as more fundamental than, because it "shelters and stores within it," the "gentle twofold of *Geschlechters,*" of sex. Unlike the dead who decay and cease to be "in the lateness of a spent life," Elis is the dead who "moves away into earliness" (175). He "unfolds the human essence forward into the beginning of what is yet to be born. This quieter and hence more stilling undelivered [*Unausgetragene*] in the essence of mortals [*Sterblichen*] is what the poet calls the unborn [*Ungeborene*]." The stranger is this unborn; "the unborn" and "the strange" "say the same" (*sagen dasselbe*). The unborn "guards and watches over the stiller childhood for the coming awakening of mankind [*Menschengeschlechtes*]. Thus at rest, the early dead *lives*" and is not spent, looking forward "into the blue of the spiritual night." What is promised is, again, the "gentler twofold of *Geschlechtes.*"

A further reflection on the lonely path of the stranger shows that it leads past, but not through, what will not receive him as a guest: "the gloomy towns, the lonely summers." His path leads *through* the "spiritual years whose days are everywhere turned toward the beginning and are ruled, that is, set right [*recht*] from there. The year of his soul is gathered into rightness [*Rechte*]" (176). This rightness, sheltered by earliness, is the "essential rightness [*Wesensgerechte*] of the unborn." The right stamping of the soul has been announced.

Heidegger's clarification of the temporal character of earliness distinguishes it as a "time of its own kind [*eigener Art*], the time of the 'spiritual years.' " The stiller childhood is the inception (*Anbeginn*) that is preceded by the end of the "decaying *Geschlechtes*," which means that the inception, the "earlier earliness" (*frühere Frühe*) "has already overtaken the end." The inception, that is, lies ahead, as it always had for Heidegger. The earliness "preserves" the "originary essence, thus far always veiled, of time." Heidegger tells us—a retrieval of one of his own early and crucial teachings—that the essence of time will remain hidden as long as the Aristotelian representation of time as the "dimension of the quantitative or qualitative calculation of duration a sequential progression" is retained. Earliness in Trakl's poetizing is inscribed in Heidegger's critical engagement with Aristotle (e.g., BPP secs. 19–20). More directly than he does in almost any other text, Heidegger offers his alternative: "True time, however, is the arrival [*Ankunft*] of that which has been [*Gewesenen*]. This is not what is past, but rather the gathering of essencings [*Wesenden*], which precedes all such arrival in gathering itself into the shelter of what it was earlier" (OWL 176–77). The attunement corresponding to the "end and its accomplishment" is, in Trakl, called "dark patience," which bears "the concealed [*Verborgenes*] toward its truth," "toward its going under into the blue of the spiritual night" (177). In contrast, the inception "corresponds to a seeing and minding which gleams golden because it is illuminated by 'the golden, the true.' " I note that Heidegger does not call this seeing and minding itself the golden or the true; the originary illuminates but is never directly seen or grasped.

The difference between the stranger and the followers is evident, for his boat tosses "playfully" on the starry pond of night, while that of the followers tosses "timorously" and sinks. It does not sink into nothingness, for the "silent face of the night" looks down upon it. The silence belongs to apartness, as do the "earliness of stiller childhood, the blue night, the stranger's nighting paths, the soul's nocturnal wing-beat, even the twilight as the gateway to going under." This gathering into apartness happens "not afterward but such that apartness unfolds within its already ruling [*waltet*] gathering." Heidegger's final teaching on spirit is reached when we learn that apartness, the site of Trakl's poetizing, is "spiritual."

"Spiritual," Heidegger writes, "means what spirit is in meaning [*Sinn*], what stems from it and follows its essence" (178). Just as he had separated "soul" from Western metaphysics earlier, here Heidegger separates "spirit" from the "spirituality" of priests and church, from

Christianity, and therewith from the Western tradition again. Trakl's adjective "spiritually" (*gesitlich*) belongs instead to his thinking of the "earliness of the long-dead which promises the 'Springtime of the Soul.'" Heidegger asks: Why did not Trakl speak of the twilight or night of the spirit—of *geistigen* twilight or night? The poet's *geistliche* is not Christian *geistige*. His answer is that "spiritual" in the phrase "of the spirit" means the opposite of "material" and this "posits" (*stellt*) the "Platonic-Western [*platonisch-abendländisch*] gulf between the supra-sensuous [*noēton*] and the sensuous (*aisthēton*)." Spirit, and both Western metaphysics and Christianity are intended here, means "rational, intellectual, ideological" and their opposites, all of which belong to the "world-view [*Weltansicht*] of the decaying *Geschlechtes*" (179). Neither the twilight nor the stranger's path can be called spiritual in these senses. "Spirit" in Trakl is distinguished from the Western *pneuma*, "the ethereal" (*spirituell*), which is a derivative and not originary sense; in speaking of the "hot flame of the spirit"—spirit as "the flaming [*das Flammende*], and perhaps it is only as such that it is a blowing [*ein Wehendes*]"—Trakl sees spirit as "flame, that inflames [*entflammt*], rouses [*aufjagt*], displaces [*entsetzt*], and takes out of reach [*ausser Fassung bringt*]."[28] The flaming is lighting; it is the "outside-itself [*Ausser-sich*] that lights and lets shine, that also can consume and reduce everything to white ashes." Thus, Trakl understands *Geist* in its "originary signification" (*ursprünglichen Bedeutung*), what is said in and by *gheis:* "burst open [*aufgebracht*], displaced [*entsetzt*], being-outside-itself [*ausser sich sein*]." Spirit, then, "presences" (*west*)—its way of movement is—in the "possibility" (*Möglichkeit*) of "gentleness" (*Sanften*), which holds its flaming "gathered in the rest [*Ruhe*] of friendship" and "destructiveness" (*Zerstörerischen*), which as "active evil" is, as Heidegger had long maintained, spiritual and not material (cf. ST 146). Evil is spiritual, he writes, "as the revolt of a blinding displacing that places into the fragmentation of the disastrous [*Unheilen*] and threatens to reduce the gathered blooming of gentleness to ash." I remind the reader that the poet as inspiriter would, in Hölderlin's poem, be almost as ash. The spirituality of evil ensures that its destructiveness can never be far from gentleness, including the gentleness of the twofold of which the poet speaks.

In order to answer the question of the site and action of the gathering of gentleness, Heidegger must ask the decisive question: "How is human essencing [*Menschenwesen*] spiritual, and how does it become so?"

The answer is that since the essence of spirit is "in inflaming," it "strikes a course, lights it, and sets man on the way" (179–80). As flame, spirit is the "storm that 'storms the heavens' and 'hunts down God,'" and "drives the soul into the under-way [*Unterwegs*] where it leads the way" (180). In so driving the soul, spirit "carries it over into the strange [or foreign] [*versetzt in das Fremde*]," which is its way of being on earth, and which, we have learned from the Hölderlin readings, is necessary for it to come into its own. Thus, spirit brings the soul into its ownmost possibility. It "bestows" (*beschenkt*) the soul; it is the "besouler" or "inspiriter" (*Beseeler*) of the soul, which in turn guards it so that without it spirit could not be spirit. That is, the soul, essentially spirit, must be inflamed in order to become what it truly is, and thereby in turn "nourish" (*nährt*) spirit by giving it the flame that is its own essence. This is a political teaching, for its structure is precisely that of the relation of spirit and people I have already shown in the Hölderlin readings. In the Trakl reading the "greatness" of the soul—may one inscribe here Nietzschean "rank"?—is indicated by "its capacity to achieve the flaming vision by which the soul becomes at home in pain." Pain, in turn, rending, tearing away, marks the movement of the soul in both its heaven-storming sweep and its "fitting submission of seeing acceptance" (180–81).[29] The shining of flaming spirit "happens [*geschieht*] in the beholding look" to which the "advent of all that shines" "appropriates itself" (*ereignet sich*) (181). The "flaming vision" that is pain "determines" (*bestimmt*) the greatness of the soul, which means that pain is the "inspiriter" (*Beseeler*). Pain is the "fundamental trait" (*Grundzug*) of the soul's essence. "Only a being that lives soulfully," Heidegger writes, "can fullfil its essential determination [*Wesensbestimmung*]" that lets it belong to the "harmony of mutual bearing by which all living beings belong together." Every being that lives thus is "fit, that is to say, good. But the good is good painfully." Both the good and the truth of the soul must *be* painfully; this is the condition for giving sheltering concealment to beings that lets them be what they are. In Trakl's poetizing, pain, concealing itself in the stone, "delivers itself into the keeping of the impenetrable rock in whose appearance there shines forth the ancient origin out of the silent glow of the earliest early, which as the prior inception, is coming toward all becoming, wandering, bringing to it the advent [*Ankunft*] of its never to be overtaken essence" (182).

Pain is conditioning; it "looks earthily [*erdhaft*] upon mortals," telling them, the wanderers who follow the stranger, that it will always be with them. Everything "troubled, hampered, disastrous, and diseased, all the distress of disintegrating, is in truth only the singular semblance [*einzige Anschein*] in which the 'truth' conceals itself: the all-pervading pain" (183). Pain is "neither repugnant nor profitable [*Nützliche*]"; it is the "favor [*Gunst*] of the intrinsic [*Wesenhaften*] of essencing." Elsewhere the "favor," concealed within the self-concealing and oblivion of Being that characterizes the age of technology, and "as yet ungranted," marks a "turning," after which world and things are given without epochal determinants (QCT 43–44).[30] If "favor," thus understood, is inscribed in the Trakl reading, we find that pain is the necessary correlate of the temporality as which giving happens. That this thought may be present in the Trakl reading is suggested when Heidegger explains that the seemingly "contradictory essence of pain—that its sweep carries us truly onward only as it sweeps us back"—conceals its "essential onefold" (*Wesenseinfalt*), that in "flaming it carries itself fathest when it holds to itself most intimately in vision" (OWL 183). Pain is the "grounding trait" (*Grundzug*) of the "great soul" that corresponds to the "holiness of the blue," which "shines upon the soul's face by withdrawing into its own depth. The holy endures, when it presences [*west*], only by keeping within this withdrawal [*Entzug*] and by turning its vision toward the fitting [*Fügsame*]." Again, this teaching is of a piece with that of the Hölderlin readings, for the holy can never be exhibited completely (G4 63–70, 148).

"Pain is truly pain," Heidegger writes, "when it serves the flame of the spirit" (184). This sentence separates the "pain" spoken in Trakl's poem "Grodek" from ordinary pain. The "grandsons yet unborn" in the poem are not, Heidegger insists, "the unbegotten sons of the sons killed in battle, the progeny of the decaying generation [*Geschlecht*]," just as "Grodek" is not a war poem but "infinitely more, because it is something other." Indeed, if the poem merely marked an "end to the procreation of earlier *Geschlechter*," the poet "would have to rejoice," rather than mourn with a "prouder mourning." The "grandsons" are rather "an other generation" (*eine andere Generation*)—(I note that Heidegger does not write *Geschlecht* for "generation" here; "generation" is the Diltheyan term of distinction as it was in his early account of the crises of science and the university)—"other" (*anders*) because it is an "other kind" (*andersartig*) from "an essentially other origin" (*anderen Wesensherkunft*) "out of the earliness of the unborn." The "great pain," then, is the "beholding vision whose flames envelop everything and which looks ahead into the still-withdrawing earliness of yonder dead one toward whom the 'spirits' of early victims have died." Time—as I interpret the "spiritual" twilight, the night, and the years that inflame in the poem—guards pain "that it may feed the hot flame of the spirit." This "spiritual" (*Geistliche*) in turn, awakens from the spirit Trakl calls "the spirit of an early dead" (*An einen Frühverstorbenen*) (185).

Apartness "essences as pure spirit"; it is the "radiance of the blue reposing in the spirit's depth and flaming in greater stillness, the blue that kindles a stiller childhood into the gold of the inception" (185). Now since it is the "gathering power," apartness, already thought as the site of Trakl's poetizing, is yet another name for sitedness as such, for the *Da:* "As a gathering, apartness has the essence of a site [*Ort*]." The gathering power returns "mortal essence" back to its "stiller childhood," sheltering it as the "kind" (*Schlag*) "whose stamp marks future generations," withholding it for a "coming rebirth of man's essence out of earliness [*das Frühe*]," which stands here, I think, for an other inception. The "gathering stills, as the spirit of gentleness, the spirit of evil." "That spirit's revolt," Heidegger writes, "rises to its utmost malice when it breaks out even from the discord of the sexes [*Geschlechter*] and invades the realm of brother and sister." In apartness, the spirit of evil, an element of the "twofoldedness of humankind," is "neither destroyed and denied, nor set free and affirmed," but rather is "transformed" (*verwandelt*). What remains unsaid is the nature of this transformation, although the soul must "turn to the greatness of its essence," which is determined by "apartness," now explained as the "gathering through which the human essence is sheltered once again in its stiller childhood, and that childhood in turn is sheltered in the earlieness of another inception." "Apartness" is not the "desolation of the departed dead" but rather a path taken by the "stranger" in Trakl's "Summer's Decline" marked off from the rest of "humankind hitherto" (*bisherigen Geschlecht*), poetized as the "music of his spiritual years" (186). Sung by the soul of the departed and taken up by his friend, the song praises and thus guards what is praised (186–87). If "apartness rings out [*entgegenklinkt*] toward him who follows," the "spirit of the early dead appears in the glow of earliness [*im Glanz der Frühe*]" (187).

"Apartness is the poem's site," Heidegger writes, "because the mu-

sic of the stranger's ringing-radiant [*tönend-leuchtenden*] passage inflames his followers' dark wandering into listening song" (188). This
inflamed motion "clears" (*lichtet*) the souls of the followers, so that the
"whole being of the singing soul is one single concentrated gaze ahead
into the blue of night which holds that stiller earliness." What completes or perfects (*vollendet*) apartness as the site for the poem is its
gathering, which lets those gathered separate from the rest of humankind. This separation is crucial for the work of the poet, which is to "say
again the music of the spirit of apartness" to which he has listened. The
"saying-after" (*nach-sagen, nachsagenden*) precisely *is* "poetry"; what
poetry speaks "shelters the poetic as essentially unspoken." Because it
must listen, poetry becomes "more pious" (*frömmer*), "more joined"
(*fügsamer*) to the "promptings of the path."

Listening after the stranger who walks along the path "out of the
dark of childhood into the stiller, brighter earliness," the poet, gazing
into earliness, is parted from the rest of humankind, wandering in an
"infinite torment" that is "consummate, perfect [*vollendete, vollkom-
mene*] pain that comes into the fullness of its own essence" (189). The
"onefold" (*Einfalt*) of pain comes into its own, into "pure play" (*reine
Spiel*) during the journey in which "spirit's gentleness is called to hunt
down God, its shy reserve called to storm heaven" (189–90). It is
essential to note that this assault does not "lay the quarry [*Erjagte*] low
but lets it [God] arise to behold the sights of heaven whose pure coolness veils the Divine" (190). What is sought, that is, is what is above
God or the gods, in a seeking conditioned by pain to which the poet
submits. The path taken by the stranger leads away from the old "degenerate [*entarteten*] *Geschlecht*" and into the "earliness of the unborn
generation" (191). The language of poetry in the site of apartness "answers to the turning-home [*Heimkehr*] of unborn mankind into the quiet
inception of its stiller essence." That inception, however, is not accomplished, but rather is still "impending" (*ungewesenen*).

The language of Trakl's poetry speaks from this "transition" (*Übergang*) from the "downfall of all that decays over to the descent into the
twilit blue of the holy." Trakl's language, spoken "from the journey of
apartness," is essentially "multivocal" (*mehrdeutig*) because it speaks
from the "innermost site" (*innersten Ort*) of poetry, and thus out of a
gathering which "for itself alone, always remains unsayable" (192).
What can be said by the poet, what must be said multivocally, is

sayable only because of the "rigor of him who leaves what is as it is, who has entered into the 'righteous vision' [*gerechten Anschauens*] and now submits to it."

Another setting-apart distinguishes Trakl's language from one of its own sources, "the world of biblical and ecclesiastical ideas" (193). Any discussion of the allegedly Christian elements in Trakl requires identification of the site of his poetry. Moreover, the thinking of any "metaphysical" or "church-based theology" is plainly inadequate for this task. Trakl's poetry, for Heidegger, in fact has *no* Christian resonances; in his words, "does not an intimate ardent simplicity ring out, the simplicity of those who remain on the journey toward the 'golden face of man,' despite the danger of the utter withdrawal of wholeness?" A passage from one of the Hölderlin lectures is apposite. In their listening, authentic poets are "no 'prophets' in the Judeo-Christian signification of the term," for such prophets do not simply say "in advance the foremost grounding word of the Holy" but go on to "utter the God well enough beforehand reckoning the certainty of salvation in supraearthly blessedness" (G4 114). Hölderlin's poetry is not to be understood in terms of the " 'religiousness' of 'religion' which remains a matter of the Roman interpretation of the relation between man and gods." As poetically said by Hölderlin, the Holy "only opens the time-space of an appearance of the gods and shows in the place of dwelling of historical men on the earth." Accordingly, "the essence of the poet may not be thought in correspondence to the 'prophets'; rather, the 'prophetic' of this poetry must be conceived out of the essence of the poetizing that foretells. Its dream is divine, but it does not dream of a god."

In the final part of his essay, Heidegger returns to the question of the location of the site of Trakl's poetry. In going down into the evening, the wanderers follow the stranger to "an open region that holds the promise of a dwelling, and provides a dwelling," a "land" (OWL 194). Finally, the sitedness (*Ortschaft*) of the site that "gathers Trakl's work into itself" is the "concealed essence of apartness," the *Abendland,* older and earlier, and "therefore promising more [*versprechender*]," than the "Platonic-Christian" or "European" West because it is the " 'first inception' [*Anbeginn*] of a mounting world-year, not the abyss of decay." In language deeply reminiscent of the Hölderlin reflections, indeed of his wartime comments in the Parmenides and Heraclitus courses, Heidegger writes: "The evening land concealed in apartness is not going under; rather, it remains, and as the land of descent into the spiritual night, it awaits those who will dwell in it. The land of going under is the transition into the inception [*Anfang*] of the early concealed in it."

What Heidegger characterizes as the "key note [*Grundton*] in which the poem of this poet silently sounds the mystery," and which is the political teaching of the essay, follows (195). Trakl sings of "*One* generation," the unity of which "arises from the kind [*Geschlecht*] which, along the 'lunar paths of the departed,' gathers together and enfolds the discord of the generations into a gentler twofold—which does so in virtue of its apartness, the stiller stillness reigning within it, in virtue of its 'forest sagas,' its 'measure and law.'"

"*One*" in "*one* generation" has nothing to do with the "monotony of dull equality," nor indeed with any "biological fact at all"; in it is "hidden that unifying force which unifies in virtue of the spiritual night's gathering blue," spoken from the "song which sings of evening." Heidegger then repeats, almost exactly, his definition offered earlier (cf. 170): "Generation" encompasses the "historical generation of man," the "races, tribes, clans, and families of mankind," and "always refers to the twofoldness of the sexes." What marks all of these as "one" acts "by prompting the soul" to begin its journey. Trakl's singing of the evening land is a "single call for the happening [*Ereignis*] of the right kind [*Schlag*], to speak the flame of the spirit into gentleness." "Spirit" as flame resembles *phusis* as sheer presencing ↔ absencing; compliance with it of necessity is action not determined by any epochal principle. The speaking correlate with it will of necessity be strange to the decaying human beings living under an epochal principle.

Such speaking—God's speaking in Trakl's poem—"assigns to man a stiller essence, and thus calls on him to give that response by which man rises up from what is authentic going under into the early" (196). "The 'evening land,'" Heidegger writes, "holds the rising of the ascent of the *one* generation." It is hardly surprising, I think, that for Heidegger, Trakl's poetry is "historical in the highest sense," for it sings of the "destiny [*Geschick*] which casts mankind in its still-withheld essence, that is, saves it." This is for Heidegger hardly "dreamy romanticism," for it concerns the "advent of a destiny which concerns man at the beginning of his essence" (197). Trakl's poetizing, like Heidegger's thinking, attempted in *Beiträge*, is already oriented toward the "other inception" in which the truth of Being and the Being of truth are understood as the same—never, for Heidegger, merely identical— as what displaces itself in its own "turning appropriation" (*kehrige*

Ereignis) and belongs to the "abyss" (*Ab-grund*) (G65 185). Heidegger does not say here that the Germans must speak the flame of spirit, must be the ground of the enfolding of discord into unity, but who else could be equal to the task?

It is necessary to refer once more to the Hölderlin readings. The coming of the holy grounds "another beginning of another history," for it decides inceptively "regarding men and gods, as to whether they are and who they are and how they are and when they are." Hölderlin's word is the "calling word," the announcement of the holy. Thus, for Heidegger, Hölderlin's word is not merely a hymn to poets or nature or the holy but a hymn *of* the holy, for it "bestows the word and comes itself in this word. The word is the eventuation of the holy [*das Ereignis des Heiligen*]" (G4 76–77). Although Hölderlin's poetry is the inceptive calling of coming itself, which makes his word "compelled by the holy" [*heiliggenothiget*], the poet's response is also characterized by sobriety. Heidegger finds this element in "German Song" (77):

> then in the deep shade, when
> Above his head the elm-tree rustles,
> By the stream that breathes out coolness the
> German poet sits
> And sings, when of the hallowed sober water
> Enough he has drunk, listening far out into
> silence,
> The song of the soul.

The shade and coolness of the stream shelters the poetic word, protecting it from the "heavenly fires." In Heidegger's words: "The coolness and shade of sobriety answers to the holy. This sobriety does not belie the inspiriting. Sobriety is already the fundamental determinant of preparedness [*Bereitschaft*] for the holy." The last two sentences of Heidegger's sounding of "As on a Holiday . . ." assert the rank of Hölderlin, of the Germans, and finally, silently, of Heidegger's thinking, in which this rank is understood. First, the penultimate sentence: "Hölderlin's word says the Holy and thus names only once the time-space [*Zeit-Raum*] of the inceptive decision for the essential joining [*Wesensgefüge*] of the future history of the gods and of humanity" (G4 77). Then the last sentence: "This word is, yet unheard, preserved in the Western language of the Germans." The words I have translated as "Western language" are in German *abendländische Sprache*. They could also be rendered as "evening-land language," the language of the world's twilight, or the world's night. In 1945 Heidegger writes that "the surmounting of nihilism nevertheless announces itself in German poetic thinking and singing," but "of this poetry, however, the Germans still have had the least understanding, because they are concerned to adapt to the measures of the nihilism that surrounds them and thus to misunderstand the essence of a historical self-affirmation" (R 498). The flame of spirit has not yet ignited the site of the historical people. The last god has not given the people their measure; the people have been unable to make it their own.

Epilogue

> To experience something means to attain it along the way, by
> going on a way. To undergo an experience with something
> means that this something, which we reach along the way in
> order to attain it, itself pertains to us, meets and makes its
> appeal to us, in that it transforms us into itself.
>
> (OWL 73–74)

HOW, FINALLY, IS Heidegger's *paideia* to be understood? Beginning
with Plato, the Western philosophical tradition was insufficiently attentive to the ambiguity inherent in *ōn*, which means that a fundamental
"thoughtlessness" constitutes the "essence of metaphysics" (HCE
108). What the tradition has not grasped is that human beings are set
between Being and Nonbeing, a location to which a "need" (*Not*) corresponds that "displaces [*versetz*] man in the inception of a grounding of
essences" (G45 161). To the "discord" (*Zweispalt*) in Being there corresponds discord in man (G51 68). We comprehend Being as what claims
human beings, to which we belong, and which is necessarily futural;
this thought seems to me essential for understanding Heidegger's political thinking (2, 3, 12, 15). Beings are subject to the rule (*Zwingnis*) of
Being; they have no force that surpasses the "constraint" (*Zwang*)
of Being. Indeed, the constraint presences *as* Being, the "most-
constraining" (*Verzwingendste*). Being plays through us and has set us
"there" where beings are (67). It is what opens domain of the *Da*, which
is the condition for living in the differentiation of Being and beings. In
this opening, Being liberates us from beings, making it thus possible
for us to be our own selves as settled into Being. Indeed this is the essence of freedom; Being as the constraining/liberating (68). Our "sojourn" (*Aufenthalt*), our setting of "inescapability" (*Ausweglosigkeit*),
in Being is the location in and from which the "way-to-be" (*Wesenart*),

rank, and essential state of our historical essence are to be decided (80–83).

Decisive as well is the thought that *all* talk of conditions, retrievals, and possibilities is determinate. Sitedness is never effaced in Heidegger; it is, rather, deepened, and in the Hölderlin and Trakl readings, as well as in the *Beiträge,* thought as the site of the *German* people. What is insufficiently well understood by postmodern Heideggerians is that Heidegger's antihumanism leaves, necessarily, a manifold of historical *peoples.* This condition of the present age is, I am convinced, as fundamental for Heidegger as is the governing of "our" situation by the withdrawal and forgetting of Being, which presences as absence in presencing as Enframing. While Heidegger believes that we live in "times of reversal" in and from which a retrieval of the inception is possible, which in turn opens to the possibility of an "other inception," I find nothing in his thinking to suggest that anything like the universality of humanism will recur. Consider once more the principles that are deconstructed at the end of metaphysics: "It becomes a destining that the suprasensory world, the Ideas, God, the moral law, the authority of reason, progress, the happiness of the greatest number, culture, civilization, suffer the loss of their constructive force and become void" (QCT 65). Shall we call "bad faith," in the fashion of an earlier French thinker indebted to Heidegger, Derrida's privileging of the "classical emancipatory idea," which does not seem to him "outdated," or Schürmann's claim that in the postmodern condition formal "rules for action" can be somehow deduced from the originary?[1] Should not postmodern talk of emancipation, transgression, and the marginalized—can German or Swabian nationalists be included?—be deconstructed in the space Heidegger opens?

Political activity remains a possibility in Heidegger's thinking. The title of the interview in *Der Spiegel* (one not chosen by Heidegger)—"Only a God Can Save Us"—resembles a Nietzschean aphorism that distracts us from what is essential. The interview is "political" in two senses: it continues the evasions and misdirections of the official account of Heidegger's involvement with National Socialism and contains some of Heidegger's most direct remarks on the political and on the relations between philosophy and the political. Thus he says that the questions developed in BT and after are "fundamental questions of thinking which in an indirect way affect even national and social questions" (Sp 270). To speak strictly, what can it mean for thought to have an "effect"? The very ideas of "effect" and "effecting" belong to metaphysics—here, philosophy—said to have ended, dissolved into the sciences. Thus, when Heidegger says that "if one thinks in different terms a mediated effect is possible, not a direct one," that "thinking, as it were, can causally change the situation of the world," what remains to be thought is how this "actualization" (*Verwirklichung*) happens (278, 279). Certainly the situation of man "in the world of global technology" is not a "fate which cannot be escaped or unravelled" (280). What is sought with regard to technology is a way in which we can respond to its essence. Indeed, Heidegger understands "the task of thought to consist in helping man in general, within the limits allotted to thought, to achieve an adequate relationship to the essence of technology," which most emphatically does not mean simply to reject it (280; cf. DT 53–57; G55 203).

Heidegger's engagement with National Socialism is reinscribed here, in a moment which could have been the occasion for a less ambiguous rejection, in the next sentence: "National Socialism, to be sure, moved in this direction. But those people were far too limited in their thinking to acquire an explicit relationship to what is really happening today and has been underway for three centuries." The failure of National Socialism, then, is one of thought—a failure to grasp what is essential, which leaves us with the question of whether this failure somehow encompasses or is responsible for what was done by National Socialism. The original of which National Socialism was the initially promising, but ultimately disastrous, image is the German people itself, rooted in its fitting place, elevated by its language, spiritual, cognizant of, and prepared for, its historical task.

That task, put simply, is to hold open the inception, to recover and stand in the site of the first inception in order to hold open the possibility of an other inception. Heidegger explains the role of the Germans in an addendum to the Parmenides lectures and in a passage from the Heraclitus lectures. In the former he writes that it is because "Being and the truth of Being are essentially beyond all men and humanities, that the 'Being' or 'Nonbeing' of man can, and therefore must, be at stake where man as historical is determined to the preservation of the truth of Being" (G54 249). A "decline" (*Untergang*) can be "overcome" (*überwunden*) when the inception is saved, that is, "allowed to be the inception it is," to be "inceptive only when thinking itself and man in his essence think inceptively," which means "to enter, by way of inceptive thinking, into a confrontation and dialogue with the inception in order to perceive the voice of the disposition and determination of the future." This voice is heard where experience, itself the "pain [*Schmerz*] in which the essential being-other of beings reveals itself in opposition to what is usual," takes place:

> The highest form of pain is dying one's death as a sacrifice for the preservation of the truth of Being. This sacrifice is the purest experience of the voice of Being. What if "the german" [*das deutsche*] is the historical collectivity [*geschichtliche Menschentum*] which, like the Greeks, is called upon to poetize and think, and what if it must first perceive the voice of Being! Must not the sacrifices, then, be as many as the causes immediately eliciting them, since the sacrifice has *in itself* [*an sich*] its own essence and does not require goals and uses! Thus what if the voice of the inception should announce itself in our historical determination [*Bestimmung*]? (G54 249–50)

In the Heraclitus lectures he writes:

> The word in which the essence of historical mankind is transferred is the word Being [*Seyn*]. This inceptional word is preserved in poetizing and thinking. No matter how the external destiny of the West will be forged, the biggest and most proper test for the Germans is still ahead, a test, that is, in which the Germans will perhaps be tested by ignorant people and against their will; that is, whether they, the Germans, are in agreement with the truth of Being, whether they are beyond readiness to die, strong enough to save the inception of inconspicuous adornment over against the smallmindedness of the modern world.
>
> The peril in which "the holy heart of peoples" of the West presently is, is not a peril of going under, but the peril that we, ourselves confounded, may surrender to the wills of modernity, driving toward it. So that this ordeal may not happen, there is, in the coming decades, need for those who are in their thirties and forties and who have learned how to think properly. (G55 181–82)

The actualization of thinking that changes the world is *not* simply the transgressive disruption of institutions and the delegitimizing of ruling principles, the comportments that enchant postmodernists. If we must, as Schürmann puts it, unlearn the "*pros hen* grammar" of Western metaphysics, we must also recognize that such unlearning is already intimated, enacted in the rootedness of a historical people, exhibited in the coming of the Germans into their own.[2] We have seen that for Heidegger, philosophy must be rooted in a people; the "philosophy of a people is that which makes the people into the people of a philosophy" (G65 43). This enactment is a guarding of the truth of Being such that the philosophy of a people is "its free and its own" that is "*over* the people because it comes *out of* the people" to the extent that its Da-sein has "decided itself." Aware of its "ownmost origin" (*eigensten Ursprung*), philosophy must always ask not only who we are but *whether* we are (48, 51). Such thinking, Heidegger tells us, with every resource at his command, is "dangerous," yet it is the only way in which the "originary saving" of the West can be reached (54). What must be said clearly is that the thinking Heidegger attempts in the *Beiträge*, indeed his very conception of essential thinking, is related essentially to the singularity of the *Volk*. This is why the *Beiträge*'s attempt to become attuned to *Ereignis*, to allow to happen *from Ereignis* "a thoughtlike-saying listening to Being and in the word 'of' Being," is inherently political (3).

Such attunement—from truth as correctness of judgment in the first inception to truth as truth of Being in an other inception—is not simply comportment oriented to an opposite; an other inception "stands *as other*" apart from opposition (187). I emphasize the radical character of Heidegger's teaching here in order to make clear what governs his understanding of *Ereignis* as the "ground and abyss of the joining of the god over man and the turning of men for the god," a joining that happens only in Da-sein (256). In a futural meaning, "being" (*sein*) has the sense of "endurance" (*Ertragsamkeit*) as a founding of *Da*, where *Da* means the lighting of Being itself, an opening of a place for possibilities and the "establishment" (*Einrichtung*) of beings in historical (*geschichtliches*) work, deeds, and sacrifice (298). That work centers, as we have seen, in the establishing of a site for a god, which is necessary if a people is to become what it essentially is. Postmodernists are, as far as I can tell, somewhat less than attentive to issues concerning God, let alone the gods. Speech about the gods cannot, for them, answer the questions of who or whether "we" are.

The people, the Germans, to the extent that they enact the motions of coming into their ownmost, thereby act in and thus enact a way of being for human beings attuned to, corresponding with, the movement of presencing ↔ absencing, hence, *poiein kata phusin* (G55 367). Heidegger's politics is not a matter of romantic or aesthetic creativity, for poetry, the highest poetry, like science in WM and in the rectoral address, "holds out in the void of darkness" (G4 48; WM 102–11; RA

473–74). Language, which is the condition for a people's historical Dasein, and which is exhibited in its deepest and most essential sense in poetry, allows what is great to be recovered and "consequently inexhaustibly disclosed in appropriation always anew, and becoming more powerful" (G39 146). The measure for man's dwelling is provided in and by poetry—and the poet of poets poetizes in German. The poet calls "that which in its very self-disclosure causes the appearance of that which conceals itself, and indeed *as* that which conceals itself. In the familiar appearances, the poet calls the alien as that to which the invisible imparts itself in order to remain what it is—unknown" (PLT 225). Thought in connection with the task of the Germans, poetic measure means that this task is intelligible under the heading of finitude, or of the resolute stand—thoroughly consistent with releasement (*Gelassenheit*)—in and exposure to darkness. When "world" is established, it is "that opening which unlocks the broad tracks of the simple and essential decisions in the destiny of a historical people" (PLT 48). A decision, moreover, conceals: "Every essential decision is the lighting of the essential injunctions with which all decision complies. Every decision, however, bases itself on something unmastered, hidden, confusing; otherwise it would never be a decision" (PLT 55; cf. ST 154–55).

"If the true as the only destiny is to come truly toward us and our descendants," Heidegger writes, "everything must remain provisional, widely expectant, cautious: we could not yet calculate when and where and in what shape that happening will occur" (G55 190). The appropriate staying of beings in the clearing of world is measured by their compliance with time (G51 100–110, 117, 120–21; EGT 40–55). Such compliance is for human beings "the knowing, voluntary, attuned moving into essencing, to stand in it and to stand it" (G45 201, 210, 218; G65 13). Comportment, action, is measured thus: "Each time, Being lets powers arise for a while, but it also lets them sink with their impotencies into the inessential" (EPh 76). Heidegger had always understood *phronēsis* as the virtue involved in knowing one's way around. Recognition of epochality is the completion of that virtue.

Finally, there is in the *Beiträge* a characterization of BT which speaks from the uttermost depth of Heidegger's philosophical sensibility, and which should not be ignored by any student of his political thinking. The earlier work, he writes, is "the self-preparatory beginning of the presencing of Being itself," of what "compels *us*, provided that we have become ripe for it, into a thinking which neither yields a doctrine, occasions a 'moral' activity, nor secures 'existence.' Rather it is something which 'only' grounds the truth as the time-play-space [Zeit-Spiel-Raum] in which beings can again come to be, that is, can become the preservation of Being" (G65 243; cf. 87–88). The realization of Heideggerian thinking would reach a site which, according to this thinking, is more fundamental than anything we might call ethics. It is worth noting that the being of essential thinkers "consists in an almost *inhuman* fidelity [*unmenschlichen Treue*] to the most covert history of the West. This history is the poetizing and thinking struggle [*Kampf*] for a word for beings as a whole. All world-historical publicity essentially lacks the eyes and the ears, the measure and the heart, for the poetizing-thinking [*dichterisch-denkerischen*] struggle for the word of Being. The struggle plays [*spielt*] beyond war and peace, outside success and defeat, is never touched by clamor and acclaim, and remains unconcerned [*unbekümmert*] about the destiny [*Geschick*] of individuals" (N3 18–19). From such texts I draw the conclusion that a way of life of the Being of Dasein, compliant with the play of Being, with *Ereignis,* would be, *radically* unlike any way of life human beings have yet lived. Its alterity has not yet been pondered deeply enough. What calls for thinking is that the political correlate of this way of life resembles most closely, for Heidegger, the rooted community of German *völkisch* nationalism.

Heidegger may be understood as having challenged the scholarly prejudice—I do not say a prejudice of philosophers—that philosophy itself is, or must be, moderate or counsel moderation with regard to political things. Thinking and action *kata phusin* are inherently radical; Heidegger makes no promise that this comportment is, or even can be, "good" in any traditional sense. This is because Being gives "good" and "evil" alike—"to healing" it "first grants ascent into grace; to raging its compulsion to malignancy" (LH 238). What Heidegger cannot provide is some way for philosophy to immunize philosophers and the rest of us from catastrophe, to prevent the thinker from making a blunder, and the greater the thinker, the stronger the guarantee is supposed to be. Heidegger's thinking repudiates the very possibility, the intelligibility, of such a guarantee, for with "inhuman fidelity" to the question of Being comes the impossibility of any such immunization. Heidegger can, and does, recognize and speak of the "boundless suffering" and "measureless sorrow" of the world in the age of the withdrawal and forgetting of Being (N4 245). Compliance with time, the awakening of the gentle unborn in the Trakl reading, the descent to the evening-land, poetic dwelling, releasement, the rooted people under the last god—none of these valorizes a way of life. Rather, each names a way of life fitting for the finitude, the proper motion, of Dasein, and each lies in a different register from the ethical. What remains to be asked is whether Germans, or anyone else, can live without a valorization.

I recall, finally, two lines from Greek antiquity.[3] Heidegger uses the line from *Ajax* to utter the Greek understanding of time; his own understanding of time does not oppose it: "All things does Time, vast and incomprehensible to calculation, bring forth to rise undisclosed, and conceals appearances (again) in itself." The second line comes from one of Pindar's Olympian Odes: "What has been done with justice or without not even time the father of all can undo" (2.15–17). These lines provide no consolation, and they justify nothing. They utter, however, what Heidegger understands to be true.

Notes

Preface

1 Philippe Lacoue-Labarthe, *Heidegger, Art, and Politics*, pp. 18–19.

2 Hugo Ott, *Martin Heidegger: Unterwegs zu seiner Biographie* (1988). This book has been translated recently by Allan Blunden as *Martin Heidegger: A Political Life* (1993).

3 Victor Farias, *Heidegger et le nazisme* (1987). A translation of this book as *Heidegger and Nazism* appeared in 1989. A complete bibliography of the ensuing controversies involving students, defenders, and critics of Heidegger would be enormous. One of the best guides to the disputes is Tom Rockmore, *On Heidegger's Nazism and Philosophy*, chap. 7. See also Richard Wolin, "The French Heidegger Debate"; and Michael E. Zimmerman, "The Thorn in Heidegger's Side: The Question of National Socialism."

4 Stanley Rosen, *The Question of Being: A Reversal of Heidegger*, p. x; Jacques Derrida, "Heidegger, l'enfer des philosophes," p. 173.

5 Luc Ferry and Alain Renaut, *Heidegger and Modernity*, p. 15.

6 Jeffrey Herf's authoritative study of this political tendency makes clear that Heidegger did not belong to it. See his *Reactionary Modernism: Technology, Culture, and Politics in Weimar and the Third Reich*, p. 109.

7 For treatments of *völkisch* nationalism, see George L. Mosse, *The Crisis of German Ideology: Intellectual Origins of the Third Reich*, and Rodney Stackelberg, *Idealism Debased: From Völkisch Ideology to National Socialism*. According to his son, Dr. Herrmann Heidegger, Heidegger voted for a conservative local winegrowers party in the 1932 Reichstag election. See Frank H. W. Edler, "Philosophy, Language, and Politics: Heidegger's Attempt to Steal the Language of the Revolution of 1933–34," pp. 237–38. Richard Rorty's playful speculation that if Heidegger had married Hannah Arendt and emigrated to the United States, he would have found kindred spirits in the Southern Agrarians is not wide of the mark. See his "Taking Philosophy Seriously."

8   John D. Caputo discusses this issue in his *Demythologizing Heidegger*, chap. 5, pp. 101–17.

9   On this point, see Otto Pöggeler, "Heidegger's Political Self-Understanding," p. 205.

10   Rockmore, *On Heidegger's Nazism*, pp. 110, 125, 239–40, 298–301.

11   Jacques Lyotard, *Heidegger and "the jews,"* p. 67. Another interpretive possibility is pursued by Harry Neumann, for whom Heidegger embodies "real nazism" and is perhaps the "only Nazi." Neumann explains: "Only real nazism is sufficiently courageous to incorporate the apolitical or anti-political thrust of science or global technology. As such it has nothing but contempt for all values (any notion of good and bad, right and wrong, true and false) or wholes or universals (anything political, anything common or communicable. Since politics always is concerned with such things, true nazis are radically apolitical. . . . science is the simple realization that whatever is experienced—a self, a world, the law of contradiction, a god or anything else—is nothing apart from its being experienced. . . . It is unscientific illusion to believe that any thoughts or words, 'scientific' or unscientific theories, are anything more than empty experiences, empty because nothing—including 'experience'—is definable or limited by anything. . . . The reality revealed by science consists quite literally of nothing, of empty, interchangeable nothings. . . . Nothing—and only nothing—exists in nazism's scientific reality. Nazism's will asserts itself in the face of its own nothingness" ("Politics or Nothing! Nazism's Origin in Scientific Contempt for Politics," pp. 226–27, 229). For discussion more directly devoted to Heidegger, see Neumann's "The Man on the Moon? The Question of Heidegger's 'Self-Assertion of the German University.'"

12   John Lukacs, *The End of the Twentieth Century and the End of the Modern Age*, p. 401.

13   Reiner Schürmann, *Heidegger on Being and Acting: From Principles to Anarchy*, p. 43. Cf. his "Legislation-Transgression: Strategies and Counter-Strategies in the Transcendental Justification of Norms," "Modernity: The Last Epoch in a Closed History?" and "Principles Precarious: On the Origin of the Political in Heidegger."

14   Stanley Hoffmann, "The Passion of Modernity," p. 101.

15   Derrida, "Force of Law: The Mystical Foundation of Authority," p. 973.

16   Gerald L. Bruns writes: "The intuition that there is some intrinsic connection between Heidegger's 'philosophy' and his political behavior needs to be worked through from many directions. I don't think we have made much of an effort to do this yet, in large part because we don't know how." Bruns characterizes Farias's book as "provocative but still intuitive," as if he already knows that the method he awaits must somehow be

more than intuitive (*Heidegger's Estrangements: Language, Truth, and Poetry in the Later Writings*, p. 201).

17 David Farrell Krell, *"Die Kehre:* Heidegger's Ostensible Turning," in his *Intimations of Mortality: Time, Truth, and Finitude in Heidegger's Thinking of Being*, p. 105.

18 Schürmann, *Heidegger on Being and Acting*, p. 3.

19 Judith N. Shklar, *Men and Citizens: A Study of Rousseau's Social Theory*, pp. 217–18. Michael Zimmerman's summary of Heidegger's "reactionary attitudes" is instructive. He notes that Heidegger "hated materialism, scientific reductionism, the decline of community, the evils of urban life, spiritual decay, atomistic individualism, and alienation from the transcendent dimension. Like other reactionaries, he rejected the economic and political values of the Enlightenment and called for a new social order that could arise only by returning to Germany's primal roots. . . . In his quest to renew Germany, Heidegger used almost all of the important terms—including degeneration, nihilism, decline, the need for rootedness, *Volksgeist*, decision, spiritual transformation, martyrdom, revelation, renewal, achievement of Germany's salvific mission—and debated with the works of many of the important authors. . . . of the reactionary political movement which helped bring Hitler to power" (*Heidegger's Confrontation with Modernity*, p. 4). I have no quarrel with such a summary. It is "correct"—although the label "reactionary" encourages us to distance Heidegger from ourselves—but is not ultimately decisive for understanding what he wrote. What must be kept in mind is that while many German intellectuals were antiliberal or reactionary or apolitical romantics, only Heidegger wrote *Being and Time*.

20 William J. Richardson, *Heidegger: Through Phenomenology to Thought*, p. 258; Harry Neumann, "The Closing of the Philosophic Mind: A Review of *The Closing of the American Mind*," p. 160.

Introduction

1 Thomas Sheehan's accounts of Heidegger's understanding of Being are especially clear explanations of this point. See his "On Movement and the Destruction of Ontology," "Introduction: Heidegger, the Project and the Fulfillment," "On the Way to *Ereignis:* Heidegger's Interpretation of *Physis*," "Heidegger, Aristotle, and Phenomenology," and "Time and Being, 1925–27." For additional commentary on the relation of Heidegger to Aristotle, see Michel Meyer, "De Aristote à Heidegger"; Rémi Brague, *Aristote et la question du monde. Essai sur le contexte cosmologique et anthropologique de l'ontologie* and "Radical Modernity and the Roots of Ancient Thought"; and Franco Volpi, *Heidegger e Aristotele*. For

a sound and comprehensive study of Heidegger's work as a whole, see Dieter Thomä, *Die Zeit des Selbst und die Zeit danach: Zur Kritik der Textgeschichte Martin Heideggers, 1910–1976.* Cf. Otto Pöggeler, *Martin Heidegger's Path of Thinking.*

2 Gerald L. Bruns emphasizes alterity in his Heidegger interpretation, to which I am deeply indebted. See his *Heidegger's Estrangements: Language, Truth, and Poetry in the Later Writings.*

3 Cited by Zygmunt Adamczewski in his "On the Way to Being: Reflecting on Conversations with Martin Heidegger," p. 26.

4 I follow Reiner Schürmann in distinguishing carefully between the "originary" (*ursprünglich*) and the "inceptive" (*anfänglich*) in Heidegger. For this reason I have always included the German word whenever either of these words appears. See Schürmann, *Heidegger on Being and Acting: From Principles to Anarchy,* chap. 8, pp. 122–51. Cf. Marlène Zarader, *Heidegger et les paroles de l'origine.*

Chapter 1 : Retrievals and Settings-Apart

1 Indispensable to the study of "early" Heidegger are Theodore Kisiel, *The Genesis of Heidegger's "Being and Time,"* and John van Buren, *The Young Heidegger,* forthcoming from Indiana University Press. For Marxist perspectives, see Wolf-Dieter Gudopp, *Der junge Heidegger: Realität und Wahrheit in der Vorgeschichte von "Sein und Zeit";* Hans-Martin Gerlach, *Martin Heidegger: Denk-und-Irrwege Eines Spätbürgerlich Philosophen;* and Pierre Bourdieu, *L'ontologie politique de Martin Heidegger.*

2 Weber identifies the thesis that "we are cultural beings, endowed with the capacity and will to take a definite attitude toward the world and to lend it significance" as the "transcendental presupposition of every cultural science" (Max Weber, *Max Weber on the Methodology of the Social Sciences,* p. 81) What may be called transcendental social theory moves from putatively invariant features of human experience to their a priori structures and, in doing so, establishes the order of inquiry appropriate to the comprehension of human conduct. Simmel exemplifies the practice of such theory when he characterizes its task as a search for "forms of sociation" or general structures of social experiences, which makes social science a "declaration of the sovereignty of the category over the material." See Georg Simmel in *Georg Simmel, 1856–1918: A Collection of Essays with Translations and a Bibliography,* ed. Kurt H. Wolff, p. 106. In addition to the works cited in the previous note, see, for discussions of connections between Heidegger's thinking and the *Geisteswissenschaften,* Jeffrey Barash, *Heidegger and Historical Meaning.*

3 John D. Caputo shows that Heidegger's appropriation of Christianity is

quite selective; Heidegger takes from it the temporal structure of experience and ignores or translates into temporal-structural terms human suffering, pain, mercy, and the experience of the marginalized. See Caputo, *Demythologizing Heidegger*, chaps. 2, 3, and 6. For additional commentary, see Thomas Sheehan, "Heidegger's 'Introduction to the Phenomenology of Religion,' 1920–21"; "Hans-Georg Gadamer, "Heidegger's 'theologische' Jugendschrift"; and Otto Pöggeler, *Martin Heidegger's Path of Thinking*, pp. 24–31.

4 There are numerous studies of Heidegger's early "logical" works. See T. C. W. Oudemans, "Heideggers 'logische Untersuchungen'"; J. N. Mohanty, "Heidegger on Logic"; and John D. Caputo, *Heidegger and Aquinas: An Essay on Overcoming Metaphysics*, chap. 1. For commentary on the role of temporality in Heidegger's early thinking, see Marion Heinz, *Zeitlichkeit und Temporalität: Die Konstitution der Existenz und die Grundlegung im Frühwerk Martin Heideggers*.

5 For good general discussions of Heidegger's understanding of Dilthey, see Charles B. Guignon, *Heidegger and the Problem of Knowledge*, pp. 45–59, and Otto Pöggeler, *Heidegger's Path of Thinking*, pp. 19–24. For a close analysis of Heidegger's appropriation of Dilthey, see Theodore Kisiel, "Why the First Draft of *Being and Time* Was Never Published." For a discussion of Heidegger and Dilthey in connection with PIA, see Rudolf F. Makreel, "The Genesis of Heidegger's Phenomenological Hermeneutics and the Rediscovered 'Aristotle Introduction' of 1922." Stanley Corngold has shown that Dilthey is a far more politically engaged thinker than is recognized by most of his interpreters. The relations between Dilthey's political thinking and that of Heidegger remain to be explored. See Corngold, "Dilthey's Essay *The Poetic Imagination: A Poetics of Force*."

6 Space prohibits a complete listing of all of Heidegger's texts concerned with Hegel. See, e.g., G32; ID; G9 255–72.

7 Cited by Victor Farias, *Heidegger and Nazism*, p. 45. For additional commentary, see Hugo Ott, *Martin Heidegger: A Political Life*, pp. 59–63.

8 In his preliminary account of historicity as constituting Dasein's happening, which in turn is the condition for any proper attribution of "history," Heidegger explains that Dasein *is* its past (BT 41). For Heidegger this means that Dasein "'happens' out of its own future"; its way of Being conditions its self-interpretation and therewith "the possibilities of its Being are disclosed and regulated." Dasein's past, moreover, "always means the past of its 'generation.'" The "full authentic happening" of Dasein is its "fateful destiny in and with its 'generation'" (436). His reference to Dilthey is to the latter's essay "Concerning the Study of the History of the Sciences of Man, Society, and the State" (*Über das Studium*

der Geschichte der Wissenschaften vom Menschen, der Gesellschaft und dem Staat) (1875), in which "generation" appears as the basic unit for the study of human history (498). Dilthey, in turn, is citing his own foreword to his *Life of Schleiermacher* (1870). For Dilthey, "generation" specifies "objective spirit," identifying a determinate world of meaning in which experience, expression, and understanding are made concrete, and is thereby "articulated as a structural order of types." Our self-knowledge, acquired in and through our comprehension of our lived experience taking place in this order, is thereby necessarily historical. See Dilthey, *Der Aufbau der geschichtlichen Welt in den Geisteswissenschaften,* pp. 256, 263, 348.

9 In Sheehan, "Heidegger's 'Introduction,' " p. 316.

10 Cited in Thomas Sheehan, " 'Introductory Note' to 'The Understanding of Time in Phenomenology and in the Thinking of the Being-Question,' " p. 199.

11 William J. Richardson, *Heidegger: Through Phenomenology to Thought,* p. 91 n. 187. I do not agree with Richardson, however, that these senses of *Schicksal* and *Geschick* vanish in "Heidegger II."

12 For a thorough discussion of Nietzsche in BT, see Jacques Taminiaux, *Heidegger and the Project of Fundamental Ontology,* chap. 6.

Chapter 2 : The Happening of Crisis

1 Jacques Derrida, *Of Spirit: Heidegger and the Question,* p. 34.

2 Ibid., pp. 5–6.

3 Gregory Schufrieder provides a thoughtful interpretation of this sentence in his "Heidegger on Community," pp. 28–29.

4 Heidegger will argue later that the notion of *Volk* is grounded in modern subjectivity (G54 203–7; cf. LH 221). He clarifies this issue still further in *Beiträge,* as we shall see in chapter 7.

5 For interpretations of these lectures, see Michel Haar, *The Song of the Earth,* pp. 25–33; David Farrell Krell, "Daimon Life, Nearness and Abyss: An Introduction to Za-ology," pp. 27–31. Cf. Krell, "Of Spirit and the Daimon: On Derrida's *De l'espirit*." Winfried Franzen scrutinizes the lectures for possible Nazi resonances. See his "Die Sehnsucht nach Härte und Schwere: Über ein zum NS-Engagement disponierendes Motiv in Heideggers 'Die Grundbegriffe der Metaphysik' von 1929/30." Krell's *Daimon Life: Heidegger and Lebensphilosophie,* forthcoming from Indiana University Press, will examine the issue of "life" in Heidegger's thinking closely. Caputo argues that Heidegger's "ominous 'Kampf-philosophy' " is first evident in the lectures. See his *Demythologizing Heidegger,* pp. 52–55. The phrase cited appears on p. 52.

6 Derrida, *Of Spirit,* pp. 39–72. The passage cited appears on p. 56. Derrida's larger claim is that it is precisely Heidegger's *humanism,* which he will reject later, that inclines him both to a repetition of the traditional opposition of spirit and nature—i.e., to humanism—*and,* paradoxically, to his engagement with National Socialism in the first place. His disengagement with National Socialism, then, is a correlate of what is understood to be his growing criticism of humanism. This is to say that National Socialism is a humanism. For a criticism of this analysis, see Luc Ferry and Alain Renaut, *Heidegger and Modernity,* pp. 46–54, 90–108.

7 Krell, "Daimon Life, Nearness and Abyss," p. 46. John D. Caputo takes this position as well in his *Demythologizing Heidegger,* pp. 124–30; cf. Haar, *Heidegger and the Essence of Man,* pp. 76–88.

8 Nietzsche, Aphorism 419, *The Will to Power,* pp. 225–26. Heidegger *does* cite this passage as the frontispiece to his lecture course on Aristotle given during the summer of 1931, which, he writes, names "the inner will of this lecture."

9 The question concerning finitude is both the "unifying and originary root" and the "middle" of the other questions (G29/30 253). Heidegger's concern is existential, not lexical, for the *"working out of these questions* is none other than as the sharpening of the possibility of [the] fundamental determinant" of deep boredom. Moreover, deep boredom—indeed, "boredom as such"—is "engrained in the *temporality* of Dasein." This means that the questions "in their origin" return to the "question concerning the essence of time," which is itself the "origin of all metaphysical questioning." Does this mean that this "metaphysical problematic" must be extended to the "totality of world history" (*ganz Weltgeschichte*) (254)? Heidegger does not claim to have decided this issue. He does assert that "the possibility of another necessity of the grounding of metaphysics must remain open"; it will not be an "empty, merely logical possibility, but must as possibility be attached to the *Schicksal* [destiny ↔ fortune] of men."

10 Heidegger provides an archaeology of metaphysics in which it is evident that his interpretation of the Greek beginnings of philosophy, to which I shall turn in a later chapter, is already well developed (G29/30 14–87). Here I note only the following: The struggles of philosophers over the questions of metaphysics are grounded in their Dasein (31–35). Heidegger does not return to the Greeks for purely etymological reasons but rather, as he had always done, to recover the force of the "basic words" of Western philosophy (44–45). Accordingly, his discussions of *logos,* alē-*theia,* and especially the *Urwort, phusis* (36, 45–48), are oriented not to philology but to what is named in and by these words (36–45). The

decline (*Verfall*) of philosophy comes with the hardening of thinking into the doctrines of philosophical schools, and transformations in the meaning of "metaphysics" in medieval and modern philosophy conceal its original sense (52–87). There is a difference, however, between merely speaking about metaphysics and speaking *from* it, and the latter is and must be the "beginning of a really lively philosophizing" (87). Heidegger is aware of the circularity involved in inquiring into a thesis in which we and our inquiry are necessarily included (265–67). It is this very circularity, however, that "is the sign that we are moving in the domain of philosophy," i.e., in a domain in which the movement of thinking differs essentially from the seeking of foundations (266).

11 Our experience of a determination is more and other than the phenomena of psychology. "How often it happens that we are not 'there' in a party conversation," Heidegger writes; "how often we notice that we have been *absent*, without being asleep. This not-being-there [*Nicht-Da-Sein*], being-away [*Wegsein*] has nothing at all to do with consciousness or unconsciousness. . . . At the end, to 'be away' pertains to the essence of Dasein" (G29/30 95). What is peculiar about being away is that it is both "being-there" and "not-being-there"; it is an exhibition of presencing and absencing located in, or perhaps it would be better to say, as, Dasein (98).

12 Richard Wolin and Winfried Franzen, on whom Wolin relies, are wrong to see in these critiques any support for "vitalism" (Wolin, *The Politics of Being*, pp. 72–74).

13 Heidegger misquotes a line from the poem "From High Mountains," which Nietzsche placed after the end of *Beyond Good and Evil* (238). Where Nietzsche writes "Nur wer sich wandelt bleibt mit mir verwandt," which Kaufmann translates as "One must change to stay akin to me" or "Only those who change remain related to me," Heidegger has "Nur wer sich wandelt, ist mit mir verwandt," which could be translated as "One must change to be akin to me" or "Only those who change are related to me." The difference between the lines is a difference between *staying* or *remaining* akin to Nietzsche by changing and *being* akin to him by changing. Does Heidegger's misquotation elevate one who already *is* akin to Nietzsche by changing over one who must change in order to *become* akin to him? Heidegger does not claim to provide a full interpretation of "Dionysus and Apollo"; I suggest that he inscribes this opposition in Nietzsche's self-knowledge. In turn, then, Heidegger takes over and surpasses this self-knowledge when he determines Nietzsche's location in and at the end of the history of Western metaphysics.

14 Hendrik J. Pois, cited in Dimitry Gawronsky, "Ernst Cassirer: His Life and His Work," p. 67.

15　The treatments of the various forms of boredom appear as follows: "becoming bored" (secs. 19–23, pp. 117–59); "being bored" (secs. 24–28, pp. 160–98); "deep boredom" (secs. 29–36, pp. 199–238). See also Eiho M. Kawahara, "Heideggers Auslegung der Langeweile," and Parvis Emad, "Boredom as a limit and a Disposition."

16　Tom Rockmore, *On Heidegger's Nazism and Philosophy*, p. 314 n. 107. Michael E. Zimmerman interprets the "manager" as an anticipation of Hitler (*Heidegger's Confrontation with Modernity*, p. 33).

17　Heidegger discusses the theories of several biologists, including the nineteenth-century Dutch scientist Johannes Muller, and his own contemporaries, F. J. J. Buytendijk, Hans Driesch, and J. J. von Uexküll. This *Auseinandersetzung* with naturalistic understandings of the essence of life is a further contribution to Heidegger's criticism of biologism. Philosophy and theology, he notes, had been rethought in accordance with what was taken to be the significance of the findings and developments of the life sciences (G29/30 378–79). There is as well a "turn" in "seeing and asking" in these sciences which as a turn is always decisive (379). Indeed, "The greatness of a science and its vitality show themselves in the strength of its possibility for this turn," as Heidegger had long argued. This turn is misunderstood either as a mere "change [*Wechsel*] in standpoint" or a "shifting" (*Verscheibung*) in what we may call the sociological condition of a science. Heidegger dismisses such accounts. Psychological or sociological "conditionality" (*Bedingtheit*) is but a "facade"; sociology stands in relation to "actual science and its philosophical understanding" as a "cat burglar" to an architect or to a truly creative handworker. Heidegger considers Driesch's *Localization of Morphogenetic Processes: A Proof of Vitalism* (1899) and von Uexküll's *Environing World and Internal World* (1909) to be "two decisive works" (379–85). They are results of critical self-reflection in biology which exhibits increasing recognition of its limits. Certainly Heidegger could be sympathetic to, if not in complete agreement with, Driesch's Aristotelianism and his attempt to update entelechy, and with von Uexküll's opposition to Darwinism and his claim that the various worlds of animal experience have determinate structures. These works, however, were incomplete, for they gave insufficient attention to life as "movement," a result of the inadequacy of their inherited understandings of "organism" (385–86).

18　Cf. Derrida, *Of Spirit*, pp. 51–53.

19　Krell, "Daimon Life," pp. 29, 51 n. 14.

20　Haar, *The Song of the Earth*, p. 160 n. 10, p. 27.

21　Ibid., p. 160 n. 10.

22　Heidegger provides a number of examples of the behavior of bees as exhibitions of compulsion/benumbedness (350–58). The main point is that all such instances are never examples of comportment. What seems like comportment is "only another manner of being-compelled/benumbed" (354). Thus, the bee can never encounter things *as* anything, and certainly not *as such*. Understood strictly, the various "drives" we attribute to it are not "had" in the way in which we "have" drives. The bee's movement can never be in a "space," and it can have no genuine "place" or "home" (354–57). The phototropism of an animal, he explains later, is radically unlike what the seeking of light is for human beings (364–67).

23 Krell, "Daimon Life," p. 31.

24 All references to Nietzsche's text are taken from the Kaufmann translation of *Thus Spoke Zarathustra*, pp. 317–24. I have benefited from Laurence Lampert's discussion in his *Nietzsche's Teaching: An Interpretation of "Thus Spoke Zarathustra,"* pp. 305–10. See also his important new book *Nietzsche and Modern Times: A Study of Bacon, Descartes, and Nietzsche*. Unfortunately, Lampert thinks that Heidegger is a "conservative" (pp. 430–31).

Chapter 3 : How It Stands with Being

1 Caputo rightly reads IM as a statement of Heidegger's political radicalism and notes the distance between its teaching and official National Socialism. See his *Demythologizing Heidegger*, chap. 5, pp. 101–17.

2 William J. Richardson, *Heidegger: Through Phenomenology to Thought*, p. 42.

3 For an exhaustive discussion of Heidegger's texts concerned with God, see George Kovacs, *The Question of God in Heidegger's Phenomenology*. Kovacs, however, fails to recognize Heidegger's deep antipathy to Christianity evident in his thinking by at least the mid-1920s. Caputo recognizes and documents Heidegger's views in his *Demythologizing Heidegger*, pp. 50–52, 56–59, 60–74, 169–85. In a discussion in 1953, Heidegger is reported to have said: "Within thinking nothing can be achieved which would be a preparation or a confirmation for that which occurs in faith and in grace. Were I so addressed by faith I would have to close up my shop. . . . Within faithfulness one still thinks, of course, but thinking as such no longer has a task. . . . Philosophy engages in a kind of thinking of which man is capable on his own. This stops when he is addressed by revelation" (PT 64).

4 The translator omits these last words.

5 Heidegger cites BGE 292: "A philosopher—is a human being who constantly experiences, sees, hears, suspects, hopes, and dreams extraordinary things," and "philosophy . . . is a voluntary living amid ice and mountain heights."

6   Here "destiny" as a translation of *Geschick* is too restrictive; I have left it untranslated because I share Reginald Lilly's concern with the manifold senses it has in Heidegger's thinking. See his "Translator's Introduction" (PR xiv–xv).

7   Zimmerman provides a useful discussion of this issue in *Heidegger's Confrontation with Modernity,* pp. 229–36.

8   In their *Heidegger and Modernity,* Luc Ferry and Alain Renaut are among the most indignant critics of Heidegger on this point.

9   Jacques Derrida, *Of Spirit,* p. 45.

10 Jacques Lyotard, *Heidegger and "the jews,"* p. 80.

11 In my view, Tom Rockmore's dismissal of Derrida's effort to interpret the senses of *Geist* in Heidegger does not succeed in showing that *Geist* is "not fundamental but ancillary to or even insignificant in his [Heidegger's] position" (Rockmore, *On Heidegger's Nazism and Philosophy,* p. 274).

12 Rorty supposes that in speaking of the "collapse of German idealism," Heidegger means merely the opinions of long-dead academic philosophers. See "Overcoming the Tradition: Heidegger and Dewey" in his *Consequences of Pragmatism,* pp. 37–59, and "Heidegger, Contingency, and "Pragmatism" in his *Essays on Heidegger and Others,* pp. 27–49. The phrase itself may derive from the title of Paul Ernst's book *Der Zusammenbruch des deutschen Idealismus* (The collapse of German idealism) (1918), although I have not found any reference to it in Heidegger's writings.

13 Among Heidegger's discussions of German idealism, see *Hegels Phanomenologie des Geistes* (G32); G65 198–204; N4 205; EPh 89; as well as HCE, PR, and ID throughout.

14 Wayne J. Froman, *"Schelling's Treatise on the Essence of Human Freedom* and Heidegger's Thought," pp. 471–78. Two good studies of Schelling are Alan White, *Schelling: An Introduction to the System of Freedom,* and Werner Marx, *The Philosophy of F. W. J. Schelling.* See also David Farrell Krell, "The Crisis of Reason in the Nineteenth Century: Schelling's Treatise on Human Freedom (1809)."

15 Manfred Frings, "Is There Room for Evil in Heidegger's Thought or Not?" Frings argues that Heidegger could have dealt with evil in his account of Dasein's "distantiality" (*Abständigkeit*) in BT but failed to do so.

16 Some interpreters of Heidegger claim that he is very nearly a Schellingian with regard to political thought, or that his thinking belongs to the tradition of the philosophy of freedom that stems from Schelling. See Fred Dallmayr, "Ontology of Freedom: Heidegger and Political Philosophy," and *Polis and Praxis,* pp. 104–32, for a somewhat more developed

version of this thesis, as well as W. R. Newell, "Heidegger on Freedom and Community: Some Political Implications of His Early Thought." This interpretation fails for two reasons. First, Heidegger believes that our time, unlike that of Schelling, does not require philosophical systems, for today has a "very definite stamp of its own and that means a direction and a manner of its historical domination over existence" (ST 22). Second, he understands that for Schelling the possibility of immediate knowledge meant that the time of historical faith is over, for we have "nature" as a revelation more fundamental than any other (ST 167). On this point he comments: "But is this true straightaway for our time, too? Or is this time, ours, different? For what law demands that thinking follow its time? Or is thinking untimely, always and necessarily? But what if the untimely were just the reversal of the timely, a still fiercer dependency on 'time'? How is 'an age' to be determinative for thinking? What if essential thinking first determines an age in what is most its own and does this without the age having or being able to have a public consciousness of its own historical essence? But then this decisive thinking must, after all, be so originary that it cannot get lost in a past epoch and calculate in it what is necessary for the present and make it compatible with the present. That calculating is the essence of 'historicism,' this making compatible is the essence of 'actualism.' Both belong together. They are the enemies, sometimes openly, sometimes hiddenly, of decisive thinking."

Chapter 4 : Properly Human Work

1 Unlike one translator of the rectoral address, William S. Lewis, I do not find anything "slightly misleading" when *Wissenschaft* is rendered as "science." To be sure, German philosophers from Fichte onward understand *Wissenschaft* to encompass a wider range of disciplines than is commonly suggested in English by "science," including "philosophy," or at least, genuine philosophy. Lewis goes too far when he writes that the word "has nothing to do with what we in English refer to as the 'natural sciences'" (RAW 30 n.). In the Heidegger texts under consideration here, I find nothing whatever to suggest that Heidegger is *not* discussing, among other possible kinds of "science," the natural sciences.

2 The Student Law of May 1, 1933, was intended to facilitate *Gleichschaltung* in German universities by organizing students.

3 Heidegger's understanding of academic freedom resonates in the position taken by Walter Schultze, leader of the National Socialist Association of University Lecturers, to which all members of university faculties had to belong, from 1935 to 1943. In an address given in 1939 he argues that academic freedom is rightly understood only when its relation to the

Volk is rightly understood. "We proceed here from a notion of freedom that is specifically our own, since we know that freedom must have its limits in the actual existence of the Volk. Freedom is conceivable only as a bond to something that has universal validity, a law of which the whole nation is the bearer." He goes on to link the "German idea of freedom" exhibited in the thinking of German idealism to its realization in the Nazi present. "This idea of freedom, which is at the same time is an idea of personality, in its deepest sense is being lived and thought through today at the university. And we must also understand the freedom of scholarship, the freedom of inquiry and teaching, on this basis, ultimately is nothing else but responsible service on behalf of the basic values of our being as a Volk" (cited in Mosse, *Nazi Culture*, pp. 315–16).

4   Among recent interpreters Jacques Taminiaux has made this argument forcefully. See his *Heidegger and the Project of Fundamental Ontology*, pp. 129–37. Taminiaux's larger claim in this connection is that Heidegger's appropriation of Aristotle's notions of *praxis* and *poiēsis* exhibits a "Platonic bias" which ignores what Taminiaux takes to be the irreducible plurality and ambiguity of human things in fact recognized by Aristotle. At issue, ultimately, is the question of the relation between philosophy and politics. For a lucid discussion of this question, see Hans Sluga, *Heidegger's Crisis: Philosophy and Politics in Nazi Germany*, pp. 245–65.

5   Lacoue-Labarthe, *Heidegger on Art and Politics*, pp. 53–54. An older and undeservedly neglected study that gives a prominent place to the theme of "the worker" is Jean-Michel Palmier, *Les écrits politiques de Heidegger*. While it is evident that Heidegger's thinking concerning "work" and the "worker" owes a great deal to Ernst Jünger, I want to emphasize that it is deeply rooted as well in his own inquiries. Heidegger appropriates Jünger's thought, to be sure, but this is a *critical* appropriation that takes Jünger as an indicator of the dominance of the will to power in and as the type of the "worker" (e.g., G51 36–38; R 484–85). For Heidegger's criticism of Jünger's thought as insufficiently radical because it remains within the Western metaphysical tradition, see QB. For a thorough examination of Heidegger-Jünger, see Michael E. Zimmerman, *Heidegger's Confrontation with Modernity*, pp. 46–93.

6   Zimmerman, *Heidegger's Confrontation*, p. 109.

7   Farias provides several pages of notes taken by Helene Weiss from Heidegger's course given in the summer semester of 1933, "The Fundamental Questions of Philosophy." See his *Heidegger and Nazism*, pp. 131–35. The words cited appear on p. 131.

8   I use the formula from Otto Pöggeler's frequently cited article "Den Führer führen? Heidegger und kein Ende."

9   A thorough comparative study would have to go back at least to the "Aristotle Introduction" (e.g., AE 254–59).

10 See Reiner Schürmann's discussion of this usage in *Heidegger on Being and Acting*, pp. 176, 358–59.

11 See Zimmerman, *Heidegger's Confrontation*, pp. 150–56.

12 "Appresentation" is a Husserlian coinage designating co-presence. For a discussion of Heidegger's use of it see Kisiel, *The Genesis of Heidegger's Being and Time*, p. 375.

13 Ibid., pp. 165–72. See also Herf, *Reactionary Modernism*, pp. 109–15.

14 For a useful discussion of this issue in connection with Aristotle, see Stanley Rosen, "Thought and Touch: A Note on Aristotle's *De Anima*," in Rosen, *The Quarrel between Philosophy and Poetry: Studies in Ancient Thought*, pp. 118–26. Many recent discussions concerning Heidegger stem from two studies by Derrida: "*Geschlecht:* Différance sexuelle, différance ontologique" (1983) and "La main de Heidegger (*Geschlecht* II: 1984–1985)," in Derrida, *Psyché: Inventions de l'autre*, pp. 395–414 and 415–51.

15 Gerald L. Bruns, *Heidegger's Estrangements: Language, Truth, and Poetry in the Later Writings*, pp. 134–35.

16 The Heidegger-Marx literature is vast. For useful introductions, see Fred Dallmayr, "Heidegger and Marxism," in Dallmayr, *Between Freiburg and Frankfurt: Toward a Critical Ontology*, pp. 160–82; David Schweickart, "Heidegger and Marx: A Framework for Dialogue"; Friedrich Vosskühler, "Praxis und Wahrheit. Ein Gang des Denkens von Marx zu Heidegger"; Danilo N. Basta, "Zu Heideggers Marx-Interpretation"; and Hans Köchler, *Skepsis und Gesellschaftskritik im Denken Martin Heideggers*, pp. 102–46.

17 Schürmann, *Heidegger on Being and Acting*, p. 322 n. 48.

18 Ibid., p. 364 n. 74.

19 Schürmann recognizes this himself (ibid., p. 197). For his masterful summary of Heidegger's teaching on this point, see pp. 175–77.

20 Noted by Zimmerman, *Heidegger's Confrontation*, p. 156. The context in the Aristotle course is Heidegger's discussion of the "faculty of producing" (*Vermögen des Herstellens*) and *logos* "as [the] innermost scaffold" (*Gerüst*) of producing, crucial for an understanding of *epistēmē poiētikē* in Aristotle.

21 For a typical example of this line of criticism, see Wolin, *The Politics of Being*, p. 90. Hugo Ott notes the need for an "in-depth study of [Heidegger's] use of the words '*Kampf*' and '*kämpferisch*,' together with their compounds and derivatives" (*Martin Heidegger: A Political Life*, p. 157).

22 Farias traces this citation to Clausewitz's *Three Confessions* and the "War Party's Agenda" of 1812 and notes its appearance in the right-wing

journal *Deutschlands Erneuerung* of Georg von Below and H. Stuart Chamberlain in 1919 (*Heidegger and Nazism*, pp. 105–7).

Chapter 5 : The Teaching on Science

1   The best survey of the relevant literature on Heidegger's view of science and technology is Albert Borgmann and Carl Mitcham, "The Question of Heidegger and Technology: A Review of the Literature." Cf. Joseph Rouse, "Heidegger's Later Philosophy of Science"; Phillip R. Fandozzi, *Nihilism and Technology: A Heideggerian Investigation;* Joseph Loscerbo, *Being and Technology: A Study in the Philosophy of Martin Heidegger;* Drew Leder, "Modes of Totalization: Heidegger on Modern Technology and Science"; and Theodore J. Kisiel, "Heidegger and the New Images of Science."

2   See the clear discussion of *Wesung* by Alfons Grieder in his superb study "What Did Heidegger Mean by 'Essence?'" pp. 72–73. Cf. Grieder, "Essential Thinking: Reflections on Heidegger's *Beiträge zur Philosophie*," and Stanley Rosen, *The Question of Being: A Reversal of Heidegger,* pp. xvi–xvii.

3   Christopher Fynsk, *Thought and Historicity,* p. 116.

4   Because Heidegger has made explicit the difference between his own understanding of freedom and that exhibited in such notions as positive or negative freedom, it seems to me unfruitful to argue that he simply does not know what freedom "really means," as if such a meaning is readily available and incontestable. For a useful discussion of Heidegger's view of freedom, see Michel Haar, "The Question of Human Freedom in the Later Heidegger."

5   William J. Richardson, *Heidegger: Through Phenomenology to Thought,* p. 214.

6   I agree with Silvio Vietta's interpretation of *Beiträge* as containing significant criticisms of National Socialism. See Vietta, *Heideggers Kritik am Nationalsozialismus und der Technik,* pp. 69–94. For Tom Rockmore, the passages cited by Vietta are ambiguous on this point. See Rockmore, *On Heidegger's Nazism and Philosophy,* pp. 176–203.

7   Vietta, *Heideggers Kritik,* p. 72.

8   Rockmore recognizes that the *Beiträge* is the "single most important text for the relation between Heidegger's later position and his Nazism" (*On Heidegger's Nazism,* p. 176).

9   Schürmann, *Heidegger on Being and Acting,* p. 252. I translate *ahnen* as "presentiment" rather than "presurmise," as Schürmann does, because I see no need for a neologism. The phrase in which *ahnen* appears reads: "Die gewährte Frist zeigt sich nur eine Besinnung, die bereits die Ge-

schichte des Seins zu ahnen vermag." The English translation reads: "The time span granted shows itself only to a reflection which is already able to glimpse the history of Being." The use of "reflection" and "glimpse" inscribes *seeing* in a context where, from Heidegger's position, it could hardly be welcome. I prefer Schürmann's rendering, substituting "already capable of having a presentiment" where he has "already capable of presurmising" (p. 251). The result: "The time span granted shows itself only to a meditation already capable of having a presentiment of the history of Being."

10 Edmund Husserl's *Die Krisis der europäischen Wissenschaften und die transzendentale Phänomenologie* (The crisis of European sciences and transcendental phenomenology) was published in 1936.

Chapter 6 : Politics at/of the Inception

1 For a discussion of this translation, see Jean-Pierre Faye, "Attaque Nazies contre Heidegger," p. 142. A more recent treatment is Bernd Martin, "'Alles Grosse ist gefährdet'—Der Fall Heidegger(s)," pp. 3–13. Wolin's remark very nearly summarizes the superficiality of much of his interpretation: "Finally, in the motto with which he concludes the address, Heidegger—the philhellene for whom etymology is *everything*—commits the ultimate sacrilege: philological apostasy" (*The Politics of Being*, p. 90). I know of no Heideggerian text in which philology is privileged.

2 Allan Bloom suggests that Socrates and Thrasymachus agree on at least the following points: "the character of the ruling group is the core of politics, that the rulers are the stronger, . . . that justice is a political phenomenon and must be embodied in the laws of a city" and that rulers, whether "perfectly publicly-spirited" (the philosopher-kings) or "perfectly selfish" (Thrasymachus's alternative), must be "knowers" ("Interpretive Essay," in his translation of Plato's *Republic*, pp. 328–29). See also Robert Bart, "The Shepherd and the Wolf: The First Book of Plato's *Republic*," pp. 7–19.

3 Making this point in ideological terms, Tom Rockmore calls the teaching of RA "a form of right-wing Platonism," a doctrine which includes the notion that "only the philosopher can secure the good life for the people" (*On Heidegger's Nazism and Philosophy*, pp. 54, 197). Philippe Lacoue-Labarthe writes that Heidegger's "commitment of 1933 is founded upon the idea of an hegemony of the spiritual and the philosophical over political hegemony itself (this is the theme of a *Führung* of the *Führung* or of the *Führer*) which leads us back to the Platonic *basileia*, if not to Empedocles." Heidegger is said to share with Plato (and Hegel) "a *similar* 'attitude' or 'gesture,' or, if one prefers, a *similar posture*" of "fasci-

nated submission to the tyrant" as evidenced in his agreement with Plato that "it is essentially necessary that philosophers be rulers" (*Heidegger, Art and Politics*, pp. 13, 27–28).

4   Karsten Harries, "Heidegger as a Political Thinker," p. 657. The allusion preceding the quote from Harries is to the title of E. M. Butler's classic study *The Tyranny of Greece over Germany* (1935).

5   Stanley Rosen, among others, makes this argument. See his *Nihilism: A Philosophical Essay*, pp. 156–63. Cf. William Galston, "Heidegger's Plato: A Critique of *Plato's Doctrine of Truth*," pp. 373–78; Robert J. Dostal, "Beyond Being: Heidegger's Plato," pp. 96–97, n. 55. See also Véronique M. Fóti, "Representation and the Image: Between Heidegger, Derrida, and Plato."

6   Heidegger gives the earlier date 1930/31 in the references to *Wegmarken* (G9 483) and the later date on the title page of that collection. The lecture course given in the winter semester of 1931/32 is *Vom Wesen der Wahrheit. Zu Platons Höhengleichnis und Theatët* (G34). For discussions of the controversy involving a request from Alfred Rosenberg to prevent the essay from being published, see Farias, *Heidegger and Nazism*, pp. 260–68, whose treatment is superficial, and Hugo Ott, *Martin Heidegger: A Political Life*, pp. 284–95, whose account is far superior to that of Farias. Ott shows that Heidegger's criticisms of humanism contradicted a propaganda line to the effect that National Socialism was a genuine, contemporary humanism.

7   It is possible to search out parallels and resemblances, intersections and accords, between Heidegger and Plato, to modulate from the confrontation Heidegger stages with Plato to an effacing of that confrontation. This is the strategy carried out with great power and originality by Jean-François Mattéi in the study which forms the center of the interpretation of Heidegger written by Dominique Janicaud and Mattéi, *La métaphysique à la limite: Cinq études sur Heidegger,* pp. 49–162. The quarrel between Heidegger and Plato, while it may appear in a different and less confrontational aspect when "Plato" is firmly, if gently, detached from "Platonism," cannot, in my view, be dissolved by hermeneutic charity. Or, if that quarrel is at bottom only one side of a more nuanced juxtaposition of the two philosophers, then my intention here is to concentrate on that side, for it is there, in my view, that Heidegger's political thinking in connection with Plato is to be found. See also Stanley Rosen, *The Question of Being*, and Alain Boutout, *Heidegger et Platon.*

8   Plato and Platonism would seem to coexist in the Platonic texts, and there can be no rule by which they can be distinguished to the satisfaction of every interpreter, just as there can be no rule by which we can decide whether or when to be philologists or philosophers. It is only by means of

historical meditative thinking (*geschichtliche Besinnung*) attuned to or corresponding with the matter of thought that Heidegger can know certain things about the Greeks and Greek thinking (G45 35–36, 39–41; cf. PLT 183–86). The following passage from MFL, in which I substitute "Plato" for "Kant," may shed light on how Heidegger understands philosophers in terms of historical possibilities: "This historical Plato is always only the Plato that becomes manifest in an original possibility of philosophizing, manifest only in part, if you will, but in an authentic part that carries in it the impact of the whole. The actuality of the historical, especially the past, does not emerge in the most complete account of 'the way it happened.' Rather, the actuality of what has been resides in its possibility. The possibility becomes in each case manifest as the answer to a living question that sets before itself a futural present in the sense of 'what can we do?' The objectivity of the historical resides in the inexhaustibility of possibilities, and not in the fixed rigidity of a result" (MFL 71–72).

9   See Rosen, *Nihilism: A Philosophical Essay*, pp. 146–53. Socrates characterizes himself as "greedy for" or "sticking close to" images (*glischros eikazō*, 488a). For further commentary see Joel Warren Lidz, "Reflections on and in Plato's Cave."

10   Schürmann translates *Fügung* as "constellation" in *Heidegger on Being and Acting*, p. 123. It is essential, however, to retain the movement character of the term, which Richardson does by translating it as "process of organizing" in *Heidegger: Through Phenomenology to Thought*, p. 263. Note also that Being is not only imageless but is said in and by an "inceptively soundless word" (*anfänglich lautlosen Wort*) (G55 27).

11   Seth Benardete, *Socrates' Second Sailing: On Plato's Republic*, p. 156.

12   In his study "Heidegger's Interpretation of Plato," Stanley Rosen recognizes that one of the most important differences between Heidegger and Plato has to do with the openness in which the movement of beings (for Heidegger) takes place or from which man "sees" into an "openness that transcends what man can see" (for Plato, according to Rosen). That is, for Heidegger "nothing can be said about openness-away-from-man," while for Plato "by a divine fate or madness we are enabled to discern the visibility of Being as open away from man." We are left, in other words, with an essential difference between what the two philosophers "see"; put perhaps too bluntly, Heidegger may be understood as claiming that Plato is *wrong*, that we cannot see Being "as open away from man." Later Rosen explains correctly that for Heidegger the "kind of motion by which we are returned to the origin" points to the "relation between motion and rest *within* the origin." Since motion is temporal for Heidegger, this means that the movement of thought back to the origin is grounded in— and, I would say, is the most fitting response to—the internal motion of

the origin. Rosen incorrectly supposes that temporality is "conceived in terms of human activity"; it is rather that temporality is the condition for human activity, the explication of which in turn clarifies temporality. Rosen's conclusion brings us to the difference between Heidegger and Plato: "By conceiving Being within the horizon of time, Heidegger never takes seriously the possibility that the temporal present is itself a derivative of the transtemporal presence of visibility." It is difficult to determine what Rosen may mean by "takes seriously"; Heidegger offers arguments and meditations to show that, to put the matter propositionally, there is no "transtemporal presence of visibility" of the sort Rosen (or Plato) requires. Rosen's essay appears in Stanley Rosen, *The Quarrel between Philosophy and Poetry: Studies in Ancient Thought*, pp. 125–47; passages cited: pp. 137, 137–38, 141.

13   Heidegger's target is *Bildung*, understood as inner cultivation or refinement. See Klaus Vondung, "Unity through *Bildung:* A German Dream of Perfection."

14   William V. Spanos, *Heidegger and Criticism: Retrieving the Cultural Politics of Destruction,* pp. 148–49, 291 n. 22. Cf. Véronique M. Fóti, "Alētheia and Oblivion's Field: On Heidegger's Parmenides Lectures," and especially Éliane Escoubas, "Heidegger, la question romaine, la question impériale: Autour du 'Tournant.' "

15   Heidegger agrees with the Brothers Grimm, who understood *falsch* as an "un-German" word. He goes on to add *verum* to this list (G54 57, 67–73). For other such words, see PR (e.g., PR 29).

16   Spanos relates LH to the Parmenides lectures (*Heidegger and Criticism,* pp. 140–49). He goes on to suggest that Heidegger's account of the "developed form of the imperial project" anticipates Althusser's understanding of ideology and Foucault's view of the subject in a disciplinary society (pp. 291–92 n. 23).

17   Fynsk's interpretation of the Heidegger-Hölderlin relationship is centered on the line and its multiple senses in Heidegger. See his *Heidegger: Thought and Historicity,* pp. 174–229. The citation in the text is found on p. 176.

18   Heidegger calls his enterprise a "genuine attack [*eigentlicher Angriff*]" against a "fundamental position of the Western spirit [*Grundstellung des Geistes des Abendlandes*]" (IM 98–99). His specific target is "intellectualism," otherwise unspecified except in contrast to those who advocate a proper use of the traditional intellect" (103). Both sides derive from the rule of thinking over Being in Western metaphysics. The "spiritual reaction" (*Reaktion des Geistes*) of traditionalists against intellectualists, "stemming partly from natural inertia and partly from conscious effort, becomes the breeding ground for political [reaction]." The prevailing

misinterpretation of thinking as logic cannot be overcome by the "rule of sheer feeling" but "only through authentic and originary thinking [*echt und ursprüngliches Denken*] and *through nothing else.*" For the immediate political context of IM, see Hugo Ott, *Martin Heidegger: A Political Life*, pp. 270–83.

19 Heidegger does not ignore the inequalities inherent in the polis, as charged by John D. Caputo. What makes Heidegger's thought difficult is his seemingly casual acceptance of them. Caputo develops his criticism in his *Radical Hermeneutics: Repetition, Deconstruction, and the Hermeneutic Project*, pp. 252–53, and in *Demythologizing Heidegger*, pp. 166–67.

20 Cf. Heidegger's discussion of this fragment in WCT 168–244 and EGT 79–101.

21 Heidegger's translation of the choral ode appears in several texts. It appears as well in G13 35–37.

22 Michel Haar draws attention to the fact that the Greek text contains neither *deinon* nor *deinotaton* but only the plural *deina* and the comparative *deinoteron* (*Heidegger and the Essence of Man*, p. 153).

23 Haar writes that *Gewalt* "designates a power maintained at an extreme but mastered by itself, devoid of disordered movements and of any of the ugliness proper to 'violence.' Moreover, how could the term *'violence'* be in accord with the continuity, if not the 'constancy,' of the opening? If the opening of being is *gewaltig*, it is by possessing the power to maintain itself and maintain man in the balance of appearance and withdrawal. The supposed 'violence' would make it a jolting palpitation, an irregular flashing entirely incompatible with the stability of disclosure" (*The Song of the Earth*, p. 106, and *Heidegger and the Essence of Man*, pp. 153–54). Haar does not consider Heidegger's own remark on "violence" that follows immediately in the text of IM.

24 Since *poros* can also mean resource, the pairing of *pantoporos* and *aporos* can mean "all-resourceful" and "without resource." Cedric Whitman proposed a translation of the line as "Resourceless man comes to the nothing(ness) that is his future." Whitman is cited by Charles Segal in *Tragedy and Civilization: An Interpretation of Sophocles*, p. 441 n. 10.

25 Michael Zimmerman, drawing upon an analysis by Kathleen Wright, argues that Heidegger's later treatment in G53 recognizes that Antigone's way of being human, the "way of the hearth," is preferable to the "violent" way presented in IM. As my discussion indicates, I do not agree, for I find that the two ways are at bottom only one way. See Zimmerman, *Heidegger's Confrontation with Modernity*, pp. 120–21. For additional commentary, see Fred Dallmayr, *The Other Heidegger*, pp. 161–65.

26 A controversy exists concerning the meaning of *hupsipolis* in Sophocles'

text. Does it refer to the city or to one's position within the city? Richard C. Jebb and Fitts and Fitzgerald choose the former, rendering *hupsipolis* as "proud stands his city" and "how proudly his city stands," respectively. Victor Ehrenbereg chooses the latter—"stands high in the *polis*." Cynthia P. Gardiner's interpretation is banal: "In the end, the chorus' view is that Man should use his skill and cleverness to protect himself, to keep himself safe and secure in the protection of a strong city rather than endangered by the absence of that protection." See Gardiner, *The Sophoclean Chorus: A Study of Character and Function*, p. 87. See Gardiner's n. 12, p. 87, for the translations of Jebb and Ehrenberg, and her bibliography for full citations. Segal's interpretation is more subtle. He argues that both Antigone and Creon claim to honor the "laws of the earth" and the "oath-bound justice of the gods" yet do not in fact do so: "Each one, therefore, is *hupsipolis* and *apolis*, though in contrasting ways" (Segal, *Tragedy and Civilization*, p. 168).

27 Gregory Schufrieder's comment is apposite: "While individual work may serve to open up various paths, even to the extremity of beings, it cannot by itself establish the further dimension of unconcealment, and the unique possibilities for being in the midst of beings, the intersection of these paths results in. In converging at the *polis*, those individual ways become something more than they alone could be; no longer, as Heidegger answers Nietzsche's lament, 'merely poet,' thinker, etc., in so far as such individual work takes on reality in contributing to the institution of a measure of 'being' for an historical community" ("Heidegger's Contribution to a Phenomenology of Culture," pp. 171–72). Unfortunately, Schufrieder does not take into account Heidegger's rejection of anything answering to the modern notion of culture.

28 Manfred Frings's accounts of these lectures, which he edited, are reliable guides to their general aims and structure. Unfortunately, he seems unaware of their political dimension. See Frings, "Heraclitus: Heidegger's 1943 Lecture Held at Freiburg University" and "Parmenides: Heidegger's 1942–1943 Lecture Held at Freiburg University." For additional commentary, see Kenneth Maly and Parvis Emad, eds., *Heidegger on Heraclitus: A New Reading*, and, for a discussion of Parmenides relevant to the study of Heidegger, Reiner Schürmann, "Tragic Differing: The Law of the One and the Law of Contraries in Parmenides."

29 I have in mind the dispute concerning Heidegger's understanding of *alētheia*. Caputo has sorted out the issues involved with great care. See his *Demythologizing Heidegger*, chap. 1. Cf. David Farrell Krell, *Intimations of Mortality: Time, Truth, and Finitude in Heidegger's Thinking of Being*, chap. 4; and Robert Bernasconi, *The Question of Language in Heidegger's History of Being*, chap. 2.

30 The Parmenides and Heraclitus lectures are crucial to Schürmann's Heidegger interpretation, yet he never mentions the philosopher's remarks
on the war or his claims about the role of Germany and the Germans in
the destiny of the West. Spanos (see nn. 14 and 16) also does not seem to
notice Heidegger's continued emphasis on the German mission.

31 Frings, "Parmenides: Heidegger's 1942–1943 Lecture Held at Freiburg
University," p. 28. For additional commentary, see Fóti, "Alēthia and
Oblivion's Field," p. 76; and Haar, *Heidegger and the Essence of Man*,
pp. 157–65.

Chapter 7 : Poetic Dwelling

1 Harries translates *Volkstum* as "popular base," which is needlessly
vague. William S. Lewis renders it as "the culture of one Volk" (RAW
31). I have, I believe, given sufficient indication of Heidegger's assessment of the concept of "culture" to cast doubt on the propriety of such a
translation.

2 According to Otto Pöggeler, Heidegger would write, in a passage omitted
from the published version of G53: "Perhaps the poet Hölderlin must
become a *Geschick* of decisive confrontation for a thinker whose grand-
father was born at the same time the 'Ister Hymn' and the poem 'Andenken' originated—according to the records, in the sheepfold of a dairy
farm in Ovili, which lies in the upper Danube valley near the bank of the
river, beneath the cliffs. The hidden history of Saying knows no accidents. Everything is dispensation [*Schickung*] ("Heidegger's Political
Self-Understanding," p. 223). It is necessary to recall that Heidegger
explicitly rejects "destiny" as a translation of *Geschick* in PR 60–61. The
English translator of Pöggeler's article, Steven Galt Crowell, renders
Geschick as "destiny."

3 I borrow "soundings" for *Erläuterungen* from Gerald L. Bruns, who seems
to me to understand Heidegger's aims quite well. He writes, concerning
an *Erläuterung* of a poem, that "it would be the light that it sheds on a
matter of concern to us, not the light we shed on its inner sanctum in our
reading of it. . . . [It] more nearly resembles the allegorization of a text
than the analysis of it. Allegory is the appropriation of dark texts; that is,
it means taking a text differently from its literal sense because there is no
taking the text literally—its literal sense is no sense at all: nothing can be
made of it. . . . Allegory is a taking-off from the text rather than an exegesis
that extracts something from the text in order to hold it up to the light.
The dark text surrenders nothing of itself" (*Heidegger's Estrangements*,
pp. 67–69). If the readings or soundings are taken as interpretations, it is
evident, as Christopher Fynsk remarks, that Heidegger's "sacralizing"

interpretation of Hölderlin is "no more benign than Plato's own similar response to the poets" (*Heidegger: Thought and Historicity*, p. 194). Heidegger's "misreadings" are examined with great care by Véronique Fóti in her *Heidegger and the Poets*. Cf. David Halliburton, *Poetic Thinking: An Approach to Heidegger*, chap. 3, pp. 59–76. The early study of Beda Allemann, *Hölderlin und Heidegger* (1956), remains an influential statement of many important issues concerning Heidegger's understanding and use of Hölderlin. For discussions of Heidegger's selection of Hölderlin to exhibit the essence of poetry, see Allemann's work just cited; Halliburton, *Poetic Thinking*, chap. 4, pp. 77–112; Fynsk, *Heidegger: Thought and Historicity*, chap. 5, pp. 174–229; Gary Aylesworth, "Heidegger and Hölderlin"; Michael Murray, "Heidegger's Hermeneutic Reading of Hölderlin: The Signs of Time"; André Schuwer, "Nature and the Holy: On Heidegger's Interpretation of Hölderlin's Hymn 'Wie wenn am Feiertage'"; Paul de Man, "Les exégèses de Hölderlin par Martin Heidegger." See also Andrzej Warminski, *Readings in Interpretation: Hölderlin, Hegel, Heidegger;* and Otto Pöggeler, "Heidegger's Begegnung mit Hölderlin." For Tom Rockmore, the turn to Hölderlin shows that Heidegger "maintained his antirationalist claim for insight into history and the future through a reference beyond the philosophical tradition." See his *On Heidegger's Nazism and Philosophy*, p. 127. David White criticizes Heidegger severely for his alleged failure to consider questions of "rightness" in connection with poetry ("Poetry and Thinking: Heidegger and the Question of Rightness"). Cf. also White's *Logic and Ontology in Heidegger* and *Heidegger and the Language of Poetry*.

4 Fred Dallmayr calls "dubious" Heidegger's "persistent reference to 'the people' (*Volk*) in the sense of a homogeneous entity or totality," finding this a theme "not entirely congruent" with the "overall direction of his thought" and suggesting that his "nonobjectivist ontology and his stress on ontological difference should have suggested to him a greater heterogeneity among people (perhaps along the lines of Arendt's notion of 'plurality')." An essential part of Heidegger's political thinking is thereby reduced to a mere inconsistency. See Dallmayr, *The Other Heidegger*, pp. 146–47. Lacoue-Labarthe exaggerates, but at least does so in the proper direction, when he writes that the lectures on Hölderlin "probably contain all Heidegger's 'political' thinking" (*Heidegger, Art and Politics*, p. 134).

5 The Hölderlin lectures set the poet over against popular and Nazi appropriations of him. Dallmayr documents this defense of Hölderlin persuasively in *The Other Heidegger*, pp. 141–48. For an argument that Heidegger's concern with the history and destiny of the German people in the first Hölderlin lectures shows that he has *not* distanced himself

from National Socialism, see Tom Rockmore, *On Heidegger's Nazism and Philosophy*, pp. 123–32.

6 See Friedrich Hölderlin, *Sämtliche Werke* 6.1, p. 426. Heidegger cites the letter in his Hölderlin lectures at G39 136ff., G4 87, and G53 154–55.

7 That there is a "secret Germany" whose essence is prefigured in Hölderlin's poetry is the interpretation of Norbert von Hellingrath, whose edition of Hölderlin revived interest in the poet. For Heidegger's agreement with this interpretation, see Frank H. W. Edler, "Philosophy, Language, and Politics: Heidegger's Attempt to Steal the Language of the Revolution in 1933–34," p. 208. "Secret Germany" is also the title of a poem by Stefan George. See Olga Marx and Ernst Morwitz, *The Works of Stefan George Rendered into English*, pp. 371–74. The poem breathes the same atmosphere as that of Heidegger's Hölderlin readings:

> Powers below pondered gravely
> Gracious celestials gave their
> Ultimate secret: They altered
> Laws over matter and founded Space—a new space in the old

The conclusion of the poem:

> Who then, who of you brothers
> Doubts, unshocked by the warning,
> That what most you acclaim, what
> Most you value today is
> Rank as leaves in the fall-wind,
> Doomed to perdition and death!

> Only what consecrate earth
> Cradles in sheltering sleep
> Long in the innermost grooves,
> Far from acquisitive hands,
> Marvels this day cannot grasp
> Are rife with the fate of tomorrow.

8 Reiner Schürmann argues (mistakenly in my view) that Heidegger's theme of "thinking's neighborhood with poetry" (OWL 69) is "soon abandoned" (*Heidegger on Being and Acting*, p. 373 n. 120) Schürmann virtually ignores poetry and Hölderlin in his influential study of Heidegger, as Bruns notes (*Heidegger's Estrangements*, p. 192 n. 11).

9 I translate *Ursprung and Völkern* as "origin" and "peoples," rather than "source" and "nations."

10 Fynsk, *Heidegger: Thought and Historicity*, p. 215. Dallmayr warns us not to understand Heidegger's designation of Hölderlin as the "poet of

the Germans" "in a restrictive ethnic, or even a directly referential, sense" but goes on to explain that his poetry "constitutes the being of Germans by opening up a historical possibility for them—albeit, a possibility they tend to ignore" (*The Other Heidegger,* pp. 135–36). I fail to understand why this role is not "directly referential."

11 John D. Caputo, *Demythologizing Heidegger,* pp. 160–62; Murray, "Heidegger's Hermeneutic Reading of Hölderlin," p. 50.

12 Although he seldom, if ever, employs the *device* of parataxis in the Hölderlin readings, there is, I think, a larger sense in which the juxtapositions and dissociations of passages from the poetry and the interweaving of Heideggerian themes with Hölderlinian language are themselves a constellation of paratactic structures. As Heidegger puts it elsewhere, parataxis speaks "where there are no words, in the field between the words which the colons indicate" (WCT 186). There is at least one massive service thereby performed for Heidegger's thinking. Express or implied, parataxis blocks dialectics; the forces that confront each other and thereby become what they truly are come into their own, undergo no dialectical resolution. Poetry, faithful to what makes it possible, never transcends its own darkness. Ultimately, this is why the poet is never solely a founder and why the orphic, constitutive talk of the first Hölderlin readings and in particular "Hölderlin and the Essence of Poetry" is Heidegger's first, and not his last, word. Darkness is "always already" there, lying within poetic saying. The founding saying of the poet is that founding is inherently riven with *polemos.* If we continue to call the founding that is thematic in the Hölderlin interpretations political founding, "politics in the highest and authentic sense," then we must say that political founding is thought as conditioned by the gatherings and dispersings, the self-refusal of language as exhibited in poetic saying, and, in more specifically Hölderlinian accents, the want of holy names and the flight of the gods. The poet, in responding to what is, exhibits the correct *paideia.* Heidegger never fails to remember: "The ownmost and its appropriation is the hardest" (G53 154).

13 Cf. Fynsk on this theme, *Heidegger: Thought and Historicity,* p. 193.

14 Cf. Gregory Friel, "Heidegger's *Polemos.*" Space precludes an inventory of interpretations of Heidegger as a bucolic or environmentalist philosopher.

15 Hegel, of course, had claimed to bring Heraclitus into German thinking, but this inscription is inadequate (G39 129–31). Heidegger characterizes Hegel's political teaching as follows: "For Hegel the reality of the spirit in history was the state . . . [which] developed the utmost opposition of the free independence of the individuals and the free power of the general community in living unity" (133). He then refers to paragraph

185 of the *Philosophy of Right,* in which Hegel explains that "ancient states . . . went under, because they lacked truly infinite strength, which lies only in that unity which allows the opposition of reason complete strength to go back and forth and so fulfill itself" (*Elements of the Philosophy of Right,* p. 222). For Hegel, the failure of the ancient city lay in its incapacity to accommodate the infinite freedom inherent in individuality, a limitation comprehended in and by Christianity. For Heidegger, it is rather Hölderlin's poetry that exhibits the "infinite strength" required by, but absent from, the ancient city.

16 See, for example, Kathleen Wright, "Comments on Michel Haar's Paper, 'The Question of Human Freedom in the Later Heidegger," p. 20.

17 Of *Geschick* Heidegger writes that we usually understand it as "that which has been determined and imposed through fate: a sorrowful, an evil, a fortunate *Geschick.* This meaning is a derivative one. For *schicken* originally denotes: 'preparing,' 'ordering,' 'bringing each thing to that place where it belongs'; consequently it also means to 'furnish' and 'admit'; 'to appoint' a house, a room, means: 'to keep in good order,' 'straightened up and tidied' " (PR 61).

18 Rockmore reads these passages as evidence of Heidegger's continuing adherence to National Socialism "as an ideal" (*On Heidegger's Nazism and Philosophy,* pp. 119–21). In my view, they are rather statements of a fundamental theme in Heidegger's political thinking that is ultimately tangential to National Socialism.

19 Lacoue-Labarthe makes this point but fails to see that Heidegger's move from science to poetry or art not only conserves the political dimension of the former but articulates more profoundly how Dasein is held into the totality of what is (*Heidegger, Art and Politics,* pp. 52–59).

20 In *Beiträge* Heidegger writes that we must think "nature" in terms of "earth," because as "historically related" in its strife with world, it is more originary than "nature" (G65 275, 29).

21 For a useful discussion of the "colony" themes in Hölderlin, see R. B. Harrison, *Hölderlin and Greek Literature,* pp. 252–62.

22 In his lectures on Hegel's *Phenomenology of Spirit* given in 1930/31, Heidegger argues that for Hegel and German idealism, spirit is ego (G32 111).

23 Schürmann, *Heidegger on Being and Acting,* pp. 223. I disagree, however, with his position that the number "four" has no importance. The deconstruction of any substantive character for the members of the four-fold does not dissolve the fourfold; its "pre-Socratic" and Hölderlinian provenances cannot be removed so easily. Michel Haar understands the fourfold as an "immemorial whole that does not concern any precise epoch" and is "prior to the primordial Greek oppositions such as being

and thinking or being and appearance and prior to every definition of man or to the appearance of this or that god." As such the fourfold is "nonhistorical." (*Heidegger and the Essence of Man*, pp. 178–79). I disagree with this interpretation because it comes perilously close to understanding the fourfold as a metaphysical foundation, which Heidegger explicitly rejects. Moreover, as what is gathered, the fourfold is necessarily "historical" in the decisive sense sought by Heidegger.

24   Derrida, *Of Spirit*, pp. 83–113. For other interpretations, see Caputo, *Demythologizing Heidegger*, pp. 149–66; Véronique Fóti, "The Path of the Stranger: Heidegger's Interpretation of Trakl"; Richard Detsch, *Georg Trakl's Poetry: Towards a Union of Opposites;* Karsten Harries, "Language and Silence: Heidegger's Dialogue with Georg Trakl"; W. H. Rey, "Heidegger-Trakl: Einstimmiges Zweigespräch."

25   Cf. David Farrell Krell, "Strokes of Love and Death," in his *Intimations of Mortality*, pp. 165–68; Derrida, *Of Spirit*, p. 89.

26   As Derrida notes, night, as spiritual, shelters the year, which makes spiritual as well "the revolutionary coming-going of the very thing which goes" (*Of Spirit*, p. 89).

27   I use Krell's translation here ("Strokes of Love and Death," p. 167).

28   The translator renders *entsetzt* as "horrifies." Derrida notes that *entsetzt* can mean "deposes or frightens, transports or transposes, deports"—that it encompasses a "whole semantics" (*Of Spirit*, p. 98).

29   Caputo argues that Heidegger's reading is a massive allegorization that displaces suffering and purges Trakl's poetry of its Jewish and Christian voice. In his view, it is the very success of Heidegger's treatment that is a "scandal," which for him shows the "offensive and insensitive" character of Heidegger's "thinking" (*Demythologizing Heidegger*, pp. 158–65; the words cited appear on p. 160).

30   Schürmann provides a concise account of "favor," noting that it also translates *philia* "as a predicate of the pre-metaphysical notion of *phusis*" in G55 (*Heidegger on Being and Acting*, pp. 215–17).

Epilogue

1   Jacques Derrida, "Force of Law: The Mystical Foundation of Authority," p. 973; Reiner Schürmann, *Heidegger on Being and Acting: From Principles to Anarchy*, p. 295.

2   Schürmann, *Heidegger on Being and Acting*, pp. 240–42.

3   Sophocles, *Ajax* 5.646; I have used Frank J. Nisetich's translation of Pindar.

Bibliography

Adamczewski, Zygmunt. "On the Way to Being: Reflecting on Conversations with Martin Heidegger." In *Heidegger and the Path of Thinking,* ed. John Sallis, pp. 12–36. Pittsburgh: Duquesne University Press, 1970.

Alleman, Beda. "Heidegger und die Politik." In *Heidegger. Perspektiven zur Deutung seines Werks,* ed. Otto Pöggeler, pp. 246–60. Cologne: Kiepenheuer-Witsch, 1969.

———. *Hölderlin und Heidegger.* Freiburg: Atlantis Verlag, 1954.

Aristotle. *The Basic Works of Aristotle.* Edited by Richard McKeon. New York: Random House, 1941.

Aylesworth, Gary. "Heidegger and Hölderlin." *Philosophy Today* 30, 2/4 (Summer 1988): 143–55.

Barash, Jeffrey. *Heidegger and Historical Meaning.* The Hague: Dordrecht, 1988.

Bart, Robert. "The Shepherd and the Wolf: The First Book of Plato's *Republic.*" In *Essays in Honor of Jacob Klein,* pp. 7–19. Annapolis: St. Johns College, 1976.

Basta, Danilo N. "Zu Heideggers Marx-Interpretation." In *Martin Heidegger—Unterwegs im Denken. Symposion im 10. Todesjahr,* ed. Richard Wisser, pp. 215–38. Freiburg: Verlag Karl Alber, 1987.

Benardete, Seth. *Socrates' Second Sailing: On Plato's Republic.* Chicago: University of Chicago Press, 1989.

Bernasconi, Robert. *The Question of Language in Heidegger's History of Being.* Atlantic Highlands, N.J.: Humanities Press International, 1989.

———. "The Transformation of Language at Another Beginning." *Research in Phenomenology* 13 (1983): 1–23.

Blitz, Mark. *Heidegger's "Being and Time" and the Possibility of Political Philosophy.* Ithaca: Cornell University Press, 1981.

Borgmann, Albert, and Carl Mitcham. "The Question of Heidegger and Technology: A Review of the Literature." *Philosophy Today* 31, no. 2 (Summer 1987): 98–194.

Bourdieu, Pierre. *L'ontologie politique de Martin Heidegger.* Paris: Editions de Minuit, 1988.

Boutout, Alain. *Heidegger et Platon.* Paris: Presses Universitaires de France, 1987.

Brague, Rémi. *Aristote et la question du monde. Essai sur le contexte cosmologique et anthropologique de l'ontologie.* Paris: Presses Universitaires de France, 1988.

———. "Radical Modernity and the Roots of Ancient Thought." *Independent Journal of Philosophy* 4 (1983): 63–74.

Bruns, Gerald L. *Heidegger's Estrangements: Language, Truth, and Poetry in the Later Writings.* New Haven: Yale University, 1989.

Butler, E. M. *The Tyranny of Greece over Germany.* Cambridge: Cambridge University Press, 1935.

Caputo, John D. *Demythologizing Heidegger.* Bloomington: Indiana University Press, 1993.

———. "Demythologizing Heidegger: *Alētheia* and the History of Being." *Review of Metaphysics* 41, no. 3 (March 1988): 519–46.

———. *Heidegger and Aquinas: An Essay on Overcoming Metaphysics.* New York: Fordham University Press, 1982.

———. *The Mystical Element in Heidegger's Thought.* Athens: Ohio University Press, 1978.

———. *Radical Hermeneutics: Repetition, Deconstruction, and the Hermeneutic Project.* Bloomington: Indiana University Press, 1987.

———. "Thinking, Poetry, and Pain." *Southern Journal of Philosophy* 28, supp: (1989): 155–82.

Corngold, Stanley. "Dilthey's Essay *The Poetic Imagination:* A Poetics of Force." *Interpretation* 9, nos. 2–3 (September 1981): 301–37.

Dallmayr, Fred. *Between Freiburg and Frankfurt: Toward a Critical Ontology.* Amherst: University of Massachusetts Press, 1991.

———. "Ontology of Freedom: Heidegger and Political Philosophy." *Political Theory* 12 (1984): 204–34.

———. *The Other Heidegger.* Ithaca: Cornell University Press, 1993.

———. *Polis and Praxis.* Cambridge: MIT Press, 1984.

De Man, Paul. "Les exégèses de Hölderlin par Martin Heidegger." *Critique,* nos. 11–13 (1955): 800–819.

Derrida, Jacques. "Force of Law: The Mystical Foundation of Authority." *Cardozo Law Review* 2, nos. 5–6 (1990).

———. "Heidegger, l'enfer des philosophes." *Le Nouvel Observateur,* November 6–12, 1987.

———. *Of Spirit: Heidegger and the Question.* Translated by Geoffrey Bennington and Rachel Bowlby. Chicago: University of Chicago Press, 1989.

――. *Psyché: Inventions de l'autre*. Paris: Galilée, 1987.

Detsch, Richard. *Georg Trakl's Poetry: Towards a Union of Opposites*. University Park: Pennsylvania State University Press, 1983.

Dilthey, Wilhelm. *Der Aufbau der geschichtlichen Welt in den Geisteswissenschaften*. Frankfurt am Main: Suhrkamp, 1974.

Dostal, Robert J. "Beyond Being: Heidegger's Plato." *Journal of the History of Philosophy* 23, no. 1 (January 1985): 71–98.

Edler, Frank H. W. "Philosophy, Language, and Politics: Heidegger's Attempt to Steal the Language of the Revolution of 1933–34." *Social Research* 57 (Spring 1990): 197–238.

Emad, Parvis. "Boredom as a Limit and a Disposition." In *Heidegger Studies* 1 (1985): 64–78.

――. "World, Finitude, and Solitude as Basic Concepts of Metaphysics: Review of *Die Grundprobleme der Metaphysik: Welt-Endlichkeit-Einsamkeit* by Martin Heidegger." *Research in Phenomenology* 15 (1985): 247–57.

Escoubas, Éliane. "Heidegger, la question romaine, la question impériale: Autour du 'Tournant.'" In *Heidegger: Questions ouvertes*, ed. Éliane Escoubas, pp. 173–88. Paris: Éditions Osiris, 1988.

Fandozzi, Phillip R. *Nihilism and Technology: A Heideggerian Investigation*. Washington, D.C.: University Press of America, 1982.

Farias, Victor. *Heidegger and Nazism*. Edited by Joseph Margolis and Tom Rockmore. Translated by Paul Burrell, Dominic Di Benardi, and Gbriel R. Ricci. Philadelphia: Temple University Press, 1989.

――. *Heidegger et le nazism*. Paris: Editions Verdier, 1987.

Farwell, Paul. "Can Heidegger's Craftsman Be Authentic?" *International Philosophical Quarterly* 29, no. 113 (March 1989): 77–90.

Faye, Jean-Pierre. "Attaque Nazies contre Heidegger." *Médiations*, no. 5 (Summer 1962): 137–51.

Fell, Joseph P. *Heidegger and Sartre: An Essay on Being and Place*. New York: Columbia University Press, 1979.

――. "Heidegger's Mortals and Gods." *Research in Phenomenology* 15 (1985): 29–41.

――. "Heidegger's Notion of Two Beginnings." *Review of Metaphysics* 25, no. 2 (December 1971): 213–37.

Ferry, Luc, and Alain Renaut. *Heidegger and Modernity*. Translated by Franklin Philip. Chicago: University of Chicago Press, 1990.

Fóti, Véronique M. "Alētheia and Oblivion's Field: On Heidegger's Parmenides Lectures." In *Ethics and Danger: Essays on Heidegger and Continental Thought*, ed. Arleen B. Dallery, Charles E. Scott, and P. Holley Roberts, pp. 71–82. Albany: State University of New York Press, 1992.

———. *Heidegger and the Poets: Poesis, Sophia, Techne.* Atlantic Highlands, N.J.: Humanities Press, 1991.

———. "The Path of the Stranger: Heidegger's Interpretation of Trakl." *Review of Existential Psychology and Psychiatry* 17 (1986): 223–33.

———. "Representation and the Image: Between Heidegger, Derrida, and Plato." *Man and World* 18 (1985): 67–78.

Franzen, Winfried. "Die Sehnsucht nach Härte und Schwere: Über ein zum NS-Engagement disponierendes Motiv in Heideggers 'Die Grundbegriffe der Metaphysik' von 1929/30." In *Heidegger und die praktische Philosophie,* ed. Annemarie Gethmann-Siefert and Otto Pöggeler. Frankfurt am Main: Suhrkamp Verlag, 1989.

Fresco, Marcel F., Rob J. A. van Dijk, and H. W. Peter Vijgeboom, eds. *Heideggers These vom Ende der Philosophie: Verhandlungen des Leidener Heidegger-Symposiums April 1989.* Bonn: Bouvier Verlag, 1989.

Friel, Gregory. "Heidegger's *Polemos.*" *Journal of Philosophical Research* 16 (1991): 145–95.

Frings, Manfred S. "Heraclitus: Heidegger's 1943 Lecture Held at Freiburg University." *Journal of the British Society for Phenomenology* 21, no. 3 (October 1990): 250–73.

———. "Is There Room for Evil in Heidegger's Thought or Not?" *Philosophy Today* 32, no. 1/4 (Spring 1988): 79–92.

———. "Parmenides: Heidegger's 1942–1943 Lecture Held at Freiburg University." *Journal of the British Society for Phenomenology* 19, no. 1 (January 1988): 15–33.

Froman, Wayne J. "*Schelling's Treatise on the Essence of Human Freedom* and Heidegger's Thought." *International Philosophical Quarterly* 30, no. 4 (December 1990): 465–80.

Fynsk, Christopher. *Heidegger: Thought and Historicity.* Ithaca: Cornell University Press, 1986.

Gadamer, Hans-Georg "Heidegger's 'theologische' Jugendschrift" *Dilthey-Jahrbuch für Philosophie und Geschichte der Geisteswissenschaften* 6 (1989): 228–34.

Galston, William. "Heidegger's Plato: A Critique of *Plato's Doctrine of Truth.*" *Philosophical Forum* 13, no. 4 (Summer 1982): 371–84.

Gardiner, Cynthia P. *The Sophoclean Chorus: A Study of Character and Function.* Iowa City: University of Iowa Press, 1987.

Gawronsky, Dimitry. "Ernst Cassirer: His Life and His Work." In *The Philosophy of Ernst Cassirer,* ed. Paul Arthur Schlipp. New York: Tudor Publishing, 1949.

George, Stefan. *The Works of Stefan George Rendered into English.* Edited and translated by Olga Marx and Ernst Morwitz. Chapel Hill: University of North Carolina Press, 1974.

Gerlach, Hans-Martin. *Martin Heidegger: Denk-und-Irrwege Eines Spät-bürgerlich Philosophen.* Berlin: Akademie-Verlag, 1982.

Grieder, Alfons. "Essential Thinking: Reflections on Heidegger's *Beiträge zur Philosophie.*" *Journal of the British Society for Phenomenology* 23, no. 3 (October 1992): 240–51.

——. "What Did Heidegger Mean by 'Essence?'" *Journal of the British Society for Phenomenology* 19, no. 1 (January 1988): 64–89.

Gudopp, Wolf-Dieter, *Der junge Heidegger: Realität und Wahrheit in der Vorgeschichte von 'Sein und Zeit.'* Frankfurt am Main: Verlag Marx-istische Blätter GMBH, 1983.

Guignon, Charles B. *Heidegger and the Problem of Knowledge.* Indianapolis: Hackett Publishing, 1983.

——, ed. *The Cambridge Companion to Heidegger.* Cambridge: Cambridge University Press, 1993.

Haar, Michel. *Le Chant de la terre: Heidegger et les assises de l'histoire d'être.* Paris: Éditions de l'Herne, 1987.

——. "The End of Distress: The End of Technology?" *Research in Phenomenology* 13 (1983): 43–63.

——. *Heidegger and the Essence of Man.* Translated by William McNeill. Albany: State University of New York Press, 1993.

——. "The Question of Human Freedom in the Later Heidegger." *Southern Journal of Philosophy* 27, supp. (1989): 1–16.

——. *The Song of the Earth.* Translated by Reginald Lilly. Bloomington: Indiana University Press, 1993.

Habermas, Jürgen. "Work and Weltanschauung: The Heidegger Controversy from a German Perspective." In *The New Conservatism: Cultural Criticism and the Historians' Debate,* ed. Jürgen Habermas, trans. Shierry Nicholsen, pp. 140–72. Cambridge: MIT Press, 1989.

Halliburton, David. *Poetic Thinking: An Approach to Heidegger.* Chicago: University of Chicago Press, 1981.

Harries, Karsten. "Heidegger and Hölderlin: The Limits of Language." *Personalist* 44 (1963): 5–23.

——. "Heidegger as a Political Thinker." *Review of Metaphysics* 29 (June 1976): 642–69.

——. "Language and Silence: Heidegger's Dialogue with Georg Trakl." In *Heidegger and the Question of Literature: Toward a Postmodern Literary Hermeneutics,* ed. William V. Spanos, pp. 155–71. Bloomington: Indiana University Press, 1979.

Harrison, R. B. *Hölderlin and Greek Literature.* Oxford: Clarendon Press, 1975.

Hegel, G. W. F. *Elements of the Philosophy of Right.* Edited by Allen W. Wood. Translated by H. B. Nisbet. Cambridge: Cambridge University Press, 1991.

Heinz, Marion. *Zeitlichkeit und Temporalität: Die Konstitution der Existenz und die Grundlegung einer temporalen Ontologie im Frühwerk M. Heideggers.* Würzburg: Königshausen und Neumann, 1982.

Herf, Jeffrey. *Reactionary Modernism: Technology, Culture, and Politics in Weimar and the Third Reich.* Cambridge: Cambridge University Press, 1984.

Herrmann, Friedrich-Wilhelm, von. *Heideggers Philosophie der Kunst.* Frankfurt am Main: Vittorio Klostermann, 1980.

———. *Hermeneutische Phänomenologie des Daseins. Eine Erläuterung von "Sein und Zeit."* Vol. 1: *Einleitung: Die Exposition der Frage nach dem Sinn von Sein.* Frankfurt am Main: Vittorio Klostermann, 1987.

Hoffmann, Stanley. "The Passion of Modernity." *Atlantic* 272, no. 2 (1993): 101–8.

Hölderlin, Friedrich. *Poems and Fragments.* Translated by Michael Hamburger. Cambridge: Cambridge University Press, 1980.

———. *Sämtliche Werke.* Grosse Stuttgarter Ausgabe, ed. Friedrich Beissner. Stuttgart: W. Kohlhammer, 1946–68.

Janicaud, Dominique. "Metamorphosis of the Undecidable." *Graduate Faculty Philosophy Journal* 13, no. 1 (1988): 125–40.

———. *L'ombre de cette pensée. Heidegger et la question politique.* Grenoble: Jérôme Millon, 1990.

Janicaud, Dominique, and Jean-François Mattéi. *La métaphysique à la limite. Cinq études sur Heidegger.* Paris: Presses Universitaire de France, 1983.

Kawahara, Eiho M. "Heideggers Auslegung der Langeweile." In *Martin Heidegger—Unterwegs im Denken. Symposion im 10. Todesjahr,* ed. Richard Wisser, pp. 87–110. Freiburg: Verlag Karl Alber, 1987.

Kisiel, Theodore. *The Genesis of Heidegger's Being and Time.* Berkeley: University of California Press, 1993.

———. "Heidegger and the New Images of Science." *Research in Phenomenology* 7 (1977): 162–81.

———. "Why The First Draft of *Being and Time* Was Never Published." *Journal of the British Society for Phenomenology* 20, no. 1 (January 1989): 3–22.

Köchler, Hans. *Skepsis und Gesellschaftskritik im Denken Martin Heideggers.* Meisenheim am Glan: Verlag Anton Hain, 1978.

Kovacs, George. "On Heidegger's Silence." *Heidegger Studies* 5 (1989): 135–51.

———. *The Question of God in Heidegger's Phenomenology.* Evanston, Ill.: Northwestern University Press, 1990.

Krell, David Farrell. "The Crisis of Reason in the Nineteenth Century: Schelling's Treatise on Human Freedom (1809)." In *The Collegium Phae-*

nomenologicum: The First Ten Years, ed. John Sallis, Giuseppina Moneta, and Jacques Taminiaux, pp. 13–32. The Hague: Martinus Nijhoff, 1989.

———. "Daimon Life, Nearness and Abyss: An Introduction to Za-ology." *Research in Phenomenology* (1987): 23–54.

———. *Intimations of Morality: Time, Truth, and Finitude in Heidegger's Thinking of Being*. University Park: Pennsylvania State University Press, 1986.

———. "Of Spirit and the Daimon: On Derrida's *De l'espirit*." In *Ethics and Danger: Essays on Heidegger and Continental Thought*, ed. Arleen B. Dallery, Charles E. Scott, and P. Holley Roberts, pp. 59–70. Albany: State University of New York Press, 1992.

Lacoue-Labarthe, Philippe. *La fiction du politique: Heidegger, l'art et la politique*. Paris: Christian Bourgois, 1987.

———. *Heidegger, Art, and Politics: The Fiction of the Political*. Translated by Chris Turner. Oxford: Basil Blackwell, 1990.

———. *L'imitation des modernes. Typographies II*. Paris: Éditions Galilée, 1986.

Lampert, Laurence. *Nietzsche and Modern Times: A Study of Bacon, Descartes, and Nietzsche*. New Haven: Yale University Press, 1993.

———. *Nietzsche's Teaching: An Interpretation of "Thus Spoke Zarathustra."* New Haven: Yale University Press, 1986.

Leder, Drew. "Modes of Totalization: Heidegger on Modern Technology and Science" *Philosophy Today* 29, no. 3/4 (Fall 1985): 245–56.

Lidz, Joel Warren. "Reflections on and in Plato's Cave." *Interpretation* 21, no. 2 (Winter 1993/94): 115–34.

Loscerbo, Joseph. *Being and Technology: A Study in the Philosophy of Martin Heidegger*. The Hague: Martinus Nijhoff, 1981.

Löwith, Karl. "Les implications politiques de la philosophie de l'existence chez Heidegger." *Les Temps Moderne* 2, no. 14 (November 1946): 343–60.

———. *Mein Leben in Deutschland vor und nach 1933*. Stuttgart: J. B. Metzler, 1986.

———. "The Political Implications of Heidegger's Existentialism." Translated by Richard Wolin. In *The Heidegger Controversy*, ed. Richard Wolin, pp. 167–85. Cambridge: MIT Press, 1993.

Lukacs, John. *The End of the Twentieth Century and the End of the Modern Age*. New York: Ticknor & Fields, 1993.

Lyotard, Jean-François. *Heidegger and "the jews."* Translated by Andreas Michel and Mark Roberts. Minneapolis: University of Minnesota Press, 1990.

———. *Heidegger et "les juifs."* Paris: Galilée, 1988.

Magnus, Bernd. *Heidegger's Metahistory of Philosophy: Amor Fati, Being and Truth.* The Hague: Martinus Nijhoff, 1970.

Makreel, Rudolf F. "The Genesis of Heidegger's Phenomenological Hermeneutics and the Rediscovered 'Aristotle Introduction' of 1922." *Man and World* 23 (1990): 305–20.

Maly, Kenneth, and Parvid Emad, eds. *Heidegger on Heraclitus: A New Reading.* Lewiston, N.Y.: Edwin Mellen Press, 1986.

Martin, Bernd. " 'Alles Grosse ist gefährdet'—Der Fall Heidegger(s)." In *Martin Heidegger und das 'Dritte Reich': Ein Compendium,* ed. Bernd Martin, pp. 3–13. Darmstadt: Wissenschaftliche Buch Gesellschaft, 1989.

Marx, Werner. *Heidegger and the Tradition.* Translated by Theodore Kisiel and Murray Greene. Evanston, Ill.: Northwestern University Press, 1971.

———. *The Philosophy of F. W. J. Schelling.* Translated by Thomas Nenon. Bloomington: Indiana University Press, 1984.

Meyer, Michel. "De Aristote à Heidegger." *Revue Internationale de Philosophie* 43, no. 168 (January 1989): 142–59.

Mohanty, J. N. "Heidegger on Logic." *Journal of the History of Philosophy* 26, no. 1 (January 1988): 107–35.

Mosse, George L. *The Crisis of German Ideology: Intellectual Origins of the Third Reich.* New York: Grosset and Dunlap, 1964.

———. *Nazi Culture: Intellectual, Cultural, and Social Life in the Third Reich.* New York: Grosset & Dunlap, 1966.

Murray, Michael. "Heidegger's Hermeneutic Reading of Hölderlin: The Signs of Time." *Eighteenth Century* 21, no. 1 (1980): 41–66.

Neske, Günther, and Emil Kettering, eds. *Heidegger and National Socialism: Questions and Answers.* Translated by Lisa Harries. New York: Paragon House, 1990.

Neumann, Harry. "The Closing of the Philosophic Mind." *Interpretation: A Journal of Political Philosophy* 16, no. 1 (Fall 1988): 157–64.

———. "The Man on the Moon? The Question of Heidegger's 'Self-Assertion of the German University.' " *Journal of Value Inquiry* 13 (1979): 274–82.

———. "Politics or Nothing! Nazism's Origin in Scientific Contempt for Politics." *Journal of Value Inquiry* 19 (1985): 225–34.

Newell, W. R. "Heidegger on Freedom and Community: Some Political Implications of His Early Thought." *American Political Science Review* 78, no. 3 (September 1984): 775–84.

Nietzsche, Friedrich. *Beyond Good And Evil: Prelude to a Philosophy of the Future.* Translated, with commentary, by Walter Kaufmann. New York: Vintage, 1966.

———. *The Will to Power.* Translated by Walter Kaufmann and R. J. Hollingdale. New York: Vintage, 1968.

Ott, Hugo. *Martin Heidegger: A Political Life.* Translated by Allan Blunden. New York: Basic Books, 1993.

———. *Martin Heidegger: Unterwegs zu seiner Biographie.* Frankfurt am Main: Campus, 1988.

Oudemans, T. C. W. "Heideggers 'logische Untersuchungen.'" *Heidegger Studies* 6 (1990): 85–105.

Palmier, Jean-Michel. *Les écrits politiques de Heidegger.* Paris: L'Herne, 1968.

Pindar. *Pindar's Victory Songs.* Translation, Introduction, and Prefaces by Frank J. Nisetich. Baltimore: Johns Hopkins University Press, 1980.

Plato. *The Collected Dialogues of Plato, Including the Letters.* Edited by Edith Hamilton and Huntington Cairns. Princeton: Princeton University Press, 1969.

———. *The Republic of Plato.* Translated by Allan Bloom. New York: Basic Books, 1968.

Pöggeler, Otto. "Den Führer führen? Heidegger und kein Ende." *Philosophischer Rundschau* 32, no. 1/2 (1985): 26–67.

———. "Heidegger's Begegnung mit Hölderlin." *Man and World* 10, no. 1 (1977): 13–61.

———. "Heidegger's Political Self-Understanding." Translated by Steven Galt Crowell. In *The Heidegger Controversy,* ed. Richard Wolin, pp. 198–244. Cambridge: MIT Press, 1993.

———. *Martin Heidegger's Path of Thinking.* Translated by Daniel Magurshak and Sigmund Barber. Atlantic Highlands, N.J.: Humanities Press International, 1987.

———. *Philosophie und Politik bei Heidegger.* Freiburg: Karl Albers, 1972.

———, ed. *Heidegger. Perspektiven zur Deutung seines Werks.* Cologne: Kiepenheuer-Witsch, 1969.

Rey, W. H. "Heidegger-Trakl: Einstimmiges Zweigespräch." *Deutsche Vierteljahresschrift* 30 (1956): 89–136.

Richardson, William J. *Heidegger: Through Phenomenology to Thought.* The Hague: Martinus Nijhoff, 1974.

Rockmore, Tom. *On Heidegger's Nazism and Philosophy.* Berkeley: University of California Press, 1992.

Rorty, Richard. *Consequences of Pragmatism (Essays: 1972–1980).* Minneapolis: University of Minnesota Press, 1982.

———. *Essays on Heidegger and Others. Philosophical Papers.* Vol. 2. Cambridge: Cambridge University Press, 1990.

———. "Taking Philosophy Seriously." *New Republic,* April 11, 1988.

Rosen, Stanley. *The Ancients and the Moderns: Rethinking Modernity.* New Haven: Yale University Press, 1989.

———. *Hermeneutics as Politics.* New York: Oxford University Press, 1987.

———. *Nihilism: A Philosophical Essay.* New Haven: Yale University Press, 1969.

———. "Philosophy and Ideology: Reflections on Heidegger." *Social Research* 35 (1968): 260–88.

———. *Plato's Sophist: The Drama of Original and Image.* New Haven: Yale University Press, 1983.

———. *The Quarrel between Philosophy and Poetry: Studies in Ancient Thought.* New York: Routledge, 1988.

———. *The Question of Being: A Reversal of Heidegger.* New Haven: Yale University Press, 1993.

Rouse, Joseph. "Heidegger's Later Philosophy of Science." *Southern Journal of Philosophy* 22, no. 1 (Spring 1985): 75–92.

———. "Kuhn, Heidegger, and Scientific Realism." *Man and World* 14 (1981): 269–90.

Sallis, John. *Echoes: After Heidegger.* Bloomington: Indiana University Press, 1990.

———. "The Origins of Heidegger's Thought." *Research in Phenomenology* 7 (1977): 43–57.

———, ed. *Heidegger and the Path of Thinking.* Pittsburgh: Duquesne University Press, 1970.

Schirmacher, Wolfgang. *Technik und Gelassenheit: Zeitkritik nach Heidegger.* Freiburg: Alber, 1983.

Schufrieder, Gregory. "Heidegger on Community." *Man and World* 14 (1981): 25–54.

Schürmann, Reiner. *Heidegger on Being and Acting: From Principles to Anarchy.* Translated by Christine-Marie Gros in collaboration with the author. Bloomington: Indiana University Press, 1987.

———. "Legislation-Transgression: Strategies and Counter-Strategies in the Transcendental Justification of Norms." *Man and World* 17 (1984): 361–98.

———. "Modernity: The Last Epoch in a Closed History?" *Independent Journal of Philosophy* 4 (1983): 51–59.

———. "Principles Precarious: On the Origin of the Political in Heidegger." In *Heidegger: The Man and the Thinker,* ed. Thomas Sheehan, pp. 245–56. Chicago: Precedent Publishing, 1981.

———. "Tragic Differing: The Law of the One and the Law of Contraries in Parmenides." *Graduate Faculty Philosophy Journal* 13, no. 1 (1988): 3–20.

Schuwer, André. "Nature and the Holy: On Heidegger's Interpretation of Hölderlin's Hymn, 'Wie wenn am Feiertage.'" *Research in Phenomenology* 7 (1977): 225–37.

Schwan, Alexander. *Politische Philosophie im Denken Heideggers.* Cologne: Westdeutscher Verlag, 1989.

Schweickart, David. "Heidegger and Marx: A Framework for Dialogue." In *Heidegger: The Man and the Thinker,* ed. Thomas Sheehan, pp. 229–43. Chicago: Precedent Publishing, 1981.

Segal, Charles. *Tragedy and Civilization: An Interpretation of Sophocles.* Cambridge: Harvard University Press, 1981.

Shahan, Robert W., and J. N. Mohanty, eds. *Thinking about Being: Aspects of Heidegger's Thought.* Norman: University of Oklahoma Press, 1984.

Sheehan, Thomas J. "Heidegger and the Nazis." *New York Review of Books,* June 15, 1988, pp. 38–47.

———. "Heidegger, Aristotle, and Phenomenology." *Philosophy Today* 19 (1975): 87–94.

———. "Heidegger's 'Introduction to the Phenomenology of Religion,' 1920–21." *Personalist* 60, no. 3 (July 1979): 312–24.

———. "Introduction: Heidegger, the Project and the Fulfillment." In *Heidegger: The Man and the Thinker,* ed. Sheehan, pp. vii–xx. Chicago: Precedent Publishing, 1981.

———. " 'Introductory Note' to 'The Understanding of Time in Phenomenology and in the Thinking of the Being-Question." *Southwestern Journal of Philosophy* 10 (1979): 199.

———. "On Movement and the Destruction of Ontology." *Monist* 64, no. 4 (October, 1981): 534–42.

———. "On the Way to *Ereignis:* Heidegger's Interpretation of *Physis.*" In *Continental Philosophy in America,* ed. Hugh J. Silverman, John Sallis, and Thomas M. Seebohm, pp. 131–64. Pittsburgh: Duquesne University Press, 1983.

———. "Time and Being, 1925–27." In *Thinking about Being: Aspects of Heidegger's Thought,* ed. Robert W. Shahan and J. N. Mohanty, pp. 177–219. Norman: University of Oklahoma Press, 1984.

———, ed. *Heidegger: The Man and the Thinker.* Chicago: Precedent Publishing, 1981.

Shklar, Judith N. *Men and Citizens: A Study of Rousseau's Social Theory.* Cambridge: Cambridge University Press, 1969.

Simmel, Georg. *Georg Simmel, 1858–1918: A Collection of Essays with Translations and a Bibliography.* Edited by Kurt H. Wolff. Columbus: Ohio State University Press, 1959.

Sluga, Hans. *Heidegger's Crisis: Philosophy and Politics in Nazi Germany.* Cambridge: Harvard University Press, 1993.

Sophocles. *The Oedipus Cycle: An English Version.* Translated by Dudley Fitts and Robert Fitzgerald. New York: Harcourt, Brace & World, 1949.

———. *Sophocles' Ajax.* Translated and edited by W. B. Standford. London: Macmillan, 1963.

Spanos, William V. *Heidegger and Criticism: Retrieving the Cultural Politics of Destruction.* Minneapolis: University of Minnesota Press, 1993.

Stackelberg, Roderick. *Idealism Debased. From Völkisch Ideology to National Socialism.* Kent, Ohio: Kent State University Press, 1981.

Taminiaux, Jacques. *Heidegger and the Project of Fundamental Ontology.* Translated and edited by Michael Gendre. Albany: State University of New York Press, 1991.

———. "The Interpretation of Greek Philosophy in Heidegger's Fundamental Ontology." *Journal of the British Society for Phenomenology* 19 (January 1988): 3–14.

———. "Poiesis and Praxis in Fundamental Ontology." *Research in Phenomenology* 17 (1987): 137–69.

Thomä, Dieter. *Die Zeit des Selbst und die Zeit danach: Zur Kritik der Textgeschichte Martin Heideggers, 1910–1976.* Frankfurt am Main: Suhrkamp, 1990.

Van Buren, John. "The Young Heidegger and Phenomenology." *Man and World* 23 (1990): 239–72.

———. "The Young Heidegger, Aristotle, Ethics." In *Ethics and Danger: Essays on Heidegger and Continental Thought,* ed. Arleen B. Dallery and Charles E. Scott with P. Holley Roberts, pp. 169–85. Albany: State University of New York Press, 1992.

Vietta, Silvio. *Heideggers Kritik am Nationalsozialismus und der Technik.* Tübingen: Niemeyer Verlag, 1989.

Volpi, Franco. *Heidegger e Aristotele.* Padua: Daphne Editrice, 1984.

Vondung, Klaus. "Unity through *Bildung:* A German Dream of Perfection." *Independent Journal of Philosophy* 5/6 (1988): 47–55.

Vosskühler, Friedrich. "Praxis und Wahrheit. Ein Gang des Denkens von Marx zu Heidegger." In *Martin Heidegger—Unterwegs im Denken. Symposion im 10. Todesjahr,* ed. Richard Wisser, pp. 183–213. Freiburg: Verlag Karl Alber, 1987.

Warminski, Andrzej. *Readings in Interpretation: Hegel, Hölderlin, Heidegger.* Minneapolis: University of Minnesota Press, 1987.

Weber, Max. *Max Weber on the Methodology of the Social Sciences.* Translated by Edward Shils and Henry A. Finch. Glencoe: Free Press, 1949.

Weinberger, David. "Earth, World, and Fourfold." In *The Thought of Martin Heidegger,* ed. Michael E. Zimmerman, pp. 103–9. New Orleans: Tulane University Press, 1984.

White, Alan. *Schelling: An Introduction to the System of Freedom.* New Haven: Yale University Press, 1983.

White, David A. *Heidegger and the Language of Poetry*. Lincoln: University of Nebraska Press, 1978.

——. *Logic and Ontology in Heidegger*. Columbus: Ohio State University Press, 1985.

——. "Poetry and Thinking: Heidegger and the Question of Rightness." *Revue Internationale de Philosophie* 43, no. 168 (1989): 64–79.

Wisser, Richard, ed. *Antwort: Martin Heidegger im Gespräch*. Pfullingen: G. Neske Verlag, 1988.

——. *Martin Heidegger—Unterwegs im Denken. Symposion im 10. Todesjahr*. Freiburg: Verlag Karl Alber, 1987.

Wolff, Kurt H., ed. *Georg Simmel, 1858–1918: A Collection of Essays with Translations and a Bibliography*. Columbus: Ohio State University Press, 1959.

Wolin, Richard. "The French Heidegger Debate." *New German Critique* 45 (Fall 1988): 135–61.

——. "Introduction. Martin Heidegger and Politics: A Dossier" *New German Critique* 45 (Fall 1988): 91–95.

——. *The Politics of Being: The Political Thought of Martin Heidegger*. New York: Columbia University Press, 1990.

——, ed. *The Heidegger Controversy*. Cambridge: MIT Press, 1993.

Wright, Kathleen. "Comments on Michel Haar's Paper, 'The Question of Human Freedom in the Later Heidegger.'" *Southern Journal of Philosophy* 28, supp. (1989): 17–22.

Zarader, Marlène. *Heidegger et les paroles de l'origine*. Paris: J. Vrin, 1986.

Zimmerman, Michael E. *Heidegger's Confrontation with Modernity: Technology, Politics, Art*. Bloomington: Indiana University Press, 1990.

——. "The Thorn in Heidegger's Side: The Question of National Socialism." *Philosophical Forum* 20 (1989): 326–65.

Index